THE MANTLE ODES

The Mantle Odes

ARABIC PRAISE POEMS TO THE PROPHET MUḤAMMAD

SUZANNE PINCKNEY STETKEVYCH

Indiana University Press
Bloomington & Indianapolis

This book is a publication of

Indiana University Press
601 North Morton Street
Bloomington, Indiana 47404-3797 USA

www.iupress.indiana.edu

Telephone orders 800-842-6796
Fax orders 812-855-7931
Orders by e-mail iuporder@indiana.edu

∞ The paper used in this publication meets the minimum requirements of the American National Standard for Information Sciences—Permanence of Paper for Printed Library Materials, ANSI Z39.48-1992.

Manufactured in the United States of America

Library of Congress Cataloging-in-Publication Data

Stetkevych, Suzanne Pinckney.
The mantle odes : Arabic praise poems to the Prophet Muhammad / Suzanne Pinckney Stetkevych.
p. cm.
Includes bibliographical references and index.
ISBN 978-0-253-35487-7 (cloth : alk. paper) — ISBN 978-0-253-22206-0 (pbk. : alk. paper) 1. Muhammad, Prophet, d. 632—In literature. 2. Laudatory poetry, Arabic—History and criticism. 3. Ka'b ibn Zuhayr—Criticism and interpretation. 4. Busiri, Sharaf al-Din Muhammad ibn Sa'id, 1213?–1296?—Criticism and interpretation. 5. Shawqi, Ahmad, 1868–1932—Criticism and interpretation. I. Title.
PJ7642.M75S74 2010
892.7'1009351—dc22

2009048138

1 2 3 4 5 15 14 13 12 11 10

FOR JULIAN, QAYS, AND KHALID

CONTENTS

PREFACE

The Mantle Odes: Arabic Praise Poems to the Prophet Muḥammad offers original translations and contextualized interpretations of the three most renowned praise poems to the Prophet (*madāʾiḥ nabawiyyah*) in the Arab-Islamic tradition. The three odes span the arc of Islamic history: the first dates from the lifetime of the Prophet (7th c. CE); the second from the medieval Mamlūk period (late 13th c.); and the third from the Modern colonial period (1910). It is the intention of this study to bring these Arab-Islamic devotional masterpieces into the purview of contemporary literary interpretation in a way that makes them culturally relevant and poetically effective for the modern reader, whether Muslim or non-Muslim.

Chapter 1: Kaʿb ibn Zuhayr and the Mantle of the Prophet. The first poem is the conversion ode of the celebrated pre-Islamic poet, Kaʿb ibn Zuhayr. The poet, who faced a death sentence for his failure to convert to Islam, in the end came to the Prophet in submission and presented the ode of praise (*qaṣīdat al-madḥ*) that opens "Suʿād Has Departed" (Bānat Suʿād). As a sign of his protection and acceptance of Kaʿb's submission, the Prophet bestowed his mantle on the poet, and the poem became known as "The Mantle Ode" (Qaṣīdat al-Burdah). Suʿād Has Departed is a striking example of the panegyric ode in the pre-Islamic tradition and demonstrates the power and plasticity of that form to become the dominant genre of the courtly and religious poetry of the Islamic tradition.

Chapter 1 opens with an introductory section that presents in a succinct manner the form and function of the pre-Islamic ode of praise to Arab kings and tribal chieftains. In light of theories of rite of passage and gift exchange, it presents the Arabic praise ode as part of a multifaceted exchange ritual, whereby a bond of mutual obligation and allegiance is formed between the poet and patron. Above all, it demonstrates that the three-part praise ode incorporates a supplicatory ritual that forms the basis for the poem's performative functions. Three renowned examples of the pre-Islamic ode, by ʿAlqamah ibn ʿAbadah, al-Nābighah al-Dhubyānī, and Zuhayr ibn Abī Sulmá, along with the prose anecdotes that contextualize them in the Arabic literary tradition, thus set the stage for the examination of the dramatic conversion narrative and celebrated ode of Kaʿb ibn Zuhayr.

The interpretation of Kaʿb's Suʿād Has Departed demonstrates that Kaʿb has captured in poetic form the life-and-death drama that is so evident in the prose narratives about his risking his life to submit to the Prophet and convert to Islam. Through viewing the poem as a ritual of submission and supplication—what I term the Supplicatory Ode—this study reveals as well how and why Kaʿb's Suʿād Has Departed has provided a spiritual model for Muslims seeking redemption throughout the ages. Chapter 1 closes with a brief look at another poem to the Prophet, the elegy of Ḥassān ibn Thābit, to demonstrate how the supplication ritual and the exchange of poem for prize in this world (i.e., the exchange of Kaʿb's poem for the Prophet's mantle) can be translated, after the death of the Prophet, to the next world.

Chapter 2: Al-Būṣīrī and the Dream of the Mantle. The second poem to receive the sobriquet of Mantle Ode is the most famous devotional poem in the Islamic world, the Mantle Ode (Qaṣīdat al-Burdah) of the 7th/13th century poet of Mamlūk Egypt, al-Būṣīrī. The legend goes that the poet, afflicted with incurable hemiplegia, composed, out of hope and despair, a praise poem to the Prophet. That night he saw the Prophet in a dream and recited his poem to him. The Prophet, delighted with the poem, bestowed his mantle on the poet. Al-Būṣīrī awoke the next day, completely cured. His Mantle Ode has, ever since, been credited in the Islamic world with curative, talismanic, and spiritual powers. The renowned 9th/14th century historian and sociologist of the Maghrib, Ibn Khaldūn, considered a copy of al-Būṣīrī's Burdah a fit gift to present to the Mongol conqueror, Tīmūrlank.[1] With the nineteenth-century Ottoman restoration project, verses of the Burdah, along with those of the Qurʾān, adorned the domes of the Mosque of the Prophet in Medina.[2]

Al-Būṣīrī's Mantle Ode generated a massive production of manuscripts, commentaries, expansions, imitations, and translations, and continues to be widely performed and printed throughout the Islamic world.

Chapter 2 begins with a brief overview of the developments in genre and style that took place in the centuries of Classical Arab-Islamic poetry that intervened between Kaʿb's poem and al-Būṣīrī's distinctly Post-Classical poem. After offering an interpretation of the narratives of the poet's miraculous cure and the talismanic powers of the verses of al-Būṣīrī's Burdah, it offers a structural interpretation on which to base the reading of the poem. It argues that the overarching structure of the poem is that of the Supplicatory Pattern examined in chapter 1 and, further, that the ritual of supplication in medieval praise poems to the Prophet invariably involves presenting the poem of praise in exchange for the Prophet's intercession on Judgment Day. It then argues that the extended poetic passages concerning themes and events from the life of the Prophet have been appended to the praise section of the poem and serve to promote an ideology of what I term "Islamic Manifest Destiny"—an argument for worldly dominion that serves as an earthly counterpart or complement to the otherworldly concern with Judgment Day. The poem as a whole and these passages about the Prophet in particular provide a window onto traditional Islamic beliefs and practices that continue until our own day.

Chapter 3: Aḥmad Shawqī and the Reweaving of the Mantle. The third poem is The Way of the Mantle (Nahj al-Burdah) by the preeminent Egyptian Neo-Classical poet, Aḥmad Shawqī (d. 1932). It is, as its title suggests, a praise poem to the Prophet composed as a formal imitation of al-Būṣīrī's Burdah. Written in 1910, it ostensibly celebrates the Ḥajj pilgrimage of the poet's patron, the khedive of Egypt, ʿAbbās Ḥilmī II. The poem continues to be widely appreciated, both in written form and in the tremendously popular musical rendition by the Egyptian singer, Umm Kulthūm (d. 1975).

Chapter 3 opens with a brief survey of the political and cultural context of early twentieth-century Egypt. Egypt finds itself politically trapped between the moribund Ottoman Empire and the British Occupation. In response to its double exposure to the West—both its liberal humanism and its brutal imperialism—the Arab world produced the literary and cultural renascence termed the Nahḍah (Arab Awakening) or Iḥyāʾ (Revival). This background material paves the way for the interpretation of The Way of the Mantle as Shawqī's literary formulation of an anticolonialist stance, what I have termed his Iḥyāʾ (Revival) Project. Through a close reading of the poem in light of the commentary by Shaykh Salīm al-Bishrī, this section demonstrates how Shawqī has "rewoven" al-Būṣīrī's Mantle into a forceful and eloquent plea for the restoration of the Islamic Ummah based on "humanistic" concepts which he locates in the Classical Arab-Islamic past.

Until now, scholarship on praise poems to the Prophet has, for the most part, been limited to descriptive accounts of their historical circumstances and thematic contents, without any recognition of their ritual structure and its relation to their poetic (and spiritual) efficacy. By interpreting these poetic works in light of the structural elements of the supplicatory ode, by highlighting the performative function of the odes as speech acts with transformative power, and by viewing them as part of the ritual exchange of poem for prize, *The Mantle Odes* demonstrates why these praise poems to the Prophet have continued through the centuries to inform the poetic and religious life of the Arab and Islamic world.

ACKNOWLEDGMENTS

This book represents work I have done over the past eight years, during which I have benefited from the kindness and expertise of many friends and colleagues. I would like to express my thanks in particular to my colleagues Professors Ḥasan al-Bannā ʿIzz al-Dīn, Muḥsin Jāsim al-Mūsawī, the late ʿIzz al-Dīn Ismāʿīl, Maḥmūd ʿAlī Makkī, Sulaymān al-ʿAṭṭār, Michael Sells, and Consuelo López-Morillas. For emergency aid with references and texts as I was finalizing the manuscript in Cairo, I am grateful to my colleague, Professor Kevin Martin, and to Indiana University graduate students Ahmad al-Mallah and Hassan Lachheb. For the typesetting of the Appendix of Arabic Texts, I thank Mike Kelsey of Inari Information Services, and for proofreading it, Indiana University graduate student Bilal Maanaki. I am likewise grateful to my copy-editor, Candace McNulty, for her diligence and expertise with a technically demanding manuscript. For her encouragement, advice, and support of this project at various stages, I thank Janet Rabinowitch, the director of Indiana University Press. A special category of thanks is reserved for my closest friend and colleague, my husband, Professor Jaroslav Stetkevych. All the shortcomings of this work are my own.

I owe a debt of gratitude as well to the institutions whose financial and material support were essential to the completion of this book. I would like to thank the National Endowment for the Humanities and the American Research Center in Egypt for a fellowship in Egypt, January–June 2001, that allowed me to undertake the initial research for this project; the Dār al-Kutub al-Miṣriyyah for providing access to microfilms and manuscripts; the Staatsbibliothek of Berlin for providing microfilms of manuscripts in its collections; the Herman B Wells Library at Indiana University for its extraordinary service in making available research materials of all kinds; and the College Arts and Humanities Institute of Indiana University for granting me a course-release research fellowship for fall semester 2005.

Finally, my thanks are due to the Library of Alexandria, Egypt, and especially its manuscript collection director, Professor Youssef Zeidan, for granting permission and providing the photograph of the *Takhmīs Qaṣīdat al-Burdah* manuscript page that graces the cover of my book, and I would like to express my appreciation to Koninklijke Brill N.V. for permission to republish: "From Text to Talisman: Al-Būṣīrī's Qaṣīdat al-Burdah (Mantle Ode) and the Poetics of Supplication," *Journal of Arabic Literature* 37 no. 2 (2006), 145–89; and "From Sīrah to Qaṣīdah: Poetics and Polemics in al-Buṣīrī's Qaṣīdat al-Burdah (Mantle Ode), *Journal of Arabic Literature* 38 no. 1 (2007), 1–52. These appear in revised form in chapter 2 of this book.

NOTE ON TRANSLATION AND TRANSLITERATION

All the translations from Arabic and other languages in this study are my own, except where otherwise noted. Particularly in the case of the poetry texts, I have tried to honor the original while at the same time taking the liberties necessary to produce a readable and, I hope, engaging English rendition. With a view to a smooth English reading of both poetry and prose translations, I have not used square brackets [/] for minor interpolations that are simply a matter of clarification or style, but rather only in cases where the interpolation is open to doubt, such as the identification of the antecedent of a pronoun. In addition, as the full repetition of the honorific of the Prophet Muḥammad, *ṣallá Allāhu ʿalayhi wa-sallama* ("God bless him and give him peace") proves cumbersome to the English reader, I have used the standard English abbreviation "pbuh" (peace and blessings upon him) in all translations, whether the original has the Arabic siglum or the full phrase. All translation is a matter of interpretation, and interpretations, especially of poetry, are often quite an individual matter. For the Arabic reader, bracketed numbers at the right-hand margin following each poetry translation serve as the key to the Appendix of Arabic Texts. Specialists will want to refer as well to the Arabic source materials for textual variants and to the commentaries for varying interpretations.

In the transliteration of Arabic, I have followed the Library of Congress system, with the following modifications: *iyy* for *īy; ay* for *ai; uww* for *ūw;* and *aw* for *au.* For the transliteration of extended phrases, sentences, and verses, I have added end-vowels and initial *hamzat al-qaṭʿ* and have included all letters as they appear in written form, not as they are elided or assimilated in pronunciation.

ABBREVIATIONS

(Consult the bibliography for complete references)

BB	al-Būṣīrī's Qaṣīdat al-Burdah
EI2	*Encyclopaedia of Islam,* New Edition
EI2online	*Encyclopaedia of Islam, Second Edition,* Brill Online
GAL	Carl Brockelmann, *Geschichte der Arabischen Litteratur*
Lane	Edward William Lane, *Arabic-English Lexicon*
Lisān	Muḥammad ibn Mukarram ibn Manẓūr, *Lisān al-ʿArab*
NB	Aḥmad Shawqī's Nahj al-Burdah
pbuh	peace and blessings upon him = *ṣallá Allāhu ʿalayhi wa-sallama* (lit. "God bless him and give him peace," the honorific phrase traditionally used after the name of the Prophet Muḥammad)
QK	al-Qurʾān al-Karīm
WN	Waḍaḥ al-Nahj, Shaykh Salīm al-Bishrī's commentary on Shawqī's Nahj al-Burdah

THE MANTLE ODES

ONE

Kaʿb ibn Zuhayr and the Mantle of the Prophet

Introduction

THE PRE-ISLAMIC PROTOTYPE

The first poem to bear the sobriquet of Mantle Ode (Qaṣīdat al-Burdah) is Kaʿb ibn Zuhayr's Suʿād Has Departed (Bānat Suʿād) that, tradition tells us, the pagan poet presented to the Prophet Muḥammad on the occasion of his conversion to Islam (see below). In many respects, then, Kaʿb's poem marks the transition from the pre-Islamic poetic tradition, the earliest extant examples of which are dated to around 500 CE, to the Islamic, which begins 622 CE = 1 AH of the Islamic calendar, i.e., the year of the Hijrah or Migration of the Prophet Muḥammad from Mecca to Medina. Kaʿb was the scion of an illustrious poetic family of the Jāhiliyyah ("the Age of Ignorance," as the Islamic tradition terms its pagan pre-Islamic past), whose most notable member was his father, Zuhayr ibn Abī Sulmá, the famed panegyrist and moralist of pre-Islamic Arabia. We therefore know from the start that Kaʿb's ode to the Prophet is based on the rich tradition of pre-Islamic poetry, especially of the panegyric genre, the *qaṣīdat al-madḥ*. This genre served as a vehicle for the praise of the kings and tribal lords of the pre-Islamic warrior aristocracy and, in Islamic times, was to become the preeminent form of courtly ode that dominated the Arab-Islamic poetic tradition until the early twentieth century.[1]

The pre-Islamic odes, especially the celebrated masterpieces among them, were orally composed and preserved, until the collecting and editing process (*tadwīn*) undertaken by Muslim scholars in the 2nd–3rdAH/8th–9thCE centuries. We must keep in mind, therefore, that the entire pre-Islamic literary corpus, including the poetic texts, the prose narratives and anecdotes that accompany them, and the extensive biographical and genealogical information, is the product of Arab-Islamic culture that over a period of centuries transmitted, selected, edited, and shaped and re-shaped—in the form of poetic *dīwāns*, anthologies, commentaries, literary compendia, etc.—the originally oral tribal materials to its own ends. It is therefore impossible when dealing with pre- and early Islamic materials to speak of the historical and textual accuracy of individual poems (*shiʿr*, pl. *ashʿār*) or prose anecdotes (*khabar*, pl. *akhbār*). Instead, our approach in this study will be to accept the pre- and early Islamic poems and anecdotes that have been preserved in authoritative works of the classical Arabic literary canon as authentic *Arab-Islamic* texts. The choice of a particular recension of a poetic text or version of an anecdote over another does not, in this case, constitute a claim to its greater authenticity or historicity.[2]

When read in the context of the prose anecdotes that accompany the poems in the classical Arabic literary compendia and, further, in light of recent work on the ritual and performative aspects of poetry, it is evident that within pre-Islamic tribal society these poems performed multifaceted ritual, moral, political, and economic functions. At the same time, the pre-Islamic poetic tradition encapsulates and preserves for us the essential features of the autochthonous Arab Semitic culture, grounded in the civilizational bedrock of the Ancient Near East and subject to Christian, Judaic, Persian, and Byzantine influences, upon which the religion and civilization of Islam were founded. It is therefore necessary, as a prelude to the study of Kaʿb's Suʿād Has Departed, to understand both the literary form of the pre-Islamic panegyric ode and the range of its sociomorphic functions. In doing so we will focus on how the pre-Islamic ode serves as a prototype for Kaʿb's Suʿād Has Departed in particular and for the Islamic tradition of court poetry in general, and further, on the way in which Islamic culture appropriated its pagan tradition by interpreting it as proto-Islamic. To begin, we will briefly examine three renowned pre-Islamic odes that will serve as paradigms for our reading of Kaʿb's ode of conversion.

1. ʿALQAMAH'S A HEART TURBULENT WITH PASSION: THE POEM AS RANSOM PAYMENT

ʿAlqamah's ode comes down to us mainly through *Al-Mufaḍḍaliyyāt,* the authoritative anthology compiled by the Kūfan philologist, al-Mufaḍḍal al-Ḍabbī (d. 164/780–81), at the bidding, it is said, of the ʿAbbāsid Caliph al-Manṣūr for the education of his son, the future Caliph al-Mahdī.[3] The anecdotes that accompany the poem in the commentary of Abū Muḥammad al-Qāsim al-Anbārī (d. 304/916 or 305/917) provide insight into the function of the poem, which, we will argue, is essentially that of a ransom payment, that is, a ritual of exchange in which the poet presents the patron a gift of praise and the patron responds with a counter-gift—normally a material prize of gold, fine steeds or camels, slave girls, etc.,—in this case, the return of the poet's brother and other captive kinsmen.

The Arabic sources tell us that the poet ʿAlqamah ibn ʿAbadah, known as al-Faḥl, "the Stallion," for his masterful poetry, composed A Heart Turbulent with Passion after the Battle of ʿAyn Ubāgh, which historians date to 554 CE. This was a battle between the two Arab kingdoms of the Jāhiliyyah: the Lakhmids with their capital at al-Ḥīrah in Iraq, who were vassals of Sāsānid Persia and professed Nestorian Christianity, and the Ghassānids, a Byzantine client state based in Syria, who were adherents of Monophysite Christianity.[4] On the battle-day in question, the Ghassānid King al-Ḥārith ibn Jabalah defeated and slew the Lakhmid King al-Mundhir ibn Māʾ al-Samāʾ. ʿAlqamah's tribe, the Banū Tamīm, were clients fighting on the vanquished Lakhmid side, and a number of them were taken prisoner, including the poet's brother (or nephew), Shaʾs. ʿAlqamah is said to have addressed his poem to the victorious King al-Ḥārith on this occasion to plead for the release of his brother. In the context of the present study, we will argue that the poem is not merely a rhymed and metered plea for a prisoner's release, but rather serves as a commodity in a complex ritual exchange that simultaneously performs a variety of functions, such as transfer of allegiance, supplication, and negotiation.

The prose anecdotes (*akhbār*) that accompany the poem in al-Anbārī's commentary on *Al-Mufaḍḍaliyyāt* serve both to indicate the standard ritual expectations of the exchange of poem (*qaṣīdah*) for prize (*jāʾizah*) and the poet's dilemma: that if he uses the poem in exchange for his kinsmen's release, he will have to forgo the material prize that he desires. Fortunately, the wily poet has a solution for this dilemma, as al-Anbārī tells us in his commentary on verse 36:

> Shaʾs was ʿAlqamah's brother. . . . When al-Ḥārith heard him say, "Then Shaʾs too deserves a bucket of your bounty's flood" [v. 36], he exclaimed, "Buckets and more buckets!" and then ordered the release of Shaʾs and all the prisoners of the Banū Tamīm. But ʿAlqamah said to al-Ḥārith, "Don't release the prisoners of the Banū Tamīm until I've gone to see them." When he went to see them, he said, "I have asked the king for you as a gift and he has given you to me [*istawhabtukum min al-maliki fa-wahabakum lī*]. Now he is going to clothe you and bestow gifts upon you; so if you give me whatever clothes and gifts he bestows upon you, I will have you released; otherwise, I'll leave you here." So they agreed to his conditions and when they were led out, he took what had been given to them and released them.[5]

He adds a variant of the same story:

> Shaʾs was ʿAlqamah's brother or some say his brother's son. He was taken captive on that day, so ʿAlqamah came seeking his release. . . . When he reached the verse, "Then Shaʾs too deserves a bucket of your bounty's flood!" al-Ḥārith exclaimed, "Yes, and many bucketfuls!" and said to him, "Choose between a generous gift [*al-hibāʾ al-jazīl*] and the captives of the Banū Tamīm." "You have exposed me to the calumny of the tongues of the Banū Tamīm," replied ʿAlqamah, "Give me a day to consider the matter." Then he went to the captives and informed them of the offer the king had made him. "Woe to you!" they replied, "Will you abandon us and go?!" So ʿAlqamah said, "The king will certainly bestow clothes and mounts and provisions upon you. So, when you reach the tribe, then the mounts, clothes, and provisions will be mine." They agreed to this and the king released them.[6]

As both the sense and the etymologically revealing diction of these anecdotes make clear, ʿAlqamah's ode to al-Ḥārith is not perceived as an "occasional poem" to plead for or thank the king for the release of the prisoners, nor to celebrate that event. Rather it clearly functions as a valuable commodity in a gift exchange. But what makes it so valuable? And how does this exchange ritual work? Marcel Mauss's seminal study, *The Gift* (*Essai sur le don*), has much to tell us about the functions and character of gift exchange. He defines gifts as

> prestations which are in theory voluntary, disinterested, spontaneous, but are in fact obligatory and interested. The form usually taken is that of the gift generously offered; but the accompanying behaviour is formal pretense and social deception, while the transaction itself is based on obligation and economic self-interest.[7]

In the case at hand, ʿAlqamah's primary obligation is to secure the release of his kinsmen. The anecdotes reveal both the elements of obligation and economic self-interest entailed in the exchange by showing the poet's ambivalence over parting with his valuable poem/commodity to no personal profit, and more explicitly in the poet's remark that he will be exposed to calumny should he choose material gifts over the release of his kinsmen. Through a clever ruse, however, the poet manages both to fulfill his obligation and to satisfy his economic self-interest.

Al-Ḥārith's behavior, too, is ruled by the imperatives of the exchange ritual, which explains first of all why he releases all the prisoners—not just Shaʾs whose release is requested in the poem—as well as bestowing generous gifts upon the released captives. As Mauss further explains, ritual exchange entails three obligations: giving, receiving, and repaying.[8] "Failure to give or receive," he remarks, "like failure to make return gifts, means a loss of dignity."[9] In other words, to accept a gift is to accept the challenge to repay that it implies. The picture becomes clearer: to maintain his prestige among the Banū Tamīm, their poet ʿAlqamah must ransom his kinsmen; as for the victorious king al-Ḥārith, to maintain his royal dignity and not lose face, he must accept the gift (poem) and the challenge to repay it *with interest.* For, as Mauss states, "no less important is the role which honor plays in such transactions.... Nowhere else is the prestige of an individual as closely bound up with expenditure, and with the duty of returning with interest gifts received in such a way that the creditor becomes the debtor."[10] In other words, the gift exchange becomes a ritual negotiation of relative rank and prestige. As Mauss expresses it: "Between vassals and chiefs, between vassals and their henchmen, the hierarchy is established by means of these gifts. To give is to show one's superiority, to show that one is something more and higher, that one is *magister.* To accept without returning or repaying more is to face subordination, to become a client and subservient, to become *minister.*"[11] It is precisely this principle that is captured in the anecdote: when ʿAlqamah requests a mere "bucket of your bounty's flood" (v. 36), "Buckets and more buckets!" exclaims the king.

What is crucial in the context of the present study is my contention that Mauss's formulation of archaic gift exchange is fully applicable to the ritual exchange of poem for prize that is characteristic of Arabic praise poetry—whether court or tribal panegyric or Prophetic praise—and is essential to our understanding of it.

The forms and functions of gift exchange have far-reaching implications for both the literary-ritual structure of the poem and the performative roles that it plays. E. E. Evans Pritchard's summary of Mauss's conclusions concerning the nature of archaic exchange will serve in the context of our argument as a starting point for understanding the multifaceted and multifunctional nature of the classical Arabic ode: "The exchanges of archaic societies . . . are total social movements or activities. They are at the same time economic, juridical, moral, aesthetic, religious, mythological and socio-morphological phenomena. Their meaning can therefore only be grasped if they are viewed as a complex concrete reality."[12] It is our contention that in the Arabic panegyric ode, too, inasmuch as it is at the heart of this "total social phenomenon" "all kinds of institutions will find simultaneous expression."[13]

Having established the role of the poem as a commodity in an exchange ritual, we will now turn to the literary form of ʿAlqamah's panegyric ode with a view to discovering what sociomorphic institutions it expresses and how. Let us begin with its poetic structure. In this respect, ʿAlqamah's poem is a paradigmatically structured three-part panegyric ode. The three thematic sections, as conventionally described, are as follows: a lyric-elegiac prelude (*nasīb*), vv. 1–10; the poet's desert journey by she-camel toward the patron (*raḥīl*), vv. 11–20; and the praise of the patron (*madīḥ*), vv. 21–37. As useful as these conventional labels are, they tell us little about the meaning of this poetic form. For this we can turn to Arnold van Gennep's formulation of the rite of passage, which will provide us with a sense of the ritual, social, and psychological trajectory that such a tripartite structure can express and enact. Van Gennep, followed by his more recent acolytes such as Victor Turner and Mary Douglas, derived from the analysis of tribal rituals a pattern of transition or passage in three identifiable phases: Separation consists of symbolic behavior expressing detachment of an individual or group from a previous fixed point in the social structure or social state; Liminality or Marginality describes an ambiguous and therefore dangerous state, outside of society, betwixt and between the normal statuses assigned by society; and Reaggregation or Reincorporation signals the completion of the passage or transition, which finds the ritual passenger in a new and stable state, i.e., a new and defined social status with the rights and obligations that society assigns thereto.[14]

What is most important in terms of the present study is the idea that the paradigm of the classical Arabic three-part *qaṣīdah* structure, with its *nasīb, raḥīl,* and *madīḥ,* is not arbitrary or static, but rather that it shapes out and indeed performs a ritual that entails an emotional trajectory of the poet/passenger from 1) a previous, invariably failed, state (which may be social, political, psychological, spiritual, etc.—any or all of these) that leads to crisis and departure, through 2) a transitional period outside or on the margins of society, of indeterminacy, uncertainty, danger, and turmoil—but always, in the full-form ode, directed to 3) the arrival at (or return to) a new and successful status (again, social, political, spiritual, etc.). The pattern of passage invites the very common imagery, in religious ritual especially, of death and rebirth, drought and fertility, etc., and by its almost universal psychosocial nature it can and does serve as a template for a vast variety of ritual and ceremonial, including literary, productions. In terms of the *qaṣīdah,* the identification of an underlying ritual pattern helps us understand that its ritual role, as demonstrated in our discussion of gift exchange, is grounded in a ritual structure, which, in turn, is capable of performing many varied functions. This goes far in explaining the multifaceted roles that the *qaṣīdah*-form and its variants play in Arabic literature and culture.

ʿAlqamah's *nasīb* begins with the theme of lost love, as the poet-speaker, now in old age, is stirred to passion by the memory of the unattainable Laylá. In this he combines two traditional *nasīb* themes, that of the description of the beloved and the poet's passion for her (termed *tashbīb* or *ghazal*) and the complaint against old age (*al-shakwá min al-shayb*):

ʿAlqamah ibn ʿAbadah: A Heart Turbulent with Passion[15]

1. A heart turbulent with passion has borne you off,
   Long after youth has passed and the time of old age come.

2. Thoughts of Laylá trouble me, though her dwelling is now far,
   Though there have come between us hostile fates and grave events.

3. She lives in guarded luxury, all talk with her forbidden,
At her door a guard wards off all visitors.

[1]

At the end of the *nasīb* we detect a shift of mood as the poet overcomes his passion and despair and regains a sense of maturity; "do not compare me to an untried youth" he states (v. 5), for,

8. If you ask me about womankind, I am indeed
Discerning in their ailments, eminently skilled:

9. Should a man's head hoary or his wealth decrease,
He will find no share in their affections,

10. For they seek abundant wealth wherever they know it's found;
In youth's first bloom alone they take delight.

[2]

ʿAlqamah provides us with a very clear sense of direction, both psychological/emotional and geographical, as he opens the *raḥīl* section with his departure by she-camel to the court of al-Ḥārith. The key element here in terms of the psychological trajectory of the *qaṣīdah* is the transition from the sense of loss and despair in the *nasīb,* to the sense of resolve and determination in the *raḥīl.* It is the poet's mental fortitude and sense of direction, expressed above all in the Arabic poetic tradition through the physical fortitude and instinctual sense of direction of the poet's mount and poetic surrogate—the she-camel—that determines the success of this dangerous desert crossing. The poet first apostrophizes himself and then turns to relate his journey in the first person:

11. So leave her and dispel your cares with a tall mount, as bold as your resolve,
That even with a second rider keeps up a lively trot.

12. To al-Ḥārith the Munificent I hastened my she-camel
At such a pace her chest and end-ribs throb.

[3]

As he reaches the end of the *raḥīl,* ʿAlqamah stresses the hardships and death-defying perils of his liminal journey, but also a celestial sense of guidance and the well-worn track of the many who have gone before him in hopes of benefiting from al-Ḥārith's fabled generosity:

17. To you—may you repel all curses!—did she direct her gait
Through signless wastes full of dreadful terrors.

18. The twin polestars guided me to you, and a clear road,
On whose stony tracts rock piles and worn traces showed the way,

19. Upon which lay the corpses of abandoned beasts,
Their bones blanched, stiff their desiccated skin.

[4]

Having thus expressed first his loss and despair in the *nasīb,* which ends in the separation and departure that initiate the liminal *raḥīl*—where hope for the patron's bounty overcomes fear of the perilous journey—the poet-passenger arrives in verse 21 at the *madīḥ* or praise section. Although the final section is indeed dominated by motifs of encomium for the patron, much else is taking place. We can clearly detect the poet's incorporation into (a new) society with a new status, as he arrives as a stranger and supplicant pleading for the Ghassānid king's (al-Ḥārith) acceptance and favor, and transferring his allegiance to him even as he renounces his former but now failed allegiance to the slain Lakhmid king (al-Mundhir):

21. Do not withhold your favor from me, a foreigner,
For amidst the king's domed tents, I am a stranger.

22. You are the man in whom I place my trust,
For lords before have ruled me, then I was lost.

23. For the Banū Kaʿb ibn ʿAwf restored their king,
While in the armies' midst another king was left for dead.

[5]

Moreover, we witness in verses 21–23 what we will term the "ritual core" of the poem. As we will see further on in other *qaṣīdahs*, the ritual core consists of eminently performative language, characterized by very simple straightforward diction, and a clarity and transparency that often stand out from the rhetorical or metaphorical opacity of the surrounding poetic discourse. It is, however, far from simple. The three verses encapsulate a rite of passage: separation from a former state—that of allegiance to the Lakhmid king, now "left for dead"; entry into a liminal state "lords before have ruled me, then I was lost," where the passenger/poet describes himself as a "foreigner," "a stranger"—that is, having lost his previous position or status as a Lakhmid client, he now finds himself, as we would say, a "stateless person"; and then, incorporation into the Ghassānid fold through his declaration of allegiance and fealty to his new king, al-Ḥārith: "You are the man in whom I place my trust." We must, above all, be aware of the performative nature not only of the full *qaṣīdah* but of these verses of the ritual core in particular. These three verses are quite explicitly speech acts, which is to say that by the very act of uttering them the poet is renouncing his former allegiance and affirming his new one; that is, a vanquished enemy is surrendering and submitting to the victorious king.[16] Through the very utterance of these verses, the poet cuts off one moral bond and ties another. We can link this ritual of transfer of allegiance to the idea of gift exchange, when we remember that the purpose of gift exchange, as Mauss clearly realized, is not the transfer of material goods as much as it is a means of establishing social bonds.[17] In the ritual exchange of ʿAlqamah's panegyric ode for the release of the captives of the Banū Tamīm, what is really occurring is a peace treaty and cessation of hostilities, whereby al-Ḥārith's former enemies become his liege men, clients, or allies—as indeed the gifts he confers upon them confirm.

The ritual core is followed by a long passage praising—as is appropriate in a poem that is, among other things, a victory ode—the king al-Ḥārith's valor on the field of battle:

25. Into the fray you advance on your steed until his pasterns' white is black
 with blood,
 And all the while you smite the casques of armor-clad foes.

26. You were clad in double coats of mail from which are hung
 The choicest of blades—the Slicer, the Gasher.

[6]

The *madīḥ* section is sealed by verses that, like vv. 21–23, are explicitly performative and exhibit the forceful clarity of the ritual core. And likewise, their apparently stylistic simplicity belies the complex social phenomena that they embody. For if the poet threw himself at the mercy of his *mamdūḥ* (the recipient of his praise, the patron) in verses 21–23, here he sets out the terms of the contract of allegiance and the exchange ritual that will confirm it: the poet is performatively giving his gift of praise—the poem; what he asks in return is the generous release of the captive Shaʾs. ʿAlqamah begins by evoking his *mamdūḥ*'s twinned virtues of might and magnanimity, then petitions for Shaʾs's release, and closes the ode with a sort of conundrum: that the king possesses on the one hand a rank that none can approach; and yet through his generosity to them, both prisoner and kinsmen feel they have been brought close to him:

35. You are the one whose traces on the enemy,
Of harm and benefit, leave lasting scars.

36. On every tribe you have bestowed a boon;
Shaʾs, too, deserves a bucket of your bounty's flood.

37. To al-Ḥārith's high rank none draw nigh, except his prisoner,
His kinsman likewise, is not abased.

[7]

Verse 35 is quite brilliant in its evocation of the power of generosity, suggesting, as it does, that bounty can establish one's permanent subjugation of the enemy as well as violence can. In this context, verse 36, requesting bounty, namely release, for Shaʾs, reads as an offer for the cessation of hostilities—that is, the king can subdue the Banū Tamīm through his generous gifts and the obligation of loyalty that they entail, rather than the brute military force that he has shown in battle. This then relates back to the hope or trust that the poet expressed in verses 21–22. While he fears the king's might, he hopes for his magnanimity.

This brings us to the final, and perhaps in the context of the present study, most important, aspect of the many-faceted social and ritual movement of ʿAlqamah's ode: the Ritual of Supplication. As we will see throughout this study, the supplicatory structure is an essential aspect of the type of praise poem to the Prophet that we will discuss, and its elements are well established in the subcategory of the *qaṣīdah* that I have termed the Supplicatory Ode.[18] The key elements of the supplicatory structure, as I have defined it, are: Lyric-Elegiac Prelude (*nasīb*), essentially an expression of Loss; Self-Abasement and Submission; Praise of the one supplicated; Supplication, that is, the poet's petition to the patron (often accompanied in Islamic poetry by the poet's Benediction for the patron). As we will see throughout this study, the order of these elements varies from poem to poem and within a single poem they often overlap. These four are easily identifiable in ʿAlqamah's *qaṣīdat al-madḥ* to al-Ḥārith: the description of the poet's passion for his long lost Laylá (vv. 1–10) forms the Lyric-Elegiac Prelude or *nasīb;* the poet's Self-Abasement can be seen in the arduous journey that he undertakes in the *raḥīl* (vv. 11–20) in the hope of reaching the patron, but also in the pleading tone with which the poet throws himself at the patron's mercy, essentially an act of Submission (vv. 21–22). This leads into a long passage of Praise (*madīḥ*), especially for al-Ḥārith's military prowess and valor, but also his generosity; and finally, the element of Supplication appears in two installments, first in the poet's plea for the patron's favor and protection (v. 21) and then in the closing petition for the release of Shaʾs (v. 36). In both cases, the object of supplication is ultimately absolution for past transgression (i.e., having been allies of al-Ḥārith's enemy) through incorporation into the king's realm. The poem not only redeems the poet's captive kinsmen, it also is the payment for the poet's own redemption. This supplicatory ritual is intimately bound up with the complex of rituals—gift exchange, transfer of allegiance, incorporation, etc.—that are performed through the utterance of the poem. What all of these ritual patterns share is the transformative trajectory of the rite of passage.

A similar ritual complex forms, to varying degrees, the performative substructure of the other pre-Islamic *qaṣīdah*s that we will examine, as well as the praise poems to the Prophet that are the central subject of this study.

2. AL-NĀBIGHAH'S O ABODE OF MAYYAH: TRANSGRESSION AND REDEMPTION

The acclaimed ode of apology (*iʿtidhāriyyah*) by one of the master poets of the Jāhiliyyah, al-Nābighah al-Dhubyānī (active 570–600 CE),[19] to the Lakhmid King al-Nuʿmān ibn al-Mundhir is, we will argue, essentially a poem of supplication for the poet's absolution and reinstatement in his patron's court. Tradition tells us that al-Nābighah, who had been the king's favorite poet and boon companion, composed his poem of apology for having had an affair with the king's wife, an accusation leveled at the poet as a result of his scandalous erotic description of the queen in his notorious Description of al-Mutajarridah ode. One version, found in Abū al-Faraj al-Iṣbahānī's (d. 356/967) *Kitāb al-Aghānī,* presents al-Nābighah's flight from his liege lord's court as the result of the jealousy and court intrigue of a poetic rival, al-Munakhkhal:

> The reason that al-Nābighah fled from al-Nuʿmān was that once he and al-Munakhkhal . . . al-Yashkurī were sitting before the king. Now al-Nuʿmān was misshapen, leprous, and ugly, whereas al-Munakhkhal . . . was one of the most comely of the Arabs, and al-Mutajarridah, al-Nuʿmān's wife, had had her eye on him. Indeed, it was rumored among the Arabs that al-Nuʿmān's two sons by her were actually al-Munakhkhal's. Thus, when al-Nuʿmān said to al-Nābighah, "O Abū Umāmah, describe al-Mutajarridah in your poetry," and he composed his *qaṣīdah* in which he described her: her abdomen, her buttocks, and her private parts, this roused al-Munakhkhal's jealousy. So he said to al-Nuʿmān, "No one could have composed such a poem except one who had tried her!" Al-Nuʿmān took this to heart, and when news of this reached al-Nābighah, he was afraid and fled to the Ghassānids.[20]

Thus, the poet fled for his life to the rival Ghassānid court, but soon desired to return to his former Lakhmid liege lord. Inasmuch as the offense was above all poetic in form, so too are the poet's plea for absolution and redemption payment.[21] The object of the poet's supplication is therefore absolution and reinstatement in the king's inner circle. We should note that in terms of the poetic text of the apology ode, there is no reference to any sexual impropriety nor is there any admission of guilt. In other words, the poet's transgression, which the anecdotes present as sexual, may well rather have been of a political nature.

In terms of the general thematic structure, al-Nābighah's poem is, like ʿAlqamah's ode, a classically structured tripartite *qaṣīdah*: the lyric-elegiac prelude (*nasīb*): vv.1–6, featuring the poet's stopping over the abandoned campsite of his beloved; the journey (*raḥīl*): vv. 7–20, presenting the poet's she-camel through its comparison to an oryx bull beset by hunters and their hounds; the praise (*madīḥ*): vv. 20–49, comparing the king to Sulaymān (Solomon), praising his generosity, comparing him in farsightedness (that is, perspicacity) to Zarqāʾ al-Yamāmah, and in might and generosity to the formidable Euphrates.

The key elements of the supplicatory structure, which are what concern us in the present context, are: Lyric-Elegiac Prelude (*nasīb*) with its evocation of Loss; Self-Abasement and Submission; Praise of the One

Supplicated; Supplication. It should be noted from the outset that the last three elements do not always occur in the same order in every supplicatory panegyric and are often not entirely distinct from one another, but these elements otherwise are fairly predictably found in what is normally termed the *madīḥ* section. In addition, elements of what could be termed Self-Abasement can often be identified in the *nasīb* and, in the tripartite ode, in the central *raḥīl* (journey) section. In general, it soon becomes evident that an essential element of the self-abasement is the poet's expression of fear and hope, that is, his throwing himself upon the mercy of the formidable *mamdūḥ*.

The element of Loss that is distinctive of the Lyric-Elegiac Prelude (*nasīb*) takes the form not of a direct description of the poet's passion for the lost beloved herself, as in ʿAlqamah's ode, but of the closely related theme of the evocation of the abandoned campsite where the poet's beloved, Mayyah, once dwelt. Termed "stopping at the traces" (*al-wuqūf ʿalá al-aṭlāl*), this is undoubtedly the most highly developed and evocative elegiac theme of the Arabic lyrical tradition.[22]

Al-Nābighah al-Dhubyānī: O Abode of Mayyah[23]

1. O abode of Mayyah on height and peak! It lies abandoned
   And so long a time has passed it by.

2. I stopped there in the evening, to question it;
   It could not answer for in the vernal camp there was no one.

. . . .

6. By evening the abode was empty, by evening its people had packed up and left;
   It was destroyed by the same fate by which Lubad was destroyed.

7. Turn away from what you see, for it is irredeemable,
   And raise the saddle-rods on a she-camel, brisk as an onager, solid.

[8]

The sense of loss in such a *nasīb* is projected onto the physical traces or remains of the campsite, which bear a metonymic relation to the lost beloved. The *nasīb* ends with the separation and departure of the tribe, or rather, the poet's recollection of it (v. 6). There he invokes Lubad, the symbol of mortality, the last of the long-lived vultures whose life-spans measured out the life of the legendary sage Luqmān and whose death marked the sage's own demise.[24] The poet's departure, which entails his abandoning the site of loss and strengthening his resolve to head for his patron's court, is expressed in the transitional verse (v. 7), which moves from despair to determination as the poet puts the past behind him and saddles up his sturdy energetic she-camel for the journey. The *raḥīl,* in turn, leads into an extended simile, comparing the poet's she-camel in her fortitude to a lone oryx bull. The oryx bull's travails and ultimate triumph, as he suffers through a cold night of freezing rain and then at dawn triumphantly fights off a hunter and his hounds, is in effect an allegory of the poet/passenger who himself undergoes a similar passage from passive suffering to life-affirming resolve (vv. 7–20).

The supplicatory element of Self-Abasement is to some extent implied in the hardships of the desert journey that the poet/passenger undergoes in the *raḥīl,* which, in effect, says to the *mamdūh* that the poet has suffered hardship and faced perils to get to him. But the element of Self-Abasement, and with it Submission, is more explicit in the expression of twinned fear and hope that occurs midway through the *madīḥ* section. These verses are, at the same time, glaringly performative and constitute what we termed above, in our discussion of ʿAlqamah's ode, the ritual core of the poem, with its characteristically transparent and straightforward diction. The poet proclaims his innocence, which he confirms with an oath, one of the major categories of speech act or performative speech (vv. 37–39):

37. No, by the life of Him whose Kaʿbah I have anointed
And by the blood I have spilled out upon stone altars,

38. And by the Protector of the birds that seek the refuge of the sanctuary,
Unmolested by the riders of Mecca between the spring and the thicket,

39. I never said those evil things that were reported to you.
If I did, then let my hand be palsied till I cannot hold a whip.

40. It was nothing but the calumny of enemies for which I suffered;
their speech was like a stab that pierced my liver.

[9]

Verse 41 conveys the sense of Self-Abasement in the fear of al-Nuʿmān that strikes the poet's heart. In verse 42 the poet begs the king to be merciful and to "go easy" on him, which is an expression of Self-

Abasement and Submission. At the same time he proposes a contract: in exchange for King al-Nuʿmān's "going easy" on him, that is, forgiving and accepting him rather than punishing him for his transgression, the poet offers his allegiance, as expressed in the Arabic tradition, "May my soul be your ransom" (*nafsī fidāka*), which is to say, "I pledge my life to you." Verse 43 reiterates the plea for mercy that opens verse 42:

41. I've been told that Abū Qābūs* has threatened me, [* = al-Nuʿmān]
And no one can withstand the lion when it roars.

42. Go easy! May the tribes, all of them, be your ransom,
And all my herds' increase, and all my progeny!

43. Don't fling at me more than I can withstand,
Even though my foes should rally to support you.

[10]

It is obvious as well that verses 42 and 43, with their pleas for mercy, involve simultaneously the elements of Self-Abasement and Supplication (see more, below).

The Praise of the One Supplicated in al-Nābighah's ode includes the standard elements of generosity and might, which we can understand as the counterparts to, respectively, the poet's hope and fear:

20. Such a she-camel conveys me to Nuʿmān,
Whose beneficence to mankind, both kin and foreigner, is unsurpassed.

. . . .

27. I see no one more generous in bestowing a gift,
Followed by more gifts and sweeter, ungrudgingly given.

28. The giver of a hundred bulky she-camels,
Fattened on the Saʿdān plants of Tūḍiḥ, with thick and matted fur,

29. And white camels, already broken in, wide-kneed,
On which fine new Ḥīran saddles have been strapped,

30. And slave girls kicking up the trains of long white veils,
Pampered by cool shade in midday heat, lovely as gazelles,

31. And steeds that gallop briskly in their reins
Like a flock of birds fleeing a cloudburst of hail.

. . . .

44. Not even the Euphrates when the winds blow over it,
Its waves casting up foam on its two banks,

45. When every wadi rushes into it, overflowing and tumultuous,
Sweeping down heaps of thorny carob bush and sticks and boughs,

. . . .

47. Is ever more generous than he is in bestowing gifts,
Nor does a gift today preclude a gift tomorrow.

[11]

However powerful and beautiful these verses are, al-Nābighah's praise also includes two more unusual passages that are particularly suited to his dilemma. One suggests the comparison of al-Nuʿmān to Sulaymān (Solomon) in such a way as to suggest that God's exhortations to Sulaymān should apply to the king's treatment of the poet:

24. Then whoever obeys you, reward his obedience
In due measure and guide him on righteousness' path.

25. And whoever defies you, chastise him with a chastisement
That will deter the evil-doer—but do not harbor rancor.

[12]

A second comparison is between al-Nuʿmān and Zarqāʾ (= Blue-Eyed) al-Yamāmah, whom legend credits with the first use of kohl and with extraordinarily keen eyesight. When she warned her tribesmen that the enemy, camouflaged with tree-branches, was approaching, they dismissed her warning and were defeated in a surprise attack.[25] In al-Nābighah's poem, a riddle based on her ability to count a distant flock of doves extends her physical ability to mental acuity and insight, hence al-Nābighah's exhortation to the king, "Judge with perspicacity like the girl of the tribe" (v. 32).

The element of Supplication itself, the poet's petition or entreaty to the patron, is evident in the many imperative pleas that punctuate the poem: v. 32 "Judge with perspicacity"; vv. 42–43 "Go easy," and the offer of allegiance that it entails. However, it comes to the fore particularly in the closing verses of the poem, vv. 48–49. These verses, too, constitute a complex social movement, for the poet does not merely present his plea for forgiveness, but encapsulates the entire exchange ritual of praise for prize that constitutes the performative core of the ode. He states clearly, however, that he desires no material gift, but only the *mamdūḥ*'s forgiveness. That is, in a sort of ritual substitution, "apology" and "forgiveness" stand in for "praise" and "prize":

48. This is my praise: if it sounds good to you,
I have alluded—may you disdain all curses—to no gift.

49. This is an apology: if it has availed me nothing,
Then its author is indeed down on his luck.

[13]

Al-Nābighah's poem succeeded, the literary tradition tells us. We read in an anecdote that the poet Ḥassān ibn Thābit (later the famed poet-laureate of the Prophet Muḥammad) had come to al-Nuʿmān's court in al-Nābighah's absence hoping to make his fortune there, only to witness, with despair, the return of the king's erstwhile favorite with his masterpiece of apology:

> At this, Ḥassān ibn Thābit declared, "I begrudged al-Nābighah three things, and I don't know which I envied the most: al-Nuʿmān's drawing him into his intimate circle once more after his estrangement and sitting up at night conversing with him and listening to him; or the excellence of his poetry; or the hundred purebred royal camels that the king bestowed on him."[26]

King Nuʿmān not only forgave the poet and reinstated him as poet-laureate and boon companion in his court, but, as we have come to expect from Mauss's rules of gift exchange and our reading of ʿAlqamah's ode in the context of its literary anecdotes, he bestowed upon him as well a gift of one hundred of the Lakhmid's coveted royal purebred camels.

As was the case with ʿAlqamah's ode, our reading of al-Nābighah's O Abode of Mayyah in the context of its literary anecdotes reveals that this *qaṣīdat al-madḥ,* here in the form of a poem of apology, likewise exhibits a multifaceted complex of ritual and performative functions. It performs the court ceremonial of the exchange of praise poem for prize: that is, a ritualized enactment of the relation of subject to ruler. The poem's tripartite structure of *nasīb, raḥīl,* and *madīḥ* (lyric-elegiac prelude, desert journey, and praise) effects a rite of passage through which the poet makes the transition, as the anecdotes tell us, from banishment to reinstatement in the Lakhmid court. The key elements of the Supplicatory Ode are likewise in evidence in the Loss expressed in the abandoned campsite of the *nasīb*, the elements of Self-Abasement in the poet's expressions of fear and hope, the Praise of King al-Nuʿmān for might and generosity, and the Supplication itself, the poet's plea for the king's forgiveness. Overtly performative acts (speech acts) such as the exculpatory oath and oath of allegiance take place within the poem as well.

Finally, once again we need to emphasize that not only does the *qaṣīdah* incorporate speech acts, but the entire *qaṣīdat al-madḥ* itself in its recitation before the *mamdūḥ* constitutes a multifaceted performative utterance. In the case of al-Nābighah's O Abode of Mayyah the overarching ritual structure is that of supplication for the king's forgiveness. In the literary tradition, the most celebrated versions identify al-Nābighah's transgression as a sexual-poetic scandal involving the king's wife. As we noted above there is no evidence of its nature in the poem itself, and the poet, rather than confessing to any wrongdoing, denies it. As we will see, below, in our discussion of Kaʿb ibn Zuhayr's ode to the Prophet, this appears to be the ritual-poetic norm for what is termed in the Arabic tradition *iʿtidhāriyyah* (poem of apology). In this case, the literary tradition, broadly speaking, presents al-Nābighah's poem describing the king's wife al-Mutajarridah in obscene terms as the transgression, which means that it does not take the poet's denial in his poem of apology to be true.[27] That being the case, we have to understand the denials and their accompanying oaths as the sanctioned form of the ritual apology. That is, the oath of denial is an element of what Mauss terms the "formal pretense and social deception" that characterize ritual exchange (cited above). Whatever precise nature of the poet's transgression, the poem of apology is the poet's redemption payment.

If, in our reading, the ritual complexes of ʿAlqamah's A Heart Turbulent with Passion and of al-Nābighah's O Abode of Mayyah feature a pronounced supplicatory aspect, in our final pre-Islamic example the supplicatory aspect is far less pronounced as other aspects of the panegyric pact between poet and patron come to the fore.[28]

3. ZUHAYR IBN ABĪ SULMÁ'S THE TRIBE SET OUT: THE TACIT PANEGYRIC PACT

It behooves us to speak of another of the master poets of the Jāhiliyyah, Zuhayr ibn Abī Sulmá,[29] in part because he is the father of Kaʿb ibn Zuhayr, whose poem to the Prophet Muḥammad, Suʿād Has Departed, is the first poem to be given the sobriquet of Mantle Ode and the most renowned poem of praise presented to the Prophet in his lifetime. But it is of further interest because the relationship between Zuhayr and his Murrite kinsman, the chieftain Harim ibn Sinān, to whom his most famous praise poems are addressed, became the proverbial and paradigmatic model throughout the Arabic-Islamic poetic tradition, especially, as we shall see (chapter 2) in the medieval *madīḥ nabawī* tradition, for the exchange of praise/poem for prize. We will term the relationship between poet and patron that is established through this ritual exchange of poem for prize the "panegyric pact."

Zuhayr is said to have been a well-to-do lord (*sayyid*) of the Banū Murrah (his father's maternal clan, whose association Abū Sulmá preferred after an act of treachery on the part of his paternal kin, the Banū Muzaynah); he was known for forbearance and possessed a reputation for piety (*al-wara*ʿ).[30] Two points are given prominence in the biographical and critical anecdotes concerning Zuhayr: that he was both the scion of a prominent poetic family of the Jāhiliyyah and the progenitor of Islamic poets (Zuhayr's father Abū Sulmá was a poet, as were his maternal uncle, Bashāmah ibn al-Ghadīr, his stepfather, Aws ibn Ḥajar, and his sisters, Salmá and al-Khansāʾ; his two sons Kaʿb and Bujayr, as we will see below, were poets who converted to Islam);[31] and that in his panegyrics he never composed praise of anyone that was not true (*lam yamdaḥ ʾaḥadan ʾillā bi-mā fīh*).[32] Inasmuch as the classical Arabic tradition came to attack the *qaṣīdat al-madḥ*, especially in the Islamic periods, as insincere flattery in exchange for material gain, this last point exculpates Zuhayr from the first part of the criticism. A charming anecdote absolves him of the second. It presents the poet not as greedy for gain but rather as somewhat embarrassed by his patron's unbounded munificence. Whereas we saw ʿAlqamah (above) scheming to maximize the return on his poem, we find Zuhayr, in an anecdote related in *Kitab al-Aghānī*, concocting a ruse to evade his patron's oath of generosity:

> [Al-Aṣmaʿī] said: It reached me that Harim had once sworn an oath that every time Zuhayr presented him a praise poem he would give him a gift, and any time he petitioned him he would grant his request, and even if the poet so much as greeted him, he would give him a gift—whether a slave, or a slave-girl, or a horse. Zuhayr became so embarrassed at how much bounty he received from Harim that, when he saw him surrounded

> by his retinue, he greeted them, "Good morning to all of you, except for Harim—and that exception is the best among you!"[33]

Thus the poet fulfills the obligation to greet and praise his patron, but with a verbal ruse that does not incur for Harim his oath-bound obligation to confer a gift. In terms of Mauss's formulation of gift exchange, we can understand that the gist of such anecdotes is that the poet should keep up the pretense of a gift (of praise) freely and spontaneously given, not merely proffered in the hope or expectation of reward. Moreover, in light of both Mauss's remarks and ᶜAlqamah's verse 35 (above) about the power of gifts to negotiate status and to force subjection and submission, we can understand Zuhayr's "gift avoidance" as a ploy to maintain his own dignity.

Zuhayr is most renowned for his panegyric ode rhymed in *mīm,* included in the most illustrious collection of pre-Islamic odes, *Al-Muᶜallaqāt* (The Suspended Odes).[34] It was composed in praise of two chieftains of the Banū Murrah, Harim ibn Sinān and al-Ḥārith ibn ᶜAwf, in honor of their having put an end to the forty-year tribal feud, the Ḥarb Dāḥis and Ghabrāʾ (between the Banū ᶜAbs and the Banū Dhubyān), a truce that they concluded by putting up their own wealth (camel herds) to pay the blood price of the unavenged dead of the Banū ᶜAbs.[35] Zuhayr's Muᶜallaqah is famous for its condemnation of the horrors of war and the series of moral *sententiae* or proverbs (*amthāl*) with which it concludes. Here, however, we will examine his renowned *qaṣīdat al-madḥ* to Harim, the poem rhymed in *qāf* that opens "The tribe set out for distant lands" (*ʾInna al-khalīṭa ʾajadda al-bayna*) that is more paradigmatic in its form and thus more suitable for our discussion of the poet-patron relationship. It is interesting, as well, that in his panegyrics to Harim, Zuhayr does not present himself explicitly as a supplicant; rather, the exchange of poem for prize seems to be implicit in his poems. Our contention in discussing The Tribe Set Out and the anecdotes surrounding Zuhayr's poetry in the classical Arabic compendia will be that, however discreet the poet may be, the panegyric poem implies a prize, just as, in terms of Mauss's formulation of ritual exchange, a gift is *ipso facto* a challenge to reply with a greater gift.

Zuhayr's *qāfiyyah,* The Tribe Set Out, is second only to his Muᶜallaqah in Thaᶜlab's recension of the Dīwān and, for example, figures prominently, again right after his Muᶜallaqah, in al-Iṣbahānī's notice on the poet in *Kitāb al-Aghānī.*[36] The poem exhibits in classic proportions the three-part structure we saw in our two earlier examples: the lyric-elegiac prelude (*nasīb*), vv. 1–16; the desert crossing (*raḥīl*), vv. 17–32; and the encomium (*madīḥ*), vv. 33–49. This *qaṣīdah* is remarkable as well for the clear and conventional articulation of its structural sections. We do not find, however, whether in the poetic text or its accompanying prose anecdotes, any explicit presentation of the poet as supplicant or as a passenger undergoing any profound transformation, such as the rituals of (re)incorporation and transfer of allegiance that were so prominent in ʿAlqamah's and al-Nābighah's poems. Rather, we will argue, in Zuhayr's poems the three-part structure of the *qaṣīdat al-madḥ* is used in a more formal way to perform a courtly ceremony of allegiance. Absent here, too, are the elements of Self-Abasement and Submission that are characteristic of the Supplicatory Ode. As a lord (*sayyid*) of his tribe, Zuhayr wants to express his allegiance and loyalty to Harim, but without the asymmetrical power relation we saw in the odes of ʿAlqamah and al-Nābighah, which are the odes of subjects to kings. Further, Zuhayr's ode seems to be confirming an already existing bond more than tying a new one. The effect of this is that the poem lacks the immediacy and urgency, the life-and-death drama, of the other two *qaṣīdah*s we discussed, but it gains instead an elegance and refinement, and a sense of timelessness or universality. This sense of refinement and polish is reflected in the critic Ibn Qutaybah's (d. 276/889) remark that Zuhayr termed his long *qaṣīdah*s "*ḥawliyyāt*," that is, odes that took a full year (*ḥawl*) to compose and polish.[37] The emotional trajectory of the three-part structure is there, but it has the more thoughtful and contemplative feel of something considered from an objectivizing distance.

The ode opens with one of the most classic *nasīb* motifs, that of the tribal departure, which is essentially an image of separation and the cutting of ties. This opening motif leads inevitably to the person of the beloved, who is duly introduced in verses 2–4: "the Bakrī's daughter." The physical separation and cutting of ties of verse 1 quickly transforms into a cutting or breakdown of emotional and moral bonds: the breaking of promises and the forfeiting of pledges:

Zuhayr ibn Abī Sulmá: The Tribe Set Out[38]

1. The tribe set out for far-off lands, till it was cut off from us,
   While my heart remained bound, tight, to Asmāʾ.

2. She left your heart pledged irredeemably to her,
But on the day of parting, she forfeited her pledge.[39]

3. The Bakrī's daughter broke her promise to you
And the bond that bound you to her is now weak and frayed.

[14]

The poet then shifts subtly into the purely passionate, to describe the beloved (vv. 5–7):

5. A neck like the white outstretched neck of a gazelle doe, newly fawned,
Lagging behind the herd and warily watching over her wobbly fawn.

6. Her mouth after slumber tastes as if she's had a drink at nightfall
Of a fine sweet wine, aged to perfection,

[15]

The poet then reverts to the image of the departing caravan of the beloved's tribe that opened the *nasīb* (vv. 8–9), to conclude the *nasīb* with an extended simile in which he describes his tears as so copious that they could fill the buckets of a camel drawing water from a well (vv.10–16):

8. I kept on gazing after them until their camels knelt
To set them down in Rākis Hollow.

. . . .

10. As if my eyes wept till they filled the two buckets
Of a worn-out water-camel watering a distant palm grove.

[16]

The effect of this long and finely achieved simile of the water-camel (*sāniyah*) is to reduce the immediacy of the sense of loss that otherwise dominates the *nasīb*. Our attention is drawn instead to the poet's artistry.

The transition from the *nasīb* to the *raḥīl* is signaled in the clearest and most classical fashion in verses 17–18 by the imperative *ʿaddi ʿan* (turn away from!). The second step of the transition, the saddling up of the she-camel, inevitably follows. This two-part process and its conventions are already familiar to us from ʿAlqamah's A Heart Turbulent with Passion (v. 11) and al-Nābighah's O Abode of Mayyah (v. 7). What is important, especially in terms of our rite of passage paradigm, is the psychological transition that this abrupt imperative effects in its poetic context: that is, the "act of will" through which the poet-passenger renounces the sorrowful past and propels himself forward into an undoubtedly dangerous but also hopeful future. The convention of the poet apostrophizing himself in such verses authentically captures the interior psychological struggle of the poet-passenger.

The bulk of the journey section (vv. 19–32) is an extended simile comparing the she-camel in its fortitude and determination to an oryx bull that grazes until the coming of the rainy season, when he spends the night overtaken by cold and rain, only to awaken to the attack of a hunter and his hounds. As we saw in al-Nābighah's treatment of the same *raḥīl* theme, the contrast between passive suffering and energetic attack against the hounds reiterates the psychological transition of the poet-passenger himself from the *nasīb* to the *raḥīl*, and we are to understand that it is just this psychological transformation and act of will and determination on the poet-passenger's part that guarantees the success of his quest, that is, his journey to the patron.

17. Then turn away from what you see, for what you sought has passed away,
And so the crow of separation has begun to caw.

18. And raise the wooden saddle-rods on a bulky high-cheeked camel
Whose braided leather reins shake when her neck is wet with sweat.

19. As if I had put my saddle and its straps and cover-pad
Upon a full-grown oryx bull, spirited and white.

. . . .

24. There he was overtaken by a rain that came in sheets,
That soaked the soil and made the flatlands flow with water.

25. Rain-soaked, he tried all night to find shelter from the cold,
While clouds, in succession, spattered him with rain.

. . . .

28. All through the night until, when the stars' gaze grew weary,
The morning light began to shine and he went forth.

29. At dawn swift hounds attacked him,
And a hunter of consummate skill.

. . . .

31. The bull stands motionless until, thinking the sun's horn has fully risen
And fearing the lunging hounds attacking on both sides,

32. He spins around and splits the first one open with a gaping wound
That sends blood spurting over his horns.

[17]

Perhaps the fact that the physical journey of the poet on his she-camel is not directly described suggests to us that the psychological transition, here expressed at one symbolic remove in the oryx bull allegory, is more essential to the poem-as-rite-of-passage than the geographical transit. But also, like the extended water-camel simile of the *nasīb,* the elision of the journey itself to the oryx bull allegory may have the effect of drawing our attention more to the poet's finely honed art than to the poet-passenger's plight.

Zuhayr then makes a dramatic poetic move: rather than rounding out the *raḥīl* by returning to the subject of the simile (the she-camel), and then presenting the arrival at the patron's court, as our experience with the *qaṣīdat al-madḥ* genre would lead us to expect, he brings us just to the point of climax—the oryx bull gores the hounds and sends their blood gushing—and cuts abruptly to the *madīḥ.* It is as if the poet says, "If you think this is exciting, wait until you hear about Harim!"

33 But let me rather speak of the best of Qays, all of them,
In lineage; the best in bounty and in virtue.

[18]

Not only is this move stunning in itself, but equally noteworthy is that Zuhayr has omitted precisely the arrival of the supplicant at the patron's court that is so central to what we have termed the "ritual core" of the Supplicatory Ode. In other words, at this crucial structural juncture and indeed throughout the *madīḥ* section, we find no Self-Abasement and no Supplication. This is especially noticeable when we compare Zuhayr's objectively distanced *madīḥ* with the impassioned direct address to the patron of ʿAlqamah ("Do not withhold your favor from me," v. 21) and al-Nābighah ("Go easy!" v. 42; "Do not fling at me more than I can withstand!" v. 43). Zuhayr never addresses Harim directly, but rather presents well-wrought verses of encomium for his *mamdūḥ*'s virtues, including magnanimity:

35. In magnanimity, he's like the winning steed, who gives its all, and,
Never forced, never flagging, outstrips the rest.

36. Harim's supplicants and those that seek his bounty
Have beaten pathways to his doors.[40]

. . . .

43. Bright and comely of countenance, overflowing with bounty,
He breaks the shackles from the captives' hands and necks.

44. In hard times whoever finds Harim
Will find that munificence and generosity are in his nature.

45. He never refuses a relative or kinsman,
Nor an impoverished supplicant who "shakes his tree."

[19]

Harim's personal valor in battle is presented in terms of leading raids against the enemy and throwing himself aggressively into combat, and has its counterpart in tribal councils in his personal authority and commanding eloquence:

37. He leads horses that have chipped the edges of their hoofs,
That are bridled with leather straps or strips of flax.

38. They leave on raids fat and return emaciated, their young aborted,
When before, full-bodied and big-bellied, they were led beside the camels,

39. He brings them back matted and ungroomed,
In pain in their hoofs, sciatic nerves, and peritoneum.

. . . .

46. Like a man-hunting lion of ʿAththar's hollow, when other lions
Hold back from their opponents, he attacks.

47. When they shoot arrows, he thrusts the spear; when they thrust the spear,
He starts the sword fight; when they take up the sword, he grabs his foe!

48. Such is he; he is not one to stammer in the midst of men,
When an authoritative speaker speaks his mind.

[20]

Harim's greatest challenge is competing in virtue and nobility with his illustrious ancestors, especially his father, Sinān. The poet presents this competition in terms of a horse race of noble steeds:

40. He races to catch up with two men who preceded him in virtuous deeds,
Who bestowed gifts on kings and subdued their subjects.

41. He is the finest steed/most generous man; so if he can catch up with them,
However great the challenge, he's just the sort that could;

42. And if, with the lead they have, they still outstrip him,
Then deeds like theirs are the sort that outstrip others.

[21]

The poem concludes in a verse that carries religious overtones:

49. If earthly creatures could reach the heavens through noble deeds,
Then surely Harim's hand would touch the skies.

[22]

What appear to be missing in Zuhayr's The Tribe Set Out in praise of Harim ibn Sinān are precisely the two most explicit supplicatory elements that were so prominent in our examples from ʿAlqamah and al-Nābighah, that is, Self-Abasement and Supplication. Or, to be more precise, Harim's unfailing magnanimity to supplicants and petitioners is celebrated in the ode (vv. 36, 44, 45), but the poet does not explicitly place himself among them. In the *nasīb,* we were distracted from the sense of Loss by the exquisitely detailed description of the water-camel. In the *raḥīl* the arduous *mamdūḥ*-directed journey of the she-camel is elided to present the finely wrought oryx bull allegory. Finally, the Supplication itself, the poet's emotive plea and the direct and impassioned address of the *mamdūḥ,* is not found in Zuhayr's poem. Rather than enacting a dramatic and self-interested supplicatory ritual as we saw in the two previous poetic examples, Zuhayr offers an elegantly wrought ceremonial piece.

Despite the absence of an explicit supplicatory performance on the part of the poet, the classical Arabic literary context insists repeatedly on the lavish gifts that Harim conferred upon Zuhayr for his panegyric odes. In terms of the ritual complex that we have described in our discussion of ʿAlqamah's and al-Nābighah's odes, we find in Zuhayr's The Tribe Set Out a stripped down or implied ritual content wherein the structure of the *qaṣīdat al-madḥ* conveys the message and performs the ceremonial or ritual function without the explicit supplicatory and performative verses that we saw in our other examples. That is, the *qaṣīdat al-madḥ* in itself, regardless of its explicit contents, is performative: it invokes the panegyric pact and demands a reward. Part of this may reflect the sociopolitical relation of the poet and patron. They are both wealthy lords (*sayyid*s) of the Banū Murrah, and although in terms of relative rank Harim seems to hold a higher position, nevertheless it is a relation of kinsmen within the tribal aristocracy, not, as in ʿAlqamah's and al-Nābighah's odes, the relation of a non-kin subject to a king. The exchange of poem for prize in this context indicates a relation of mutual dependency: the panegyrics express Zuhayr's allegiance to Harim more than his subservience, and the counter-gifts suggest Harim's awareness that to maintain his dignity and status as chieftain he must lavishly reward such finely wrought panegyrics. The hierarchical relation may be less pronounced than in the two earlier examples, which were both panegyrics addressed to kings, but the panegyric pact is nevertheless binding, as Zuhayr and Harim compete for status within the warrior aristocracy of their tribe.

In terms of ritual exchange, the element of competition for status through the relative value of the objects of exchange comes to the fore in several anecdotes set in the Islamic period. We can begin to understand how the Islamic period valued and evaluated the poetic masterpieces of the Jāhiliyyah in the relative value assigned to Zuhayr's poems and Harim's prizes. Two anecdotes from the *Kitāb al-Aghānī* feature the stern and uncompromising second Orthodox Caliph, ʿUmar ibn al-Khaṭṭāb (r. 13–23/634–644):

> ʿUmar said to one of the sons of Harim, "Recite to me some of the panegyric that Zuhayr composed for your father." So he recited some to him. Then ʿUmar said, "He certainly did well by you in his speech!" "And, by God," Harim's son replied, "we certainly did well by him in our gifts!" "Yes, but what you gave him is long gone," retorted the Caliph, "while what he gave you [i.e., *qaṣīdahs*] still remains!"[41]

A variant conveys the same idea in terms of the *ḥulal* (robes of honor; sets of clothes, sing. *ḥullah*) that were one of the traditional gifts conferred on poets:

> ʿUmar said to [Kaʿb] ibn Zuhayr, "Whatever became of the robes of honor that Harim bestowed upon your father?" "The passage of time wore them out," he replied. "But," retorted the Caliph, "the passage of time has not worn out the robes [i.e., *qaṣīdahs*] that your father bestowed upon Harim!"[42]

THE PRE-ISLAMIC AS PROTO-ISLAMIC

The term Jāhiliyyah signifies that the pre-Islamic past was for the Islamic generations a time of ignorance, but also impetuousness and immorality, before the mission of the last and best of the Prophets, Muḥammad, to whom the definitive word of Allāh, the Qurʾān, was sent down. At the same time, it was among these pre-Islamic Arabs that the Qurʾān was sent and in the powerful language in which they prided themselves that Allāh's final revelations was expressed (the Qurʾānic *bi-lisānin ᶜarabiyyin mubīnin*, "in a clear Arab tongue") (al-Qurʾān al-Karīm [hereafter QK] 26:195). For Islamic culture, therefore, the pre-Islamic past possessed a certain ambiguity: on the one hand, it was a misguided and repudiated pagan age—perhaps best exemplified by the master poet Imruʾ al-Qays, "the leader of the poets into hell-fire"—and, on the other hand, it was the fertile moral and cultural seedbed for the new religion—what I term the "proto-Islamic" aspect of the Jāhiliyyah.[43] Perhaps nothing better exemplifies the proto-Islamic perception of the Jāhiliyyah than the persona and poetry of Zuhayr ibn Abī Sulmá, who, especially for his Muᶜallaqah, was renowned for the celebration of the virtues of peace, and who makes mention therein of Allāh and of the Day of Reckoning (*yawm al-ḥisāb*):

> You can never hide from Allāh what is in your souls, so it's concealed;
> Whatever you try to hide, Allāh will find out:
>
> Either it will be postponed, put in a book, and stored till Reckoning Day;
> Or else it will be summarily punished here on earth.[44]
>
> [23]

The perception of Zuhayr as proto-Islamic must certainly be the intent of the story of his testament to his sons Kaᶜb and Bujayr:

> It is related that Zuhayr saw in his sleep a rope that hung down from heaven to the earth and people were holding onto it. But every time he tried to grab hold of it, it would recede from him. He interpreted this to mean that a prophet would come at the end of time and would be a mediator between God Almighty and mankind, but that his own life span would not reach the time of the prophet's mission. So in his dying words to his sons he bade them to believe in this prophet when he appeared.[45]

What is most important here, however, is not so much the individual poet and his works, but rather the concept that the cultural inheritance of the Arabs was the root of Islamic culture. We read, for example, in *Kitāb al-Aghānī*:

> When someone recited to ᶜUmar ibn al-Khaṭṭāb verses that Zuhayr had said praising Harim ibn Sinān:

Leave off that and turn to speak of Harim,
The most seasoned of men, the lord of the settled tribes.

Had you been anything other than human
You would have been the full moon that illumines the night.

Of all the men I've heard of, you are the one who binds most firmly
The bonds of maternal and paternal kin.

How well you fill your coat of mail when the cry,
"Dismount and fight!" is heard, and panic grips men's hearts.

I see that you cut what you measure,
While other men measure, but then don't cut.

I praise you with what I know of you first-hand
And with the reputation that precedes you for courageous deeds.

Veils hide vile deeds,
But virtue is not veiled.

[24]

"That is the Messenger of God (pbuh)!" exclaimed ᶜUmar.[46]

This anecdote is telling us, in other words, that in the eyes of the Islamic age, it is as though the Jāhiliyyah produced *madīḥ nabawī* (praise to the Prophet) "*avant la lettre.*"

Kaᶜb ibn Zuhayr's Suᶜād Has Departed

The first poem upon which the sobriquet "Mantle Ode" (*Qaṣīdat al-Burdah*) was conferred is the poem rhymed in *lām* that opens "Suᶜād has departed" (*bānat Suᶜādu*) by the renowned poet and scion of renowned poets, Kaᶜb ibn Zuhayr.[47] According to the Islamic-Arabic literary tradition, Kaᶜb presented his ode to the Prophet Muḥammad on the occasion of his conversion to Islam, given as 9 AH/630 CE, and, in turn, the Prophet conferred upon the poet his mantle (*burdah*). As is the case with the pre-Islamic tradition, we do not possess written sources for the events under discussion dating to the time of the Prophet. Rather, our written sources are from a century and a half or more later and record, therefore, the culturally sanctioned (re)collection and/or (re)construction of the poem and of the events that surround Kaᶜb's composition and performance of it before the Prophet.[48] It should be noted that the most canonical compendium of the

Prophet's life, and the main source for the literary and poetic materials for our reading of Kaᶜb's Suᶜād Has Departed, is Ibn Hishām's (d. 218/833) *Al-Sīrah al-Nabawiyyah*, itself an edition of Ibn Isḥāq's (d. 150/767) *Al-Sīrah*.[49] The authoritative scholar Ibn Sallām al-Jumaḥī (d. 231 or 232/845 or 846) credits Ibn Isḥāq with expertise in Sīrah and Maghāzī (the military campaigns of the Prophet), but not in poetry, and castigates him for the uncritical inclusion in his *Al-Sīrah* of all sorts of unattested poetry: "He corrupted and adulterated poetry. . . and included, in his biographical accounts, poems attributed to men who never composed a line of poetry, to women, and even to ᶜĀd and Thamūd."[50] My point is that we are dealing with the cultural formation of early Islam rather than historically verifiable events and poems.

I would like to explore how the art of the *qaṣīdah* transforms an actual event or circumstance (the conversion of the pagan Arab tribes to Islam) into ritual or myth, thus changing it from an ephemeral and transient occurrence to a permanent and transcendent message.[51] Studies in the field of orality and literacy have demonstrated that the function of poetry, including all those devices we term "poetic," is essentially mnemonic, for in nonliterate, oral societies the only way to preserve information is to memorize it. As Eric Havelock has shown, rhyme, meter, assonance, alliteration, antithesis, parallelism, etc., all serve to stabilize and preserve the oral "text."[52] The same holds true for simile, metaphor, and pun.[53] Furthermore, we can add to these rhetorical elements the ritual and ceremonial structure of the classical Arabic *qaṣīdah* and the sequence of themes that traditionally occur within its structural units. That is, Havelock's words "Ritualization becomes the means of memorization" are applicable to the formal structure of the *qaṣīdah* as well to its prosodic and rhetorical features.[54] A further corollary of Havelock's definition of "poetic" elements as essentially mnemonic is that Kaᶜb ibn Zuhayr's rhetorically rich and highly formal "pre-Islamic" *qaṣīdah* should have a greater claim to authenticity than the prose anecdotes and generic occasional *Ayyām al-ᶜArab* poetry that accompany it in *Al-Sīrah*, and therefore it anchors the rest of the materials. The poeticization, i.e., the ritualization and mythicization of the historical event, in this case the mission of the Prophet Muḥammad and the conversion of the Arab tribes to Islam, does not, however, merely endow it with mnemonic stability, but, what is more important, it imbues it with suprahistorical significance. It thus functions, as Havelock has shown for poetry in oral cultures and as we will argue here for Kaᶜb's *qaṣīdah,* Suᶜād Has Departed, as "the instrument for the establishment of a cultural tradition."[55]

The gist of my argument will be that Kaᶜb's *qaṣīdah* Suᶜād Has Departed and its surrounding literary anecdotes have the effect of ritualizing and mythicizing the poet's conversion so that it encodes and embodies the conversion of the pagan Arabs of the Jāhiliyyah to Islam, and, moreover, the submission to Islam, or cooption by Islam, of the pre-Islamic poetic tradition.[56] The Arabic poetic, and especially the panegyric, tradition becomes the major literary-ceremonial expression of Arab-Islamic legitimacy and allegiance. Furthermore, in my reading, Kaᶜb's Suᶜād Has Departed, as contextualized in the Sīrah literature, encodes a spiritual trajectory from despair and doubt to hope and redemption, so that it becomes, in the Arab-Islamic tradition, a paradigmatic devotional poem whose "performance" by the believer entails the reenactment of the same moral and spiritual journey.[57] In this respect, we find, particularly in the Post-Classical period when the literary genre of *madīḥ nabawī* (praise poem to the Prophet) most flourished, myriad commentaries, contrafactions (*muᶜāraḍāt,* imitation poems in the same rhyme and meter), and expansions (*tashṭīr, takhmīs,* etc.),[58] that serve as devotional performances and reenactments of the spiritual transformation perceived in Suᶜād Has Departed.

In examining this ode, and with it the anecdotal prose (*akhbār,* sing. *khabar*) and poetic (*ashᶜār,* sing. *shiᶜr*) materials that accompany it in the classical Arabic literary tradition, I would like to demonstrate how the structure and themes of the tripartite pre-Islamic ode—the elegiac prelude (*nasīb*), the desert journey (*raḥīl*), and the praise section (*madīḥ*)—that we examined above are employed by Kaᶜb ibn Zuhayr to express on the political level a transfer of allegiance from his tribe, the Banū Muzaynah, to the Prophet Muḥammad and the nascent Islamic state and, on the religious level, the conversion from the beliefs and mores of the Jāhiliyyah to Islam. In doing so we will take as our interpretative foundation the concept of the panegyric ode (*qaṣīdat al-madḥ*), presented in the introduction to this chapter, as comprising a multifaceted "ritual complex" that interweaves the poetics of supplication and submission and ritual and ceremonial patterns such as Mauss's formulation of gift exchange and van Gennep's of the rite of passage to form a complex social movement. Inseparable from this, as we also established in the introduction, are the performative and performance aspects of the ode that, as a whole as well as in its parts, comprises speech acts effecting change of status, the cutting and binding of ties of allegiance, obligation, rites of incorporation, etc. Thus, the tripartite pattern of van Gennep's rite of passage—Separation, Liminality, and Aggregation—will be aligned with the three parts of the *qaṣīdah* to highlight the change in status and the psychological transition involved in the conversion process. In order to more fully understand the symbolic ramifications of the poet's offering a *qaṣīdah* and the Prophet's conferring of his mantle to form a bond of allegiance between subject and ruler, and a promise of protection in this world and the next, we will draw once more on the insights of Mauss's formulations concerning ritual exchange. Finally, attention to the performative aspects of the ode will help us understand how the verbal, physical, and symbolic actions of these rites enact and encode political, moral, and spiritual transformations.

THE CONVERSION NARRATIVE

Let us begin with the anecdotal and poetic context of Kaᶜb's presentation of his renowned ode, Suᶜād Has Departed, to the Prophet Muḥammad. The conversion narrative appears in the classical literary and religious sources, such as the Baghdādi philologist al-Sukkarī's (d. 275/888) collection of and commentary on Kaᶜb's poetry and the Egyptian scholar Ibn Hishām's (d. 218/833 or 213/828) Life of the Prophet (*Al-Sīrah al-Nabawiyyah*).[59] A number of points of similarity are to be noted when we compare the materials concerning Kaᶜb with those relating to al-Nābighah's O Abode of Mayyah (above): the poet is in mortal danger, with a death sentence on his head; the *qaṣīdah* is presented as part of a ceremony of submission and declaration of allegiance; in both, the *qaṣīdah* plays a role in the redemption of the poet. Further, as will be discussed below, the story of Kaᶜb ibn Zuhayr's and his brother Bujayr's conversion to Islam forms a prose conversion narrative that serves in the Arab-Islamic literary tradition to contextualize and elucidate the ritually structured conversion poem. We can appreciate how the process of oral transmission of pre-Islamic and early Islamic poetic and prose materials transforms the arbitrary and historical into the significant and mythical through Gregory Nagy's remarks concerning the mythicization of the poet in the classical Greek tradition:

> . . . the identity of the poet as composer becomes progressively stylized, becoming ever further distanced from the reality of self-identification through performance. . . . Once the factor of performance slips out of the poet's control, even if the performers of his poetry have a tradition of what to say about the poet as a composer, nevertheless, *the poet becomes a myth; more accurately, the poet becomes part of a myth, and the mythmaking structure appropriates his identity.*[60] [Emphasis mine]

Al-Sukkarī's version of the events surrounding Kaᶜb's presentation of his conversion ode, Suᶜād Has Departed, begins with the conversion of Kaᶜb's brother, Bujayr:

> Bujayr ibn Abī Sulmá al-Muzanī converted to Islam, and his people, including his full brother Kaᶜb, got angry with him. Bujayr met the Prophet during the Hijrah. Then Kaᶜb sent the following message to him:
>
> Take, you two, a message to Bujayr from me,
> "Did you accept what you said at al-Khayf, did you?[61]
>
> You drank with al-Maʾmūn a thirst-quenching cup,
> He gave you a first draught, then a second.
>
> You abandoned the ways of right guidance and followed him,
> To what was it, woe to you, that he guided you?
>
> To a religion no father or mother of yours ever followed,
> Nor any one of your kinsmen!"
>
> [25]
>
> When these verses reached Bujayr, he recited them to the Prophet who exclaimed, "He speaks the truth, I am al-Maʾmūn [the trustworthy one] and he is a liar; and certainly he found no father or mother of *his* following Islam." Then Bujayr replied to his brother:
>
> Who will take Kaᶜb a message, "Will you accept the religion for which
> You falsely blame me, though it is the more judicious course?
>
> To God alone, not to al-ᶜUzzá nor al-Lāt,
> Make for safety, while you can, and submit,
>
> Before a day when no one is safe or escapes from the Fire,
> Except the submissive Muslim, pure of heart.
>
> To me the religion of Zuhayr—and it is nothing—
> And the religion of Abū Sulmá are now forbidden."
>
> [26]

When the Apostle of God returned to Medina from al-Ṭāʾif, Bujayr wrote to Kaᶜb: "The Prophet is intent upon killing all of the polytheist poets who attack him, and Ibn al-Zabaᶜrá and Hubayrah ibn Abī Wahb [two poets of the Quraysh tribe] have fled. So if you have any use for your life, then turn to the Messenger of God, for he does not kill anyone who comes to him repentant. If you won't do this, then flee to safety." When Bujayr's message reached him, Kaᶜb became greatly distressed and anxious, and those in his tribe spread alarming news about him, saying, "He is as good as dead," and the Banū Muzaynah [his clan] refused to shelter him. So he made his way to Medina and stayed with an acquaintance of his there. Then he came to the Apostle of God. The Prophet did not recognize him, so he sat down before him and said, "O Apostle of God, if I were to bring you Kaᶜb ibn Zuhayr, repentant and submitting to Islam, would you accept him?" "Yes," he replied. Then he said, "I am Kaᶜb." Suddenly one of the Anṣār [Medinese Helpers] leapt up and cried, "Let me cut off his head!" But the Prophet restrained him, whereupon Kaᶜb recited his panegyric to the Prophet.[62]

The story of the conversion of Kaᶜb and Bujayr, the two sons of the master poet of the Jāhiliyyah and paradigm of pre- or proto-Islamic virtue, Zuhayr ibn Abī Sulmá, is one that points to the inner conflict involved in conversion. For embracing Islam involved the transfer of loyalties, renunciation of the inherited ancestral ethos of the Jāhiliyyah, of which Zuhayr ibn Abī Sulmá had been the noblest embodiment, to a new religion founded by an orphaned upstart from the politically powerful Meccan tribe of Quraysh. The prose anecdotes and the poetic exchange that they contain first indicate that it is virtue, not inherent viciousness, that holds Kaᶜb back from Islam: *pietas,* piety and devotion to the ways and religion of his ancestors. A closer look at the first poem indicates that, from the tribal point of view, Bujayr's conversion is nothing but opportunistic treachery. For whereas from the Islamic point of view to be given a drink by or share a cup with the Messenger of God suggests the cup of immortal life, from Kaᶜb's perspective, it is the commensal cup of tribal membership. In drinking from it Bujayr has renounced his own kin and the right guidance (*al-hudá*) of the ancestral ways (vv. 3–4). Nor does Bujayr deny this in his reply: he has abandoned the goddesses of the Jāhiliyyah to worship the one God; the religion of his kinsmen is nothing to him; the religion of his grandfather, Abū Sulmá, he now considers forbidden. His reason: that on Judgment Day only the Muslim, pure of heart, will escape perdition.

That this is treachery by Jāhilī standards is clear if we compare it to the celebrated statement of that ethos by the last and greatest of the Jāhilī "Arab Knights" (*fursān al-ʿArab*), Durayd ibn al-Ṣimmah, who lived until the coming of Islam, but did not convert. When he advised his kinsmen, the Banū Ghaziyyah, against fighting on the side of the Meccan polytheists against the Prophet at the Battle of Ḥunayn (8/630), they rejected his advice. Nevertheless, out of loyalty, he led them in battle. Mortally wounded, his dying words, which became a byword for loyalty even against one's better judgment and at the price of one's life, were:

> I gave my orders at the twisted sand dune,
> But they did not see that I was right till the next morning.
>
> When they defied me, I went along with them,
> Although I saw their error and that I was led astray.
>
> For am I not of the Banū Ghaziyyah? If they err, I err with them;
> And if they are rightly guided, so am I.[63]

[27]

Returning to Kaʿb, we note that the prose narrative, further, constitutes a prosaic or literalist version of Kaʿb's poem. The brief exchange of poems between Kaʿb and his brother Bujayr epitomizes the conversion process, with its renunciation of tribal religion and loyalty and its submission and allegiance to Islam and its promise of salvation. The Messenger of God has outlawed Kaʿb; his choice is to flee or else to submit and convert. The situation becomes clear to him when his own tribesmen consider him "as good as dead" (*maqtūl*) (which is the equivalent of disowning him, since it implies that they will neither defend nor avenge him), and finally his own clan, the Banū Muzaynah, refuse him shelter and protection. Kaʿb does not betray the ancestral ways; his kinsmen do. And it is only when he sees that the "religion of Abū Sulmá," his grandfather, is no more and the old social order is extinct that he heads for Medina to embrace the new one, Islam, and submit to its Prophet. Inasmuch as the anecdotes serve as a commentary (*sharḥ*) to the *qaṣīdah*, they explain the poem as an expression of transfer of allegiance, as the poet's renunciation of his former tribal allegiance and an oath of fealty to the Prophet of Islam. That the poem is likewise a redemption payment is also apparent from the anecdotes, in Muḥammad's outlawing the poet and his kinsmen's disowning him and declaring him *maqtūl* (already slain, as good as dead). It is the poem, then, that redeems Kaʿb, both in this world and, as Bujayr's poem within the conversion narrative tells us, the next. To make the point more explicit, the anecdotes present a "prosaic" (in both senses of the word) version of "salvation." They depict Muḥammad as saving Kaʿb's life in this world by restraining the zealous Anṣārī (the Anṣār, "Helpers," were the Medinese supporters of the Prophet) who would behead him on the spot. Further, as the Prophet's acceptance of the poet into the Islamic fold implies and as his saving him from the Anṣārī's sword symbolizes, he confers salvation in the world to come. As if to make the exchange of his life for his poem explicit, it is at precisely this point, according to the anecdotal narrative, that Kaʿb recites his renowned ode.

In terms of the ritual patterns on which our interpretation of this *qaṣīdah* is based, a rite of passage from the Jāhiliyyah to Islam is clearly detectable in this prose narrative: the Separation of the poet-passenger, Kaʿb, from a previous social state (the tribal loyalties of the Jāhiliyyah); Liminality, Kaʿb's dangerous "betwixt and between" outlaw status in which his tribesmen refuse him protection, on the one hand, and the Prophet threatens him with death on the other; Aggregation, that is, the poet-passenger's incorporation into a new community with the rights and obligations that this entails—in particular his submission to the Prophet and the Prophet's protection of him. The elements of the Supplicatory Ritual are in evidence as well, the poet's Loss of his Jāhilī tribal position, his Self-Abasement and Submission to the Prophet, his Supplication of the Prophet and his Praise of the one supplicated, that is, the poem of praise (*qaṣīdat al-madḥ*). It should be clear from the complex of ritual patterns inherent in the conversion narrative that it is not a mere recounting of events, but what we have termed a mythicization of the events so that they convey a permanent and transcendent spiritual message. Those who read the conversion narrative at a merely literal level and proceed to condemn Kaʿb's poem as a clever stratagem to save his skin have missed the point, both of the narratives and of the poem.[64]

THE CONVERSION ODE

Although differing somewhat in its proportions and its choice of traditional themes, Kaᶜb's ode follows the same full formal tripartite structure of the pre-Islamic panegyric ode that we presented in the Jāhilī examples of the introduction. The poem opens with 1) the elegiac prelude (*nasīb*): vv. 1–12, constructed on the traditional motif of the bereft lover describing his departed mistress, Suᶜād (Felicity), first her beauty, then her perfidy. This is followed by 2) the journey section (*raḥīl*): vv. 13–32/33, devoted to a detailed description of the fortitude of the she-camel that alone can reach the distant dwelling of Suᶜād (which now must mean the "felicity" of Islam), a final passage comparing the she-camel's unrelenting gait to the violent lamentations of a bereft mother, and the conclusion that Kaᶜb, abandoned by his kinsmen, is "as good as dead." The poem concludes with 3) the praise section (*madīḥ*): vv. 33/34–55, comprising the poet's submission and declaration of allegiance to the Prophet Muḥammad and his conversion to Islam (vv. 33–41), a comparison of the Prophet with a lion (vv. 42–48), and praise of the Emigrants (Muhājirūn), the early group of loyal Muslims who accompanied the Prophet Muḥammad on the Hijrah from Mecca to Medina (vv. 49–55).

The significance of this three-part structural sequence is perhaps most easily grasped if viewed in light of the van Gennepian formulation of the rite of passage. The elegiac prelude, desert journey, and praise (with submission and conversion) can be aligned, respectively, with the Separation from a past social state, the outcast Liminality phase outside the bonds and bounds of society, and the Incorporation phase in which the passenger (re)enters society, but with a new status, rights, and obligations. As mentioned above, my interpretation is that the rite of passage pattern inherent in this ode not only conveys the conversion of Kaᶜb from his ancestral tribal religion to the new religion proclaimed by the Prophet Muḥammad, but also operates emblematically in Islamic tradition to convey the cultural transition from the Jāhiliyyah to Islam.

KAᶜB IBN ZUHAYR'S SUᶜĀD HAS DEPARTED[65]

PART 1: LYRIC-ELEGIAC PRELUDE (*NASĪB*) (VV. 1–12)

1. Suᶜād has departed and today
   my heart is sick,
   A slave to her traces,
   unransomed and enchained.[66]

2. On the morning of departure
when her tribe set out,
Suʿād was but a bleating antelope
with languid gaze and kohl-lined eye.
3. When she smiles she flashes
side teeth wet
As if with a first draught of wine
or with a second,
4. Mixed with cool water from a wadi's bend,
in a pebbled streambed limpid
And sparkling in the noontime sun,
chilled by the north wind,
5. Cleansed by the winds
of all dirt and dust,
And by white cumuli left overflowing
with a night cloud's rain.
6. Alas! what a mistress, had she been true
to what she promised,
Had true advice not gone
unheeded.
7. But she is a mistress
in whose blood are mixed
Calamity, mendacity,
inconstancy, and perfidy.
8. She never stays the same
but is as mutable
As the *ghūl* in her garb
ever-changing.
9. Nor does she hold fast love's bond,
once she has claimed it,
Except as sieves
hold water.
10. The false promises of ʿUrqūb
were her model;
Her promises were nothing except
empty prattle.
11. I hope and pray that in the end
they'll be fulfilled,
But they will remain forever
unfulfilled.
12. Don't be deceived by the desires
she aroused, the promises she made,
For hopes and dreams
are a delusion.

[28]

The Lyric Elegiac Prelude (Nasīb)*: Verses 1–12.* Kaᶜb's elegiac prelude is constructed of the traditional motif of the bereft lover describing his departed mistress, here Suᶜād. If we note the derivation of the name Suᶜād, from the root *s-ᶜ-d,* whence *saᶜādah,* prosperity, good fortune, happiness, felicity,[67] it is possible to read this passage allegorically as an elegy to a bygone Golden Age, an elegy to the Jāhiliyyah. Suᶜād and all her etymological baggage—prosperity, happiness, good fortune—have departed. The forlorn poet is left behind, raving over the traces of the now-empty encampment. In the context of our argument, this must be read as a metaphor for the poet's political situation: the ethos of the Jāhiliyyah is obsolete; the poet has been abandoned and betrayed by his kinsmen. He is "unransomed, unredeemed" (*lam yufda*), or, as al-Sukkarī's recension has it, "unrequited" (*lam yujza*).[68] On the surface this diction refers metaphorically to Suᶜād's failure to return the poet-lover's affections in kind; on a deeper level the literal usage suggests the treachery of kinsmen who have failed in their reciprocal obligations to him, which are, above all, to ransom and to avenge.

In the description of the lost "felicity" that ensues, two aspects of the beloved are emphasized: first, in verses 2–5, her beauty and purity: her glance like the antelope's, her flashing teeth that taste of the finest wine mixed with the cool limpid waters of rain-fed mountain streams. In verses 6–12, however, purity gives way to perfidy: beautiful as the promise of "felicity" may have been, it was ultimately a broken one.[69] We can detect in Kaᶜb's *nasīb* the complex of traditional motival elements that we saw in The Tribe Set Out, the panegyric of his father, Zuhayr ibn Abī Sulmá: the departed beloved, the poet's passion, the cutting of bonds, the breaking of promises. As in al-Nābighah's O Abode of Mayyah with the cases of Sulaymān, Lubad, and Zarqāʾ al-Yamāmah, here too the poet draws upon mythic-folkloric materials, a process that anchors the poem in deeper and broader layers of culture, even as it serves as vehicle and vessel to convey and preserve that culture. In verse 8, Suᶜād's inconstancy is likened to that of the Protean *ghūl.* Of this creature the lexicographer Ibn Manẓūr (d. 711/1311–12) writes, "*ghūl,* pl. *ghīlān,* is a species of *shayṭān* or *jinn.* The Arabs claim that the *ghūl* appears to people in the desert and then transforms itself, that is, it changes into all sorts of different shapes; then it takes them away, that is, leads them astray and kills them."[70] In the classical Arabic literary lore, the *ghūl* appears most characteristically in the anecdotes of the pre-Islamic *ṣuᶜlūk* (brigand) poet Taʾabbaṭa Sharran, in which the siren-like (female) *ghūl* assumes the form of a hideous and deformed sphinx-like hybrid.[71]

Verse 10 describes Suʿād's faithlessness with the proverbial phrase "the [false] promises of ʿUrqūb" (*mawāʿīdu ʿUrqūbin*). This proverb encapsulates the story of ʿUrqūb, which the philologist al-Maydānī (d. 518/1124) relates in his renowned collection of Arab proverbs (*Majmaʿ al-Amthāl*) as follows:

> According to Abū ʿUbayd, ʿUrqūb was one of the Amalikites (ʿAmālīq). One day, one of his brothers came to him importuning him, and ʿUrqūb replied, "When this date palm puts forth shoots, you can have them." When it put forth shoots and his brother came to claim what was promised him, ʿUrqūb said, "Leave them until they become green dates." When the dates were green, he said, "Wait till they are colored." When they were colored, he said, "Wait till they are ripe." When they were ripe, he said, "Wait till they are dry." When they dried, ʿUrqūb went out at night and gathered them and didn't give his brother anything. Thus ʿUrqūb became proverbial for breaking promises.[72]

Betrayed hopes and desires, deception and delusion complete the *nasīb*.

Given the Islamic context in which this *qaṣīdah* has come down to us, the closing verses of its *nasīb* are striking for two elements of diction that have an eminently Qurʾānic resonance. The first is *abāṭīlū* ("empty prattle," rhyme word, v. 10), which occurs in the Qurʾān principally in the form *bāṭil* (false, falsehood, vanity, lie) in association with *kufr* (disbelief) and in opposition to *ḥaqq* (truth) and *niʿmat Allāh* (God's blessing) (QK 31:30; 22:62, etc.). The second is *taḍlīlū* ("delusion," rhyme word, v. 12, from form II *ḍallala,* to lead astray, into error), which occurs most often in the Qurʾān in form I *ḍalla/yaḍillu* (to stray, err), in association with *kufr* (unbelief), *shirk* (polytheism), and *ẓulm* (oppression, injustice) and in opposition to *hudá* (right guidance) (QK 41:1; 13:14; 34:24; 4:116; 19:38; 53:30, etc.). The effect of employing moral diction that had or would come to have Qurʾānic associations is to point out the analogy between Qurʾānic and poetic discourse, to alert the audience to the poet's true intent. For in the poet's mind his kinsmen's failure to fulfill the Jāhilī obligations toward kin reveals the bankruptcy, the ultimate falsehood and error, of the ancestral ways, and can be equated with the Qurʾānic *kufr* and *shirk* (unbelief and polytheism).

Most curious in this *qaṣīdah,* and yet what most confirms our reading, are the transitional verses from the elegiac prelude (*nasīb*) to the journey section (*raḥīl*) (vv. 13–14). Whereas we normally find the poet eschewing the distant and unattainable mistress and declaring his intention to seek his fortune elsewhere, verse 13 of Kaᶜb's poem states quite precisely that it is to regain "Suᶜād" that he undertakes the desert journey. This only makes sense, both poetically and politically, if we take this to mean "a new Suᶜād," the "prosperity, good fortune, and felicity" of Islam. In terms of the poetics of supplication, the Loss element, in both its emotional and moral senses, is palpably present in this *nasīb*.

PART 2: DESERT JOURNEY (*RAḤĪL*) (VV. 13–31)

13. Suᶜād alit at nightfall in a land
    unreachable
  But by the best of she-camels
    of noble breed and easy pace,
14. Never to be reached but by a she-camel
    huge and robust
  That despite fatigue sustains
    her amble and her trot,
15. Sweat gushing from the glands
    behind her ears,
  Eager for the nameless road,
    its way markers effaced,
16. With the eyes of a lone white antelope
    she pierces the unknown
  When badlands and sand dunes blaze
    in high noon's sun,
17. Stout where the pendant hangs,
    full where the shackle binds,
  Her build, the best of all
    the stallions' daughters,
18. Huge as a mountain, her sire her sibling,
    by a dam blood-stallion bred,
  Her uncle by sire and dam the same,
    She is long-necked, brisk-paced.
19. The tick walks on her hide,
    but then the smoothness
  Of her breast and flank
    makes it slip off.
20. Sturdy as the onager,
    her sides piled with meat,

Her knees set wide, clear of
  the breastbone's daughters,
21. As if her muzzle and
  the two sides of her jaw
Between her eyes and throat
  were an oblong stone.
22. She brushes with a tail
  like a stripped palm branch, tufted
Over a dry udder,
  its milk ducts unimpaired,
23. Hook-nosed, in her ears the expert eye
  discerns nobility of breed,
In her two cheeks,
  great smoothness.
24. Overtaking others, she speeds
  on legs lance-like and nimble,
Like an oath annulled they barely
  touch the ground,
25. Brown their sole sinews, they scatter
  pebbles in their wake,
So tough no shoes protect them
  on the hilltops
26. On a day when the chameleon
  is as burnt as if
His sun-scorched parts were bread
  baked on hot rock.
27. As if the repeating motion of her forelegs—
  when she is drenched in sweat
And when the narrow mountain peaks
  are cloaked in the mirage,
28. And the camel driver, his song their goad,
  says to the tribe
When ashen locusts kick up pebbles,
  "Stop and rest,"—
29. At high noon were the arms of a woman
  tall and middle-aged,
Risen in lament, then others,
  near-barren and bereft, respond,
30. Wailing, arms flailing,
  when the heralds announced
The death of her firstborn,
  bereft of reason,

31. Tearing her clothes from her breast
 with her bare hands,
Her woolen shift ripped from her collarbone
 in shreds.

[29]

*The Journey Section (*Raḥīl*): Verses 13–31.* The entire journey section of Kaᶜb's ode is devoted not to the recounting of any particular journey but to the description of that certain she-camel of verse 13 that alone can reach the distant dwelling of "Suᶜād." As we saw in the introduction, this ostensibly realistic and visual depiction of the physical and instinctual attributes of the poet's mount must be understood allegorically as ultimately referring to the poet's own resolve, his inner moral fortitude. For Kaᶜb's passage, the transition from the pagan *pietas* of the Jāhiliyyah to Islam, is primarily a moral and political, not a physical, journey. Thematically, in its focus on the camel description and journey, this *raḥīl* most resembles that of ᶜAlqamah's A Heart Turbulent with Passion, lacking, as does his, the extended animal simile, such as the oryx bull of al-Nābighah's O Abode of Mayyah, or Zuhayr's The Tribe Set Out. Kaᶜb's camel mare is thus described as being "the best," "of noble breed and easy pace" (v. 13), huge, indefatigable (v. 14). The sense of aspiration (*himmah*), usually attributed to the poet himself at the end of the elegiac prelude or at the beginning of the journey section, appears in verse 15 as an attribute of his mount. For *ᶜurḍah* (suited to, fit for) is taken by the commentators to mean *himmah* (ambition, aspiration, zeal).[73] To be "fit" or "eager" for the unknown road whose way markers are obliterated then indicates an instinctive sense of direction, which serves as a figure for the poet's "moral compass." Undaunted by the midday heat, her glance pierces the unknown (v. 16).

Verse 17 describes the she-camel in terms that define her domestication, for if she combines the attributes of wild animals—the gazelle's piercing glance (v. 16), the onager's sturdiness (v. 19)—these have been tamed to serve mankind: her neck is thus termed *muqallad* (II pass. part. as noun of place), the place-where-the-halter (*qilādah,* more precisely, what is hung about the neck of beasts being brought to Mecca for sacrifice, Lane, *q-l-d*)-goes; her pastern *muqayyad,* the place-where-the-shackle (*qayd*)-goes. The best qualities of the natural world have been harnessed to serve the cultural or even sacrificial one. The same idea is given voice in verse 18, where the natural law of survival of the fittest is displaced by the cultural laws of animal husbandry. This camel mare is "in and inbred twice" (Sells's translation), so inbred that she was sired on her dam by her brother, and her maternal uncle is her paternal uncle too (v. 18). Verse 22 seems likewise to allude to nature serving culture: her tail is likened to a stripped palm branch, that is, a plant domesticated; her dry udder indicates perhaps first of all that she is barren, and such she-camels make sturdier mounts, but further that she serves to transport humans: she is not a milch camel, nor has she perpetuated her own species. By contrast it is her animal strength that is emphasized in verse 25: her pads are so tough that even on the roughest ground they need no shoes. This message of the subordination of brute strength to cultural imperatives applies to the poet/passenger as well.

Most curious here is verse 24. As a simple simile it is quite appropriate: so nimble is the she-camel's pace that her feet look as though they are about to touch the ground, but are raised again so quickly that it seems they never do—like an oath about to be fulfilled, then suddenly annulled. Read in the context of verses 6–12, however, it seems that what speeds the poet on his journey is the annulment or abrogation of the obsolete ethos of the Jāhiliyyah. In all, the mixture of natural and cultural attributes amounts to an apt characterization of the she-camel as "betwixt and between" categories and classes: the most domesticated of the beasts, she is yet the most beast-like of the domesticated animals in physical power and strong instincts. She thus embodies the liminal qualities of the poet/passenger himself who must make the transition from the law of the Banū Muzaynah to the law of God's Messenger. Verse 26 alludes to the purifying, purgative aspect of the liminal journey through a transformation from living flesh to baked bread. The effect of heat and hardship is to weed out the weak and unfit; the strong survive, but transformed and reborn.

The final passage of the journey section (vv. 27–31) consists of an unusual simile which likens the relentless motion of the she-camel's forelegs in the hottest part of the day—when camel-caravans normally stop to rest, when locusts, lest they burn their feet, kick aside the scorching pebbles to find cooler ground—to that of the bereaved mother's arms as she frantically tears at her clothes. The more common simile in the journey section of the *qaṣīdah* is, for example, the likening of the she-camel to the oryx bull who endures a cold and rainy night only to be attacked at daybreak by the hunter and his hounds, as we saw in al-Nābighah's and Zuhayr's poems, or the pathos-laden simile of the oryx doe whose calf has been slain by wolves, who, as in the oryx bull simile, likewise suffers through a cold and rainy night only to fight off a hunter and hounds when morning comes, for example in the Muᶜallaqah of Labīd.[74] In Kaᶜb's ode the more familiar similes are replaced by an image of grief and loss that is at once instinctual and ritual: the mythic dementia of the Middle Eastern female lamentation (Adonis, the Three Maries, etc.). This culturally conditioned hysteria triggered by the slain youth endows the female mourners with the strength to shred their clothes with their bare hands, to tear their hair and scratch their faces. It is precisely the "unnatural" strength that the ritual dementia of female mourning unleashes that is likened to the unflagging energy of the she-camel. And it is ultimately the poet's own relentless drive, spurred on by the bereavement of the elegiac prelude, that is implicit in this simile and explicitly expressed in the coming verses (32–33). The bereft woman is termed "middle-aged" (*naṣaf*), which implies that she is no longer of childbearing age, thereby intensifying her sorrow through the irreplaceable loss of her firstborn (v. 30). Her sister mourners are likewise "near-barren" (*nukd*) and "bereft" (*mathākīlū*) (v. 29). This powerful image of bereavement contributes to the Supplicatory element of Loss already detected in the *nasīb.*

Then, too, given the anecdotal context and the poetic text itself, and the implied ritual of "death and rebirth" that is expressed in the perilous liminal journey of the rite of passage pattern, this description suggests the poet's vision of his own mother and womenfolk mourning his death.[75] In this respect it adds to the liminal sense that the poet is in mortal danger and risks his life in approaching the Prophet of Islam. At the same time, it expresses the symbolic "death" of the poet as the necessary precursor to his salvation and "rebirth."

PART 3: PRAISE (*MADĪḤ*) (VV. 32–55)

32. My slanderers at her two sides
    denounced me saying,
"You, O Son of Abū Sulmá, are
    as good as dead."

33. And every trusted friend in whom
    I put my hopes
Said, "I cannot help you, I am occupied
    with other things."
34. So I replied, "Out of my way,
    you bastards!"
For all that the All-Merciful decrees
    will come to pass!
35. For every man of woman born,
    though he be long secure,
Will one day be borne
    on humpbacked bier.
36. I was told God's Messenger
    had threatened me,
But from God's Messenger
    pardon is hoped.
37. Go easy, and let Him be your guide
    who gave to you
The gift of the Qurʾān in which
    are warnings and discernment!
38. Don't hold me to account for what
    my slanderers have said,
For, however great the lies against me,
    I have not sinned!
39. I stood where I saw and heard
    what would have made
The mighty pachyderm,
    had it stood in my stead,
40. Quake with fear unless
    the Messenger of God,
By God's leave,
    granted it protection,[76]
41. Until I placed my right hand,
    without contending,
In the hand of an avenger,
    his word the word.
42. He is more dreaded by me
    when I speak to him
And I am told, "You will be questioned
    and must answer,"
43. Than a lion,
    snapping and rapacious,
Its lair in ʿAththar's hollow,
    thicket within thicket,

44. Who in the morning feeds flesh
to two lion whelps
That live on human flesh,
flung in the dust in chunks,
45. Who when it assaults its match
is not permitted
To leave its match
unnotched,
46. For whom the braying onager
falls silent,
In whose wadi no hunters
stalk their prey,
47. In whose wadi lies an honest man,
his weapons and torn clothes
Flung in the dust,
his flesh devoured.
48. The Messenger is surely a sword
from whose flash light is sought,
One of the swords of God,
an Indian blade unsheathed,
49. In a band of Qurashis whose spokesman
said to them in Mecca's hollow
When they submitted to Islam,
"Depart!"
50. They departed, but no weaklings
departed with them,
None who flee the battle,
none unsteady in the saddle, none unarmed.
51. Haughty, high-nosed champions,
who on battle day
Don shirts
of David's weave,
52. White, ample, their rings
interlocking
As if they were the qafʿāʾ plant's
interlocking rings.
53. They walk as the white camels walk
when kept in check by blows,
While the stunted black ones
go astray.[77]
54. Neither jubilant when their spears
strike down a tribe,
Nor distraught when

they are struck,
55. The spear does not pierce them
except in the throat,
Nor do they shrink from
death's water troughs.

[31]

*The Praise Section (*Madīḥ*): Verses 32–55.* At verse 32 there occurs a sudden break in subject and style that signals what we have termed in the introduction the "ritual core" of the poem, which in this case forms a transitional passage that bridges over to the *madīḥ* section. The poet abruptly shifts from the lexically rich and metaphorically dense poetic metalanguage that has characterized the elegiac prelude and the journey section to a stripped-down, univocal, apparently "prosaic" style, as we observed in verses 21–22 of ʿAlqamah's A Heart Turbulent with Passion and verses 37–43 of al-Nābighah's O Abode of Mayyah, the ritual core of the poem. He describes his calumniators, by the two sides of his she-camel, who declare that he is "as good as dead" (*maqtūl*). A ritual pattern of death and rebirth, or rite of passage, is discernible in these verses (32–36): they begin with the poet's Separation or social "death" in the eyes of his friends and kinsmen, and, as we saw in the case of ʿAlqamah and his slain king, a loss of hope as a former allegiance fails and is cut off (v. 33). If the poet's passive suffering of his kinsmen's betrayal of trust is the subject of verses 32 and 33, verses 34 and 35 present the poet-passenger's forceful act of will as he cuts the ties from his side now ("Out of my way!") and surrenders himself to the will of the All-Merciful—an expression of hope. It is followed in verse 35 by the concomitant expression not so much of fear as of resignation to his fate. The important point in terms of our discussion of ritual and especially of the emotional trajectory of the *qaṣīdah* is the poet-passenger's reiteration of the act of will and determination that first appeared at the transition from the *nasīb* to the *raḥīl*.

We must be attuned to the expressly performative nature of the speech acts of verses 32–35. When the poet-passenger's slanderers, i.e., kinsmen, denounce him saying "You are as good as dead" (v. 32), they declare that he is socially dead to them—i.e., with the utterance of this expression, the poet-passenger becomes an outcast, a "non-person," to whom they will no longer offer the protection due a kinsman; in modern terms, a "stateless person" whom no government is obligated to protect. Again, it is a speech act: the excommunication comes into effect with the uttering of these words. So, too, the poet-passenger's reply of verses 34–35: when he cries "Out of my way" and accepts his probable fate (death), he is, on his side, cutting his tribal bond and entering a dangerous social no-man's-land, a liminal state. He accepts the inevitability of death (v. 35) even as invocation of the "All-Merciful" (v. 34) hints at a hope for salvation and clearly points the direction in which the poet-passenger is headed. These performative verses of the cutting of tribal bonds thus set the stage for the tying of new bonds that duly takes place in verses 36–41. If verses 32–35 express the Supplicatory element of Loss, then we can expect the remaining elements to follow in short order. Likewise, in terms of the rite of passage, the poet, having encapsulated in verses 32–35, in the simplified language of the ritual core, the Separation and Liminality phases, can now be expected to complete the Incorporation phase as he enters into the *madīḥ* (praise) section of the ode. Not unexpectedly, then, this passage reaches its dramatic climax in verse 36 where in the most forceful but simple diction the Messenger of God is twice invoked—once in terms of fear ("has threatened me") and again in terms of hope ("pardon is hoped").

The passage of verses 32–36 is set off not only by the abrupt change in style (diction, etc.) that occurs between verses 31 and 32, but also by the maintenance throughout the five verses of the Form I passive participial form (*mafʿūl*) as the rhyme word: *maqtūlū* (slain); *mashghūlū* (occupied); *mafʿūlū* (enacted); *maḥmūlū* (borne); *maʾmūlū* (hoped for). The effect of this morphological repetition is rendered especially emphatic by the fact that the long vowel preceding the rhyme-consonant (termed *ridf*) for this *qaṣīdah* can be interchangeably *-īlū* or *-ūlū* and is apparently randomly varied throughout the poem, except in this passage where all lines end in *-ūlū*. Here the rhyme functions semantically as well as acoustically, for it brackets the conversion that generated the entire *qaṣīdah* from *maqtūlū* (slain) in verse 32 to *maʾmūlū* (hoped for) in verse 36, from death to hope. The transition from lost hope (v. 33, cf. also vv. 11–12) to hope renewed, from death—as portrayed in the bereft woman simile and the denunciation of Kaʿb's calumniators (vv. 29–32)—to rebirth, points once again in the direction of the ritual form and antecedents of Kaʿb's *qaṣīdah,* and also to its ultimate intent. In terms of the Supplicatory Ode, the elements of Loss,

Self-Abasement/Submission and Supplication all make their appearance in this ritually condensed passage: Loss is most explicit in verses 32–33 in the form of the poet-supplicant's lost hope and trust in his erstwhile friends and natal tribe. Self-Abasement/Submission and Supplication before the Prophet are all in evidence in the strikingly condensed formulation of fear and hope of verse 36.

The poet begins by claiming that he was falsely accused by his calumniators who would see him dead (v. 32). He then presents himself before the Prophet as a helpless supplicant, betrayed by friends or kinsmen in whom he had put his hope and trust (v. 33). In both verses the poet is portrayed as passive victim—he hopes ("in whom I put my hope," *ʾāmuluhū*) (active), but is rebuffed. This is in contrast to verses 34–35 in which the forceful active voice of verse 34, "So I said (*fa-qultu*) 'Out of my way! . . . ,'" makes it clear that the poet has some hand in his own salvation—i.e., that he is in some sense worthy. But—and this is the essence of "Islām"—the poet's forceful act is to submit to God's will, to admit his own mortality. Moreover, he must be willing to sacrifice his own life, and this is precisely the intention of verse 34: that he will face possible death and leave the outcome in God's hands. It is this sacrifice that is the necessary requirement for the poet's redemption. To put it more clearly, the drama of Kaᶜb's submission, (*islām*/Islam), and its moral value as well, requires that he face the risk of death to do it. This, as pointed out above, is made abundantly, if prosaically, clear in the anecdotal passage cited above by the attack of the Anṣārī zealot. Without this element of risk, of putting his life in God's hands, Kaᶜb's conversion would have been mere opportunism. The poet does make some attempt to positively dispose the Almighty when, in verse 34, he chooses of the epithets of God "al-Raḥmān" (the Merciful).

The poet's act of Submission (*islām*)/Self-Abasement and Supplication are expressed with masterful concision in verse 36: *ʾunbiʾtu ʾanna rasūla Allāhi ʾawᶜadanī / wa-al-ᶜafwu ᶜinda rasūli Allāhi maʾmūlū* (I was told God's Messenger had threatened me / But from God's Messenger pardon is hoped). The first hemistich expresses Muḥammad's power; the second Kaᶜb's submission to it. Verse 36 bears a close resemblance to the cognate passages in ᶜAlqamah (vv. 21–22) and al-Nābighah (vv. 41–43) and like those pre-Islamic antecedents comprises a strikingly succinct expression of supplication, self-abasement, and declaration of allegiance. It also shares their stylistic characteristics: simplicity of diction combined with rhetorical complexity. In Kaʿb's verse this takes the form of antithesis imbedded in chiastic (*abba*) structuring. The chiasmus proceeds from a passive configuration of soft consonants *n, b, n,* then "Rasūl Allāh" (Messenger of God), to climax with the harsher and active *w,* ʿ, *d* of the threat; its antithesis, pardon, also in ʿ, *w, d,* begins the counter-movement, followed by another "Rasūl Allāh," and the chiasmus then concludes as it opened with the passive in the soft liquids *m* and *l.* "Islām" as willing self-effacement is conveyed through the use of the passive voice. Whereas in verse 33 the poet says, "I hope" (*ʾāmulu*) in the first person active, in verse 36, when confronting the Messenger of God, the poet hardly dares to hope, but employs instead the passive participle *maʾmūl* (to be hoped for). "I was informed that the Messenger of God had threatened me" (*ʾunbiʾtu . . . ʾawʿadanī*)—the poet is passive subject (*nāʾib fāʿil*) and direct object (*mafūl bih*), but no longer actor/agent (*fāʿil*).

Through the parallel placement of Rasūl Allāh (Messenger of God) in the middle of each hemistich this verse expresses both recognition and submission. The rhetorical power of this repetition is all the more striking in that no mention has been made of Muḥammad up until now. The way was perhaps prepared by the mention of the All-Merciful in verse 34, but it is only with verse 36 that the poet's *shahādah* (creed) is completed. The religious message, the essence of Islamic faith, is also stated here: God, as represented by His Messenger, threatens perdition—an expression of might—but at the same time is capable of pardon, forgiveness. It is the submission to this divine power and authority and the hope for His mercy that constitutes Islam. Verse 36 is thus rhetorically, acoustically, and semantically the crux of the *qaṣīdah,* what Arabs term *bayt al-qaṣīd.*

It is evident that this core passage of Kaʿb's *qaṣīdah,* inasmuch as it offers a concise statement of the ritual paradigm that informs the whole work, is, like Mauss's ritual exchange, a total social phenomenon. Simultaneous expression is given to all kinds of institutions: the poet redeems himself (economic), he swears his fealty to the new order (sociopolitical), he recognizes God's Messenger and submits to Islam (religious, moral) through a *qaṣīdah* whose power, value, and durability are functions of its artistry (aesthetic). The mythological aspect is expressed in the mythic/ritual pattern of death and rebirth (*maqtūl* → *maʾmūl*); its mythogenic aspect, as will be discussed further on, in its creation of the conversion of Kaʿb ibn Zuhayr as a mythos of the transition of Arab society from the Jāhiliyyah to Islam.

The tension of the climax of verse 36 is broken in verse 37 by its opening word *mahlan* ("go easy") and equally by a relaxation of the rhetorical intensity and the alteration of the rhyme from the fivefold repetition in the rhyme of the *mafʿūlū* pattern to *tafʿīlū* (*tafṣīlū,* discernment), after which the poem resumes an apparently random alternation of the *ridf* of the rhyme between *ī* and *ū*. The verse comprises a Supplication in which the poet-supplicant submits to the *mamdūḥ,* the Prophet, but at the same time invokes a higher authority, Allāh. The poet exhorts the Prophet to follow the guidance of God and the Qurʾān and to go easy on him. At this point the near identity of key phrases in verses 36–37 of Kaʿb's poem to verses 41–42 of al-Nābighah's alerts us to the fact that we are dealing not merely with poetic influence (allusion or intertextuality), but also with explicit elements of established ritual and ceremony. Thus we find the pattern: *ʾunbiʾtu ʾanna . . . ʾawʿadanī . . . mahlan . . .* in al-Nābighah:

41. *I've been told* that Abū Qābūs *has threatened me,*
And no one can withstand the lion when it roars.

42. *Go easy* on me! May the tribes, all of them, be your ransom,
And all my increase both of herds and progeny!

And in Kaʿb:

36. *I was told* God's Messenger *had threatened me,*
But from God's Messenger pardon is hoped.

37. *Go easy,* and let Him be your guide who gave to you
the gift of the Qurān in which are warnings and discernment!

These are really nothing but two interrelated aspects of the *qaṣīdah*-as-ritual. On the literary side, the allusion to a renowned masterpiece creates a mythic concordance between the supplicant/supplicated pairs: al-Nābighah/King al-Nuʿmān and Kaʿb/the Prophet Muḥammad. The effect of this is to confer poetic authority on Kaʿb and moral-political authority on Muḥammad. On the ritual side these flagged terms signal a specific step in the ritual of Supplication. We also see more clearly the relation between Supplication and Submission: that is, what we have termed Self-Abasement is really the submission to the superior might or authority of the one supplicated that serves, in turn, as a necessary prerequisite to the supplication or petition. Thus we witness in this *qaṣīdah* the Islamic cooptation of Jāhilī ritual and ceremonial forms to buttress the authority of the Prophet and the nascent Islamic state by identifying them with the authoritative models of the past.

Verses 38–41 constitute a reiteration of the ritual pattern of the poet's conversion (*islām*). The message is bracketed in rhyme words from the same root (*q-w-l,* to speak), each made more emphatic by *tajnīs* (paronomasia, verbal play on words of the same or related roots) within the verse: *aqwāl* and *aqāwīlū* in verse 38 refer to the fabrications and false accusations of the poet's calumniators; in verse 41 *qīluhu al-qīlū* refers to the veracity and authority of the Prophet's speech, his power and intention to carry out what he says. The direction of the passage is thus from falsehood to truth. The terror and danger of the transition are expressed in the "fear and trembling" of the poet, or elephant, before God's Messenger (vv. 39–40). We must keep in mind here, as Maḥmūd ʿAlī Makkī points out, the use of the elephant as a formidable and terrifying beast of battle, as is conveyed in the elephant of the army of the South Arabian king Abrahah, when he attacked Mecca, in what was termed the Year of the Elephant (traditionally considered the year of the Prophet Muḥammad's birth) (cf. the Sūrah of the Elephant/QK 105 Sūrat al-Fīl), or the elephants in Hannibal crossing the Alps.[78] The point here is that the *mamdūḥ*, Muḥammad, has power over life and death, and only with his granting Kaʿb protection does the poet's fear abate. Verse 40 reiterates in *yurʿadu . . . tanwīlū* (quake with fear . . . granting [protection]), the same antithesis as verse 36 between the threat of punishment and hope for forgiveness.

We can draw yet another comparison between al-Nābighah's *qaṣīdah* and Kaʿb's: although both poems are classified in Arabic as *iʿtidhāriyyah* (poem of apology) the wrongdoer-supplicant does not confess and beg forgiveness, as we would understand the term, but rather, the poetic ritual seems to require that the offender deny the accusations against him and swear that he is the victim of calumniators and slanderers and, on that ground, beg for mercy (al-Nābighah, vv. 39–40; Kaʿb, v. 38). As in the case of al-Nābighah, the explanation for this seems to lie in the "formal pretense and social pretension" (Mauss's terms) that are essential to ritual and ceremonial (think of the white bridal gown). The apparent dramatic and narrative realism of these passages in both al-

Nābighah's and Kaʿb's *qaṣīdahs* is revealed by such parallel constructions to be instead the reenactment of an established ritual or ceremony.

The closing verse of this passage, verse 41, is like verse 36 an expression of submission to authority. As for the meaning of the poet's placing his hand in that of the Prophet without contending (*waḍaʿtu yamīnī lā ʾunāziʿuhu fī kaffi . . .*), the editor of al-Sukkarī's recension explains: "That is, 'I placed my right hand in his by way of submission, not contention'; i.e., he surrendered himself to him and acknowledged him. For the Arabs, when they swore an oath to something, would strike each other on the right hand."[79] To describe Muḥammad as an "avenger" or "exacting vengeance" (*dhī naqimātin*) (*naqimah* = vengeance, penal retribution, punishment, Lane, *n-q-m*) is to indicate that he is a man to be feared. If the ritual core is the poem's performative nexus in terms of a speech act, verse 41 depicts the bodily enactment or physical performance of submission, of the sort that Paul Connerton terms "the choreography of authority."[80]

This entire passage (vv. 32–41) must be read, too, in light of verses 6–11 of the elegiac prelude. For there the Separation phase of the rite of passage is expressed as the failure or breakdown of trust, the abrogation of the Jāhilī social contract: mendacity, inconstancy, perfidy, the failure to fulfill promises. Of special interest here is the antithesis between "her promises were nothing except empty prattle" (*mā mawāʿīduhā ʾillā al-ʾabāṭīlū*) of verse 11 and "his word the word" (*qīluhu al-qīlū*), i.e., who keeps his word, whose word is law, which in the Islamic context can also refer to the Qurʾān—the ultimate speech of God conveyed to Muḥammad—of verse 41; failed hope as opposed to hope fulfilled; the seduction and misguidance (*taḍlīlū*) of misplaced trust (v. 12) as opposed to the right guidance (*hadá,* to guide aright), exhortation, and the discernment of right from wrong (*tafṣīlū*) (v. 37). The passage from verses 32 to 41 thus constitutes a ritual kernel whose form is the key to that of the *qaṣīdah* as a whole and whose conclusions provide the recompense for the loss expressed in the elegiac prelude. This movement from Loss to Fulfillment is expressed in a variety of ways, but especially in the movement from unfulfilled promise to fulfilled promise, and—in the most morally evocative and Qurʾānic of terms—from misguidance (*taḍlīl*) to right guidance (*hudá*). The effect is to identify the "falsehood" of Suʿād in the *nasīb* with the falsehood of the poet's slanderers and calumniators.

In the following passage (vv. 42–47) the subject is the fear engendered by the Messenger of God. The fear of the temporal judgment of Muḥammad when Kaʿb revealed himself and his identity and had to answer for his deeds (v. 42) was bound to generate an "Islamic" reading, as indeed we find cited in al-Tibrīzī's commentary.[81] Although the text of the poem contains no explicit mention of the Day of Judgment or of the Afterlife, for the traditional Muslim reader this verse must have suggested both temporal and divine judgment, a reading reflected in the Bujayr poem of the conversion narrative. The elative form "He is more dreaded" (*la-dhāka ʾahyabu*) serves as a pivot point for the poet to modulate from the "prosaic" style of the poem's semantic core via the simile back into the imagery and diction of the poetic world. In terms of the Supplicatory Ritual, the theme of fear is an expression of Self-Abasement and Submission before the one supplicated, but it also serves here as a transition into the fourth requisite Supplicatory element, that is, Praise of the one supplicated.

The description of the warrior, by metaphor or simile, as a lion is a traditional one, as we have seen in Zuhayr's The Tribe Set Out (v. 46). The rhetorical effect of the elative here is to magnify the Prophet and the fear he inspires. In terms of the present argument, this intensifies both sides of the fear/hope equation, for the value of a man's mercy is directly commensurate with the power of his wrath: the mercy or pardon of a weakling is worthless. The lion that feeds flesh to its cubs is a metaphorical variant of the more common expression in the poetry of the warrior aristocracy, that of the warrior revitalizing his kin group by slaying the enemy, here captured with bold concision: *ʿayshuhumā laḥmun* (literally, "their life is meat") (v. 44).[82]

The change from the object to the subject of the simile occurs in verse 45 in the change from the animal to the martial. Verse 46 appears to shift back to the lion, describing the terror, both instinctual and rational, that both beast (the onager) and man feel for the formidable lion. But the barrier between the subject and the object of the simile is becoming more and more attenuated. In the context of the *qaṣīdah* the ravaged corpse of verse 47 suggests what the poet's own fate might have been had he contended with Muḥammad rather than submitting to him.

The concept of might as the prerequisite for generosity and mercy—so powerfully conveyed in the image of the lion feeding his cubs human flesh—was already apparent in the praise sections of the three pre-Islamic odes we examined in the introduction. The "lion of ʿAththar's Hollow" (v. 43) we have already seen in Zuhayr's The Tribe Set Out (v. 46). In Kaʿb's poem the image of the warrior—Muḥammad—as a lion feeding human flesh to its two cubs serves to evoke both a sense of the poet-supplicant's terror, as its victim, but also his hope for its protection and bounty.

The image of the Prophet as lion-warrior dominates the Praise element of the Supplicatory Rite of this ode even as it effectively buttresses the fear-hope axis of that rite. We should keep these ritual aspects of Kaʿb's ode and its pre-Islamic precedents in mind as the literary-ritual antecedents of the praise passages, especially the martial ones, of al-Buṣīrī's Burdah (chapter 2) and Aḥmad Shawqī's Nahj al-Burdah (chapter 3). The closing passage of Kaʿb's ode (vv. 48–55) opens with a final martial metaphor that depicts the Prophet as a sword of Allāh, an image that would later achieve great popularity in Islamic military and caliphal panegyric. Verses 48–50 constitute a semantic core of the poem much as do verses 32–36 and display the rhetorical features that we have come to associate with such sections. In verse 48 we find the description of the Prophet as the sword of Allāh structured in very simple, straightforward diction in chiastic (*abba*) form—*ʾinna* al-rasūla la-sayfun *yustaḍāʾu bihī / muhannadun min* suyūfi Allāhi *maslūlū* (The *Messenger* is surely a *sword* from whose flash light is sought, / One of the *swords of God*, an Indian blade unsheathed)—to reiterate the Islamic message of right guidance and divine might. This leads into a description of the Emigrants (Muhājirūn), Muḥammad's early Meccan supporters who emigrated with him from Mecca to Medina. This migration, the Hijrah, is presented here as a spiritual one, for the Emigrants, for Kaʿb at least, are the core of Muḥammad's tried and true followers. The passage that they make is thus identified with Islam itself. Four words from verses 49–50, *ʾaslamū zūlū / zālū fa-mā zāla* (whose spokesman [Muḥammad?] said when *they submitted to Islam, "Depart!" They departed,* but the weaklings, etc., *did not depart*), constitute a remarkably concise definition of Islam and, at the same time, a separation of the wheat from the chaff: those who obey the Prophet's command are Muslims and heroes; those who do not are "damned" cowards. In Kaʿb's hands the Hijrah is thus above all a moral test that functions as a passage from the Jāhiliyyah to Islam, and, as in all such rites, only the morally and physically strong complete the passage. Kaᶜb's conception of the Hijrah as a crucial initiatory rite in the formation of an Islamic community helps us understand why its date is taken as the beginning of the Islamic calendar.

In the ensuing description of the Emigrants that closes the poem (vv. 51–55), the poet once more reimmerses himself in the diction and imagery of the classical *qaṣīdah*. The Emigrants form an elite of proud high-nosed warriors, clad in chain mail of David's weave (Dāwūd, identified with King David of the Bible and Qurʾān, is credited in Islamic lore with being the first to make chain-mail) (vv. 51–52). In verse 53 the Emigrants in their battle ranks are described as a troop of majestic white camels that are kept in line by the stick, whereas the scrawny black ones, traditionally said to refer to the Medinese Helpers (Anṣār) of the Prophet, "stray from the road" (*ᶜarrada*), i.e., flee the field of battle.[83] Despite the apparent Jāhilī imagery and diction and political reference to the Munāfiqūn (Hypocrites, those members of the early Islamic community who shirked going into battle with Muḥammad), the allusion in the Islamic moral context must certainly be to the antithesis in the opening sura (Sūrat al-Fātiḥah) of the Qurʾān (1:7) between those God blesses and "guides on the straight path" (*ihdinā al-ṣirāṭa al-mustaqīm*) and the misguided (*al-ḍāllīn*) with whom He is angry (see above on *ḍalāl* and *hudá*). Finally, Kaᶜb ibn Zuhayr seals his *qaṣīdah* with two verses of praise for the Muhājirūn that are as purely Jāhilī as those that opened it. Both closing verses combine antithesis with litotes to express in the understated tone of the negative the equanimity of the hero in battle, and in death. And yet, however purely Jāhilī in diction and imagery, the Islamic context has utterly transformed the meaning of the closing verse. For the draught from death's water troughs (*ḥiyāḍi al-mawti*) in pre-Islamic times expressed death on the field of battle. But for the Muhājirūn, as for any Muslim, death in battle "in the way of God" (*fī sabīl Allāh*) is an act of self-sacrifice and martyrdom that guarantees salvation and life everlasting.[84]

In light of our understanding of Kaᶜb's political position within his newly adopted religious community, we should keep in mind that one of the roles of the ritual patterns that we have discussed is the restoration or restructuring of a legitimate social structure, starting from the top down. As we saw in the pre-Islamic examples, the first goal of the panegyric is to negotiate the relation—the relative rank and status—between the poet and the patron. This is done through the ceremony of submission and praise, what we have termed the Supplicatory Ritual, and the ritual exchange of poem and prize. The prize or countergift is thus an expression of the patron's estimation not only of the poem, but of the poet. The poet, from his side, uses the praise section (*madīḥ*) in the first place to express the legitimacy and authority of the patron at the top of the social hierarchy. Often, the poet also attempts to promote his own vision of the political hierarchy, thereby to negotiate his rank vis-à-vis others in the polity. If we keep in mind that in the conversion narrative it was one of the Medinese Helpers (Anṣār) who attempted to kill Kaᶜb when he first identified himself to the Prophet, it becomes apparent that the poet, having established the position of the Prophet at the head of the community, is expressing his support for another political faction, that is, the Emigrants (Muhājirūn) who accompanied the Prophet from Mecca. He thus identifies them as the true core of the Islamic community, as being, like the Prophet, of the Meccan tribal aristocracy of the Banū Quraysh, and as proven by the test of the Hijrah to be tried and true to the Prophet and Islam. Thus, through the comparison of the Emigrants and Helpers, respectively, with noble-bred white camels that walk in a line and ill-bred scrawny black camels that go astray, Kaᶜb depicts the Meccan Emigrants as nobler, both genealogically and morally, than the Medinese Helpers.

Returning to the critical premises of the ritual complex upon which our analysis was based, we can begin to draw together the various aspects of the poem. First of all, in terms of ritual exchange, we find in Kaᶜb's poem a total social movement in which multiple institutions find simultaneous expression. The institution of redemption, as we saw in the pre-Isalmic odes of ᶜAlqamah and al-Nābighah, is an economic, legal, and sociomorphic one. In Kaᶜb's case, through the payment of the *qaṣīdah,* the outlawed poet is admitted as a legal member of society; the legally or socially "dead" Kaᶜb is "alive" to society once more and assumes all the rights and obligations entailed in that membership. This in and of itself indicates the poem's function in a rite of passage in which the ritual passenger effects a transition from one social status to another and, in particular, a rite of incorporation whereby, just as in the case of al-Nābighah, the outlaw comes as a supplicant and is admitted into society. In addition, the poet puts forth his vision of the proper political structure of the polity—the sociomorphic aspect of the *qaṣīdah*. In Kaᶜb's poem, with the addition of the Islamic element, the residual mythic aspects of sacred kingship already apparent in ᶜAlqamah's and al-Nābighah's *qaṣīdahs* are reactivated; so too the moral and religious aspects, such as we saw in Zuhayr's ode, are intensified. The transfer of allegiance is not from one Bedouin liege lord to another (the Ghassānids to the Lakhmids or vice-versa), but from the poet's natal tribal society to a radically new social order, from the Jāhiliyyah to Islam. It is not merely Kaᶜb's life in this world that is redeemed, but his life in the world to come. It is at this point that poesis becomes mythopoesis, and—insofar as this poem appears likely to have generated its prose anecdotes and in doing so to have made the conversion of Kaᶜb ibn Zuhayr paradigmatic for all Muslims—mythogenesis. At this point, too, Kaᶜb's poetic pedigree enters the picture. Inasmuch as he is the scion of one of the premier poetic families of the Jāhiliyyah, Kaᶜb's redemption by means of a *qaṣīdah* therefore represents as well the redemption of the Jāhilī poetic tradition in Islam. His composing an "Islamic" *qaṣīdah* so fully in the tradition of the Jāhiiyyah has the effect of rendering the pre-Islamic *qaṣīdah*, not anti-Islamic, but proto-Islamic.

The ritual patterns that have informed our discussion of the *qaṣīdah*—the rite of passage with its Separation, Liminality, Aggregation phases, and the Supplicatory Ode with its elements of Elegiac prelude (*nasīb*) expressing Loss, Self-Abasement/Submission, Supplication, and Praise—are expressions of the psychosocial mechanisms for personal and societal transition. In this respect, the *qaṣīdah* as a literary form can be viewed as a culture-specific manifestation of a universal human, both individual and corporate, process. The *qaṣīdah* thus is able to impose form and meaning on changing human and societal relationships and, by explaining and directing change, exert control over it. The ritual structure of the *qaṣīdah* allows for a multivalent layering of meaning, and hence enables the poem to give simultaneous expression to a variety of institutions. Thus, as embodied in the tripartite elegiac prelude-journey-praise (*nasīb-raḥīl-madīḥ*) form of the classical *qaṣīdah*, the ritual structure gives expression first to Kaᶜb ibn Zuhayr's political conversion from his tribe to Muḥammad, in terms analogous to al-Nābighah's transfer of allegiance from the Ghassānids to the Lakhmids; then to the religious conversion of Kaᶜb from the ancestral religion of the Banū Muzaynah to Islam; this in turn becomes paradigmatic of the conversion of Arab society from the Jāhiliyyah to Islam and, further, of the subjugation of the pre-Islamic poetic tradition to the Islamic.

If the theory of ritual exchange explains how and why the *qaṣīdah* was composed, the ritual pattern explains why it was preserved and repeated. Walter Burkert's remarks on ritual will provide some insight here:

> Since the work of Sir Julian Huxley and Konrad Lorenz, biology has defined *ritual* as a behavioural pattern that has lost its primary function—present in its unritualized model—but which persists in a new function, that of communication. . . . this communicating function reveals the two basic characteristics of ritual behaviour, namely repetition and theatrical exaggeration. For the essentially immutable patterns do not transmit differentiated and complex material information but, rather, just one piece of information each. This single piece of information is considered so important that it is reinforced by constant repetition so as to avoid misunderstanding or misuse. . . . Above all, then, ritual creates and affirms social interaction.[85]

The immediate function, or occasional purpose, of Kaᶜb's poetic ritual of supplication is to redeem the poet, that is, to save his skin in this world and, at least in the larger Islamic context reflected in Bujayr's poem in the conversion narrative, the next. Its new ritual function is then to convey that single most vital piece of information in the Islamic culture that preserved and ritualized it, that is, the Islamic message of spiritual redemption and salvation. Just as the ritual of royalty in ᶜAlqamah's and al-Nābighah's poems is reenacted to ensure and reaffirm the authority and legitimacy of Arab kingship, or the ritual of tribal allegiance is performed through Zuhayr's, so too the recitation of Kaᶜb ibn Zuhayr's *qaṣīdah* serves as a reaffirmation of Islamic faith. In our interpretation, the reason for the celebration and preservation of Kaᶜb's Suᶜād Has Departed in Arab-Islamic culture is that for the Muslim, to read the poem, in a performative sense, is to undergo for oneself the spiritual transition it embodies in its three parts: from doubt (or disbelief) and despair to belief in and hope for salvation. Furthermore, Burkert's remarks on repetition in ritual, especially when coupled with the phenomenon of redundancy that is characteristic of orally transmitted poetry, go far in explaining the numerous reiterations of the ritual pattern *within* the *qaṣīdah*—first in the overall structure, then in the series of shorter repetitions (vv. 32–36, 37–42, 44, 49–51, 53)—and through a variety of metaphors. That is, the internal repetition of the ritual pattern functions to ensure that even if parts of the text are lost, corrupted, or misunderstood, the *qaṣīdah*'s vital message of sacrifice and redemption will not be lost.

MYTHOGENESIS: THE DONATION OF THE MANTLE

No discussion of Kaᶜb ibn Zuhayr's Suᶜād Has Departed would be complete without addressing the anecdote about the mantle (*burdah*) of the Prophet, so closely associated with this *qaṣīdah* that it is commonly referred to as the Mantle Ode (*Qaṣīdat al-Burdah*). The Arab-Islamic tradition relates that when Kaᶜb recited this ode to the Prophet Muḥammad, he conferred upon the poet a mantle, which, it is said, was later purchased by the Umayyad caliph Muᶜāwiyah from Kaᶜb's heirs for twenty thousand dirhams and worn by the caliphs on feast days. Although it is cited in the literary compendia of such venerable scholars as Ibn Sallām al-Jumaḥī (d. 231/845 or 232/846) and Ibn Qutaybah (d. 276/889), this anecdote does not appear, as the initial stories of Bujayr and Kaᶜb (cited above) do, in the conversion narrative of traditionally accepted biography of the Prophet, Ibn Hishām's (d. 218/833 or 213/828) edition of Ibn Isḥāq's (d. 150/767) *Al-Sīrah al-Nabawiyyah,* nor in sources derived from it, such as al-Sukkarī's recension of the *dīwān;* nor is it found in any of the orthodox Ḥadīth collections (*al-kutub al-sittah*) (which did not, as Michael Zwettler has established, prevent it from making its way into third/ninth century collections of *ḥadīth nabawī*).[86] This, however, is only a problem if by "authenticity" we mean "historicity"; and, furthermore, our discussion has discounted the (verifiable) historicity even of those anecdotes traditionally considered authoritative. Rather, our concern in this study with early Islamic materials, as with the pre-Islamic prose anecdotes we discussed in the introduction, is the meaning of the anecdotes or stories as literary constructs.

In the context of this study, we must understand the donation of the mantle above all as part of a ritual exchange: the *qaṣīdah* functions as a symbolic gift in a ritual of allegiance or fealty, and the robe or mantle then functions as the symbolic countergift. As Carl Brockelmann and Georg Jacob noted, the conferring of a robe of honor (*ḥullah*) upon poets as a reward for their verse was a well-established custom among the Arabs.[87] In the Arabic literary context, to have one's poetry rewarded with a royal robe of honor was, as the Umayyad poet al-Farazdaq (d. 110/728) attests in a verse about the renowned pre-Islamic poet ᶜAlqamah (above), a distinction tantamount to having one's verse immortalized in the hearts or on the tongues of the people:

> The Stallion ᶜAlqamah upon whom kings' robes were bestowed
> Was proverbial among the people for his words.[88]
>
> [32]

Furthermore, as we saw in the case of Zuhayr ibn Abī Sulmá and his patron Harim ibn Sinān, the rank and renown of both poet and patron was bound up in this ritual exchange.

In the case of ᶜAlqamah's A Heart Turbulent with Passion and the king al-Ḥārith (above), the poet faces the dilemma of choosing between the two gifts that the king offers him as the prize for his magnificent ode: his kinsmen's release or the lavish robes. In either case, the gift serves as a token or emblem of the end to hostilities and the tying of bonds of allegiance—loyalty on the part of the subject and protection on the part of the king. In such rituals of allegiance as al-Nābighah's O Abode of Mayyah, the supplicant offers his life or something of himself to the ruler, and the ruler, in accepting his allegiance, grants him his protection and virtually confers life, or new life, upon his vassal. The gift and countergift of the fealty ritual, especially when we keep in mind Mauss's remark that the gift contains something of the giver or soul of the giver (see below), embody the essence of fealty: that each owes the other his life, that each will protect the other with his life. If Kaᶜb's recitation of Suᶜād Has Departed constitutes his gift of submission, allegiance, and praise of the Prophet, the Prophet's countergift of the mantle betokens his acceptance of Kaᶜb into the Islamic Ummah and his promise of protection. It is at once an "outward and physical sign of an inward and spiritual" transaction and, at the same time, as with performative utterances, the physical act of the donation of the mantle in itself constitutes the Prophet's acceptance of the poet's allegiance and conferral of the Prophet's protection. Further, more than serving as a symbol or emblem, a ritual token, of the Prophet's acceptance and protection, the garment is a symbol of the soul or self. Given the astounding emblematic value that would accrue to a garment of the Prophet, it is not surprising that the Umayyad and ʿAbbāsid caliphs would be eager to possess it. For the leader of the Islamic Ummah, the mantle of the Prophet conveys his protection and, therefore, the legitimacy of its wearer's rule. That is, the robe or mantle functions likewise as a symbol of legitimacy.[89] Rudi Paret, giving the biblical example of the miraculous mantle of the Prophet Elijah (II Kings 2:13–15), thus quite correctly explains the interest of the Umayyad caliphs in obtaining and retaining this relic.[90]

The symbolic function of the mantle conferred upon the poet saved by Islam becomes even clearer when contrasted with the function of garments in the story of the most celebrated Jāhilī poet, whom the Prophet is said to have condemned as "the leader of the poets into Hellfire,"[91] Imruʾ al-Qays. Unable to find supporters among the Arabs to aid him in his quest for extravagant vengeance for his slain royal father, Imruʾ al-Qays abandons his suits of ancestral armor (hereditary legitimacy) and seeks support from the Byzantines. When a slanderer at Caesar's court informs the emperor that Imruʾ al-Qays has an illicit liaison with his daughter, Caesar, who had sent the Arab prince forth with an army, sends him an embroidered robe interwoven with gold, but also laced with poison. The overjoyed prince no sooner dons it than his skin breaks out in sores and sloughs off, and he dies.[92] If, as I have argued elsewhere, his ancestral armor symbolizes hereditary legitimacy, then surely the lethal foreign robe of honor symbolizes illegitimacy.[93] Moreover, if the Byzantine Christian robe brings perdition to the renegade Arab who dons it (surely the true sense of Imruʾ al-Qays's sobriquet "the Errant/Erring King [*al-malik al-ḍillīl*]),[94] then the Mantle of the Prophet must confer salvation. If Kaʿb, as the scion of Zuhayr ibn Abī Sulmá, represents that aspect of the Jāhiliyyah that was proto-Islamic, Imruʾ al-Qays is perceived as the embodiment of all that was anti-Islamic.

In this light, the Prophet's conferring his mantle on Kaʿb was not merely, as Paret would have it, a sign of recognition of his poetic achievement, but a sign of the legitimacy of poetry under Islam. We need to reiterate at this point that, as we saw in all three of our pre-Islamic examples, the exchange of *qaṣīdah* and *jāʾizah* constitutes the sealing of a contract between the poet and the patron, in this case between Kaʿb and the Prophet Muḥammad, and further, symbolically, between the pre-Isalmic tradition and the Islamic. Thus, I maintain, the submission (*islām*) of the poet to the prophet became paradigmatic of the submission of the poetic to the prophetic in Islamic culture. And just as the poet had to submit to be saved, so too did the poetic tradition.

Finally, our evaluation of the ritual exchange of *qaṣīdah* for mantle must consider the basis for equating these two symbolic and ceremonial currencies. In the case of Kaʿb ibn Zuhayr and the Prophet Muḥammad, what is exchanged are symbols of immortality, one poetic, the other prophetic. This concept was noted by Mauss in his discussion of the archaic exchange:

> We can see the nature of the bond created by the transfer of a possession. . . . it is clear that . . . this bond created by things is in fact a bond between persons, since the thing is a person or pertains to a person. . . . It follows clearly from what we have seen that in this system of ideas *one gives away what is in reality a part of one's own nature and substance, while to receive something is to receive part of someone's spiritual essence.*[95] [Italics mine]

I believe we will have a much better grasp of the nature of the Arabic panegyric ode and the gift or prize (*jāʾizah*) that is traditionally conferred on the poet in return if we consider them in light of Mauss's further remarks concerning "the power of objects of exchange": "Each of these precious things has, moreover, a productive capacity within it. Each, as well as being a sign and surety of life, is also a sign and surety of wealth, a magico-religious guarantee of rank and prosperity."[96]

We must finally recognize that the panegyric ode was understood to confer immortal renown on both poet and patron, the subject of its praise (*mamdūḥ*), and that its worth to the patron was thus commensurate with its aesthetic worth, which was the sole guarantee of its preservation and thus his immortal renown. In this respect, the idea that Kaʿb's gift of a *qaṣīdah* could elicit as a counter-gift the Prophetic mantle, an emblem of the salvation and immortality conferred by Islam, reflect the Prophet's—or more precisely the Arabic literary tradition's—estimation of the ode.

In sum, the poem itself, as I see it, has generated the "myth" of the donation of the mantle. Furthermore, the myth then generated an actual relic. Although some claim that the references of the mantle in Caliphal times (as in al-Buḥturī's (d. 231/845) celebrated ode to the ʿAbbāsid Caliph al-Mutawakkil for ʿĪd al-Fiṭr)[97] confirm the historical veracity of the story, my argument is rather that belief or myth actually generates physical relics—like the discovery of the "true cross" in Crusader times. In other words, once the story circulated it was only a matter of time before an actual mantle became identified with the mythical one. Clearly, in Kaʿb's conversion poem the real prize is the gift of life—the revocation of his death sentence—which functions above all as a synecdoche for the gift of salvation and life immortal in the heavenly garden; this, in turn, is what his forgiveness and incorporation among the community of believers entails. The effect of the myth of the mantle is to provide a tangible gift whose symbolic value is that of the forgiveness, blessing, and protection of the Prophet. In other words, the donation of the mantle confirms literally and symbolically the full enactment of the ritual exchange and the Prophet Muḥammad's fulfillment of the contractual obligation incurred by the presentation of the panegyric ode.[98]

Conclusion

We have seen the transformation from the royal and tribal court panegyrics of three of the master poets of the Jāhiliyyah, ʿAlqamah, al-Nābighah, and Zuhayr ibn Abī Sulmá, to Kaʿb ibn Zuhayr's poem of conversion to Islam and praise of the Prophet. In both the pre-Islamic and Islamic cases, the ritual exchange of poem and prize, however much it may symbolize otherworldly matters, is set (traditionally, even if not historically verifiably) in real time and space. The massive production of *madāʾiḥ nabawiyyah* (praise poems to the Prophet), however, occurred not during the lifetime of the Prophet, nor even during the classical Arabic poetic period (1–5/7–12 centuries), but rather during the Post-Classical period (6–13/12–19 centuries), conventionally termed the Age of Decline (*ʿAṣr al-Inḥiṭāṭ*). What happens to the idea of the ritual exchange of poem and prize when the *mamdūḥ* is no longer of this world? Kaʿb's poem, as contextualized with Bujayr's poem in the conversion narrative, already conveys the idea of a spiritual as well as worldly reward, but the presentation of the *qaṣīdah* and the conferral of the prize take place on *terra firma*.

ḤASSĀN IBN THĀBIT'S AT ṬAYBAH LIES A TRACE

A brief look at the *marthiyah* (elegy) for the Prophet that opens *bi-Ṭaybatah rasmun,* by his poet laureate, Ḥassān ibn Thābit (d. before 40/661), will help show how the literary transition from panegyric to the living Prophet to that of the Prophet after death was effected.[99] As with Kaʿb ibn Zuhayr's poem and associated anecdotes, we cannot claim in Ḥassān ibn Thābit's case to be speaking of verifiable historical events and texts from the time of the Prophet, but rather with the tradition-sanctioned recollection or reconstruction of them. Indeed, the authenticity of poems attributed to Ḥassān has long been subject to doubt, and that of At Ṭaybah Lies a Trace in particular. It is found in Ibn Hishām's *Al-Sīrah,* but not in the transmissions of Ḥassān's *dīwān.*[100] What is important in our discussion, however, is that this elegy attributed to Ḥassān ibn Thābit is given pride of place in Ibn Hishām's *Al-Sīrah* narrative of the death of the Prophet and therefore in the Islamic tradition constitutes the expression of the communal (re)construction of that event (see chapter 3 for Shawqī's treatment of the subject in Nahj al-Burdah).

Although traditionally classified as *rithāʾ* (elegy), the poem is curiously anomalous and can be viewed, at least in light of its role in the development of *madīḥ nabawī,* as a hybrid between *rithāʾ* and *qaṣīdat al-madḥ,* between elegy and panegyric or, more precisely, what we have termed the supplicatory-panegyric ode, that serves as a transitional poem toward the formation of the Post-Classical genre of *madīḥ nabawī.* The original sense of *rithāʾ* in the Jāhiliyyah was that the poet gave of himself, his poetry, selflessly, to perpetuate or immortalize the name of a kinsman who had sacrificed his life on the field of battle. The ritual exchange of poetry for blood, intimately linked to that of blood-vengeance (blood for blood), was a confirmation of bonds of kinship, and the obligations incurred, like blood-vengeance, had a self-perpetuating concatenating effect: one warrior died, was avenged and elegized by a kinsman, who in turn was slain on the battlefield, avenged, and elegized. With the advent of Islam much of this changed, especially since the promise of immortality in the afterlife made, or should have made, immortalization through poetry redundant. Blood vengeance, likewise, was to have become obsolete.

In the case of Ḥassān's *rithāʾ* for the Prophet, the situation is quite different from that of the Jāhilī ritually obligatory elegy. The Prophet was not slain on the battlefield, but died of natural causes, and the poet is not his kinsman. What Ḥassān's poem has achieved, however, is an original and brilliant poetic formulation: it combines elements of elegy and supplicatory panegyric to create a poem that both comforts the bereft community and exhorts their *continued allegiance* to Muḥammad, the Prophet whose leadership or guidance of the community is not terminated by his death. The poem opens with a *nasīb* in the form of the lyric-elegiac prelude theme of the ruined abode (vv. 1–6), now Islamized to express the loss not of a departed mistress but of the deceased Prophet.

Ḥassān ibn Thābit: At Ṭaybah Lies a Trace[101]

1. At Ṭaybah lies a trace of the Messenger
   and a place thronged and luminous,
   While other traces lie barren and effaced.
2. The signs are not erased from that inviolate abode
   In which stands the minbar that the Guide would mount.
3. Its signs yet clear, its waymarks standing still,
   And his quarter where his mosque and prayer-place stood.

[33]

For those critics, classical and modern, who fault this poem on the grounds that in *rithā*ʾ there should be no *nasīb,* our contention that the poem is actually a hybrid informed by the genre requirements of the Supplicatory Panegyric, among them the *nasīb,* serves as refutation. The *nasīb* is followed by a long lament section, followed by a praise section that could belong equally to an elegy or a panegyric (37–42). What concerns us most, however, is the two-verse closure: here the poem is revealed to be above all a supplicatory panegyric for which a reward is expected—life eternal in the immortal garden, and, in a manner that reminds us of the ritual aspect of Aggregation and Incorporation of the other *qaṣīdahs* we have examined in this chapter, that the poet will be brought once more into the inner circle of his lord:

45. I will never cease desiring to praise him, for perhaps thereby
    I will dwell in the immortal garden forever.
46. With al-Muṣṭafá, God's chosen, I desire by this praise
    to dwell in his protection,
    And for the reward of that day, I strive and strain.

[34]

Thus, even though it is generally, and correctly, termed an elegy, the ritual-thematic intent of the poem is clearly that of the praise for prize exchange of the panegyric ode, and the prize that the poet wants is to be brought into the company of the Prophet—now in the immortal garden. Notice his use of the precise diction of the Supplicatory Ode: "I desire thereby to dwell in his protection."

When we then place the poem in the context of the death of the Prophet and the challenge that it presented to the nascent Islamic community, we can appreciate the genius of Ḥassān's formulation even more. For if, as I have argued above, and extensively elsewhere, the *qaṣīdat al-madḥ* serves to establish a bond of allegiance, especially between subject and ruler,[102] then by incorporating it into his "elegy," Ḥassān has not merely offered comfort to the bereft believers but has solved the crisis of the Islamic community: the supplicatory-panegyric exchange of poem and prize between the poet and deceased Prophet confirms that the Prophet was not merely a temporal ruler whose passing marks the abrogation of obligations of allegiance (as the Murtaddūn [Apostates] claimed, thereby setting off the Ḥurūb al-Riddah [Wars of Apostasy]), but is indeed a Prophet whose mutual bonds of obligation with his community of believers still stand (see chapter 3).

In sum, what all the poems we have examined in chapter 1 have in common is their supplicatory-panegyric structure and function: a poem of praise and entreaty is presented to a *mamdūḥ* with the expectation, indeed requirement, that he give something in return. The exchange pattern of gift and counter-gift is ritually and morally binding on both the poet and the patron, and the performance of this ritual, in which the poem constitutes a speech act, establishes a contractual bond of obligation and allegiance between the two. This ritual complex that determines the contents, structure, and function of the Supplicatory Panegyric Ode will serve as the basis for our reading of al-Būṣīrī's Burdah (chapter 2) and Aḥmad Shawqī's Nahj al-Burdah (chapter 3).

TWO

Al-Būṣīrī and the Dream of the Mantle

Introduction

Indisputably the most renowned poem of praise to the Prophet Muḥammad (*madīḥ nabawī*) and arguably the most famous poem in the Arabic language is that known as the Mantle Ode (Qaṣīdat al-Burdah) by the thirteenth-century poet of Mamlūk Egypt, Sharaf al-Dīn Abū ʿAbd Allāh Muḥammad ibn Saʿīd al-Būṣīrī (d. 694–96/1294–97), originally titled by its author Al-Kawākib al-Durriyyah fī Madḥ Khayr al-Bariyyah (Pearly Stars in Praise of the Best of All Creation).[1] It is difficult to enumerate the tremendous array of literary, liturgical, and religious functions that al-Būṣīrī's Burdah performed: it generated hundreds of commentaries, expansions (s. *tashṭīr, takhmīs,* especially, and *tasbīʿ*),[2] a new subgenre of *madīḥ nabawī,* the *badīʿiyyah,*[3] and contrafactions (*muʿāraḍāt*), i.e., counter-poems or imitations that emulate the original in the same rhyme and meter—a celebrated example of which is Aḥmad Shawqī's Nahj al-Burdah (The Way of the Mantle, 1910), the subject of chapter 3 of this study. Further, there are numerous translations into Persian—most notably that of Jāmī (d. 898–99/1492)—Turkish, and Urdu, and innumerable translations into virtually all of the languages of the Islamic world, from Indonesia and the Indo-Pakistani subcontinent, central Asia, the Middle East, North Africa, and Islamic areas of sub-Saharan Africa.[4] The Arabic manuscripts alone must number in the thousands, given the hundreds in the major catalogued archives.[5] These range from elaborate gilded polychrome court (*khazāʾinī*) manuscripts to the crudest copies for personal devotional use.

The same is true of the numerous print editions, beginning from the mid-nineteenth century and continuing to today, which range from elaborate lithographed and later typeset texts with commentaries to the ubiquitous cheap, popular, chapbook-like printings.

The liturgical uses of al-Būṣīrī's Burdah are also extensive and varied. They range from personal acts of piety and devotion to the Prophet, to Ṣūfī (in particular the Shādhiliyyah order) in chanted or sung form with decidedly mystical intent (especially to see the Prophet in one's dreams), to its widespread public recitation, especially, in many areas, on the Prophet's birthday (*mawlid al-nabī*), at funerals, or weekly recitations associated with the Friday prayer. The uses vary from location to location and no doubt have varied over time.[6]

There are, in addition, the practical, psychological, spiritual, and medicinal properties ascribed to specific verses and properly made talismans and amulets—most often involving explicit recipes for philters such as writing the lines and dissolving them in rose-water and saffron, etc.—assigned to particular lines or passages (see below). The properties or benefits of specific Burdah lines or groups of lines are termed in the Arabic sources *khāṣṣiyyah,* pl. *khawāṣṣ, khāṣṣah,* pl. *khaṣāʾiṣ,* or *fāʾidah,* pl. *fawāʾid,* words which are otherwise used for, among other things, medicinal properties and benefits. The aim of chapter 2 will be to explore why al-Būṣīrī's Burdah came to be the locus of so much literary, religious, and talismanic activity.

POETIC GENRE

Although praise poetry addressed to the Prophet in his lifetime came, in retrospect, to be termed *madīḥ nabawī,* in fact the distinct poetic genre did not crystallize until the Post-Classical period. The praise poems dedicated to the Prophet during his lifetime, such as Kaʿb ibn Zuhayr's celebrated Suʿād Has Departed (Bānat Suʿād), the poem upon which the epithet Qaṣīdat al-Burdah, or Mantle Ode, was first conferred (see chapter 1), follow the generic strictures of the pre-Islamic *qaṣīdat al-madḥ* (panegyric ode), or else, like the many shorter pieces contained in *Al-Sīrah* of Ibn Isḥāq/Ibn Hishām, resemble the pre-Islamic *Ayyām al-ʿArab* battle poetry.

Arabic poetry of the Classical Age (the Umayyad and ʿAbbāsid periods, late 1st/7th–5th/11th c.) was dominated by court panegyric (*qaṣīdat al-madḥ*) devoted to establishing and celebrating the legitimacy and might of the caliphs and lesser potentates (see below). During these four centuries, as literary scholars such as Zakī Mubārak and Maḥmūd ʿAlī Makkī have established, the theme (although not the genre) of praise of the Prophet was developed within the context of Shīʿite praise poetry (*madīḥ*) or elegy (*rithāʾ*) for the Āl al-Bayt (the family of the Prophet). In accord with their belief that the descendants of the Prophet's cousin and son-in-law ʿAlī ibn Abī Ṭālib and daughter Fāṭimah were the only legitimate rulers of the Islamic Ummah, Shīʿite poets employed the *qaṣīdah* to promote ʿAlid claims, air their grievances over ʿAlid disenfranchisement, and mourn, in a manner that expresses their political as well as personal sorrows, the ʿAlid dead, especially al-Ḥusayn, the Prophet's grandson who was martyred at Karbalāʾ.[7] Although the praise of the Prophet is poetically subordinated to that of ʿAlī and his descendants, these Shīʿite poems provide not only poetic precedents for the themes and motifs of medieval *madīḥ nabawī* but also the elements of otherworldly supplication and intercession and the heightened emotive tone that characterize the medieval genre.

Also deserving of further study is the complex and obscure process of emergence and formation of the medieval *madīḥ nabawī*. Its flowering in the medieval period is undoubtedly part and parcel of the medieval cultural religious phenomenon of heightened personal devotion to and celebration of the Prophet, especially as intercessor on Judgment Day. In addition to elements that derive from Shīʿite poetry, it is intimately bound up in the pilgrimage rituals of the Ḥajj, or more precisely with the attendant visit to the Prophet's tomb in Medina, which at that period was considered an essential part of the pilgrimage. Whether the poet was able to perform the Ḥajj or merely yearned to do so, the result was a highly lyrical poetry of personal piety and devotion to the Prophet Muḥammad. This, in its form and lyricism, seems to me to have close ties to Ṣūfī devotional poetry, as well as Shīʿite poetry to Āl al-Bayt. The Ṣūfī mystical journey of the way-stations pilgrimage route and sacred sites of the Ḥajj gives way in the *madīḥ nabawī* of this sort to a devotional poetic pilgrimage. This form seems to have been especially popular in al-Andalus. Another aspect, which also appears in al-Andalus, is *madīḥ nabawī* in response to the fall of Muslim cities to the Reconquista. Here worldly politics comes to the fore, as poems of praise to the Prophet become one of several literary vehicles to plead for intercession against the Infidel—not merely from divine agency, but from the rulers of the Muslim East.[8]

Given that the *madīḥ nabawī* of the seventh/thirteenth century, at least in the Arab East (Mashriq), was predominantly the lyric of personal devotion, we can appreciate the novelty of al-Būṣīrī's choice of structuring his Burdah along the lines of a classical panegyric and, in particular, of the supplicatory type, i.e., like Kaᶜb's Suᶜād Has Departed—while at the same time alluding quite explicitly in its imitation (*muᶜāraḍah*) of the rhyme, meter, and *nasībic* diction to a Ṣūfī *ghazal* by the sixth/twelfth-century Egyptian mystic Ibn al-Fāriḍ (see below).[9] In literary historical terms, al-Būṣīrī's Burdah, in its heightened rhetorical expression, motifs, themes, and structure became the genre-defining paradigm for *madīḥ nabawī*.[10]

As we saw in chapter 1, the classical Arabic panegyric (*qaṣīdat al-madḥ*), of which the *madīḥ nabawī* of al-Būṣīrī's type is a derivative, is an eminently courtly ode intimately engaged in the politics and polemics of the ruling elite. As I argued at length in my book *The Poetics of Islamic Legitimacy*, one of the key functions of the Islamic courtly *qaṣīdat al-madḥ*, whether explicitly of the supplicatory form or not, is to construct and perpetuate a legitimizing myth of Arab-Islamic rule and, in particular, to establish the legitimacy of the *mamdūḥ*'s rule or role. This perforce means that the *qaṣīdat al-madḥ* is polemical in nature: that Islam is to be promoted as the true religion and the royal patron as the divinely appointed ruler, to the exclusion of other claimants and pretenders. This is achieved primarily through the celebration of the recognized virtues of the religion and the ruler, and the argument, whenever possible, is sealed with compelling external validations of both propositions—above all, the prosperity of the realm and military victory. It is in this light that al-Būṣīrī's adoption or adaptation of this form to introduce a polemical (and political) dimension into a *madīḥ nabawī*, as I will argue, especially with regard to the Sīrah-derived themes of Burdah parts 4–8, must be understood. Certainly his Burdah's sweeping domination of the genre up until the present day attests to the success of al-Būṣīrī's poetic venture.

POETIC STYLE: CLASSICAL AND POST-CLASSICAL *BADĪᶜ*

Just as we must interpret the form of al-Būṣīrī's Burdah in light of the cultural history of Arabic poetic structures and genres, so too must we understand its stylistic and rhetorical features within the history of Arabic poetics and rhetoric. Those of us whose literary sensibilities have been shaped by Modernist aesthetics in general, and the assault of Egyptian Modernists such as Maḥmūd ʿAbbās al-ʿAqqād (d. 1964) on classical Arabic poetic language in particular—and more especially the consensus of both the Arab Neo-Classicists and Modernists that Post-Classical or Medieval Arabic poetry is the mediocre product of an Age of Decline (ʿAṣr al-Inḥiṭāṭ)—will be disinclined to appreciate al-Būṣīrī's rhetorically ornate style and self-consciously Classical poetic diction. The general view is summed up by ʿUmar Mūsá Bāshā, who, in the introduction to his edition of al-Ghazzī's commentary on the Burdah, concludes his discussion of al-Būṣīrī's use of rhetorical devices (*al-ṣuwar al-balāghiyyah*) with the remark: "[These examples] are sufficient for us to conclude that the poet affected the most important aspects of *badīʿ* known in his age and that this affectation was the malady of the age that afflicted poets and prose writers alike."[11] A more useful starting point for us is the observation with which he opens his discussion of what he terms "*badīʿ* images" in al-Būṣīrī's Burdah: "We are in the age of *badīʿ*, when the poet whose poetic compositions were not replete with *badīʿ* images was considered to fall short of his peers in the [poetic] race."[12] In this we have the recognition that the aesthetic expectations or requirements of the Medieval or Post-Classical period differ not only from our Modernist tastes, but even from the less rhetorically laden prescriptions for nobility and sweetness of language found in the Classical Arabic formulations of proper poetic style, termed *ʿAmūḍ al-Shiʿr* (the pillar of poetry).[13]

Furthermore, we must keep in mind that with al-Būṣīrī we are *not* in the *Classical* Age of *Badīʿ*, the second–third/eighth–ninth century florescence of the high classical rhetorical style, termed *badīʿ*, of such ʿAbbāsid masters as Bashshār ibn Burd (d. 167/783), Abū Nuwās (d. 199 or 200/814 or 815), Muslim ibn al-Walīd (d. 208/823), al-Buḥturī (d. 284/897) and, above all, Abū Tammām (d. 231 or 232/845 or 846). The *badīʿ* style of the ʿAbbāsids is celebrated by its supporters, and decried by its detractors, as innovative and original in the dramatic intensity of its use of rhetorical devices—such as *istiʿārah* (metaphor), *tashbīh* (simile), *jinās* (paronomasia, root-play), *ṭibāq* (antithesis), *radd al-ʿajuz ʿalá al-ṣadr* (repetition of an early word in a line in the rhyme-word), and *al-madhhab al-kalāmī* (abstruse logical constructions, conceits that are abstract, conceptual, or far-fetched). By the medieval period, however, the categories and subcategories of rhetorical devices had been exhaustively classified and catalogued, but the luster of originality or innovation, at least by our standards, had worn off.[14] In other words, what in its High ʿAbbāsid heyday constituted bold, even scandalous, innovation (as the term *badīʿ* derived from *b-d-ʿ*, to originate, to invent, to do something new, for the first time, indicates; Lane, *b-d-ʿ*) had in the medieval period become a matter of filling *de rigueur* production quotas of such rhetorical constructs in imitation of those of the ʿAbbāsid masters. This tendency reached its climax in the subgenre of *madīḥ nabawī* termed *badīʿiyyah,* which consists of a *muʿāraḍah* following the rhyme, meter, and poetic structure of al-Būṣīrī's Burdah in which each line illustrates a particular rhetorical device.

Central to the present argument is my claim that the distinctive poetics of the *badīʿ* style came to be identified as a rhetoric of Arab-Islamic hegemony, indeed triumphalism. To trace this development briefly, let us begin with the chief stylistic features of *badīʿ* poetry. The first, as described by Ibn al-Muʿtazz (d. 296/908), is the sudden proliferation of rhetorical devices, such as *istiʿārah, jinās* and *ṭibāq,* which he claims are already present in the poetry of the Ancients.[15] Somewhat distinct from this is the fact that, upon analysis, we find that the rhetorical devices of the *badīʿ* poets tend to be abstract or conceptual, and involve conceits that are far-fetched or require what I term "mental gymnastics" to disentangle the meaning. In these respects, the *badīʿ* style is comparable to English Metaphysical poetry, or Spanish Gongorism, or may be termed mannerist.[16]

I have analyzed elsewhere the emergence of *badīʿ* from Muʿtazilite views on language, especially Qurʾānic language, and more generally the distinctive modes of expression developed by the science of Kalām (dialogical disputation, speculative theology).[17] What concerns us here, however, is how this particular style came to be associated with religious, cultural, and political hegemony. In this respect, I see two interrelated phemonena. The first is that with the transition of Arab culture from orality to literacy, there occurred a stunning florescence, described by al-Jāḥiẓ, of (analytical) sciences expressed in written prose. This entailed the coining of technical terms, the analysis and classification of materials of a vast cultural scope, and above all the development of a "language" of "scientific" discourse, that is, the dialectical mode of expression (*mujādalah*) that typifies *ʿilm al-kalam* (speculative theology), but quickly spread to all areas of literary discourse. This included, of course, the development of the linguistics sciences, such as grammar, including syntax and morphology (*al-naḥw, al-ṣarf*), etymology (*ishtiqāq*), and, for poetry in particular, al-Khalīl ibn Aḥmad's (d. 175/791) systematization of the poetic meters (*ʿilm al-ʿarūḍ*), and the description (by al-Jāḥiẓ, d. 255/868) and analytical classification (beginning with Ibn al-Muʿtazz, d. 296/908) of rhetorical devices. This vast scientific-cultural movement of analysis and classification entailed above all the mental processes of abstraction and conceptualization, which thus typify all the discourses of the period—and poetry was no exception.[18]

Further, the sciences and the analytical methods they involve give their practitioner a sense of control and mastery over his scientific domain. For the poet, for example, the sciences of *ishtiqāq, naḥw,* and *ṣarf* allow for the invention of new words and constructs never before imagined. Thus, much to the horror of conservative critics, such as al-Āmidī (d. 370/981) in *Al-Muwāzanah,* we see Abū Tammām, the most celebrated, or notorious, proponent of *badīʿ* poetry, coin new words such as *tafarʿana* (to be despotic), which he derived from *firʿawn* (pharaoh); and devise, through a process of grammatical analogy to such Kalām postulates about the Divine as *huwa huwa* (He is He), unheard-of constructions, such as *lā anta anta* (you are not you).[19] Nor was this power to analyze and innovate limited to individual expressions; rather we see in Abū Tammām's most celebrated ode, on the conquest of Amorium, his ability to recast the entire structure of the *qaṣīdah* so that he omits the prescribed lyrical elegiac opening section of the genre, the *nasīb,* to surprise and dazzle his audience with a dramatic unannounced martial entrance: *al-sayfu aṣdaqu ʾanbāʾan min al-kutubī* (The sword is more veracious than the book).[20]

The point I am trying to make is that in such rhetorical moves the poet has a conscious conceptual mastery of language and literary form that he did not possess before. In this respect, let me reiterate my earlier work to stress that the *badīʿ* style is not merely the mechanical proliferation of rhetorical devices that are already found in the Ancients, as Ibn al-Muʿtazz argued, but rather reflects, along the lines of al-Jāḥiẓ's thinking, a new conceptual and analytical control of language, and with it the metalanguage of poetry, one that allows for, indeed requires, the innovative manipulation of language at various levels.

Even within the realm of established rhetorical devices, we find distinctive differences between *badīʿ* poetry and that of the Ancients. Even familiar devices now come with a complex conceptual twist. Thus, Ibn al-Muʿtazz chooses, as a typical example of the metaphor of the Ancients, the Mukhaḍram Abū Dhuʾayb al-Hudhalī's use of personification to express the ineluctability of fate or death:

> When fate digs in her talons
> You will find every amulet useless.[21]
>
> [35]

How much more complex is his example from Abū Tammām, the *badīʿ* poet's abstraction and inversion of the concept of time that destroys all things, as he personifies time itself as "perishing" (a reflection perhaps of the disputes of the Mutakallimūn over whether time is finite or infinite, now subordinated to the poet's panegyric purpose) to praise to his longtime friend and patron, the general Abū Saʿīd Muḥammad ibn Yūsuf al-Thaghrī:

> When your fated time comes, you will not perish,
> But time, that has destroyed others like you, will perish.[22]
>
> [36]

The gist of this rhetorically complex line, which exhibits *radd al-ʿajuz ʿalá al-ṣadr* as well as metaphor, is the inversion of the commonplace mortality of man and immortality of time or fate: for the *mamdūḥ* will be immortal and time/fate will perish. The idea of one's appointed time to die is construed as a metaphor of heroic "mortal" combat between Abū Saʿīd and Fate or Time, from which the ʿAbbāsid general emerges victorious. In other words, his heroic deeds fighting for Islam will win him immortality in terms of both the poet's verse and the heavenly garden. Thus, the *badīʿ* poet is not merely clothing old ideas in new rhetorical garb; he is inventing rhetorically complex conceits that delight us by turning conventional commonplaces on their heads.

Particularly important in this respect is Ibn al-Muʿtazz's category of *al-madhhab al-kalāmī* (the method of Kalām, or, in Ignatius Kratchkovsky's apt translation, "dialectical mannerism"), which to him means convoluted expressions that need to be disentangled by the application of logic, as is the case with all three of the examples from Abū Tammām that we have just discussed.[23] As I have argued elsewhere, we can usefully extend this term beyond its denotation of particular rhetorical device to a habit or method of analytical conceptual thought that pervades all aspects of poetic production, and indeed characterizes the cultural production of the High ʿAbbāsid period. I believe that this broader understanding of *al-madhhab al-kalāmī,* which is extrapolated from al-Jāḥiẓ's insightful, if not systematic, remarks, provides a far better basis for understanding the accomplishments of the *badīʿ* poetry of the ʿAbbāsid masters than Ibn al-Muʿtazz's limited definition of the *badīʿ* style as merely a proliferation of rhetorical devices that are already present in the poetry of the Ancients.[24] In the context of the present study, I would like to emphasize the newfound sense of mastery over language and literary form that the analytical sciences of the age provided to the *badīʿ* poet.

The second step of this argument for the association of the *badīʿ* style with Arab-Islamic hegemony is one of historical context. In my view, the *badīʿ* style is an organic part and parcel of the development of the analytical sciences in the High ʿAbbāsid period, and these in turn were the result of the cultural and political dominion of the ʿAbbāsid state. It is, in my estimation, no accident that *badīʿ* poetry emerged and flourished during the Golden Age of the ʿAbbāsids (132–334/750–945). This was precisely the period of the apex of ʿAbbāsid politico-cultural hegemony and military might, and, I argue, the *badīʿ* style evolved precisely to express, celebrate, and immortalize that hegemony and that might. In other words, the transformation of Arab civilization in the first three centuries of Islam and the astounding political dominion and cultural florescence of the High ʿAbbāsid Age demanded that the expressive capabilities of the Arabic language, and its poetic metalanguage in particular, be expanded to convey ideas and experiences hitherto unknown.[25] More simply put, the *badīʿ* style in practice is precisely the dominant mode of expression of the High ʿAbbāsid court panegyric, a body of poetry that celebrates Arab-Islamic political and cultural hegemony, military might, and religious authority as vested in the caliph himself or, in a subordinate manner, in lesser patrons of the court. *Badīʿ* is, I argue, the "linguistic correlative" of Islamic might.

No single poem demonstrates this claim better than Abū Tammām's most celebrated panegyric, The Sword is More Veracious, to the Caliph al-Muʿtaṣim (r. 218–27/833–42) on the conquest of the Byzantine city of Amorium, arguably the most influential and formative poem produced in the ʿAbbāsid period.[26] Opening, as mentioned above, with an aggressive martial image, "the sword," the ode is not a historical narrative of the military campaign and conquest, rape, and pillage of the Byzantine city. Rather, through the rhetorical magic of *badīᶜ*, the political military event is recast as a perduring cultural myth of a cosmic battle between good and evil, that is, Arab Islam versus Byzantine Christianity, championed by, respectively, the divinely appointed, virtuous, and heroic Caliph al-Muᶜtaṣim and the craven and despotic Emperor Theophilus. The key point in the context of the present argument is that through the process of recasting the contemporary military event as a *qaṣīdat al-madḥ*, a panegyric ode to the victorious caliph, the poet *politicizes* and *polemicizes* the event as not merely a martial success, but a divinely ordained victory achieved by a divinely appointed ruler, a victory that, moreover, takes its place in the teleological progression of what I have termed the ideology of Islamic Manifest Destiny.[27] The expression of so self-confident an ideology of God-given dominion and destiny required a poetic metalanguage equally robust and confident. This is precisely what the taut muscularity, palpable intensity, and bold innovation of the *badīᶜ* style provided. Consider the rhetorical intensity and rousing momentum of Abū Tammām's morphologically based (*muftaᶜil*, form VIII act. part.) expression of the caliph's divine appointment and equally divine mission:

37. Directed by one relying on God, avenging for God,
Striving and yearning toward God.

[37]

Or the complex interplay of antitheses (*muṭābaqāt*) of darkness and light to describe in cosmic terms the caliph's power to overturn the natural cycle of night and day through the smoke and fire of battle:

26. You left in [Amorium] a black night bright as forenoon
For in her midst a dawn of flame dispelled the dark.

. . . .

28. There was light from the fire while darkness still clung
And dark from the smoke in the pale noonday sun.

[38]

Or the erotic excitement of the rape that is rhetorically stimulated/simulated through the double root-play (*jinās*) derived from traditional metaphors for male and female:

65. How many a reed trembling on a sand-dune
Did the drawn and trembling Indian swords obtain.

[39]

These compelling and innovative images of domination and conquest are achieved through a formidable command of rhetorical tools and an astounding audacity in their use. It is my argument that through imperial panegyrics such as the Amorium *qaṣīdah,* Abū Tammām achieved so perfect a fusion of style and subject matter that ever after the two were identified. That is, the *badīᶜ* style became inseparable or indistinguishable from the ideology of Arab-Islamic hegemony and triumphalism.

ᶜAbbāsid political dominion declined precipitously after the reign of al-Muᶜtaṣim, so that even Abū Tammām's younger contemporary, pupil, and rival, al-Buḥturī, could not match in his panegyrics to caliphs such as al-Mutawakkil (r. 232–47/847–61) or al-Muntaṣir (r. 247–48/861–62) and the men of their courts the unwavering rhetorical conviction that informs his master's panegyrics. Ever after, poets seeking to praise the princes and kinglets of lesser Arab-Islamic domains could most effectively do so by conjuring up the heyday of Arab-Islamic dominion, and this, in turn, was most effectively done by invoking the style and images of Abū Tammām's masterful *qaṣīdahs*. In this respect, the clearly discernible Abū Tammāmian influence on the most celebrated of the classical Arabic poets, al-Mutanabbī (d. 354/965), comes to mind. In sum, the *badīᶜ* style in and of itself, whether specifically that of Abū Tammām or more generally that of the ᶜAbbasid master panegyrists—Abū Nuwās, Muslim ibn al-Walīd, Abū Tammām, al-Buḥturī, Ibn al-Rūmī, al-Mutanabbī—became an expression of Arab-Islamic hegemony and an allusion to the cultural and political dominion of the High ᶜAbbāsid Age.[28]

A further crucial step provides a more purely religious dimension for the Post-Classical insistence on the rhetorical aspects of literary language, especially poetry: the formulation of the Islamic doctrine of the miraculous inimitability for the Qurʾān (Iᶜjāz al-Qurʾān) in the fourth–sixth/tenth–twelfth centuries in terms of its rhetorical beauty. This led to the absorption of the study of rhetoric into the field of Iᶜjāz al-Qurʾān, and to the valorization of the study and exercise of rhetoric as religious duties or undertakings allowing the believer to more fully understand, indeed witness, the evidentiary miracle of the Qurʾān (below, Burdah, part 6).[29]

THE POET AND HIS TIMES

Al-Būṣīrī's century was one to shake the foundations of Arab-Islamic self-confidence, if not faith itself. The Mongol invasions, culminating in the sack of Baghdād in 656/1258, marked a horrific and decisive end to Arab dominion and definitively shifted the Arab cultural center of gravity to Egypt. Even there, the reins of political power were not held by Arab hands. The Kurdish Ayyūbids had replaced the Fāṭimids in Egypt in 566/1171 and, under the leadership of Ṣalāḥ al-Dīn (d. 589/1193), had driven most of the Crusaders from Palestine and Syria. The seventh/thirteenth century was marked by two military crises: the Crusade of St. Louis (647–49/1249–50) and the Mongol invasion, after their conquest and devastation of Baghdād (656/1258), of Syria (657–58/1259–60). In the context of the latter, after the defeat of the Mongols at ʿAyn Jālūt (658/1260), the Baḥrī Mamlūks, of Qipchak Turkish origin, under Baybars, replaced the Ayyūbids as the masters of Egypt, only to be themselves replaced by the Barrī/Burjī Mamlūks when Qalāwūn usurped the throne in 678/1279. Although less dramatically devastating than the Mongol invasions, the remaining Frankish Christian states in Syria and Palestine took a toll on Muslim self-confidence. A particular fear was a coordinated Frankish-Mongol pincer attack against Mamlūk lands. Within the Mamlūk leadership, through the end of the seventh/thirteenth century, political intrigue and instability continued to rule the day.[30]

Sharaf al-Dīn Abū ʿAbd Allāh Muḥammad ibn Saʿīd ibn Ḥammād al-Ṣanhājī al-Būṣīrī was born in 608/1212 in Būṣīr (Abūṣīr) or Dalāṣ in Upper Egypt of Ṣanhājah Berber origin. He is said to have been skilled as a scribe, traditionist, and Qurʾān reciter, to have studied for a time under the Ṣūfī Abū al-ʿAbbās Aḥmad al-Mursī, and to have been involved in the early Shādhiliyyah Ṣūfī order. After spending ten years in Jersualem, then in Mecca and Medina, he took up a minor administrative post in Bilbays, in the eastern Delta. He died in Alexandria 694–696/1294–97 and is said to be buried either in Alexandria or in Cairo in the Muqaṭṭam. Although his *dīwān* contains a variety of occasional poetry—ranging from court panegyrics to Egyptian officials to jocular verse mocking the foibles of Egyptian society of his day—his fame derives from his *madāʾiḥ nabawiyyah,* his praise poems to the Prophet.[31] Among these are his Hamziyyah (ode rhymed in the letter *hamzah*), titled Umm al-Qurá fī Madḥ Khayr al-Wará (The Mother of Villages in Praise of the Best of Mankind), like the Burdah the basis of many commentaries, expansions, and contrafactions, and his Lāmiyyah (ode rhymed in *lām*), which, as is clear from its title Dhukhr al-Maᶜād fī Wazn Bānat Suᶜād (The Storehouse [of good deeds] for Judgment Day in the Meter of "Suᶜād Has Departed"), is a contrafaction of Kaᶜb ibn Zuhayr's renowned poem (see chapter 1).[32] None can compare, however, to the fame achieved by his Mīmiyyah (ode rhymed in *mīm*), on which he bestowed the title Al-Kawākib al-Durriyyah fī Madḥ Khayr al-Bariyyah (Pearly Stars in Praise of the Best of all Creation) and on which posterity has bestowed the epithet: Qaṣīdat al-Burdah (The Mantle Ode).

THE MIRACLE AND THE POEM

A fair amount of al-Būṣīrī's biography has been reconstructed, primarily on the basis of his poetic *dīwān* and several literary-biographical compendia.[33] Nevertheless, throughout the rich manuscript and print tradition that surrounds the Burdah and his several other famed poems of praise to the Prophet, a single episode only of his life is related: namely, the circumstances surrounding his composition of the Burdah, from which the poem, which al-Būṣīrī originally titled Al-Kawākib al-Durriyyah, came to be most popularly known by the epithet Qaṣīdat al-Burdah (The Mantle Ode) and sometimes Qaṣīdat al-Burʾah (The Poem of the Cure).[34] A number of variants and elaborations of this episode exist, and the popularity of the poem suggests extensive oral as well as literary transmission. We read an example of the narrative in its simplest form in the Egyptian scholar Muḥammad ibn Ibrāhīm al-Bājūrī's (d. 1276/1860) *Ḥāshiyah* (Gloss), as he introduces al-Būṣīrī's Burdah and explains the reason for its epithet:

> Because when he composed it, seeking a cure from the disease of hemiplegia which afflicted him, leaving him semiparalyzed and baffling his physicians, he saw the Prophet, pbuh, in his sleep. Then the Prophet stroked him with his hand and wrapped him in his mantle, so he was cured immediately, as the poet mentions in his comment on the poem. Some say that it is more appropriate to call it Qaṣīdat al-Burʾah (Poem of the Cure) because its composer was cured by it, and that the poem that is rightfully called al-Burdah is Bānat Suᶜād (Suᶜād Has Departed), the poem by Kaᶜb ibn Zuhayr, because the Prophet, pbuh, rewarded him (*ajāzahu*) for it with a mantle when he recited it before him.[35]

Charming and more elaborate is the oft-cited version given in the Syrian historian Muḥammad ibn Shākir al-Kutubī's (d. 764/1363) biographical dictionary, *Fawāt al-Wafayāt*:

> Al-Būṣīrī said: I had composed poems of praise to the Messenger, pbuh, among them those that al-Ṣāḥib Zayn al-Dīn Yaʿqūb ibn al-Zubayr had suggested to me. Then it happened after that that I was stricken with hemiplegia that left me half paralyzed, so I thought of composing this Burdah poem, and I did so. And with it I asked for intercession with Allāh the Exalted for Him to forgive me, and I recited it over and over again, and wept and prayed and entreated. Then, when I had fallen asleep, I saw the Prophet, pbuh. He stroked my face with his blessed hand, then threw a mantle over me. When I awoke, I found my health restored [*wajadtu fiyya nahḍah*], so I arose and went out of my house, and I had not told a soul about this. Then a Sufi mendicant met up with me and said to me, "I want you to give me the poem with which you praised the Messenger (Peace upon him)." "Which one?" I replied. "The one you composed when you were sick," he said, and recited the beginning of it. And he continued, "By Allāh, I heard it last night when it was recited before the Messenger of Allāh, pbuh, and I saw the Messenger of Allāh, pbuh, sway with delight at it, and throw a mantle over the one who recited it." So I gave it to him, and the Ṣūfī mendicant mentioned this and the dream became widely known.[36]

Thus, the poem generated many blessings: a dream-vision of the Prophet, a miraculous cure, its mysterious revelation to, or witnessing by, a Ṣūfī adept. As a first step in our investigation, then, we can understand the massive literary engagement of al-Būṣīrī's Burdah—the manuscripts, expansions, commentaries, imitations, etc.—as attempts to appropriate the blessing (*barakah*) inherent in this poem, a blessing whose efficacy has been proved or established by the poet's miraculous cure and its attendant miracles. Its talismanic uses, too, can be understood as a further extension and application of the same principle.

This story is virtually inseparable from the poem throughout its literary and religious-liturgical itinerary. Nevertheless, in order to understand the literary and religious phenomenon of al-Būṣīrī's Burdah, we must investigate, on a level far deeper than the ultimately irrelevant and unanswerable issue of its historicity, the relation of the story to the poem. To do this we have to examine the two texts and their contexts. Let us first note, in examining the poem itself, that there is no indication in the text that the poet suffers from a physical affliction or is praying for a physical cure. Muḥammad Kīlānī's attempt to determine on the basis of al-Būṣīrī's references to ailments elsewhere in his *Dīwān* that he may indeed have suffered from hemiplegia is, therefore, both inconclusive and, ultimately, irrelevant.[37] More to the point is Stefan Sperl's remark concerning spiritual malady and its cure:

> Although the poem makes no mention of a physical illness on the part of the poet it certainly contains evidence of a spiritual crisis: at the beginning of the work, the poet is in a state of despair and expresses bitter remorse over his moral failings. Through depicting and eulogizing the great example of the Prophet, he regains a sense of confidence, and, at the end of the poem, sees grounds for hope that his sins will be forgiven. This therapeutic element, inherent in the very structure of the work, may go some way towards explaining its immense popularity.[38]

Above all, at this point, we must build upon our interpretation in chapter 1 of the relationship between the original Mantle Ode, Kaᶜb ibn Zuhayr's Bānat Suᶜād, and the myth of the donation of the Prophet's mantle that has become so intimately associated with it. We argued there that Kaᶜb's poem was a supplicatory ode, a performance of the poet's spiritual transformation from the Jāhiliyyah, a state of disbelief (or belief in an obsolete tribal religion) to allegiance to and belief in the Prophet Muḥammad and his message, Islam. Inasmuch as the supplicatory ode partakes as well of the ritual of gift exchange inherent in the panegyric pact—the poet presents a "gift" of praise and the patron responds with a (greater) "counter-gift"—we interpreted the Prophet's donation of his mantle to the poet as the completion, through a powerfully symbolic or metaphorical act, of the ritual: i.e., the patron's counter-gift. We understood the gift of the mantle to be a symbol or token of the Prophet's acceptance of the poet's (poem of) submission, the Prophet's protection, in this world, *and the next.* Further, we interpreted the appearance in the Umayyad and ᶜAbbāsid caliphal courts of (what was believed to be) the very mantle given to Kaᶜb by the Prophet, now worn ceremonially by the caliph on the major Islamic feast-days of ᶜĪd al-Fiṭr and ᶜĪd al-Aḍḥá as an emblem of the Prophet's recognition and protection (i.e., legitimacy) of his rule, to be the result of a myth generating a relic.

Our argument will be that in composing this *madīḥ nabawī,* al-Būṣīrī is implicitly following in the steps of Kaᶜb's master poem and in the performance of the spiritual transformation that it entails. One effect of the Dream of the Mantle is to explicitly establish poetic and spiritual cognation with Kaᶜb ibn Zuhayr and his celebrated Suᶜād Has Departed. That is, al-Būṣīrī's Dream of the Mantle, through its identification with Kaᶜb ibn Zuhayr's Donation of the Mantle, establishes a mythic concordance between the two poets and the two poems. As in Kaᶜb's case, so too in al-Būṣīrī's, the myth of the mantle provides a symbolic or metaphoric completion of the ritual of exchange of praise for prize, with the difference that for the Mamlūk period poet, the entire exchange has been translated from the realm of an earthly encounter, understood to be historical, to that of the dream vision. And again, the Prophet's acceptance of the poet's poem/performance of submission, repentance, and praise is betokened by the conferring of the mantle, just as the poet's spiritual transformation is betokened by his physical cure. In other words, al-Būṣīrī has appropriated Kaᶜb ibn Zuhayr's myth with all that it entails of religious and symbolic authority and interpretative significance for his poem. And, whereas Kaᶜb's myth generated a relic, al-Būṣīrī's generated a miracle.

The *barakah* (blessing), that is, the performative efficacy inherent in al-Būṣīrī's Burdah, is incontrovertibly demonstrated in the dream vision of the Prophet, the Prophet's donation of his mantle to the poet, and the poet's miraculous cure. It is no wonder then that in medieval and popular Islam believers sought to appropriate the poem's power. Literary appropriation was achieved through recitation, copying, commentary, imitation-contrafaction, translation, expansion, etc. All of these forms of engagement involve an identification with al-Būṣīrī's original experience and a mythic concordance with it. They constitute performances of the text, through which the performer reenacts and recreates al-Būṣīrī's poem/performance, in a manner we could understand in terms of mimesis whereby imitation generates identity, or in terms of sympathetic magic whereby an equally effective analog is created or performed. By "performance," here as elsewhere in this study, I mean a ritual reenactment whereby the performer or ritual subject through the ritual mimetic repetition of an originary event himself undergoes—that is, experiences for himself—the spiritual (or social, etc.) transformation that it entails.

But something else has also transpired: whereas in Kaᶜb's case the myth produced a relic, in al-Būṣīrī's case, the poem becomes the relic, that is, the physical remnant, of the miraculous cure. On this basis, particularly in the extraliterary world of popular piety, we find—through processes we could understand as synecdoche (the part for the whole) or metonymy (association through attribute) or contagious magic—the widespread use of al-Būṣīrī's Burdah for amulets, talismans, and philters to cure a vast range of bodily and spiritual maladies, and to solve myriad problems of a more practical nature. In other words, through its association with al-Būṣīrī's miracle the poetic text of the Burdah, or parts of it, serve as vessels or conduits for its spiritual and physical powers. Thus, in al-Bājūrī's *Ḥāshiyah,* we read of the following applications of selected verses:

Vv. 1–2:

> The beneficial property of these two verses is that if you write them on a cup, that is, a glass, and dissolve them in rainwater and then give this drink to an untrainable or intractable beast, it will become tractable, docile, and quick to learn. And if you have a foreign slave who is slow to learn Arabic, write these two verses on a piece of gazelle parchment, hang it on his right arm, and he will speak Arabic in no time. (al-Bājūrī, p. 5)

Vv. 3–7:

> If a man is suspicious of his wife, daughter, or female relative, he should write these verses on a citron leaf and put it on her left hand as she sleeps. If he then puts his ear to her mouth, she will tell him everything that she has done in his absence, whether good or bad. Similarly, if he suspects someone of stealing from him, let him write these verses on a tanned frog skin, then take the tongue of the frog and put it in the skin, then hang the skin around the suspect's neck, and, out of surprise, he will confess immediately. (al-Bājūrī, p. 9)

V. 8.

> The virtue of this verse is that whoever repeats it after the evening prayer until he is overcome by sleep will see the Prophet Muḥammad Muṣṭafá, pbuh, in his sleep, if Allāh the Exalted wills. (al-Bājūrī, p. 10)

Other verses, properly applied, will guarantee success in licit love (al-Bājūrī, p. 12), turn the unrepentant soul toward repentance (p. 13), make the hard-hearted and willful kindhearted and repentant (p. 18), give the lazy the energy to stay up late at night to pray and to do good works (p.

23), strengthen the heart of the warrior who fights in Allāh's way and the heart of the deceased to answer the dreaded questions of the angels Munkir and Nakīr in the grave (p. 32). Further examples from al-Bājūrī include cures for epilepsy (p. 53) and stuttering (p. 57); protection for one's house and garden against wild beasts, thieves, and worms (p. 76); amulets for children against Satan, disease, etc. (p. 82).

A twelfth/eighteenth-century manuscript now housed in Berlin that records the special properties of Burdah verses (*Khawāṣṣ al-Burdah*) compiled by one Ibn ʿAbd al-Salām gives fairly close variants of what we find in al-Bājūrī, but some others as well:

Vv. 145–147

> The special property of these verses is that if they are engraved on a silver signet ring when the moon is out, they are beneficial for all bodily ailments from the head to the navel: they will cure ailments of the head and face, the eyes, nose and ears, the teeth, neck, shoulders, flanks, stomach, chest, and heart, with the permission of Allāh the Exalted; this is tested and sound. However, if they are engraved on an iron signet ring, then they are beneficial against all diseases from the navel to the foot: they will cure numbness, colic, and trembling, ailments of the kidneys and spleen, hemorrhoids, pains of the uterus, diarrhea, all diseases of the male and female genitals, and everything in the thighs. All of this is tested and sound, without a doubt. You put the silver ring on the head and the iron ring on the belly. (Ibn ʿAbd al-Salām, folio 253b) [39]

Vv. 152–160:

> The special property of these verses is for the dying. When someone is giving up the ghost, write these lines on a piece of his shroud and put it on his head, moistened with his sweat, then perfume this scrap of cloth with the perfume with which the dead are anointed. If the dying man is at the tomb of the Messenger, pbuh, you should place the piece of cloth in the noble Rawḍah [the Prophet's Meadow, just west of his tomb in Medina] and let it become blessed there, so that when it is placed on the dying man's head, the departure of his soul will be easy for him, with the permission of Allāh the Exalted, and he will remain calm in the face of death. And after it is brought from the Rawḍah to the tomb of the Prophet, pbuh, then someone must go to the dying man while he is still conscious and tell him that he is going to the best of places because of the blessing of these verses. (Ibn ʿAbd al-Salām, folio 254b)

The argument advanced in chapter 2 will be that in its ritual structure and thematic purport al-Būṣīrī's Burdah is essentially an Arabic panegyric ode (*qaṣīdat al-madḥ*) of the supplicatory variety, addressed to the Prophet Muḥammad as the *mamdūḥ,* and pleading for his intercession on Judgment Day. It follows that only through analyzing the supplicatory-panegyric structure of the poem itself within the context of the overarching classical Arabic-Islamic panegyric tradition can we understand the Burdah's power to generate, or perpetuate, the myth of the miracle—the healing of the poet's physical malady, in other words, the metaphorical leap from spiritual to physical cure, and further, within the popular Islamic tradition, the variety of talismanic and therapeutic properties attributed to the Burdah.

ʿUMAR IBN AL-FĀRIḌ'S WAS THAT LAYLÁ'S FIRE

Technically, as has been generally recognized and widely pointed out, al-Būṣīrī's Burdah is a *muʿāraḍah* (contrafaction, imitating the rhyme and meter) of an eighteen-verse Ṣūfī lyric (*ghazal*) by the Egyptian mystical poet ʿUmar ibn al-Fāriḍ (d. 632/1235).[40]

ʿUmar ibn al-Fāriḍ's Was That Laylá's Fire[41]

1. Was that Laylá's fire ablaze in the night at Dhū Salam
   Or was it a lightning-bolt flashing at al-Zawrāʾ, then at al-ʿAlam?
2. O winds of Wadi Naʿmān, is there at dawn no breath of air?
   O water of Wajrah, is there for the thirsty mouth no drink?
3. O driver of the laden camels, who rolls up the wayless desert
   Like a scroll, at the Wormwood Trees of Iḍam,
4. Turn aside at the protected precinct, may God guide you,
   And head for the Lote-Thicket with its sweet bay and lavender.
5. And stop at Mount Salʿ and ask at the wadi's bend
   If the tamarisk saplings on the valley's sides have been watered by
   a streaming rain.
6. I beseech you by God, if you have crossed the ʿAqīq in the forenoon,
   Do not be bashful, but greet its people with "Peace!"
7. And say, "I have left a man fallen in your abodes,
   Alive but like dead, lending malady to malady."

8. In my heart is a flame of passion that could light a fire,
In my eyes are tears that pour like ceaseless rains.

9. Such is the lot of lovers: when they fall in love with a fawn
No part of their body is free from pain.

10. O you who, out of impudence, blame me for my love
Stop your blaming: if you had ever loved, you would not blame me.

11. By the sacred union and the ancient love,
By the firm covenant and what was of old,

12. I have found no consolation or replacement for them,
For it is not my nature to be consoled or to replace.

13. Return sleep to my eye, for perhaps then your phantom
Will visit my bed in the heedlessness of dream.

14. Alas for our days at al-Khayf, if only they had lasted tenfold!
O how was it that they did not last!

15. Far from it! O, if only my sorrow and regret
Could recover what is lost!

16. O gazelles of the sloping dune, out of kindness, turn away from me,
For I have trained my gaze to look at no one but them,

17. Out of obedience to a judge who has issued an awful fatwa:
To shed my blood in both profane and sacred months.

18. He is deaf to my complaints; mute, giving no reply;
To the plight of the lover, he is blind.

[40]

What those who mention this relationship fail to point out, however, is that despite this technical fact and al-Būṣīrī's elegant evocation of the base-text in the *nasīb* (elegiac prelude), verses 1–11 of his long ode, there is no further structural or thematic resemblance between the two poems. That is to say, they belong to two different poetic genres. Ibn al-Fāriḍ's is a Ṣūfī *ghazal* of rhapsodic love, essentially, as Jaroslav Stetkevych has demonstrated in his discussion of one of its sister-poems in the *Dīwān* of Ibn al-Fāriḍ, a mystical distillation of the motifs and structure of the classical *nasīb* (the opening section of the bipartite or tripartite classical *qaṣīdah*), rapturous love and yearning for the lost or departed beloved, to create the self-contained *ghazal*-form, in which the poet quite explicitly (vv. 12, 16) refuses to move psychologically or poetically beyond his love obsession.[42] By contrast, al-

Būṣīrī's Burdah, as we shall see below, takes as its overall framework the structure, themes, and motifs of the classical Arabic *qaṣīdat al-madḥ* (panegyric ode) of the supplicatory type. In the *qaṣīdah* form, the poet concludes the *nasīb* by repenting of and abjuring the passions indulged therein and moving on, often by means of the *raḥīl,* or desert journey section, to a world of new affections and allegiances, of a more mature and stable nature, in the *madīḥ,* or praise, section.

The Mantle Ode

Let us turn to the Burdah itself: it consists of 160 lines (give or take a few in various recensions; it is also very common to add additional lines at the end of the poem to specify additional persons and groups of people to be blessed). It is in the meter al-Basīṭ (*mustafʿilun fāʿilun*), rhymed in *mīm.*

THE STRUCTURE OF AL-BŪṢĪRĪ'S BURDAH

In many of the manuscript and print traditions, the Burdah is divided into ten sections. This division is neither original nor essential to the poem and has the effect of breaking up the poetic sequence or flow of the lines and the transitional passages. However, for the purposes of a thematic and structural overview, it proves useful. The titles or labels of the sections vary somewhat, but the divisions themselves are consistent. Badr al-Dīn Muḥammad al-Ghazzī (d. 984/1577), in his commentary *Al-Zubdah fī Sharḥ al-Burdah,* labels the sections as follows (emphasis mine):

Thematic Sections of al-Būṣīrī's Burdah

1. *Al-nasīb al-nabawī* (Prophetic *nasīb*): vv. 1–11 = lyric-elegiac prelude
2. *Al-taḥdhīr min hawá al-nafs* (Warning against the desires of the self): vv. 11–28
3. *Madḥ al-Rasūl al-karīm* (Praise of the noble Messenger): vv. 29–58
4. *Al-taḥadduth ʿan mawlidih* (What is related about his birth): vv. 59–71
5. *Al-taḥadduth ʿan muʿjizātih* (What is related about his miracles): vv. 72–87
6. *Al-taḥadduth ʿan al-Qurʾān al-karīm* (What is related about the noble Qurʾān): vv. 88–104
7. *Al-taḥadduth ʿan al-Isrāʾ wa-al-Miʿrāj* (What is related about the Night Journey and Ascension): vv. 105–17
8. *Al-taḥadduth ʿan jihād al-Rasūl wa-ghazawātih* (What is related about the jihād and military campaigns of the Messenger): vv. 118–39

9. *Al-tawaṣṣul wa-al-tashaffuʿ* (Supplication and Plea for Intercession): vv. 140–51
10. *Al-munājāh wa-al-taḍarruʿ* (Fervent Prayer and Petition): vv. 152–60[43]

If we omit all the sections that al-Ghazzī labels as *taḥadduth,* that is, "relating what is said about something" (which deal with elements from the life of the Prophet), we find that the remaining parts of the poem (1–3 and 9–10) in sequence, themes, and motifs, constitute a classically structured supplicatory panegyric ode. The sequence is: lyric-erotic prelude and complaint of passion—conventional subjects of the classical *nasīb,* the opening section of the panegyric ode (parts 1–2); praise of the *mamdūḥ* (one praised, patron), in this case the Prophet Muḥammad (part 3); the poet's self-abasement and supplication (parts 9–10). The thematic structure of the two-part *qaṣīdat al-madḥ,* consisting of *nasīb* (lyric-elegiac prelude) and *madīḥ* (praise section) with little or no indication of a *raḥīl* (journey section), as has long been recognized, came to dominate the Arabic panegyric tradition from the ʿAbbāsid period onward. The formative structural role that supplication (including self-abasement and plea) plays in the Arabic panegyric tradition had, however, been largely overlooked prior to my recent studies of what I have termed the Supplicatory Ode.[44]

We argued in chapter 1 that Kaʿb ibn Zuhayr's Suʿād Has Departed owes its poetic and ritual efficacy to its structural, thematic, and motival incorporation of the supplicatory elements already established in the pre-Islamic odes of that type—for example al-Nābighah's poem of apology, O Abode of Mayyah, or ʿAlqamah's poem for the release of his captive kinsmen, A Heart Turbulent with Passion. Even in panegyric odes that are less explicitly supplicatory, such as Zuhayr's poems to Harim ibn Sinān, the effect of this supplicatory structure, as we saw in chapter 1, is to render the poem a performative speech act that establishes a mutual bond of obligation and allegiance between the supplicant and supplicated, that is, between the poet and the *mamdūḥ.* In other words, with the poet's recitation of the poem before the patron, a mutual contractual obligation comes into effect—a "panegyric pact"—and, further, the poem constitutes both the performance and the documentation of that contract. The forging of this contractual bond takes place through a ritual exchange, in the terms formulated by Marcel Mauss, in which the poet's gift (the poem of praise) obligates the patron to make a counter-gift (termed in Arabic *jāʾizah* or prize), and the gift and counter-gift then serve as tokens of the bond of allegiance established between the two.[45] It is of note that al-Bājūrī's version of the Burdah of Kaᶜb ibn Zuhayr story uses the verbal derivative of *jāʾizah* (prize, award), that is, *ajāza* (he bestowed a prize, award; see text cited above).

The present argument is, in essence, that the efficacy, both poetic and religious, of al-Būṣīrī's Burdah lies in large part in its ritual structure, which is that of the Supplicatory Ode of the Classical tradition and which is also, potentially, a liturgical structure—the distinction lying solely in the identity of the *mamdūḥ,* i.e., whether he is royal or divine, political or religious. The story of al-Būṣīrī's Dream of the Mantle (whatever its precise provenance) should alert us to the cognation between not merely the two stories but also the two poems. Our argument here is that al-Būṣīrī's Burdah, however thematically distinct, shares with Kaᶜb's Suᶜād Has Departed the same supplicatory structure with its four basic elements: 1) Lyric-Elegiac Prelude (*nasīb*); 2) Self-Abasement and Submission; 3) Praise of the one supplicated; and 4) Supplication. These, as we will see further below, are set out in Burdah parts 1, 2, 3, 9, and 10. The additional sections, parts 4–8, comprise major thematic elements in the life of the Prophet and, I will argue, are incorporated structurally as a series of extensions to the praise section, part 3. These structural supplements are not, however, mere versified narratives of episodes from the life of the Prophet; in fact, they are not narratively or chronologically structured. Rather we find there that major themes from the life of the Prophet are poetically performed to produce a polemic in defense of an ideology of Islamic Manifest Destiny.

With this contextual and conceptual framework in mind, let us now turn to our reading of the poetic text itself.

The Beginning of the Supplicatory Pattern: Parts 1–3
The Mantle Ode of Al-Būṣīrī[46]

PART 1: PROPHETIC *NASĪB* (VV. 1–12)

1. Was it the memory of those you loved at Dhū Salam
 That made you weep so hard your tears were mixed with blood?

2. Or was it the wind that stirred from the direction of Kāẓimah
 And the lightning that flashed in the darkness of Iḍam?

3. What ails your eyes? If you say, "Cease!" they flow with tears;
What ails your heart? If you say "Be still!" its passion flares once more.

4. Does the lover think that his passion can be concealed
When his tears are flowing with it and his heart inflamed?

5. But for passion you would not shed tears over a ruined abode,
Nor spend nights sleepless from remembering the ben-tree's fragrance and the supple banner-spear.
OR: from remembering the ben-tree and the mountain peak.

6. How can you deny your love when two upstanding witnesses,
Tears and lovesickness, have testified to it?

7. And passion has borne witness to it
With two streaks of tears upon your cheeks, as red as ʿanam-boughs, and a sickly face, as yellow as the blossoms of bahār?

8. Oh yes, the phantom of the one I love did come by night
And leave me sleepless; love does indeed impede delight with pain.

9. O you who fault me for chaste ʿUdhrī passion, forgive me!
For were you fair, you would not censure me.

10. May you be stricken with the same affliction!
My secret is not hidden from my enemies; my sickness never ends!

11. You gave me sound counsel, but I didn't listen,
For lovers are deaf to those that reproach them.

12. Even the advice of grey hair I held suspect,
Though grey hair is the least suspect of all reproachers.

[41]

The *nasīb,* as discussed above in the context of Ibn al-Fāriḍ's Ṣūfī *ghazal,* is a model of the intriguing ambiguity of poetic language. Al-Ghazzī tells us in his commentary (v. 2 and n. 1) that Dhū Salam, Kāẓimah, and Iḍam are places (or the last perhaps a mountain) near Mecca, the site of the Ḥajj, and Medina, the city of the Prophet; and that the use of such pilgrimage-related place-names is a sign that the poem will be a *madīḥ nabawī.*[47] Yet, at the same time, we should note that the evocation of pilgrimage-route place-names in the *nasīb,* a convention traceable to the later ʿAbbāsid Shīʿite poets al-Sharīf (descendant of the Prophet) al-Raḍī (d. 406/1016) and his devoted pupil, a convert from Zoroastrianism, Mihyār al-Daylamī (d. 428/1037), became highly developed in Ṣūfī poetry. There, the identity of the "beloved" is either Allāh or His Prophet, and, as J. Stetkevych has shown, the place-names evocative of the pilgrimage route and sacred cities serve to create a spiritual itinerary.[48] We must keep in mind, however, that at this point in the Arabic poetic tradition, the use of these names evokes poetic precedents and their lyric-elegiac mood-associations rather than geographical locations. Further, in composing his poem as a *muʿāraḍah* of Ibn al-Fāriḍ's *mīmiyyah,* a Ṣūfī *ghazal* of unrepentant devotion to the b/Beloved, al-Būṣīrī employs the same poetic motifs and diction to evoke the memory of and passion for a lost beloved.

In the reading of verse 5 that I have chosen to translate, "the ben-tree's fragrance" and "the supple banner-spear" (*ʿalam,* literally "the ben-tree" and "the banner-spear") serve as traditional metaphors (or similes) for the beloved's delightful fragrance (a synecdoche, really) and supple figure. Following Nicholson's choice of the other meaning of *ʿalam* that the commentarists proffer, "mountain tip," the result is, as al-Ghazzī tells us, that both elements now serve as synecdoches for the places of verses 1 and 2: the ben-trees of Dhū Salam and the tip of Mount Iḍam (al-Ghazzī, v. 5).[49] In effect, the semantic interplay of conventional elements of the intimately related imagery and diction of the abode and the beloved has been so intensified in the Arabic poetic tradition that the strict distinction of rhetorical function—simile, metaphor, synecdoche, or metonymy—breaks down until everything is a metonymy of everything else—that is, any one element has the effect of evoking the others.

Technically, within the *nasīb* itself (vv.1–12), the identity of the b/Beloved is not revealed: is this a worldly passion or is al-Būṣīrī describing his passionate devotion to the Prophet Muḥammad or the Divine? In the end—and this is where the metalanguage of poetic form (i.e., of the difference between the self-contained *ghazal*-form and the *nasīb,* which is only the first part of the structural-thematic trajectory of the bi- or tri-partite *qaṣīdah*-form) comes into play—the *nasīb* (vv. 1–12) of al-Būṣīrī's *madīḥ nabawī* veers away from the concluding reaffirmation of unrepentant passion of the self-contained (Ṣūfī) *ghazal.* It follows instead the structural dictates of the panegyric ode (*qaṣīdat al-madḥ*), that is, it invokes the memory of and passion for what is revealed to be an earthly beloved, but in the end abjures that passion and moves on to regret and repentance—as we saw in the *qaṣīdahs* of chapter 1. By contrast, the self-contained Ṣūfī *ghazal* stubbornly maintains the ambiguity—or identity—of the earthly and divine b/Beloved.

PART 2: WARNING AGAINST THE DESIRES OF THE SELF (VV. 13–28)

13. My willful wicked soul in its folly refused all warnings
From the harbingers of grey hair and old age.

14. It did not prepare a repast of good deeds to welcome
The guest (grey hair) that, unabashed, alighted on my head.

15. Had I known that I could not honor this guest,
I would have concealed his arrival with katam-dye.

16. Who will restrain my defiant soul from error
The way that bolting steeds are curbed by yanking back the reins?

17. Don't hope to curb her craving for defiance by indulging it,
For food only increases the glutton's appetite.

18. The self is like a little child: if you ignore it, it won't outgrow
Its love of suckling; only if you wean it will it stop.

19. Curb the passion of your willful soul; don't let it rule you!
When passion reigns it brings death or disgrace.

20. Watch over her when she is grazing freely among deeds:
If she finds a pasture sweet, don't let her graze there.

21. How often has she made the deadly seem delicious,
So man doesn't know that his rich dish holds poison.

22. Fear the tricks that hunger and satiety can play!—
An empty belly can do as much harm as a full one.

23. Purge with tears an eye sated with forbidden sights;
Adhere to a strict diet of repentance.

24. Disobey your willful soul and Satan, defy them!
And if they offer you advice, don't trust them!

25. Don't let them play litigant or judge in your deliberations,
For you know the tricks that litigants and judges play.[50]

26. I seek God's forgiveness for my saying what I do not do;
It's as though I've claimed a sterile man has children.

27. I ordered you to do good, but I did not obey my own command;
I have not done right, so how can I tell you "Do right!"?

28. I have not set by, before death, a store of extra prayers;
I've prayed only the required prayers, and have not fasted more than is required.

[42]

The imposition of thematic sectional divisions upon the poem may obscure the masterful transition of verses 11–13 through which the ambiguous b/Beloved of the Ṣūfī-influenced *nasīb* is revealed to be an earthly beloved who represents the vanities and passions of the world. In the end, al-Būṣīrī's *nasīb* thus resembles Kaʿb's *nasīb* (chapter 1) more than it resembles Ibn al-Fāriḍ's *ghazal*. Further, for al-Būṣīrī, inasmuch as the *nasīb* functions as an emblem or synecdoche of poetry as whole, what the poet is really rejecting is worldly poetry (see below). By verse 13, then, the passion of the *nasīb* is described as a folly from which the willful self or soul will not desist (al-Būṣīrī's *ʾammārati bi-al-sūʾi* invokes the Qurʾānic *ʾinna al-nafsa la-ʾammāratun bi-al-sūʾi*, "Surely the willful soul commands one to evil," of Sūrat Yusūf [QK 12:53]). In verses 13–15, al-Būṣīrī employs the conceit of grey hair (a reminder of man's mortality and a harbinger of death) as a pushy guest who arrives unannounced and for whom the poet/host is caught unprepared. As al-Ghazzī's editor, Bāshā, and Sperl note, the second hemistich of verse 14, "The guest (grey hair) that, unabashed, alighted on my head," is a direct quote of the opening hemistich of a poem by al-Mutanabbī.[51] Nevertheless, the classical *nasīb* motif of the unrepentant aging lover railing against old age (*al-shakwá min al-shayb*) is somewhat twisted here. Instead of defying or denying the unwanted guest, he recognizes his obligation to honor him. The poet is ashamed of his arrested moral development and repents of having clung to the things of this world, "the follies of youth," rather than preparing a store of good deeds for the "guest," for the life to come. These verses thus signal a moral and emotional transition.

This reading should help us understand that in the classical *qaṣīdat al-madḥ*, too, the *nasīb* is not an extraneous element nor merely a seductive "come-on," but the necessary starting point for the psychological and moral trajectory of the poem. Unlike the static single-themed *ghazal*-form that so admirably expresses (especially) erotic fixation or obsession, the *qaṣīdah* in its tripartite or bipartite form is a structure that expresses transition, indeed, transformation. So far in this poem, we have made the transition from erotic suffering (part 1) to repentance, contrition, and the poet's moral admonition, to himself as well as others, to curb the appetites of the "willful ego" (part 2). With this, the elements of self-abasement that most concern us in the context of the present argument come to the fore. They are most apparent in the confession and plea for absolution in verses 26–29.

Once again the section heading of part 3 obscures the subtlety of the transition, whereby the poet moves from the self-reproach and repentance of part 2 into the Praise for the Prophet Muḥammad of part 3: ". . . / I've prayed only the required prayers, and have not fasted more than is required // I have profaned the Path of him whose night prayers brought the darkness to life / . . ." (vv. 28–29). It should be further noted here that Part 2: Warning against the Desires of the Self serves as a passage of self-abasement and transition in the same way the *raḥīl,* the central journey section, of the tripartite *qaṣīdat al-madḥ* does.

PART 3: PRAISE OF THE NOBLE MESSENGER (VV. 29–58)

29. I have profaned the Path of him whose night prayers brought the darkness to life
Until his feet complained of pain and swelling,

30. Who tied a stone to his belly to blunt the hunger pangs,
Concealing beneath the stone his tender flank.

31. Haughty mountains of pure gold sought to tempt him,
But, oh, with what disdain he turned them down!

32. His need served only to strengthen his renunciation,
For necessity cannot prevail against the sinless.

33. How could need tempt with this world's vanities one who, but for him,
The world would never have emerged from nothingness?

34. Muḥammad, the master of all who dwell in both the seen and unseen worlds,
Of both corporeal species, men and jinn, of the two races, ʿArab and ʿAjam.

35. Our Prophet, the commander of good and forbidder of evil;
No one was more just than he when he said "yes" or "no."

36. He is the beloved of God whose intercession is hoped for
In the face of every dread and unexpected horror.

37. He called mankind to God, so whoever clings to him
Clings to a rope that will never be broken.

38. He surpassed all other prophets in form and character;
They could not approach him in knowledge or in magnanimity.

39. Each of them beseeching God's Messenger
For a handful of the sea of his knowledge or a sip of the unceasing downpour of his munificence.

40. Standing before him, lined up by rank,
Like points on the letters of his knowledge or vowel-marks on the text of his wisdom.

41. He is the one whose spirit and form were perfected,
Then the Creator of mankind chose him as His beloved.

42. In inner and outer beauty he is free from any partner,
For in him the essence of beauty is indivisible.

43. Don't claim what the Christians claim for their prophet,
But praise him as you judge best and proper.

44. Ascribe to him as much honor as you wish;
Assign him as much majesty as you desire,

45. For surely the merit of God's Messenger is without limit,
And so exceeds what any tongue could ever express.

46. If his miracles were as mighty as his rank, the mere mention of his name
Would bring decaying bones of dead men back to life.

47. He did not test us with more than human minds could grasp,
So we never harbored doubts nor fell into confusion.

48. But his true nature defies human understanding:
There is no one, near or far, who is not dumbfounded by it,

49. Like the sun that from afar seems small to the eye,
But is too bright to look at directly.

50. How can mankind in this world, asleep and distracted by dreams,
Comprehend the Prophet's true nature?

51. The utmost extent of our knowledge of him is that he is human,
And that he is the best of all of God's creation.

52. And all the miracles that other noble messengers have brought
Have reached them only through his light.

53. He is the sun in virtue; the others, stars
Whose lights appear to mankind only at night.

54. How noble is the form of a Prophet adorned with good morals,
Cloaked in comeliness, marked by a radiant face!

55. A tender blossom in complexion, the full moon in nobility,
The sea in magnanimity, in aspiration as limitless as time itself.

56. Even alone in his majesty, he seems, when you meet him,
Surrounded by an army and an entourage.

57. As if the pearls secreted in their oyster shells
Were from the two mines of his speech and of his smile.

58. No perfume is as redolent as the dust that holds his bones;
Whoever inhales or kisses it is blessed.

[43]

The *madīḥ* (praise) section weaves together threads of several different strains, which, when analyzed, give us some idea of the literary genealogy of al-Būṣīrī's *madīḥ nabawī*. First, as expected, there are elements deriving from Islamic religious sources, the Qurʾān and the life of the Prophet, the latter sometimes traceable to Ibn Hishām/Ibn Isḥāq's *Al-Sīrah al-Nabawiyyah* and to standard Ḥadīth collections, such as those of al-Bukhārī and Muslim, as noted by the commentators, but also to later though authoritative sources, such as the Traditionists al-Ḥākim al-Naysābūrī (d. 405/1014) and his pupil Abū Bakr al-Bayhaqī (d. 458/1066). Particularly proximate to the Burdah in time and materials pertaining to the Prophet is the enormously successful *Al-Shifāʾ bi-Taʿrīf Ḥuqūq al-Muṣṭafá* by the celebrated Mālikī scholar of the Muslim West, al-Qāḍī ʿIyāḍ ibn Mūsá (d. 544/1149), a work that continues to play an important role in popular Muslim piety.[52] A compendium of traditional beliefs concerning the Prophet and the obligations of the Muslim to him, *Al-Shifāʾ* provides a convenient prose reference, if not indeed a source, for many of the traditions concerning the Prophet covered in parts 3–8 of the Burdah, and is cited often, sometimes by name, sometimes not, by the Arab commentarists relied on in this study. We should not lose sight of the fact, however, that al-Būṣīrī's most direct sources for the Burdah were no doubt his literary predecessors in the genre of *madīḥ nabawī* and in the broader Arabic poetic tradition.

Except for some of the Qurʾānic references, it is impossible to say precisely what al-Būṣīrī's sources were, but we can conclude from the corroborating evidence of the sources adduced by the commentators that the Burdah expresses traditional beliefs that were accepted in his time and long thereafter. Further, we should note that what in historical terms we would call Post-Classical Islamic developments are seamlessly integrated here and elsewhere in the poem. In the initial passage describing the Prophet's suffering and renunciation, elements attested by al-Bukhārī and *Al-Sīrah* of Ibn Hishām, such as the Prophet placing a stone on his belly to ward off hunger pangs (vv. 29–30) lead to an episode (which we might otherwise recognize from the Temptation of Christ) in verse 31, attested to in *Al-Shifāʾ* of al-Qāḍī ʿIyāḍ, in which Jibrīl tempted or tested the Prophet with a mountain of gold.[53] Likewise, later neo-Platonic–influenced concepts of the Prophet Muḥammad are reflected in verse 33, for which al-Ghazzī and al-Bājūrī cite a *ḥadīth* given by al-Ḥākim and his pupil al-Bayhaqī concerning the concept of *al-ḥaqīqah al-Muḥammadiyyah,* i.e., that the Prophet Muḥammad was the goal of God's creation:[54]

> When Ādam committed a sin, because he had seen written on the feet of God's throne: "There is no god but God and Muḥammad is the Messenger of God," he asked if he could be forgiven in Muḥammad's name (*bi-ḥaqq Muḥammad*). God Almighty replied, "If you are asking me in his name (*bi-ḥaqqih*), then you are forgiven, for if it were not for Muḥammad, I would not have created you." And God had created for the progeny of Ādam all that is on the earth and subjected to them the sun and the moon and the night and the day, etc." (al-Ghazzī, al-Bājūrī, v. 33)

It is curious that, whereas al-Ghazzī interprets verses 52–53 more conservatively, saying that Muḥammad's *nūr* (light) means his knowledge, and that the image of the sun and stars is a simile, meaning that the *sharīʿah* of Muḥammad abrogated those of the earlier prophets, al-Azharī and al-Bājūrī both add further that these lines refer to *al-nūr al-Muḥammadī.*[55] The analogy is quite compelling—the sun has light in itself, whereas the light of the planets is only borrowed from the sun; the sun's light is not at all diminished by its lighting the planets, etc. (al-Ghazzī, al-Azharī, al-Bājūrī, vv. 52–53). Not surprisingly, such elements of the poem elicited condemnation from certain conservative quarters, most notably the celebrated Ḥanbalī theologian Ibn Taymiyyah (d. 728/1328), who took particular exception to verses 43–46.[56]

Some Qurʾānic references are more straightforward, such as verse 37 in its poetic paraphrase of QK 2:256: "Whoever denies Satan and believes in Allāh has grasped a firm handle that will never break" (. . . *fa-*

man yakfur bi-al-ṭāghūti wa-yuʾmin bi-Allāhi fa-qad istamsaka bi-al-ʿurwá al-wuthqá lā infiṣāma la-hā. . . .), and which also plays with the use of this expression as an epithet for the Prophet.[57] Other elements reflect the Islamic beliefs of the medieval period, deriving from neo-Platonic, Ṣūfī, and popular devotional sources, for example, verses 33–34, 36, 42, 46, 50–52.

Most important are the two interrelated and interwoven themes that dominate Part 3: Praise of the Noble Messenger: the Intercession of the Prophet on Judgment Day, and his rank, as Seal of the Prophets (Khātam al-Anbiyāʾ), above that of all other prophets. Both reflect the medieval development of personal devotion to the Prophet Muḥammad, and both perform the standard function of classical Arabic panegyric (*madīḥ*), that is, of establishing the unique qualifications of the *mamdūḥ* for his position, to the exclusion of all other claimants or contenders. On the Prophet as Intercessor on the Day of Judgment, both al-Ghazzī and al-Bājūrī cite a passage from the renowned Shāfiʿī jurist and traditionist of Damascus, Muḥyī al-Dīn al-Nawawī (d. 676/1277) on the types of intercession that the Prophet can or will provide (al-Ghazzī, al-Bājūrī, v. 36). Muḥammad's unique role among the prophets as intercessor for his community on Judgment Day is dramatically related by al-Qāḍī ʿIyāḍ in *Al-Shifāʾ*:

> It was related that Abū Hurayrah said: The sun will draw near and the people will suffer the most unbearable affliction, until they say, "Don't you see anyone who can intercede for you?" So they come to Adam and say, "O Adam, father of all mankind! God created you with His own hand, and breathed some of His own spirit into you, and set you to dwell in His garden, and made the angels prostrate themselves before you, and taught you the names of all things! Intercede for us with your Lord so He will release us from this terrible state! Don't you see what distress we're in?" Adam replies: "My Lord is very angry today—angrier than He ever was before or ever will be! He forbade me to taste of the tree and I disobeyed! I fear for my own soul! Seek help from someone else! Go to Noah!" So they come to Noah and say, "You are the first Messenger God sent to the people of the earth, and God named you His grateful servant. Don't you see what distress we are in? Don't you see what's happened to us? Won't you intercede for us with your Lord?" Noah replies: "My Lord is very angry today—angrier than He ever was before or ever will be! I fear for my own soul! . . . Go to Abraham!"

> [The story repeats itself with Abraham, Moses, and finally Jesus, who directs them to Muḥammad. The narration continues, now in Muḥammad's words:]
>
> Then they come to me, so I say: "I'm the one to do it. I will go and ask permission to go before my Lord and He will grant it to me. And when I see Him I will prostrate myself before Him. . . . Then a voice will say "O Muḥammad, raise your head. Ask and you will be given, intercede and you will be granted intercession." Then I will raise my head and say, "O Lord, my people (*ummatī*)! O Lord, my people!" Then He will say, "Bring in your people without any reckoning through the right-hand gate of the gates of the garden."[58]

The intimate connection between the twin elements of Muḥammad's intercession on Judgment Day and his superiority to the other prophets is made explicit in this prose narrative.

The insistence on Muḥammad's rank as the highest of the prophets that continues in verses throughout much of part 3 is a theme that reflects the intercommunal polemic distinctive of the Burdah and others of al-Būṣīrī's poems, and which comes to the fore in the Burdah, Part 7: The Night Journey and Ascension.[59] Al-Būṣīrī, in his argument and polemic against Christianity, faces a complex rhetorical challenge. The Christians, in claiming that Jesus is divine, make a higher claim for him than the Muslims do for Muḥammad. In Islamic doctrine Muḥammad is the best and last of all the prophets (the Seal of the Prophets/Khātam al-Anbiyāʾ), but he is human and not divine. Thus al-Būṣīrī cannot merely exchange their positions: while demoting Jesus from divine to prophetic status, he cannot correspondingly elevate Muḥammad to the Godhead. Additionally, as Jesus is recognized as a prophet in Islam, al-Būṣīrī cannot attack him, but only his followers who (falsely, in the Islamic view) claim divinity for him. In this respect, al-Būṣīrī's greatest rhetorical challenge is to elevate Muḥammad as far as possible above the other prophets without committing *shirk*, that is, polytheism, assigning partners to Allāh (precisely the abomination of Christianity, in Muslim eyes), i.e., claiming divinity for him.

Verses 38 to 40 are devoted to the first step of al-Būṣīrī's argument: the demonstration, in ritual terms that we now understand, of the inferior status of the other prophets vis-à-vis Muḥammad. In verse 39 they are portrayed as supplicants (with all that that entails of self-abasement, etc.) begging for even a handful of the sea of Muḥammad's knowledge or a sip of the downpour of his bounty. Their subordination is bodily enacted or performed in verse 40 as they stand by rank lined up before him, like courtiers before their king, or soldiers before their commander, to be understood in terms of Connerton's "choreography of authority."[60] The second hemistich of verse 40 then switches from the bodily to the conceptual (*badīʿ*) expression: Muḥammad's knowledge (= the Qurʾān) is the main text (= the ultimate divine revelation) while theirs (the Torah, the Psalms, the Gospels), like letter points and vowel marks, are ancillary to the main text.

The second step is the elevation of the Prophet Muḥammad. Verses 41 and 42 perform this function, attributing to the Prophet perfection and moral and physical beauty. In verse 42 the poet elevates Muḥammad as much as "humanly" and rhetorically possible. Al-Būṣīrī suggestively employs diction that is commonly associated with Allāh Himself: "free of any partner" (*munazzahun ʿan sharīkin*) is uncomfortably close to the Islamic deific formula for Allāh "who has no partner" (*lā sharīka lahu*); likewise "indivisible . . . essence" (*jawharu . . . ghayru munqasimin*) echoes the formulations of the Mutakallimūn (speculative theologians) on the nature of Allāh. Of course, in terms of elevating the status of Muḥammad this is as rhetorically striking as it is daring. As an escape clause, al-Būṣīrī offers verse 43, "Don't claim what the Christians claim for their prophet [Jesus]"—carefully leaving the unthinkable (the divinity of Muḥammad) unspoken. Yet we find in verse 46, carefully couched in a conditional sentence, a similar appropriation of divine attributes to the Prophet. The Qurʾān is, of course, replete with expressions of Allāh's reviving the dead on Resurrection Day. Al-Būṣīrī's verse 46 plays explicitly, however, on one instance, through the conjuncture of the verb *ʾaḥyā* (to give life, to revive) with the rhyme word *al-rimami* (decaying bones). This is an evocation of the Qurʾānic exchange in which Allāh instructs Muḥammad that, if a doubter should challenge him saying, "Who can revive (*yuḥyi*) dead bones after they are decayed (*ramīm*)?" he should reply, "He [Allāh] who gave them life in the first place will revive them (*yuḥyīhā*)" (QK 36:78–79).

Another feature of part 3 is one that distinguishes al-Būṣīrī's Burdah from the more purely lyrical devotional tone of much of the medieval *madāʾiḥ nabawiyyah:* al-Būṣīrī's introduction of the rhetoric and motifs of the Arab-Islamic court panegyric tradition. This poetics or rhetoric of political power originated in the Jāhiliyyah with poets such as al-

Nābighah (see chapter 1), was appropriated in the Umayyad period by poets like al-Akhṭal, Jarīr, and al-Farazdaq, and reached its apex in the ᶜAbbāsid period in the highly rhetorically ornate *badīᶜ*-style panegyrics of poets like Abū Tammām (d. 231/845), al-Buḥturī (d. 284/897), and al-Mutanabbī (d. 354/965; chapter 2, introduction). This High ᶜAbbāsid panegyric style became the consummate expression of divinely appointed Arab-Islamic hegemonic rule. It is most salient in this section in verses such as 33, which despite its neo-Platonic precept exemplifies the verbal and mental play that defines *al-madhhab al-kalāmī,* that most distinctive element of the *badīᶜ* style that we have described as "mental gymnastics." Typical, too, of the high panegyric *badīᶜ* style is verse 40, discussed above, with its conceit that the other prophets are to Muḥammad as "points on the letters of his knowledge or vowel-marks on the text of his wisdom." Verses 53–57, except for the word Prophet in verse 54, could be taken directly from court panegyric of the Abū Tammāmian sort. Despite its lyrical first hemistich, verse 55, as has been noted by al-Ghazzī's editor, Bāshā, boasts precisely the parallel phrases (*tashṭīr* or *tarṣīᶜ*) of Abū Tammām's celebrated praise of the Caliph al-Muᶜtaṣim:

> Directed by one relying on God, avenging for God
> Striving for God and yearning for God.[61]
>
> [44]

Verse 56 in particular is straight out of the ᶜAbbāsid military panegyric motif catalog: the image of the caliph-commander who incites as much awe when alone as when surrounded by his mighty army is now applied to Muḥammad. The double-simile of pearls in verse 57, as al-Ghazzī (v. 57) notes, is based on a verse by al-Buḥturī:

> Pearls she reveals when she smiles,
> And pearls she lets fall, one by one, as she speaks.[62]
>
> [45]

In terms of our discussion of the rhetorically ornate *badīᶜ* style, we can note that al-Būṣīrī's verse, like al-Buḥturī's, is a double inverted simile. The poet has taken two traditional similes: first, that beautiful words are like pearls (cf. the English "pearls of wisdom" for "wise sayings") and second, that beautiful white teeth are like pearls (cf., again, the English "pearly whites" for "teeth"); then, al-Ghazzī continues, the poet has inverted each one of them (pearls are like the Prophet's words and like the Prophet's teeth) and combined them in a single verse (al-Ghazzī, v. 57). That one simile is physical and the other conceptual adds further rhetorical refinement.

In a curious and moving manner, after this complex interweaving of various religious and political panegyric strains, al-Būṣīrī closes the *madīḥ* section proper (part 3) with a delicately lyrical verse (v. 58), "No fragrance is as redolent as the dust that holds his bones," that evokes the elegiac mood of both *nasīb* and *rithā᾽* that we know from Ḥassān ibn Thābit's elegy to the Prophet (chapter 1). The section closes with a theme so prominent in both the *madīḥ nabawī* and popular piety of the medieval period, the devotional visit to Medina and the grave of the Prophet after completing the pilgrimage rites at Mecca.[63] Indeed, verse 58, "No perfume is as redolent as the dust that holds his bones; / Whoever inhales or kisses it is blessed" virtually reiterates the prescription of al-Qāḍī ᶜIyāḍ's *Al-Shifā᾽* concerning the place where the Prophet's skin first touched the earth after his death: "Its courtyards should be glorified, its fragrant odors should be inhaled, and its abodes and walls should be kissed" (*᾽an tuᶜaẓẓama ᶜaraṣātuhā wa-tunassama nafaḥātuhā wa-tuqabbala rubūᶜuhā wa-judrānuhā*).[64]

The delicate lyricism of verse 58 should not blind us to its rhetorical sophistication, most notably in the *jinās* (root-play) between *ṭīb* (fragrance or perfume) and *ṭūbá* (blessing), one conveying sweetness and purity on the physical level, the other on the spiritual. The commentarists insist on telling us that *aᶜẓum* (bones) is to be understood as a synecdoche for the entire body, because Muḥammad's body, like those of other prophets, is incorruptible and does not decompose in the grave (al-Bājūrī, v. 58). This should serve to remind us that especially in the Islamic context, *ṭīb* and *ṭūbá,* perfume and blessing, are both associated with immortality and salvation, a point further corroborated by the name (or epithet) of the Prophet's grave-site, Ṭaybah (see chapter 1, Ḥassān ibn Thābit's elegy). The emotional and literary effect of this verse serves as genre signpost to alert us once more to the fact that this is not, after all, court panegyric, but al-Būṣīrī's (at its time) curious hybrid, *madīḥ nabawī,* with its distinctive structural and motival combination of the lyric elegiac elements of *nasīb* and *rithā᾽* with the masculine and hegemonic elements of *qaṣīdat al-madḥ,* and, finally, the projection into the future of the completion of the ritual exchange that the classical *qaṣīdah* embodies and implies—i.e., *shafāʿah* and *ṭūbá,* intercession on Judgment Day and blessing.

It is important to realize that part 3, the *madīḥ* or praise section of the Burdah, is not merely a string of encomiastic verses, but rather it exhibits a clear psychological or spiritual progression or transformation. The poet (and reader) begins part 3, verse 29, in a state of self-reproach and despair over his sins: "I have profaned the Path [*sunnah*] of him whose night prayers . . . ," but emerges from it with the hope of intercession, blessing, and spiritual renewal. Thus in itself, part 3 encapsulates the structure of ritual exchange of the *madīḥ nabawī*: the poet opens with self-abasement and contrition, then offers a gift of praise, and closes with a blessing.

In terms of the full supplicatory structure of the poem, the *madīḥ* section can be understood as the countermovement to elements 1) *Nasīb* and 2) Self-Abasement. Supplication by its very nature requires the abasement, physical or psychological, of the supplicant and the elevation, physical or psychological, of the one supplicated.[65]

The Sīrah-Derived Passages: Parts 4–8

The structural-thematic elements of the Arabic Supplicatory Ode—1) *Nasīb;* 2) Self-Abasement and Submission of the supplicant/poet to the one supplicated/praised (the *mamdūḥ*); 3) Praise of the one supplicated; and 4) the Supplication itself; and in addition (especially from Umayyad and ʿAbbāsid times) one more element, 5) Benediction of the *mamdūḥ*—constitute, in my reading of al-Būṣīrī's Burdah, the framework of the poem. In terms of the traditional thematic headings of the Burdah the first three of these five supplicatory elements can be located, as we have seen above, in parts 1–3 (Prophetic *Nasīb,* Warning against the Desires of the Self, Praise of the Noble Messenger), and the last two figure most prominently, as we will see later in this chapter, in parts 9 and 10 (Supplication and Plea for Intercession, Fervent Prayer and Supplication). As we have seen, these structural-thematic elements of the supplicatory ode do not occur in strict isolation; rather, although the *nasīb* is generally quite thematically and structurally distinct and normally occurs at the beginning of the poem, the remaining elements do not exhibit a set order and are often intermixed. Apart from these requisite structural elements of the supplicatory framework are those parts (4: The Birth of the Prophet; 5: The Miracles of the Prophet; 6: The Noble Qurʾān; 7: The Night Journey and Ascension; 8: The Messenger's Jihād and Campaigns) that feature major thematic elements derived from the Sīrah (biography) of the Prophet and are incorporated, structurally, as a series of extensions to the praise section (part 3).

POETICIZATION AND POLEMICIZATION

The argument here will be that parts 4–8 are by no means merely versified versions of events that are related in the Sīrah of the Prophet, as al-Ghazzī's labels might suggest; in fact they are not narratively constructed, nor chronologically structured, nor "historically" presented. It is my contention, rather, that particular elements from the Sīrah of the Prophet have been carefully selected and masterfully poeticized to forge an Islamic polemic, which, however much it was grounded in the contemporary politics of al-Būṣīrī's day, has retained its validity and popularity throughout the centuries. Above all, I will argue that the *poeticization* of these originally prose materials achieves an increased *polemicization,* that is, it constitutes a transformation from the prosaic narrative-historical presentation of events in Sīrah and Ḥadīth works into a mythicization that aims at incorporating them into a grander cosmic plan of what I have termed Islamic Manifest Destiny.[66] This is not to say that the Sīrah and Ḥadīth versions of these events are verifiable historical fact, but rather that, although they contain mythic and folkloric as well as historical elements and are controlled by an overarching Islamic polemic, the format and presentation are those of historical narrative authoritatively related and transmitted. As we will see, the poetic rendition of these events, by contrast, dispenses with the narrative "historical" framework to foreground the mythic and cosmic significance of these events.

I am using the term "Sīrah-related" somewhat broadly to refer to elements in the Burdah that express Muslim beliefs concerning the life of the Prophet Muḥammad, some of them grounded in the Qurʾān, but more generally attested in the prose narratives of such widely accepted Islamic sources as Ibn Hishām/Ibn Isḥāq's *Al-Sīrah al-Nabawiyyah,* the canonical Ḥadīth collections (*al-Kutub al-Sittah*), such as those of al-Bukhārī and Muslim, as noted by the Burdah commentators, but especially al-Tirmidhī's influential work on *shamāʾil* (the excellent qualities of the Prophet); and also to later though authoritative sources such as the Traditionists al-Ḥākim al-Naysābūrī (d. 405/1014), author of *Al-Mustadrak ʿalá al-Ṣaḥīḥayn,* and his pupil Abū Bakr al-Bayhaqī (d. 458/1066), author of *Kitāb al-Sunan al-Kubrá,* but also of *Dalāʾil al-Nubuwwah.* As we have already noted, the very popular *Al-Shifāʾ bi-Taʿrīf Ḥuqūq al-Muṣṭafá* of al-Qāḍī ʿIyāḍ ibn Mūsá (d. 544/1149) is particularly proximate to al-Būṣīrī's Burdah and evidently relied upon by many of its commentators. Annemarie Schimmel's remarks provide a succinct description of these materials that is particularly appropriate to our discussion of the Burdah:

> In the early days . . . there was a genre called *dalāʾil al-nubuwwah,* "proofs of Prophethood," complemented by that of the *shamāʾil,* literary expositions of the Prophet's lofty qualities and outward beauty. Two of the earliest *dalāʾil* and *shamāʾil* works were composed by Abu Nuʿaim al-Isfahani (d. 1037), a mystic and historian, and by al-Baihaqi (d. 1066). Both are more or less biographies of the Prophet, studded with evidentiary miracles—those that happened before and after Muḥammad's birth as well as before and after his call to prophethood, and those that pointed to his exalted status as the last Prophet. Both sources speak of his noble genealogy and his qualities and indulge in telling many of the miracles through which men and animals recognized him as God's special messenger. Such tales formed the bases for legends and poems in which popular views about Muḥammad were to be reflected throughout the centuries.
>
> Almost two hundred years before al-Baihaqi, the traditionist Abu ʿIsa al-Tirmidhi (d. 892) compiled the first basic book about *shamāʾil al-Muṣṭafā,* in which the Prophet's external form as well as his moral superiority was described in great detail. Muḥammad appears here as the model of moral perfection, and it is not surprising that Tirmidhi's collection was used as a source by that medieval author who composed the most extensive work about the greatness of the Prophet, Qadi ʿIyad. He was a stern Malikite theologian, noted enemy of the Sufis, and much-feared judge in Ceuta and Granada. His *Kitāb ash-shifāʾ fī taʿrīf ḥuqūq al-Muṣṭafā,* however, has been widely used by nonmystics and mystics alike. In fact, it is perhaps the most frequently used and commented-upon handbook in which the Prophet's life, his qualities, and his miracles are described in every detail. The *Shifāʾ* was so admired in medieval Islam that it soon acquired a sanctity of its own and was even used as a talisman, protecting the house of its owner. . . . For surely a book that is exclusively devoted to the admiring description of the

noble Prophet partakes of the Prophet's *baraka*. Its very name, *shifāʾ*, "cure, healing," points to its healing power.[67]

The argument I will try to present is that parts 4–8 of the Burdah, which take as their subject matter elements from the biography of the Prophet, are not merely versified versions of the prose narratives from which their subject matter derives. Nor do they, or the Burdah as a whole, constitute merely, as commonly described, a versified encapsulation of Muslim beliefs of the medieval period. Rather, the specific topics that have been carefully selected from a vast body of prose materials concerning the life of the Prophet are those that can be poetically recast to serve what we described above as the polemical purposes of the *qaṣīdat al-madḥ,* that is, to establish that Islam is the true religion and that the *mamdūḥ* is the legitimate and divinely appointed leader. Curiously, in the case of *madīḥ nabawī,* these two propositions boil down to one: the veracity of Muḥammad's prophethood, that is, the authenticity of Muḥammad's mission. Given that al-Būṣīrī's age was one in which the popular religious imagination was dominated by *karamāt,* the blessings or miracles conferred on saints and holy men (of which the many miraculous cures and benefits procured through al-Būṣīrī's Burdah were to play a major role), it is not surprising that the elements he chooses are precisely the miracles (s. *āyah, muʿjizah*) associated with the Prophet—i.e., elements quite close in content and intent to the *dalāʾil* and *shamāʾil* works (see Schimmel quote, above). That is, those supernatural events that confirm his divine appointment as God's Messenger and Prophet, "evidentiary miracles" in Schimmel's term, form the subject matter of Parts 4: His Birth; 5: His Miracles; 6: The Noble Qurʾān: and 7: The Night Journey and Ascension. In Part 8: The Messenger's Jihād and Campaigns, however, the logic is turned around to follow that of the traditional Arabic victory panegyric: the Prophet's and early Muslims' worldly success on the field of battle serves as an objective validation to their claim to divine appointment and support and, as we shall see, seems to be a back-formation from High ʿAbbāsid military-political panegyric.

Before examining the individual sections, it is important to observe as well that al-Būṣīrī does not present episodes from the Prophet's Sīrah in narrative form, nor do the sections, taken together, constitute a condensed biography of the Prophet. Whether we turn to Ibn Hishām's

Al-Sīrah al-Nabawiyyah, the canonical Ḥadīth collections, or more immediate (and more polemical) sources on the life and status of the Prophet Muḥammad, such as al-Qāḍī ʿIyāḍ's *Al-Shifāʾ*, we find that in their prosaic, and often narrative, form individual motifs are subordinated to a literary form intended to establish the historicity of events. In the first two, *Al-Sīrah* and the Ḥadīth collections, this is done principally through citing authoritative sources, chains of transmitters (s. *sanad*), of the orally preserved statements (s. *matn*) of the probative witnesses to the events. In *Al-Shifāʾ* it appears that materials deriving from the first two sources, as well as others, are already widely accepted, for the author does not provide citations (although its commentators and editors diligently trace al-Qāḍī ʿIyāḍ's materials to authoritative sources). His purpose rather seems to be to organize these accepted materials into a systematic and somewhat polemical presentation of Islamic beliefs and practices concerning Muḥammad's life and his status as Prophet and Messenger. Both the sense of historicity and the narrative cohesion are achieved through the prosaic presentation of motifs/events that emphasizes their status as factual occurrences, rather than developing the symbolic and metaphorical aspects of meaning. Needless to say, the *dalāʾil al-nubuwwah* type of compilation (including, generally speaking, al-Qāḍī ʿIyāḍ's *Al-Shifāʾ*) focuses and organizes the materials toward a polemical end, a process that al-Būṣīrī takes a couple of steps further.

Extracted from their original "historical" and often narrative environment and recast paratactically in *badīʿ* poetic form, these motifs are now subordinated not to the dictates of prosaic historicity or one-dimensional logical narrative cohesion but to the poet's focused mythopoetic logic. The rhetorical structures in which they are recast create or elicit multiple dimensions of meaning—symbolic, metaphoric, metonymic, semantic—and weave these motifs in a new poetic-polemic, and eminently non-narrative, texture. In brief, whereas the Sīrah-related prose materials are structured so as to convey the motifs or events as, above all, historical, factual occurrences, al-Būṣīrī's poetic recasting of these motifs or events (which, no doubt, takes their historical occurrence for granted) forges or foregrounds their metaphysical or metahistorical, that is, mythic and cosmic, dimensions and connections.

It is my contention that through the fusion of Sīrah-related motifs and themes with the *badīʿ* style al-Būṣīrī isolates them from their original prosaic narrative context and encodes them in a metalanguage that reveals their place in the grander cosmic plan of Islamic Manifest Destiny. Further, inasmuch as the *badīᶜ* style in and of itself had come to express the divine providence and political legitimacy that guaranteed the Islamic dominion and hegemony of the High ᶜAbbāsid Age, the presentation of the miracles of the Prophet's age in the metalanguage of *badīᶜ* constitutes a declaration of the manifest destiny of the Prophet's Ummah (community). Above all, it confers on the signs and proofs of Muḥammad's prophethood the robust self-assurance and unwavering certainty that characterized the age of unquestioned Arab-Islamic hegemony and that were expressed in its distinctive poetic metalanguage of *badīᶜ*. Finally, inasmuch as virtually all the motifs or events concerning the Prophet Muḥammad in parts 4–7 of al-Būṣīrī's Burdah can be located in al-Qāḍī ᶜIyāḍ's *Al-Shifāʾ* (which is undoubtedly a definitive compendium of beliefs current in al-Būṣīrī's time), we will take it as our main point of reference for the prose antecedents of these sections.[68]

Let us keep in mind, too, that the poeticization and polemicization of the Sīrah-related prose materials does not consist merely in imposing rhyme and meter and recasting them in the rhetorical formulations of the *badīᶜ* style to create and/or elicit additional semantic dimensions; it also involves subordinating them to the overall structure and purpose of the *madīḥ nabawī* as supplicatory ode. As extensions of the *madīḥ*-section, their purpose is to establish the *mamdūḥ*'s legitimacy and authority, that is, the veracity of Muḥammad's prophethood. The extension of Muḥammad's authority from the worldly and historical to the otherworldly and cosmic—which is achieved through *badīᶜ*—is necessary in order for him to be able to confer the otherworldly prize or reward that the poet requests—his intercession (*shafāᶜah*) on the Day of Judgment. Thus, through *badīᶜ* the poet establishes his own mastery in creating a novel and dazzling gift of praise, and, at the same time, the Prophet's ability and authority to confer the countergift—*shafāᶜah.* With these matters in mind let us turn to the individual sections.

PART 4: THE BIRTH OF THE PROPHET (VV. 59–71)

59. His birth revealed the purity [*ṭīb*] of his lineage:
How noble [*ṭīb*] its beginning [Ādam]; how noble its end [Muḥammad].

60. It was a day on which the *Persians perceived* [*tafarrasa . . . al-Fursu*]
That affliction and chastisement would befall them.

61. That night the Arch of Chosroes broke in two
Like the breaking up of Chosroes' armies.

62. The fire of their temples, out of grief for him, expired;
Out of sorrow for him, the river was distracted from its course.

63. It saddened Sāwah that her lake dried up
And those that came to drink thirsty, left angry.

64. As if grief had made the fire wet as water
And made the water blaze like fire.

65. The jinn shrieked in terror; the lights shone abroad;
The truth of signs and predictions was made manifest.

66. Blind and deaf, the Meccan polytheists could not hear the glad tidings,
Nor could they see the warning of the lightning-flash.

67. After the soothsayer informed the Meccans
That their crooked religion could no longer stand straight,

68. And after they had witnessed falling stars on the horizon
Crashing down, even as, on earth, idols came crashing down,

69. Until the defeated devils, one after another, were driven
From the celestial highway of revelation,

70. As if, as they fled, they were the warriors of Abrahah
Or an army pelted with pebbles from Muḥammad's two palms,

71. Pebbles flung, after praising God in the hollow of his hands,
Just as Jonah, praising God, was flung from belly of the whale.

[46]

This part evokes the miraculous events that took place at the birth of the Prophet in ways that are extremely condensed and poeticized so as to support the poet's aim of demonstrating their place in a grander teleological myth of Islamic destiny, which is projected both backward and forward in time.

As noted previously, the traditional section headings of al-Būṣīrī's Burdah often distract us from the connections and continuities of the text. Although the poem clearly strikes out in a new thematic direction with verse 59, it is rhetorically tied to the final verse 58 of the preceding, explicitly *madḥ* (praise) section:

58. No fragrance [*ṭīb*] is as redolent as the dust that holds his bones,
Blessings [*ṭūbá*] fall upon whoever inhales or kisses it.

The two verses are connected by antithesis, inasmuch as verse 58 deals with the Prophet's death—his incorruptible bones in his grave—whereas verse 59 deals with his birth. Furthermore the *jinās* (root-play) on the root *ṭ-y-b,* which conveys sweet and pure fragrance, both literally and figuratively, connects the two verses in both sound and sense. Verse 59 is more multivalent in its meanings than the translation suggests. The Prophet's pure origin (*ṭībi ʿunṣurihi*) can be taken to mean his noble ancestry, and the beginning and end to be, as al-Bājūrī maintains, Ādam and Muḥammad himself, or perhaps more precisely the Prophet's father ʿAbd Allāh (al-Bājūrī and al-Ghazzī offer other interpretations as well, v. 59). Or in keeping with the tradition that the Prophet's body was completely clean when he was born, to refer to his own purity, bodily and spiritual, at birth and at death (see al-Ghazzī, v. 59). The latter reading again links up semantically with the belief alluded to in verse 58, that the Prophet's pure corpse lay incorruptible in the grave.

After this transitional verse, al-Būṣīrī has chosen from the miraculous occurrences associated with the birth of the Prophet those events that have a political-historical, as well as cosmic and supernatural, dimension and can therefore be incorporated into the larger sweep of teleological history (vv. 60–64).[69] The fall of the Sasanian Persian Empire to the Muslims is rendered inevitable by projecting it back in history through a fanciful etymology of the name Furs, Persians. Although normally the Arabs derive Furs from *fāris* (knight or horseman; see al-Bājūrī, v. 60), through the *jinās* (root-play) of *tafarrasa . . . al-Fursu* (the Persians perceived) the verbal identity suggests that this historical outcome was "built in" to the very name and identity of the Persians, that they were predestined through the principle of *nomen est omen* to be defeated by Islam. This technique of Arabic etymologizing of foreign names to express their destiny had already been perfected by Abū Tammām.[70] Similarly in verse 61 the cracking of the Arch of Chosroes (Īwān Kisrá) at the birth of the Prophet is taken to be both portent and metonymy of the fall of the Persian Empire. In Arabic this is etymologically suggested by the repetition of the name Kisrá, whose root *k-s-r* in Arabic means "to break." This subliminal sense of the name Kisrá is brought to the surface by the rhetorical interplay of synonyms and antitheses of "split" (*munṣadiʿ*), "unity" (*shaml*), "not united" (*ghayra multaʾimi*); in brief, the great "breaker" and his empire are "broken."

Other unnatural occurrences are cited as portents in verses 62–64: the extinguishing of the fire of the Zoroastrian temple, which, it is said, had not gone out for a thousand years, and the drying up of the lake of the Persian city of Sāwah. The fire and the city are personified to express the grief and anguish of the Persians. In verse 64 the conceit of producing a fanciful cause, termed by the Arab rhetoricians *ḥusn al-taʿlīl*, is employed to attribute to the fire and water such grief that their intrinsic nature is reversed. Just as Abū Tammām described the flames and dust as overturning the natural cycle of night and day to convey the cosmic significance of the defeat of Amorium (see above), so, too, al-Būṣīrī conveys the cosmic dimension of the birth of the Prophet through the denaturing of two of the most basic natural elements: it is as if fire has become wet and water has burned like fire.

Verse 65 continues the projection of the significance of the birth of the Prophet into various cosmic and temporal dimensions. A large amount of traditional prose material is condensed into a single line: supernatural beings, like the Jinn, shrieked or cried in recognition of the Prophet's birth (al-Ghazzī, v. 65), and, as related in Ibn Hishām's *Al-Sīrah* and in al-Qāḍī ʿIyāḍ's *Al-Shifāʾ*, upon his birth a light emanated from his body that illumined the horizon so those present could see all the way to the palaces of Shām (Syria); finally, in the second hemistich, the truth of predictions of the coming of the Prophet contained in the Holy Books, the Tawrāh and the Injīl (the Torah and the Gospel), and by Jewish rabbis, Christian monks, and pagan soothsayers, has now been made manifest.[71] Once again the effect is to ground the portentous events in a teleologically conceived sense of history.

The last half of this section, verses 66–71, features an extraordinarily dense concatenation of what are, on the surface, unrelated events from the Islamic tradition or history. There is also a chronological collapsing of events: for example, the Meccan polytheists' (*kuffār*) rejection of Muḥammad's message did not, historically speaking, occur until he proclaimed it as an adult. Verse 66 does not actually name the *kuffār* (Meccans) but rather identifies them through its allusion to the Qurʾānic description of moral or spiritual deafness and blindness (*ṣummun bukmun ʿumyun*, deaf, dumb, blind [QK 2:18, 2:171]) of those who reject the faith, which is traditionally understood to refer, in the first place, to the recalcitrant Meccans. In verse 66 the antithesis between *muʿwajj* (crooked) and *(lam) yaqumi* ([not] stand) alludes to the epithet of Islam as the "straight" or "upright" religion, *mustaqīm*.

Verses 68 and 69 begin a process of combining two apparently unrelated images so as to elicit their shared significance: verse 68 describes the *kuffār* after they have seen on the horizon the meteors that God sent to drive out of the heavens the devils (*shayāṭīn*) who were eavesdropping on the angels on the night of Muḥammad's birth.[72] The crashing down of meteors to drive out the devils is then compared to the crashing of idols to the ground that occurred (or was portended) upon the birth of the Prophet.[73] The poet thus reveals through the play on "crashing down" (*munqaḍḍah*), applied both to the meteors and the idols, the analogous defeats of devils and idol worshippers.

This concatenation of images reaches its climax in verses 69–71: once more the poet's purpose is to discover and reveal the single divine purpose that lies behind apparently disparate events, and once more he achieves this through rhetorical means. Verse 69 describes the devils fleeing the hail of meteors, as we know from verses 67 and 68. The flight of the devils is then subject to two comparisons (v. 70). *First,* the devils' flight is described as the fleeing of the armies of Abrahah, the South Arabian Christian king of Yemen. According to Islamic sources, Abrahah led an assault against the Kaʿbah in the Year of the Elephant (the year of Muḥammad's birth, ca. 570 CE, so named for the battle-elephant in Abrahah's army) but was repelled when first the elephant refused to attack Mecca and then God sent a flock of birds that pelted the army with pebbles that proved lethal to everyone they struck. *Second,* the flight of devils is compared to the fleeing of Meccan polytheists at the battle of Badr and/or of Ḥunayn, when Muḥammad threw a handful of pebbles at them (see al-Ghazzī, al-Bājūrī, v. 70). This event is associated with the Qurʾānic exhortation concerning the Battle of Badr, "You did not kill them, but God killed them; you did not throw when you threw, but God threw" (*fa-lam taqtulūhum wa-lākinna Allāha qatalahum* <u>*wa-mā ramayta ʾidh ramayta wa-lākinna Allāha ramá . . .*</u> [QK 8:17]), where commentarists take *ramá* (throw, shoot) to refer to Muḥammad's throwing a handful of pebbles. This is by no means a simple simile to adorn a text; rather the poet performs a masterful rhetorical feat whereby, through the comparison of one miraculous event to two others, he reveals the shared religious significance of all three. In this way three apparently unrelated religio-historical events are revealed or interpreted to be cognate events that simultaneously convey the same message, that of falsehood defeated by truth. Al-Būṣīrī does not stop there.

The pebbles then constitute the link to verse 71, for they had miraculously cried out God's praises (*musabbiḥ*) while in the hollow of Prophet's hands.[74] The image, or concept, of piety (*tasbīḥ*, praising God) from within a hollow before being flung out sparks (for the poet, at least) another analogous image: that of Yūnus (Jonah) singing out God's praises from the belly of the whale before he was cast forth. This is an altogether unexpected connection. To modern sensibilities it is probably what the classical critics termed "far-fetched" (*mustabʿad*); to a more traditional sensibility, it is *badīʿ*. What is essential here is that through this convoluted rhetorical play, al-Būṣīrī has established a "mythic concordance" between God's saving Jonah from the belly of the whale and His saving Muḥammad and his vastly outnumbered army of Muslims at the Battle of Badr.[75] Again, for the poet, and for the believer, the analogical or metaphorical connection between these events—i.e., the shared message that praise of God leads to salvation—trumps their "historical" discreteness.

This chaining of images operates in an associative manner in which a particular word or phrase strikes the poetic imagination and creates an altogether unexpected (and on the surface "illogical") link to a new image, which, amazingly, turns out to be an entirely "logical" metaphor of the first. What is important in the context of our argument is that this novel concatenation has the effect of eliciting or establishing *through a complex rhetorical strategy* semantic connections between what previously had seemed to be disparate images or events. However "disconnected" they may seem on the surface, in a prosaic or historical sense, the poet's masterful rhetorical skills elicit from them—or impose upon them—a single essential message: the triumph of truth over falsehood, or, as expressed in Islamic terms, that the denial of Muḥammad's prophethood leads to defeat and damnation and, conversely, acceptance of his mission and praise of Allāh lead to victory and salvation. What is noteworthy here is that events taken to have occurred before Muḥammad's proclaiming his prophethood (Jonah and the Whale, Abrahah and the Year of the Elephant) have, through this rhetorical process of "mythic concordance," been subsumed into the Islamic message.

PART 5: THE MIRACLES OF THE PROPHET (VV. 72–87)

72. The trees answered his beck and call, bowing before him,
Walking to him on a leg without a foot,

73. As if they drew a ruled line down the middle of the road
On which their branches wrote in a novel [*badīʿ*] script,

74. Like the cloud that followed him wherever he went,
Protecting him when the midday heat blazed like a furnace.

75. I swear by the moon that he split in two an oath truly sworn
That the moon is akin to his heart.

76. And by the virtue and nobility that the cave contained
When every unbeliever's eye was blind to it,

77. So the Truth [*al-ṣidq*; Muḥammad] and the Truthful One [*al-ṣiddīq*;
Abū Bakr] stayed stock-still in the cave,
While the unbelievers said, "There is no one in there,"

78. For they thought that doves and spiders would not
Weave and hover over the Best of All Creation—

79. But he whom God protects has no need
For double-knit chain-mail nor lofty strongholds—

80. That never did I suffer injustice and seek his protection
But that he extended his protection over me and I met no harm,

81. Nor did I ever beseech from his hand the riches of the two abodes
But that the best of bounties was bestowed on me.

82. So, do not deny the divine inspiration of his dream visions,
For he has a heart that, though his eyes are sleeping, never sleeps.[76]

83. The visions came when he had reached the age of prophethood,
And dream-visions of grown men are not to be denied.

84. God be blessed! Divine inspiration cannot be earned through effort;
What a prophet says of the unseen cannot be doubted.

85. How many an invalid was cured by the touch of his hand?
How many a madman was released from his affliction?

86. His prayer revived the blanched drought-stricken year
Till it shone like a blaze on the forehead of the black ages

87. With a rain-cloud that poured down so hard you'd think
The lowlands aflow with the ocean's stream or ʿArim's torrent-flood.[77]

[47]

In this part of the poem al-Būṣīrī turns from the miraculous events that occurred at the time of the Prophet's birth to signs or miracles that the Prophet himself performed.[78] In this respect the concluding simile of part 4, verses 70 and 71, which compares the devils' fleeing the meteor shower at Muḥammad's birth to the miracle of the pebbles in his hand at the Battle of Badr, serves as a transition. The heading and surface topics of part 5 should not lead us to assume that this is a mere register of prophetic miracles; rather, as we shall see, its central "event" is the oath, a speech act whose performance dominates the central portion (vv. 75–81).

Part 5 opens (vv. 72–75) by recounting in short order several well-known miracles of the Prophet: the trees that obeyed his command and came to him bowing down before him; the clouds that followed over his head to shade him; his splitting the moon in two.[79] The first and last of these are presented in the traditional sources as challenges: a Bedouin asked Muḥammad for a sign, whereupon he said to him, "Tell that tree that the Messenger of God is calling it." Whereupon the tree leaned right and left, backward and forward, until it uprooted itself. Then it dragged its roots until it stood before Muḥammad and greeted him saying, "Peace upon you, Messenger of God," and then returned and re-rooted itself in the earth.[80] Muḥammad's splitting of the moon, associated with Sūrat al-Qamar (*iqtarabati al-sāʿatu wa-inshaqqa al-qamaru*, The hour approached and the moon was split [QK 51:1]), is also said to be in response to the people of Mecca demanding from Muḥammad a sign of his prophethood. That is, these verses play a role in the overarching performative purpose of the poem: to establish the truth of and faith in the prophethood of Muḥammad.

What is important in al-Būṣīrī's poem is that the condensation of three miracles into three verses provides a panorama of the natural world, the entire cosmos—plants, clouds, heavenly bodies—submitting to the Prophet, breaking the "rules of nature" to become signs of his divine mission, that is of the cosmic power behind him. Further, as we saw in part 4 of the Burdah (above), the poet elicits, through rhetorical means, further semantic or symbolic connections. Thus through the simile of verse 73, the "novel" (*badīʿ*) script of the dragging branches of the tree suggests an affinity between the tree's act of submission and recognition and that of the poet—his *madīḥ nabawī*. So, too, as al-Ghazzī (v. 75) points out, the splitting of the moon (*shaqq al-qamar*) is likened to the angels' splitting open and cleansing of Muḥammad's breast (*shaqq al-ṣadr*), an event placed variously in Muḥammad's childhood or else just prior to his Ascension.[81] Once again, through rhetorical means, namely the alliteration on the letter *qāf* compounded with the *radd al-ʿajuz ʿalá al-ṣadr* (*ʾaqsamtu bi-al-qamari al-mushtaqqi ʾanna lahu//min qalbihi nisbatan mabrūrata al-qasami*), the poet insinuates the semantic links between the key elements: *qasam* (oath), *qamar* (moon), *qalb* (heart), and splitting (*shaqq*), with the result that the discrete miracles of the splitting of Muḥammad's breast and the splitting of the moon reveal their shared message—the truth of his prophethood—and thereby confirm the veracity of the poet's oath.

In addition, through the oath upon a heavenly body like the moon, al-Būṣīrī alludes to the Qurʾānic usage of the early Meccan Sūrahs, of opening with oaths: "By the sun and its light and by the moon . . ." (*wa-al-shamsi wa-ḍuḥāhā wa-al-qamari . . .* [QK 151:1–2]); "By the night . . ." (*wa-al-layli . . .* [QK 152:1]); "By the morning light . . ." (*wa-al-ḍuḥā . . .* [QK 153:1]), thereby evoking the ultimate veracity of the sacred text.[82]

The one-line oath of verse 75 sets the stage for the extended oath of verses 76–81. Of note in verse 77 is the poet's use of *jinās* not merely to denote Muḥammad and Abū Bakr as the two who hid in a cave during the Hijrah as God camouflaged them from the pursuing Meccan polytheists with spider webs and circling doves, but, in a manner consonant with our argument concerning the use of *badīʿ*, to elicit new dimensions of meaning, to evoke through etymology (*ishtiqāq*) the relationship between the two. So, if Muḥammad is the Truth (*al-ṣidq*—or, as al-Bājūrī, v. 77, insists, an elision of [*dhū*] *al-ṣidq*, possessor of Truth), then Abū Bakr "al-Ṣiddīq," one of the first to accept Islam, is, as his traditional epithet indicates, "trustworthy, sincere, loyal" (intensive form of *ṣādiq*) to Muḥammad, but also "the believer," or the one who gives credence (*muṣaddiq*) to Muḥammad's prophetic mission and message.[83] In other words, the poet uses rhetorical means, *jinās* on the root *ṣ-d-q* (truth, veracity) to reveal through etymological means the natures of Muḥammad and Abū Bakr and of the intimate bond between the two men.

The miracles of the splitting of the moon and of God's hiding Muḥammad and Abū Bakr in a cave from the pursuing Meccans are thus not prosaically or narratively recounted; rather they are rhetorically subordinated to the structure of the oath (*qasam*). This is particularly interesting because the logic of the oath structure, in Arabic as elsewhere, is that the first element, the oath (*qasam*) consists of invoking something absolute and unchallenged to both swearer and witness; whereas the second element, the sworn statement (*jawāb al-qasam*) is the proposition that the swearer is trying to confirm through the oath. In accord with this grammatical logic, the veracity of the first elements, Muḥammad's splitting the moon in two, God's camouflaging Muḥammad and Abū Bakr with spider webs and circling doves (vv. 76–77),[84] the signs or miracles, is unquestioned. The proposition the poet wants to confirm is that of verses 80–81: the poet's, that is, the individual believer's, own experience of presenting himself as a supplicant to the Prophet and of invariably being granted the protection or sustenance (in this world or the next) that he requested. The effect of these verses is very powerful because it bridges the gap between miracles that occurred in the lifetime of the Prophet—which could otherwise be merely a historical matter—and the poet's own lived religious experience. Above all, within the overarching purpose of al-Būṣīrī's poem, these verses affirm the Prophet's continued ability to bestow gifts, that is, the continued efficacy of the ritual exchange of praise (poem) today for intercession on Judgment Day that subtends the supplicatory structure of *madīḥ nabawī.*

The poet's lived experience, as testified to in his "sworn statement" of verses 75–81, of the Prophet's protection and bounty then provides the basis for his admonition of verses 82–83: "Do not deny the divine inspiration of his dream visions . . . ," that is, the revelations of the Qurʾān that came to Muḥammad as he slept. After declaring that prophecy is God-given and incontestable, the poet evokes the Prophet's miraculous cures of the sick and insane (vv. 84–85).[85] The section closes with a metaphorical variant of the miracle of bringing the dead back to life: the Prophet's prayers have brought rain to revive the drought-stricken land.[86] The allegory of verse 86, as al-Ghazzī (v. 86) explains, likens the "white" year of drought after the Prophet's prayer has brought rain to produce the "blackest" (that is, darkest green) most fertile years, to the white blaze on the face of a dark horse.

Verse 87 operates metaphorically to extend the idea of "revival" from plant life to bounty, generosity, and salvation. The verb *jāda* and its VN *jawd,* originally denoting abundant rain, have long since come, along with other terms in this verse, such as *baḥr* (sea) and *sayl* (torrent flood), to connote munificence and generosity. Further, in using the word *al-ʿArim* (whether taken as a common noun denoting a dam of some sort or as a proper noun, the name of a riverbed in Sabaʾ) al-Būṣīrī echoes the Qurʾānic destruction of Sabaʾ through the breaking of the Dam of Maʾrib: *fa-ʾaʿraḍū fa-ʾarsalnā ʿalayhim sayla al-ʿArimi* (Then they turned away [from Us/God], so we sent against them the torrent of al-ʿArim [QK 34:16]; al-Ghazzī, al-Bājūrī, v. 87). This allusion to the divine retribution against those who turn away from belief serves to express the threat of damnation that is the converse of the promise of salvation. Those who believe in Muḥammad's miracles and accept him as God's Messenger are saved; those who do not are damned. Through its allusion to the destruction of Sabaʾ, God's past destruction of nations who turned away from Him, verse 81 reinforces the theme of Islamic Manifest Destiny, which is essentially the projection of this past pattern into the future.

PART 6: THE NOBLE QURʾĀN (VV. 88–104)

88. Let me then describe those of Muḥammad's signs (*āyāt*) that appeared
As clear as the night-fire kindled on a mountain height for night-farers to see,

89. For pearls increase in beauty when they're strung,
Though their value does not diminish if they're loose.

90. But how could my hopes aspire to a poem of praise
That could ever express the nobility of his character and traits?

91. For the Qurʾān's verses are signs of a truth from the Most Merciful,
At once created in time and timeless, they are an attribute of the Eternal.

92. They exist beyond the bounds of time, yet they inform us
Of the Resurrection, of ʿĀd, and of the many-columned Iram.

93. They are everlasting before us and thus they surpass
All miracles of other prophets, which occurred but did not last.

94. So imbued with wisdom, so masterfully wrought, that they leave no uncertainties
For those who would sow discord, and they require no arbiter.

95. They have never been attacked but that the most hostile of enemies
Have been utterly defeated and surrendered to them.

96. Their eloquence repelled the claim of all who challenged them,
As a jealous husband repels the hand that would defile his wives.

97. Their meanings are vaster than the ocean's waves
And exceed its gems in beauty and in worth.

98. Their marvels are innumerable, incalculable,
But despite their number they are never tedious to recount.

99. They cool the eye of him who recites them, so I said to him:
"You have seized the rope of Allāh, so hold on tight!"

100. If you recite them out of fear of Hellfire,
You will extinguish the infernal flames with their cool water.

101. They are like the Basin of pure water from which
The soot-stained faces of the sinful emerge pure white,

102. Like the Straight Path Bridge and the Scales of Judgment Day in justice,
For justice based on other sources cannot stand.

103. Don't be surprised if someone, out of envy, denies these signs,
Feigning ignorance, despite acumen and discernment,

104. For the eye, when inflamed, can't see the sunlight;
The mouth, when diseased, cannot taste water.

[48]

As the previous part, as well as sources such as al-Qāḍī ʿIyāḍ's *Al-Shifāʾ*, demonstrates, a variety of traditional miracles (*muʿjizāt*) were attributed to Muḥammad and taken to be proof of his prophethood. Nevertheless, in Islamic belief, the essential and incontrovertible sign of Muḥammad's divine mission and proof of his prophethood is the Qurʾān itself. Muslims believe that the Qurʾān is God's word presented to Muḥammad by the angel Jibrīl (Gabriel) and, furthermore, that the Qurʾān is in and of itself, in its rhetorical beauty, inimitability, and other marvelous features, eminently miraculous. The beliefs and disputes concerning the nature of the miraculous inimitability of the Qurʾān are gathered in the Islamic tradition under the rubric of Iʿjāz al-Qurʾān, a field whose major accepted tenets form the basis for part 6.[87]

Iʿjāz means, essentially, to confound an opponent, to render him powerless; hence *muʿjizah,* a miracle, i.e., a feat that utterly confounds one's opponent. We must therefore keep in mind in reading part 6 that the concept of the miraculous inimitability of the Qurʾān was understood and developed above all in terms of the unmatchable beauty and effectiveness of its rhetoric (*balāghah*); it is, in von Grunebaum's concise term, "rhetorically unsurpassable."[88] A corollary of the tenet of the inimitability of the Qurʾān is that to attempt to challenge, imitate, or match the Qurʾān in linguistic beauty is tantamount to challenging Muḥammad's prophethood and claiming it for oneself. Thus for the poet to try to compose the most beautiful possible description of the Prophet's literary miracle is a particularly complex and complexed poetic challenge. For if Islam claims that the Qurʾān's unsurpassable rhetorical beauty and eloquence are in themselves incontrovertible proof of Muḥammad's prophethood, then the poet who tries through his own powers of rhetoric and eloquence to convince the reader of the Qurʾān's miraculous rhetorical beauty, is, *ipso facto,* competing with or undermining the Qurʾān's own claims, or at least usurping a Qurʾānic function or prerogative. It is only by a careful process of subordination of his own claims and goals to the miraculousness of the Qurʾān that the poet can effectively meet this challenge. Finally, we must understand, in the context of the overarching polemic of parts 4–8 of the Burdah, that to prove the superiority of the Qurʾān to the miracles of other prophets not only confirms Muḥammad's prophethood, but also establishes the superiority of Islam and its community over all other religions and communities.

The transition from the section on general miracles to the miracle of the Qurʾān in particular is gracefully achieved through the pivot-word *āyāt,* which in its general meaning refers to the "signs" or "miracles" of part 5, while at the same time, in its particular meaning of "Qurʾānic verses," introduces the specific topic of the coming section, the miracle(s) of the Qurʾān.

Verse 88 opens part 6 with a variant of the traditional poetic challenge in the imperative, "describe!" (*ṣif*), now phrased as a self-imposed challenge, "Let me describe" (*daʿnī wa-waṣfī*). Al-Bājūrī (v. 88) takes this to be addressed to those who would deny the prophethood of Muḥammad (v. 82) and in this respect we can understand that the presentation of Muḥammad's miracles is intended to play a role in the poem's political-religious polemic. Declaring these signs/Qurʾānic verses to be "as clear as day," al-Būṣīrī compares them to the conventional image of Arab generosity: the fire kindled on a hilltop for night-travelers to see and be given food and shelter, which here appears to be a metaphor for Islam's evident truth and clear offer of salvation. Verses 89–90 deal further with the issue of the poetic challenge of describing the Prophet's miracles, above all the Qurʾān.

He declares in verse 89 that, like precious pearls when strung, the Prophet's miracles may appear more beautiful when expressed in poetry, but their essential value is not diminished if they are unstrung, that is, in prose. Through the *badīʿ*-style paired antitheses of "increase" and "decrease" and "strung" (in verse) and "unstrung" (in prose), the verse rhetorically exemplifies the very concept it seeks to express. In verse 90 he engages the convention of the poet's modesty present in the idea that the nature of the Qurʾān is beyond what he or any poet can express, thereby in effect invoking once more the principle of Iʿjāz al-Qurʾān. In other words, the inimitable language of the Qurʾān is what proves the prophethood of Muḥammad, not the language of mortal poets.

In verses 91–93 the poet exploits the expressive capacities of *al-madhhab al-kalāmī,* here in the rhetorical sense of the *badīʿ* figure that employs "mental gymnastics" typical of the Mutakallimūn (speculative theologians) to express complex concepts. Through the antithesis of *muḥdathah* (newly created, recent) and *qadīmah* (ancient, eternal), verse 91 expresses the idea that the Qurʾān is sempiternal, co-eternal with God, of whom it is an attribute, while at the same time having been revealed to mankind within chronological, historical time. Al-Bājūrī (v. 91) discusses this in terms of the rhetorical device of "joining of two opposites," normally a logical impossibility. For the purposes of the present argument we can say that the poet performs the rhetorical "miracle" of joining two opposites, in the course of attempting to convey the miraculousness of the Qurʾān. The second hemistich of the verse displays double *jinās* in elegant chiastic (*abba*) form: *//qadīmatun ṣifatu al-mawṣūfi bi-al-qidami.* Similarly, verse 92 expresses the idea that, as eternal, the Qurʾān exists beyond the bounds of time, and yet informs us both of past events, such as the destruction of the ancient peoples—for example, ʿĀd with its many-columned city of Iram—and future events such as the Resurrection.

Verse 93 employs another rhetorical device, what in *ʿilm al-badīʿ* is termed *radd al-ʿajuz ʿalá al-ṣadr* (repeating an earlier word at the end of a verse) and in English terms is something of an alliterative chiasmus (*abba* pattern) to express a tenet of Iʿjāz al-Qurʾān that is central to the polemic of his poem: *dāmat ladaynā . . . lam tadumi* (the miracles/verses of the Qurʾān are everlasting . . . the miracles of other prophets did not last). The superiority of Muḥammad's miracle, the Qurʾān, over those of the other prophets constitutes, of course, the superiority of Islam over other religions—in particular Judaism and Christianity. The idea is that miracles, such as Moses' turning a rod into a snake to defeat Pharaoh's magicians or Jesus' raising the dead, occurred, historically, and confirmed the prophethood of Moses and Jesus, but are now done and gone. The Qur'ān, by contrast, is an eternal miracle, permanently operative and efficacious. The point seems to be that Moses and Jesus, for example, are both recognized by Muslims as prophets and messengers of God who performed miracles and brought divine scriptures, the Torah and the Gospel. However, they, their miracles, scriptures, and religions are things of the past that have been replaced or abrogated by the Seal of the Prophets, Muḥammad, with his permanent, eternal miracle, the Qurʾān, and the ultimate true religion, Islam.

Returning to verse 89, we can understand that in recasting in *badīʿ* poetry these well-established tenets of Iʿjāz al-Qurʾān, the poet is not claiming to increase their value (thereby to compete with the Qurʾān), but to make them more beautiful in such a way as to be more convincing to those who would deny them (v. 82)—exactly what is conveyed in the Arabic term for rhetoric, *balāghah*. In verses 94–98 the poet continues the poeticization of Iʿjāz tenets to strengthen his polemic against deniers and infidels.

Verse 94 is particularly compelling and subtle in its rhetorical expression of this idea and as an example of the complex tension and intertextuality involved in a poet describing the Prophet's literary miracle. First there is the *radd al-ʿajuz ʿalá al-ṣadr* and *jinās* of *muḥakkamāt* (imbued with wisdom, or masterfully wrought) and *ḥakam* (arbiter). Then there is a partial *jinās* between *yubqīna* (leave) and *yabghīna* (require). *Muḥakkamāt* itself is at once a pun and a Qurʾānic allusion: the most literal meaning, as a Form II (*ḥakkama*) passive participle, would be "imbued with wisdom," or "wisely made," which would allude to the self-referential epithet of the sacred text as *al-Qurʾān al-ḥakīm* (the Qurʾān full of wisdom [QK 36:2]; al-Ghazzī, v. 94). At the same time it alludes to another Qurʾānic self-referential description and the Form IV (*aḥkama*) meaning of the same root: *kitābun ʾuḥkimat ʾāyātuhu* (a book whose verses are well-wrought [QK 11:1]). In both senses al-Būṣīrī's verse 94 describes the wondrous rhetorical beauty of the Qurʾān that made unbelievers abandon all doubt and surrender to Islam (see further discussion in al-Ghazzī and al-Bājūrī, v. 94). Moreover the poet in his verse is clearly "imitating," indeed rhetorically intensifying, Qurʾānic meaning and diction through his use of *badīʿ* constructions: that is, he intends his own verse, in the Qurān's own self-referential manner, to likewise be "well wrought" and to dispel all doubt. What is crucial here, however, is that he is in no way trying to "compete" with the Qurʾān, as the term *muʿāraḍah* would suggest, rather, in what amounts to a form of submission, his own "well wrought" verses are composed solely for the purpose of expressing the miraculousness of the Qurʾān's "well wrought" verses. Verse 94 thus brilliantly encapsulates both the challenge and dilemma of the poet who directs his full poetic powers to *madīḥ nabawī.*

By contrast, verses 95–96 describe the defeat of those who would attempt to challenge the veracity or authenticity of the Qurʾān, but in the end surrender to it (v. 95). Of particular note in the context of the present argument is the poet's specifying that it is the rhetorical beauty or eloquence, the *balāghah,* of the Qurʾānic verses that repels the opponent or challenger (*muʿāriḍ*). Verses 97 and 98 seek to capture the inestimable beauty and marvels of the sacred text.

The salvific effects of the Qurʾān are the subject of verses 99–102. The spiritual comfort and salvation proffered by the Qurʾān are expressed in general terms in verse 99, with its allusion in "the rope of Allāh" to the Qurʾānic *al-ʿurwah al-wuthqá* (firm handle [QK 2:256]: Whoever denies Satan and believes in God has grasped a firm handle that will never break; and QK 31:22), as al-Bājūrī points out (v. 99) a metaphor for faith; here, more precisely, a metaphor for the Qurʾān as a means to salvation. The poet then specifies instances: the recitation of Qurʾānic verses will quench the flames of Hellfire like cool water (v. 100); they purify the believer of sins, like the Basin in which the Muslim souls will cleanse themselves of sins on Judgment Day (v. 101; al-Ghazzī, v. 101 [see chapter 3, Nahj al-Burdah, v. 48]); as a source for dispensing justice in this world, they are like the narrow Bridge over Hellfire over which only the saved will cross, and the Scales on which men's deeds will be weighed on Judgment Day (see al-Bājūrī, v. 102).

In closing this passage, al-Būṣīrī returns to the issue of the clarity of the Qurʾānic verses with which he opened part 6 (v. 88) and to the underlying polemic against unbelievers and infidels. As if in answer to the question, "If the Qurʾān's verses are so clear, why are there still disbelievers and infidels in the world?" he states, in essence, that such people are spiritually blind or sick: like the inflamed eye that cannot see the light of the sun, or the diseased mouth that cannot taste water (vv. 103–104; al-Bājūrī, v. 104).

In sum, we have argued in our discussion of part 6, with its heavily rhetoricized (*badīʿ*) poeticization of prose materials, such as al-Qāḍī ʿIyāḍ's *Al-Shifāʾ*, concerning Iʿjāz al-Qurʾān, that the poet is not merely "adorning" these tenets with literary embellishments. Rather their *poeticization,* particularly in what we would describe as *al-madhhab al-kalāmī* (the manner of Kalām, both as a device of logical complication within one verse and as a conceptual approach to poetry), aims at rendering them rhetorically compelling and effective, i.e., at achieving their *polemicization.* In other words, the *badīʿ* style constitutes the use of rhetoric in the sense of the "art of persuasion." The poet is not merely trying to express these tenets more beautifully; he is, moreover, trying to make the argument for the miraculousness of the Qurʾān, the prophethood of Muḥammad, and the ultimate truth of Islam more convincing. In a manner that compellingly underlines the message and purpose of *madīḥ nabawī,* al-Būṣīrī is placing his own poetic marvels (*badāʾiʿ*) at the service of Muḥammad's miracle, the Qurʾān.

PART 7: THE NIGHT JOURNEY AND ASCENSION (VV. 105–117)

105. O best of those whose courtyard the supplicants seek, hastening on foot
Or on the backs of she-camels whose heavy tread leaves traces
on the ground,

106. You who are the greatest sign to him who considers
And the greatest benefit to him who will seize it.

107. You traveled by night from one sacred precinct, Mecca, to the other,
Jerusalem,
Like the full moon traversing the pitch-dark sky.

108. Through the night you ascended until you reached a station two
bows' length from Allāh,
A station that no one else had ever attained or even dared desire.

109. To it the other Prophets and Messengers bade you precede them,
Like servants giving deference to him they serve,

110. As you, passing by them, pierced the seven levels of heaven,
In a procession of angels of which you were the standard-bearer,[89]

111. Until you left no goal that any rival could approach
Nor any height that a competitor could scale,

112. And you reduced every station to the possessive case,
Since you were called to high station, in the nominative of a tribal chief or proper noun.

113. So that you won a union with God entirely hidden
From the eyes of all creation, and a secret utterly concealed.

114. You gathered every uncommon virtue
And passed through each uncrowded rank.

115. Exalted beyond measure are the ranks assigned you;
Great beyond grasp the blessings bestowed on you.

116. Good tidings are ours, O community of Islam,
For we have a pillar of Providence that cannot be toppled:

117. When God called him who called us to obey
"The noblest of Messengers," we became the noblest of nations.

[49]

One of the Islamic beliefs that has most inspired the literary and pictorial imagination is Muḥammad's miraculous Night Journey and Ascension (*al-Isrāʾ wa-al-Miʿrāj*).[90] Although the details are subject to variation and debate (particularly as to whether the journey and ascension were physical or spiritual), the general consensus is as follows: Muḥammad was physically transported by night, borne on the magical winged mule-like creature Burāq, from Mecca to Jerusalem, where he met ʿĪsá (Jesus) and Mūsá (Moses) and led them in prayer; from there he experienced a bodily ascension on a splendid ladder (*miʿrāj*), accompanied by Jibrīl, through the seven levels of the heavens, where he encountered and surpassed the other prophets, until his arrival before the throne of Allāh, who confided secrets to him alone; he awoke the following morning back in Mecca. The origins of this narrative are traced to the Qurʾānic passages, QK 81:19–25 and 53:1–21, which describe visions in which a divine messenger appears to Muḥammad, but most explicitly in QK 17:1 (*subḥāna alladhī ʾasrá bi-ʿabdihi laylan mina al-masjidi al-ḥarāmi ʾilá al-masjidi al-ʾaqṣá . . .*, Praise be to Him who carried his servant by night from the Sacred Place of Prayer to the Furthest Place of Prayer). These have been elaborated upon in canonical sources such as Ibn Hishām's *Al-Sīrah*, Ḥadīth, and Qurʾānic commentaries, but also in many popular extracanonical forms, both written and oral, of Night Journey and Ascension narratives. It is, as both Jamal Eddine Bencheikh and Annemarie Schimmel note, an eminently initiatory journey.[91]

In the context of the present study, what is remarkable in al-Būṣīrī's poeticization of the Night Journey and Ascension is that he foregoes the many lyric and dramatic possibilities offered by the materials we find, for example, in Ibn Hishām's *Al-Sīrah al-Nabawiyyah* or in al-Qāḍī ʿIyāḍ's *Al-Shifāʾ*: the description of the magical beast Burāq; the etiological myth of Abū Bakr's being dubbed *al-Ṣiddīq* (in this context, "the believer," for giving credence to Muḥammad's remarkable account when others did not); the story of Moses helping Muḥammad to haggle the number of daily prayers required of Muslims from fifty down to five; Muḥammad's confounding the doubters with miraculous knowledge of caravans heading toward Mecca; or, especially in the overarching context of the Burdah as a supplicatory ode pleading for the Prophet's intercession on Judgment Day, we might have expected the poet to distinctly evoke the episode in which Allāh grants Muḥammad the right to intercede for his community.[92] Instead, al-Būṣīrī focuses his poetic treatment on one particular aspect; he limits his presentation to precisely those elements from the Night Journey and Ascension accounts that mark Muḥammad's entry or acceptance into the ranks of the Prophets and, above all, that signal Muḥammad's unique status as the Seal of the Prophets, i.e., the last and foremost of all of God's Prophets. In other words, as we shall see below, he selects those elements that support his polemic for the superiority of Islam over competing religions, above all, Judaism and Christianity. The initiatory nature of these events is evidenced particularly in the aspect of the competition or contest, the trial by which Muḥammad establishes his preeminence over all previous prophets, and his reward, that is, his unique proximity to and intimacy with Allāh, and the secret knowledge that is confided to him alone.

Part 7 opens with an evocation of the Burdah's overarching supplicatory theme, with a vocative addressing the Prophet as the best of benefactors (v. 105), before reverting to the subject of signs and miracles (v. 106), to introduce the Night Journey and Ascension (vv. 107–115). In Islamic belief, Muḥammad's bodily journey to Jerusalem, ascension to the heavens, and return to Mecca in the course of a single night is considered miraculous; indeed, the standard refutation of those who claim it was merely a spiritual journey or a vision is that in that case it would not have been a miracle.[93] However, in the Burdah, al-Būṣīrī does not dwell on this issue and in no way presents a complete or narrative rendition of the well-known events of that night. Rather in two verses he condenses the barest essentials: the night journey from one sacred precinct (Mecca) to another (Jerusalem) (v. 107); the ascension to within the Qurʾānic "two bows' length" of Allāh (*thumma danā fa-tadallá fa-kāna qāba qawsayni ʾaw ʾadná*, Then he approached and drew near until he was two bows' length [from Allāh] or closer [QK 53:8–9]); and, finally, the main thrust of his polemic, Muḥammad's reaching a station that no other man, or prophet, has ever attained or even dared to desire (v. 108). Having thus encapsulated the main points and confirmed the result—that Muḥammad has achieved an unparalleled proximity to and intimacy with God—the poet then backtracks to fill in those details of the Ascension that highlight Muḥammad's precedence over the other prophets. Again, we should note that the poet does this in an eminently non-narrative fashion. He is not (re)telling a story—the narratives, whether popular or canonical, concerning the Night Journey and Ascension were already common knowledge; rather, he is employing certain aspects of it poetically, or rhetorically, to construct his polemic.

Verses 109 to 112 convey the message of the Prophet Muḥammad's precedence over the other Prophets and Messengers that culminates in verse 113 with his obtaining union (*waṣl*—I take it to mean coming into His presence) with Allāh and receiving from Him exclusive confidences or esoteric knowledge. Verse 109 depicts the other Prophets and Messengers deferring to Muḥammad, as servants to their masters, to precede them. Verse 110 condenses the narrative of the Ascension through the seven levels of the heavens into a single verse. As he ascends through one level of the heavens after another toward Allāh, Muḥammad, leading a procession—of angels, as al-Azharī tells us—passes by, that is, surpasses, the other prophets. Al-Ghazzī cites Muslim to the effect that "in the lowest heaven he passed by Ādam; in the second, ʿĪsá and Yaḥyá (Jesus and John); in the third, Yūsuf (Joseph); in the fourth, Idrīs (Enoch); in the fifth Hārūn (Aaron); in the sixth Mūsá (Moses) and in the seventh, Ibrāhīm (Abraham), God's blessing and peace upon all of them" (al-Ghazzī, v. 110). The initiation ritual that structures this Ascension passage, as well as Ibn Hishām's *Al-Sīrah* rendition of Muḥammad's Ascension, is of the same pattern familiar to us from mystery cults. It is particularly apparent in the elements of trial and contest, the progression through a series of ranks or stations, here in the form of the seven levels of the heavens and their attendant prophets, and especially in the arrival at the highest rank and acquisition of esoteric knowledge. Verse 111 reiterates the idea of competition for ranks—the trial part of the initiation rite—and Muḥammad's overcoming all rivals and competitors—i.e., the other Prophets and Messengers.

In verse 112 the poet plays on Arabic grammatical terms to the same effect. On the surface, it means that you, Muḥammad, subordinated all other ranks to your rank when Allāh called you to a high station the way a chieftain or notable is called (al-Azharī). On this level, al-Ghazzī (v. 112) tells us that "calling" here refers to Allāh's addressing the Prophet, "O Muḥammad, come near, come near!" (*yā Muḥammadu udnu udnu*). And the "elevated station" refers to the distance of "two bows' length," the proximity to God that Muḥammad alone achieved (see above, verse 108). At the same time, *khafaḍta* (reduce, lower) also means to put in the genitive case; *iḍāfah* means the possessive genitive construct; *nūdīta bi-al-rafᶜ* means for the vocative to be used in the nominative case, as in *yā Muḥammadu* cited above, but also, "be called to high rank"; and *al-mufrad al-ᶜalam*, as well as meaning a unique chieftain, means a singular proper noun. If to the modern sensibility this verse seems excessively contrived (especially in English), we should keep in mind that Arabic grammatical terminology is simply the technical use of what are otherwise quite ordinary everyday words, so that the punning of this line is far smoother and more charming in Arabic than in translation. Verse 112 nevertheless clearly qualifies as an example of *badīᶜ*, the complex and self-conscious rhetorical play that requires some mental effort in order to elicit the full meaning.

The climax of this initiatory ascent is reached in verse 113, as the prophet-initiate Muḥammad, having overcome all rival prophets, "wins" (*tafūza;* al-Bājūrī, v. 113, glosses it as *ẓafira,* which, like *fāza,* means to be victorious as well as to obtain) union (i.e., proximity, intimacy) with Allāh and secret knowledge from Him. Verses 114 and 115 conclude the Ascension passage by reiterating Muḥammad's achievement of a uniquely exalted rank and status. As we saw in verse 42, once more in verse 115 al-Būṣīrī, in his determination to elevate the status of the Prophet Muhḥammad, employs diction—"exalted" (*jalla*) and "great" (*ᶜazza*)—that inevitably, and intentionally, evokes the Islamic deific formula, *Allāhu ʿazza wa-jalla* (= God Almighty). In accordance with Islamic creed, al-Būṣīrī does not claim divinity for Muhḥammad, but he certainly wants to assure that Muhḥammad has no contenders when it comes to proximity to Allāh.

The two remaining verses serve to integrate the Night Journey and Ascension passage into the larger polemic of the poem. In verse 116, Muḥammad is evoked metaphorically as a pillar of the Muslim community that has been erected by God and can never be toppled. The argument for the superiority of Islam and of the Islamic community over all other religions, especially Judaism and Christianity, is clinched in verse 117: if God has declared Muḥammad the noblest of Messengers, then it follows that his community is the noblest of nations. The "chain of command" from God through his Prophet Muḥammad to the Islamic community is rhetorically achieved through the *jinās* on *daʿā* (call, call out, name) of "God called Muḥammad the noblest of Messengers" and *dāʿīnā* (Muḥammad, "the one who called us [the Muslims]" to obey God), in the first hemistich, followed by the repetition of *ʾakram* (noblest) first for Muḥammad and then for his community, in the second.

In sum, as we have seen in the earlier Sīrah-related sections of the Burdah, al-Būṣīrī has selected elements from the narrative materials concerning the Night Journey and Ascension of the Prophet and has poetically recast them in a highly rhetoricized non-narrative form. His purpose in this is to buttress his polemic in support of the preeminence of Islam and the Islamic community as a corollary to the unique and superior position of the Prophet Muḥammad vis-à-vis the other, Jewish and Christian, Prophets and Messengers. The closing verse of part 7, 117, constitutes a virtual declaration of Islamic Manifest Destiny, the guarantee of the worldly success and victory of Islam, its Prophet, and his community, which is the subject of part 8.

PART 8: THE MESSENGER'S JIHĀD AND CAMPAIGNS (VV. 118–139)

118. The news of his message struck terror in the hearts of his enemies,
Like the roar of the lion that startles the heedless sheep.

119. He fought them on every battleground
Till the spears left them like meat exposed in the sun to dry.

120. They were so eager to flee that they envied the limbs of the slain
That were carried off by eagles and vultures.

121. In their terror they lost count of the passing nights,
Except in the Sacred Months when no battle is waged.

122. As if Islam were a guest that alighted in the enemies' courtyard
Bringing with it every brave Muslim warrior greedy for enemy flesh.[94]

123. The Prophet draws behind him a five-part army like a bounding sea, which,
Mounted on swift-swimming steeds, flings dashing waves of warriors at the foe.

124. Each of its warriors, consecrated to God and reckoning God's heavenly reward,
Assaults with weapons that exterminate the Infidel,

125. Until, through them, the community of Islam was bound together
Like blood-kin, after they had been like strangers.

126. In them it is forever protected by the best of fathers and husbands,
So the Muslim community is never orphaned or widowed.[95]

127. The Companions are as steadfast as mountains, so ask
Their battle-foe how they find them on every battleground.

128. Ask Ḥunayn and Badr and Uḥud about them, they will reply:
"The ways they kill the Infidel are more deadly than the plague."

129. They are the ones who return from battle with their white blades red
From drinking the blood of every black-locked foe,

130. Who write using the brown-hued Khaṭṭī spears,
Whose pens leave no letter on an enemy corpse undotted,

131. Who are bristling with weapons, but marked by the same sign
That tells you the rose from the thorn-tree.

132. When the winds of victory spread the sweet fragrance of their news,
You think each armor-clad warrior has blossoms in his sleeves.

133. Like clinging hilltop plants, they are rooted to the backs of their steeds
From firm resolve, not from firm saddle cinches.

134. The enemy's hearts were so flustered by fear of the Muslims' fierce fighting
That they couldn't tell sheep [*bahm*] from brave warriors [*buham*].

135. Whoever is succored by the Messenger of God, if lions
Were to find him in their lair, they would fall silent.

136. You will find no friend of his who is not victorious;
Nor any foe who is not broken.

137. He settled his community in the stronghold of his creed,
Like a lion with its cubs in its lair.

138. How many an opponent did the Words of God refute,
How many an adversary was vanquished by the Proof.[96]

139. It is miracle enough for you that an illiterate should achieve such knowledge
In the Age of Ignorance, that an orphan should acquire such refinement. [50]

By now we realize that the titles assigned to the traditional divisions of the Burdah provide only a general indication of the main subject matter. Once again, as we have come to expect, the poet does not offer an encapsulation of historical events, but rather a carefully constructed polemic aimed at establishing the terror and cowardice of the enemies of the Prophet and of Islam as opposed to the courage and determination of the Prophet's warriors, who have consecrated their lives to Allāh. Above all, in the context of the present study, we find that al-Būṣīrī does not in any way follow the extensive and largely narrative sections on the Prophet's battles or raids such as we find in Ibn Hishām's *Al-Sīrah al-Nabawiyyah* (and notably al-Qāḍī ʿIyāḍ does not cover these topics in *Al-Shifāʾ*); rather he casts this passage on the military prowess and victory of the Prophet and his Companions as a High ʿAbbāsid military panegyric with its characteristic *badīʿ* style, which we have identified in the beginning of chapter 2 as the expression of Arab-Islamic hegemony. This means that the poem has moved from employing the rhetorical techniques of the *badīʿ* style to adopting its subject matter. What is equally significant is that we have moved from the domain of miracles to the concrete real-world proving ground of the ideology of Islamic Manifest Destiny.

Although the theme of contrasting the nobility of one's own forces to the depravity of the foe is, no doubt, universal in martial polemics from the crudest propaganda to the most sublime poetry, in the case of Arab poetry the rhetorical techniques for achieving this antithesis were most highly developed in the High ʿAbbāsid period and within the specific context of the nearly perennial military encounters between the Muslims and the Byzantines along the constantly shifting borderlands known as the *thughūr*. In part 8, then, the rhetoric, diction, and imagery that grew out of those later hostilities are projected back to a much earlier period, onto the rivalry between the Prophet Muḥammad's nascent Muslim community and the Meccan polytheists. This has the effect of detaching the events from their historical chronological moorings and conferring upon them a mythic, timeless—that is, paradigmatic—quality.[97] This sense of timelessness is further enhanced by the striking absence of proper names in this passage, which is presented largely in the most general of terms, such as "the enemy" (*al-ʿidā*, vv. 118, 122) versus the warriors of Islam. Even the invocation (v. 138) of the Prophet's most famous battles against the Meccan polytheists—Ḥunayn (8 AH), Badr (2 AH), and Uḥud (3 AH)—which had soon taken on an emblematic more than historical quality, does little to dispel the sense of timelessness.

Through a process of chronological and rhetorical retrojection, a mythic concordance is established between victorious ʿAbbāsid caliphs such as al-Muʿtaṣim and their imperial armies and the Prophet and his Companions as warriors. What is particularly important from a literary point of view is that despite the Qurʾānic sources for these battles and their extensive coverage, including large amounts of poetry as well as prose, in Ibn Hishām's *Al-Sīrah al-Nabawiyyah*[98] this poetic passage has not been shaped by these, nor has it been shaped by works such as al-Qāḍī ʿIyāḍ's *Al-Shifāʾ*, in which, though mentioned in the context of various miracles, these battles have no formative presence. Rather, both in terms of subject matter and in style, the sources for this passage are the rich Arabic poetic tradition of battle poetry, rooted in the Jāhiliyyah. Closer at hand is Kaʿb ibn Zuhayr's description of the Prophet and the warriors of the Muhājirūn (the Emigrants, who accompanied Muḥammad in his flight from Mecca to Medina) in his celebrated Suʿād Has Departed, the subject of chapter 1. The main source here, however, is the *badīʿ*-style High ʿAbbāsid battle panegyric for caliphs, princes, and generals, typified by Abū Tammām's Amorium Ode (see chapter 2 and the introduction). In this respect, we must realize that it is the structural and thematic imperatives of such *qaṣīdah*s, which in the High ʿAbbāsid period required military prowess and God-given military success as signs of legitimate rule and hence as necessary components of the *madīḥ* (praise) section, that explain the presence of this passage in al-Būṣīrī's poem.

In a manner closely resembling that of Abū Tammām's description of the moral and spiritual depravity of the Byzantine Christian foe in his Amorium Ode,[99] al-Būṣīrī opens part 8 describing the terror that Muḥammad's mission struck in the hearts of the enemy, who are defined by the commentarists as "al-Kuffār," meaning in general the Infidel, but also, specifically at the period of the Prophet's early battles, the Meccan polytheists who refused to accept Muḥammad's prophethood and message (vv. 118–122). Grounded in images that are rooted in the Jāhiliyyah—the lion startling the heedless sheep (v. 118); meat on a drying block (v. 119) to describe those slain in battle—the passage soon picks up distinctly *badīᶜ* features: the conceit of terrified soldiers so eager to flee that they are jealous of the limbs of the slain that are carried from the battlefield by birds of prey (v. 120). Verse 121 plays on the pre-Islamic custom of abstaining from warfare in the Sacred Months of Dhū al-Qaᶜdah, Dhū al-Ḥijjah, Muḥarram, and Rajab, to say that the terrified enemy lost all sense of time during the Profane Months when they were in perpetual fear of the Prophet's attacks, as opposed to the Sacred Months when they could relax. Even more distinctively *badīᶜ* is the complex (and, to the commentators, the subject of some confusion) conceit of verse 122. In its personification of Islam, it adds a level of conceptualization and Islamization to a pre-Islamic metaphor. In the Muᶜallaqah of ᶜAmr ibn Kulthūm, for example, we find the obligation to feed the guest as a metaphor for its counterpart, the obligation to slay the enemy, for, the commentarist tells us, the verse means "we took the initiative to attack you first rather than wait for you to revile us for cowardice":

> You alighted as guests alight in our courtyard
> And we hastened to provide hospitality lest you revile us.[100]
>
> [51]

Al-Būṣīrī's verse likens the Muslim warriors in their battle-lust against the Infidel to hungry guests that Islam has brought to the enemy's courtyard, and whom, custom requires, the host, however unwilling, must provide with the flesh that they crave—i.e., of the slain enemy (following al-Bājūrī, v. 122).

Verses 123 to 133 or 134 counter the depiction of the terrified foe with that of the majestic sweeping Muslim army led by the Prophet. This central passage of part 8 is not a narrative of historical account of the Prophet's battles and raids, but rather a *madḥ* (praise, panegyric) of the Prophet's Companions (the commentaries identify them as "al-Ṣaḥābah," see al-Ghazzī, al-Bājūrī, v. 127) in their capacity as warriors for the faith cast in the *badīʿ* style of the *qaṣīdat al-madḥ* (panegyric ode) of the High ʿAbbāsid period. Although it is clear from the context that the Prophet is the referent of the pronoun, the verse itself is purely in the High ʿAbbāsid *badīʿ* in both its diction and the complex rhetorical play on the comparison of the sweeping five-part army to the sea. The crux of the word-play is *sābiḥah,* that is, "swimmers," a conventional epithet for swift-paced steeds. This prepares us stylistically for verse 124, which, in the exhilirating momentum of its rhythmic repetition of participial forms—*muntadib* (consecrating), *muḥtasib* (reckoning), *mustaʾṣil* (eradicating), *muṣṭalim* (exterminating)—is styled quite explicitly on Abū Tammām's famous and much imitated line (cited in chapter 2), describing the Caliph al-Muʿtaṣim on the Amorium campaign: *muʿtaṣim* (relying), *muntaqim* (avenging), *murtaqib* (striving), *murtaghib* (yearning).

Verses 125 and 126 continue to describe the warriors for the faith, now through similes involving kinship: it is through them that the community of Islam is bound together and it is they who protect the community as husbands and fathers protect their wives and children. The sense seems to be that the community was forged, and is maintained and protected, by the sword.

Verses 127 to 133 or 134 combine the conventional Jāhilī *fakhr* (boast) strategy of the rhetorial question, *sal fūlānan ʿannā . . . [yujib]* (Ask so-and-so about us, [he/they will answer]), as, for example in the pre-Islamic warrior poet Bishr ibn Abī Khāzim's verse:

> And ask Banū Tamīm about us on the Day of al-Jifār and ask
> Banū Laʾm about us, when they turned tail and would not stand
> in battle.[101]
>
> [52]

Verse 127 asks their foes about the warriors for the faith in battle; verse 128 intensifies the rhetoric to personify the renowned battles of the Prophet and the nascent Muslim community against the Meccan polytheists: Ḥunayn, Badr, and Uḥud, who are asked and respond. This serves as the transition into a passage based on another Jāhilī-rooted structure, the descriptive passages in *fakhr* (boast), *madḥ* (panegyric), or *rithā*ʾ (elegy) based on a series of what I have termed elsewhere active participial epithets:[102] *al-muṣdirī al-bīḍi* (those bringing back the white swords, v. 129); *al-kātibīna bi-sumri al-Khaṭṭi* (those writing with the brown spears of al-Khaṭṭ, v. 130); *shākī al-silāḥi* (those bristling with weapons, v. 131). Indeed, the commentators explain the accusative case of these participles as the direct object of an elided verb of praise (al-Ghazzī, al-Azharī, al-Bājūrī, v. 129). This structure is now cast, however, in purely Abū Tammāmian *badī*ʿ: the intensified play on color epithets of verses 129 and 130; the conceit of verse 130 comparing spears leaving puncture-wounds in the bodies of the foe to pens putting dots on letters; the complex conceit and word-play of verse 131 which, the commentarists explain, means that the Muslim warriors in their weapons are distinguished from the foe by their moral or spiritual sweetness just as the rose bush is distinguished by the beauty and fragrance of its blossoms from the thorny salam-tree (al-Ghazzī, al-Bājūrī, v. 130).

The metaphor of sensory sweetness for spiritual purity is taken up once more in verse 132, where it is compounded with the metaphor of the wind spreading redolent fragrances for the spreading of the good news of Muslim victory. Again, the verse is closely modeled on verses like Abū Tammām's description of the "sweetness" of Muslim victory over the Byzantines at Amorium:

> 60. How many a bitter soul was sweetened when [the enemies'] souls
> were plucked from them,
> Had it been drenched in musk it would not smell so sweet.[103]
>
> [53]

The following two verses exhibit once more precisely the sort of word-play that defines the *badī*ʿ style: verse 133 contrasts the firm physical steadfastness of tightly cinched saddle girths to the psychological fortitude of the Muslims warriors on their mounts through a compound *jinās*: they cling to their saddles through the firmness of their resolve (*min shiddati al-ḥazmi*) not from the tightnening of their saddle-girths (*lā min shaddati al-ḥuzumi*). Verse 134 returns to the subject of the terror-stricken foe, whose mental confusion is expressed through the verbal confusion suggested by another double *jinās,* first of *faraq* (fear) and *tufarriqu* (distinguish), and especially between *al-bahm* (sheep) and *al-buham* (brave warriors).

What we should understand above all from this recasting of the battles and raids of the Prophet and the warriors of the nascent Muslim community into the rhetorically complex and eminently imperial or hegemonic discourse of the *badīᶜ*-style *qaṣīdat al-madḥ* of the High ᶜAbbāsid period is that a chronologically reversed process of mythic concordance has taken place. If Abū Tammām achieved a mythic concordance between the Prophet's Battle of Badr and the Caliph al-Muᶜtaṣim's victory over Amorium with his lines

69. If among fate's vagaries there is
Any tie of kinship or unsevered bond

70. Then the closest lineage connects
The days of Badr to your victorious days.[104]

[54]

then al-Būṣīrī, by clothing the Prophet and his Companion warriors in the rhetorical garb that Abū Tammām had produced for al-Muᶜtaṣim and his victorious Muslim forces, has achieved a timeless, mythic image of Islam victorious, of an Islamic Manifest Destiny.

We can better appreciate the emphasis on the warrior Companions in this passage if we keep in mind that, inasmuch as the *qaṣīdat al-madḥ*, as I have demonstrated elsewhere, constitutes a declaration of allegiance, it also presents a hierarchical model or paradigm of the polity or community of which the *mamdūḥ* is the legitimate leader.[105] Thus we found in chapter 1 that Kaᶜb ibn Zuhayr's Suᶜād Has Departed devotes the major portion of its *madīḥ* section to describing the Prophet in martial terms as more dreadful than a lion, as one of the swords of God (chapter 1, Suᶜād Has Departed, vv. 43–48), before concluding with a description of the Muhājirūn (the Emigrants, those who followed Muḥammad from Mecca to Medina) as noble warriors for the faith and the Anṣār (Medinese Helpers) as wretched runts (chapter 1: Suᶜād Has Departed, vv. 51–55).

It is significant, then, that the climactic emphasis on the Sīrah-related parts of al-Būṣīrī's Burdah falls on the militant Ummah or Community in a passage whose principle components are the divinely appointed Muslim leader, his warriors, and the adversary. It is interesting, too, that the Meccan polytheists, termed merely "the enemy" (*al-ᶜidā*, v. 118) and "the Infidel" (*al-kufr*, v. 124), through their description in the High ʿAbbāsid panegyric descriptions of the enemy, acquire a mythic cognation with the Byzantine (Christian) Infidel of that period, as found, for example in the martial panegyrics of poets such as Abū Tammām, al-Buḥturī, and al-Mutanabbī. For al-Būṣīrī's contemporaries the further identification of the infidel enemy of this passage with the Crusaders was, no doubt, inevitable.

The remainder of part 8, verses 135 to 139, explicitly names the Messenger of God for the first time in part 8, effects a transition away from the martial imagery that dominates the earlier verses of this passage, and redirects our attention to Muḥammad's defining miracle, the Qurʾān. Within the Arabic poetic context, however, the lion is the staple metaphor for the fierce warrior, so that verse 135, in which the Prophet defends those he succors against lions, and verse 137, in which he himself is likened to a lion, both have a martial tone and, indeed, recall the comparison of the Prophet to a lion in Kaʿb ibn Zuhayr's Suʿād Has Departed (chapter 1, vv. 44–46).

Nevertheless, verse 137 refers to Muḥammad's creed as a stronghold or refuge, conveying the concept of a protection that is spiritual rather than military. Finally, the two closing verses of this section move away from the martial theme of the main passages and revert to the broader theme of the Sīrah-related passages: the Prophet's miracles. Verse 138 quite cleverly maintains the adversarial tone while invoking the Prophet's greatest miracle, the Qurʾān as the Word of God and as the ultimate Proof of Muḥammad's Prophethood that defeats and vanquishes opponents and adversaries. Verse 139 offers a corollary to the Iʿjāz al-Qurʾān tenet, again through the rhetorical device, a double antithesis that produces an impossible (i.e., miraculous) combination of opposites: that an illiterate (the general understanding of QK 7:157, *al-nabī al-ummī*)[106] should achieve knowledge in the Age of Ignorance and that a (poor, neglected) orphan (Muḥammad's father, ʿAbd Allāh, died before he was born; his mother, Āminah, died when he was six years old) should achieve such refinement of language are proof of the divine inspiration of the Qurʾān and therefore of Muḥammad's prophethood.

Through these closing verses part 8 redirects us out of the martial world of military victory and conquest and back into the spiritual domain of Muḥammad, the succor and support of his community (vv. 135–137), whose prophethood is confirmed above all by the miracle of the

Qurʾān (vv. 137–138). This then sets the stage for the introduction of the two final sections of the overarching supplicatory structure of the Burdah—Part 9: Supplication and Plea for Intercession, and Part 10: Fervent Prayer and Petition.

It is essential to understand how the Sīrah-related polemical sections of al-Būṣīrī's Burdah, parts 4–8, function within what we have argued is the overarching supplicatory structure of the ode. On the one hand, in terms of their placement and themes, these sections serve as extensions of the *madīḥ* section and perform its assigned function of demonstrating the legitimacy of the *mamdūḥ*. Inasmuch as the poem is addressed to the Prophet, this amounts first of all to confirming his claim to prophethood and particularly of establishing his claim to be the Seal of Prophets; hence the polemical trajectory of these sections. The recasting of Sīrah-related materials into poetic structures, especially the highly rhetoricized poetics of *badīʿ*, has the effect of downplaying the chronological or historical narrative aspect of these materials and foregrounding their cosmic dimensions and associations, in particular through establishing a mythic concordance between the events of the Prophet's lifetime and the apex of Arab-Islamic hegemony in the High ʿAbbāsid age.

This process of mythicization creates a sense of teleological time, and with it a sense of the continued efficacy of the Prophet's connection with the Islamic Ummah, both corporately—what I have termed the ideology of Islamic Manifest Destiny—and individually. This, in turn, is essential to the ritual exchange that is at the core of the supplicatory ode—i.e., that the poet-supplicant presents a gift or offering of praise and requests a boon; and, in return, the patron-benefactor fulfills that request, thereby confirming the poet's words. Furthermore, part of this poetic ritual involves the poet's establishing the *mamdūḥ*'s ability to grant the supplicant's wish. For *madīḥ nabawī,* this means that the poet must establish Muḥammad's prophethood, for only if he truly is God's prophet can he bestow the boon of intercession (*al-shafāʿah*) on Judgment Day.

Completion of the Supplicatory Pattern: Parts 9–10

Let us now turn to parts 9 and 10, whose traditional titles tell us quite directly that they are concerned with Supplication and Plea for Intercession. Part 9 can be termed the ritual contractual core of the poem.

PART 9: SUPPLICATION AND PLEA FOR INTERCESSION (VV. 140–151)

140. I hereby serve him with praise whereby I seek forgiveness
For a life spent in poetry and service to worldly masters,

141. Which had led me to deeds of dreadful consequence,
Till I was like a sacrificial sheep led to the slaughter.

142. I obeyed the temptations of youth in both poetry and worldly service
And from them I obtained nothing but sin and regret.

143. What a loss for my soul in her commerce! She did not purchase
the next world
With this world; she did not even put this world up for sale!

144. Whoever sells the world to come to buy this fleeting world
Will soon see he's been defrauded in the sale and in the purchase.

145. If I have committed sins, yet my pact with the Prophet is not broken,
Nor is my bond with him severed.

146. Surely by my name Muḥammad I fall under his protection,
And he is the most faithful of all creation to his covenants.

147. If on Resurrection Day he does not take me by the hand,
Then say, "Oh, how his foot does slip from the Bridge into Hellfire!"

148. No one who hopes for his generous gifts is ever denied;
No one who seeks his protection is ever dishonored.

149. Since I have committed my thoughts to his praise,
I have found him most committed to my salvation.

150. His wealth will never fail the dusty outstretched hand,
For surely the rain makes flowers bloom even on hilltops.

151. —And I don't mean the blossoms of this world
That Zuhayr's hands plucked for his praise poems to Harim.

[55]

As we saw in chapter 1 on Kaʿb ibn Zuhayr's Suʿād Has Departed, the ritual core of the supplicatory ode is signaled by a change in style from the rhetorically laden and heavily metaphorical opaque poetic language to a more transparent, straightforward, prosaic language.[107] Again, we must insist that the ritual core is the most essentially performative part of the poem, that is, it is in no way a description or poetic recounting of the poet's making a pact with the Prophet; rather it is a speech act: as the poet utters the words, the pact assumes moral force. In essence, part 9 sets forth and confirms the supplicatory panegyric pact between poet and patron, specifying for this *madīḥ nabawī* the moral, spiritual, and otherworldly—that is to say, religious—dimensions of the covenant. Verse 140 succinctly reiterates the pact: that the poet is presenting praise to the Prophet Muḥammad in return for his intercession for God's forgiveness, on the Judgment Day, for the sins of a life spent devoted to the praise and service of worldly masters (al-Ghazzi, Bājūrī, v. 140). At the same time, this verse confirms our suggested reading of Part 1: *Nasīb* Lyric-Erotic Prelude, that the passions of youth and adolescent erotic suffering are figurative expressions for worldly poetry—or vice versa, as the following verses further confirm. At the same time, part 9 reiterates the key elements of the supplicatory ritual: verses 141–144 recapitulate the pattern of *nasīb*ic youthful passion that leads to sin and regret, followed by self-abasement in the form of confession and repentance. Note, too, the insistence on the use of commercial terms (vv. 143–144) that underline the concept of contractual exchange, while at the same time contrasting the inevitably fraudulent and unprofitable commerce of this world with the success of the otherworldly commerce—i.e., selling this world to gain the next. These mercantile metaphors are reminiscent of and derived from religious discourse on the subject, but also have a poetic precedent in lines such as al-Buḥturī's, from his renowned poem on Īwān Kisrá (the Arch of Chosroes, in Ctesiphon):

> In my purchase of Iraq I was swindled,
> After my selling Syria at a loss.[108]
>
> [56]

The despair of self-abasement ("like a beast /sheep to the slaughter," v. 141) and the failure of worldly commerce yields to hope and praise in verses 145–148, with particular emphasis on pacts and their binding nature: verse 145 insists that between the poet and the Prophet, "my pact (*ʿahdī*) . . . is not broken, . . . my bond (*ḥablī*) is not severed"; verse 146, the poet's "covenant of protection" (*dhimmah*) balanced with the Prophet's "covenants" (*dhimam*); verse 148, likewise, among many possible virtues he chooses the Prophet's honoring his obligation to those who have sought his protection (*al-jār . . . muḥtaram*). In verse 149, the panegyric compact is reiterated yet again: as the poet "commits" or binds himself to praising the Prophet, the Prophet thereby becomes reciprocally committed or bound to the poet's salvation. The sense of this mutually binding obligation is expressed with utter clarity in the Arabic through the *jinās* (root-play) of *ʾalzamtu* (I bound myself) in the first hemistich and *multazim* ([he was] bound, committed) in the second, both deriving from the root *l-z-m* and evoking its core meanings of clinging and sticking, obligation and duty.

The final couplet of part 9, too, reaffirms the panegyric pact, in a way that makes explicit once more the distinction between court panegyric, that is, worldly poetry, and *madīḥ nabawī*—the very distinction with which verse 140 opened the section. Now, however, the poet begins with a straightforward line of praise: just as a heavy rain makes the flowers bloom even on the driest hilltops, so too the boundless generosity of the Prophet reaches even to the poorest hand. This leads, however, in verse 151, to the poet's renouncing earthly rewards, as he insists that these flowers—the rewards for his poetry that the Prophet would bestow—are not the flowers or splendors of this world (the Qurʿānic *zahrata al-ḥayāta al-dunyā,* QK 20: 131), like the lavish robes bestowed on Zuhayr (his name means "little blossom") ibn Abī Sulmá by his patron Harim ibn Sinān (see chapter 1), but rather the flowers or rewards of the world to come.

PART 10: FERVENT PRAYER AND PETITION (VV. 152–160)

152. O most generous of all Creation, I have no one to turn to
But you, when the dreaded Day of Judgment comes.

153. O Messenger of God, it will not offend your dignity to help me
When God, the Generous One, is endowed with the name of the Avenger.

154. For indeed both this world and the next come from your generosity,
And our knowledge of the Pen and Tablet comes from your knowledge.

155. O my soul, do not despair of pardon for a sin, however grave,
For mortal sins in God's forgiveness are like venial ones.

156. I hope that my share of my Lord's mercy, when He apportions it,
Will be in equal portion to my disobedience and sins.

157. O my Lord, ensure that my hope for Your mercy is not disappointed,
And ensure my account is not left unsettled.

158. Be gracious to your servant in both abodes, for his resolve is weak:
Whenever terrors call out to him, he flees.

159. And let clouds of prayer from You rain down unceasingly upon the Prophet
In heavy downpours and in steady rains

160. For as long as the eastern breeze stirs the boughs of the ben-tree
And the camel driver stirs his light-hued beasts with song.

[57]

Part 10 seals the poem and, in the context of the present reading, also seals the contract that the poet has so explicitly and insistently spelled out in part 9. At this climactic point the poet voices what is undoubtedly the most emotive verse of the poem. Abandoning the "objective" third person of part 9, the poet now turns directly to apostrophize the Prophet and, in an expression of total self-abasement, submission, and helplessness, throws himself upon the mercy of the Prophet and begs for his intercession. As we witnessed elsewhere, both in this poem and in the examples of ʿAlqamah, al-Nābighah, and Kaʿb in chapter 1, the elements of praise, submission, confession, and supplication are so intimately bound together as to be hard to isolate. Al-Būṣīrī's plea for the Prophet's intercession on his behalf on the Day of Judgment is couched in terms familiar to us from traditional court panegyric: verse 152, he seeks refuge; verse 153, he seeks to be included in the ranks of those protected by the *mamdūḥ*/Prophet. Further, although in religious terms we are dealing with a rite of pleading for intercession (*shafāʿah*), in terms of the poetic tradition, the poet is pleading for forgiveness and incorporation, to be brought near, into the patron's inner circle—in this case those who on the Day of Judgment will be spared the horrors of the Last Judgment and be led under the Prophet's banner into the heavenly Garden.[109]

The last six verses of the poem, verses 155–160, signal a transition from entreaty to the Prophet to a plea for mercy from Allāh himself; and, finally, the poem closes with the Benediction of the Prophet. This concluding passage constitutes a second, more elevated, supplication to Allāh Himself, as the poet now places his hope in Allāh (v. 156) and abases himself before Him. Once again, the tropes and diction are those of hope and fear, and include the mercantile image of the Day of Judgment (or Day of Reckoning, Yawm al-Ḥisāb) as a balancing of accounts (v. 157). Finally, the poem closes with the poet calling upon Allāh to bless the Prophet Muḥammad.

The ritual and structural purpose of this begins to emerge if we follow Annemarie Schimmel's discussion of Muḥammad as intercessor, where she states that the blessing of Muḥammad, most commonly in the formula *ṣallá Allāhu ʿalayhi wa-sallama* (termed *taṣliyah*) is a ritually required element of supplication: "The blessing has also been regarded as a necessary condition for the granting of a prayer of petition: 'The personal supplication (*duʿā*) remains outside the heavens until the praying person utters the blessing upon the Prophet.'"[110] Although Schimmel makes no connection between this and the classical court panegyric, those familiar with the poetic tradition will recognize that the poet's *duʿāʾ* or benediction, calling Allah's blessing down upon the *mamdūḥ*, performs a similar function there. In terms of our argument concerning ritual exchange, this means that part, indeed a requisite part, of the poet's (verbal, performative) gift to the patron is the blessing—the power of which may be more palpable to us when we consider it as the opposite of a curse. Further, we can now say that the blessing and the boon are intimately linked together, both in the supplicatory panegyric poetic tradition and in the supplicatory prayer.

In this case al-Būṣīrī has subtly melded the religious and the poetic, the *taṣliyah* (blessing) of the Islamic Prophetic tradition with the most traditional *duʿāʾ* (benediction) of the panegyric *qaṣīdah* tradition, that is, the *istisqāʾ* or prayer for rain. An example from a supplicatory panegyric by the celebrated Umayyad poet al-Akhṭal (d. ca. 92/710) will give us some idea of the poetic pedigree of al-Būṣīrī's closing lines, and of the traditional association of rain with fertility and abundance of every kind:

52. May God water a land the best of whose people is Khālid,
With a cloud whose spouts keep on disgorging abundant rain.

53. When the east wind cuts through its crotches,
Its water-laden lower parts flow like milk.

54. When the wind shakes it, it drags its trains,
Like the ponderous gait of newly calved she-camels, tending their young.

55. Pouring incessantly, the lightning-bolts on its sides like lamps aglow
in the darkness
Or the flanks of piebald steeds in panic bolting.[111]

[58]

Al-Būṣīrī's closing line deserves some comment of its own. Its surface sense is entirely clear: forever.

160. For as long as the eastern breeze stirs the boughs of the ben-tree
And the camel driver stirs his light-hued beasts with song.

On the literal level it also combines the elements of nature and culture—as long as the easterly breeze blows through the boughs of the ben-tree and as long as camel drivers sing to hasten their camels along. But in a tradition as rich as the Arabic one, all of these terms are laden with further meanings and associations that have accumulated over the centuries. In the poetic tradition, the *ṣabá* or easterly breeze, whether blowing through the ben-tree or from the highlands of Najd, is the breeze that bears the fragrance of the place where the poet's now distant beloved or loved ones dwell or dwelt, and that stirs the memory of the beloved in his heart.[112] And, further, this then serves as a trope for poetic inspiration, which begins with the sparking of a memory of loss. The ben-tree, too, has a complex poetic history. As a trope for the beloved, we have seen it already in verse 5—the image of the poet spending the night sleepless remembering the fragrance of the ben-tree—i.e., of the supple figure of his beloved. In the Post-Classical period, the beloved and with it the ben-tree are transformed, first by Sufism into symbols of the Divine (Allāh as the Beloved), but then further, from the sixth-century Hijrah on, to descriptions of the Prophet Muḥammad, Allāh's beloved. The longing and memory that are stirred in the context of sixth/thirteenth century *madīḥ nabawī* are for the visit to the city of the Prophet, Medina, and his tomb, after the pilgrimage to Mecca.

This further level of interpretation then colors our reading of the second hemistich: the camel driver assumes the identity, too, of a pilgrim headed to the Holy Places, and specifically to the city of the Prophet and his grave. The song with which he hastens and delights the camels, which serve additionally or essentially as a metonymy for their riders, can then be nothing other than *madīḥ nabawī*. The poem thus closes with an intriguing metapoetic and self-referential image that also reflects the exchange ritual that has formed the basis of our argument and of our reading of the poem. For the closing line comes to express a curious reciprocity or circularity: the poet prays in a *madīḥ nabawī* for Allāh to rain His blessings down upon the Prophet for as long as the remembrance of the Prophet stirs poets to compose *madīḥ nabawī*.

Conclusion

Now that we have unearthed the ritual-liturgical structure of the poem we are in a far better position to offer an assessment of its literary and religious success. We have determined through a close analysis of the text, in comparison with other supplicatory *qaṣīdahs*, that al-Būṣīrī's Burdah is thematically structured as a ritual of supplication for the Prophet's intercession on the Day of Judgment; and further, that the ritual of supplication is essentially a ritual exchange—a mutually binding contract whereby the poet-supplicant presents the *qaṣīdah* to the supplicated *mamdūḥ* who, in turn, must present a counter-gift, i.e., grant the supplicant his wish. This finding is confirmed by the statements repeated in the manuscripts and print editions of various forms of the Burdah, that the author, translator, scribe, *mukhammis* (composer of *takhmīs*), etc., did so in the hope of intercession. It is this full (and efficacious) ritual structure, as I see it, that allowed the Muslim faithful to employ the poem in this way, i.e., as a liturgical text whose recitation constituted a reenactment of al-Būṣīrī's experience of offering a gift of praise to the Prophet and receiving in return the gift of spiritual transformation or healing. In other words, the supplicatory ritual structure, much more than the religious content per se, meant that to recite (or imitate, translate, copy, etc.) the poem was to perform a religious rite. The generation of the myth of the cure and the mantle then has the effect of symbolically underlining the efficacy of this performative recitation. As we argued in the case of Kaᶜb ibn Zuhayr's Suᶜād Has Departed, so with al-Būṣīrī's Burdah, for a believer to perform the poem is to undergo a transformation that leaves him spiritually cleansed or cured or healed and, in particular, renews his hope for the intercession of the Prophet on Judgment Day and salvation in the world to come. The story of the dream vision and cure serves, as the Anglican Church says of the Christian sacraments, as "an outward and physical sign of an inward and spiritual grace."

Surely the Ṣūfīs who have widely adopted this poem as part of their mystical practice exercised great literary perspicacity in sensing that at the root of the supplicatory-panegyric ritual is admission into the presence and inner circle of the *mamdūḥ*. It was precisely this idea that we found so charmingly expressed by the Ṣūfī in al-Kutubī's version of the Dream of the Mantle in the introduction to this chapter.

The performative concept of the efficacious word was then expanded, metaphorically we would say, on the popular level to include cures and preventions other than the purely spiritual. For if the full Burdah poem can usher the believer into the (dream) presence of the Prophet and procure both earthly, physical cure and otherworldly intercession and salvation, it follows that its parts should have their own special properties (*khaṣāʾiṣ*), that is, spiritual or psychological benefits of a more limited nature; and further, following the metaphorical relation between the poem and the story of its composition—the relation between the spiritual cure and the physical cure—specific parts of the poem should have specific properties to produce specific physical benefits as well. Although the present discussion is confined to understanding these matters in literary terms of metaphor, metonymy, and synecdoche, the range of efficacy of the Burdah in traditional Islamic society and the associative logic behind it suggest that our literary concepts are grounded in broader psychological and psychosomatic experience.

The present study has focused on establishing the ritual supplicatory structure of al-Būṣīrī's Burdah, derived from the supplicatory court panegyric, as a major determinant of its performative liturgical function in a ritual exchange of poem for prize and blessing for boon. It has argued that the function of the story of its composition, including the dream vision of reciting it to the Prophet and the miraculous cure, is to confirm the ritual efficacy of the Burdah. Whereas modern literary critics understand the story as a metaphorical expression of the poem's ritual and spiritual efficacy, centuries of believers took the story more literally and sought to employ the poem as a means not only to achieve a spiritual healing, but to cure or prevent a wide range of psychological and physical ailments.

Many other aspects of al-Būṣīrī's Burdah remain to be explored: the Burdah's preeminent position in the massive production of *madāʾiḥ nabawiyyah* in Post-Classical Arabic poetry and in other Islamic literatures; its textual history, in both manuscript and print; its commentaries and translations; its past and current private devotional and public liturgical performance by Muslims in general and Ṣūfīs in particular; and its poetic progeny, such as *takhmīsāt, badīʿiyyāt,* and *muʿāraḍāt;* its performance history generally, including contemporary recitations and contests, commercial music videos, and Internet-based (YouTube, etc.) video productions.[113] We will turn now in chapter 3 to the most celebrated of the innumerable contrafactions or imitations of al-Būṣīrī's Burdah: Nahj al-Burdah (The Way of the Mantle) by the preeminent Egyptian Neo-Classical poet, Aḥmad Shawqī. With Shawqī's poem we move beyond the Medieval and Post-Classical periods to the age of the encounter of the Arab-Islamic world with Western ideas and Western imperialism, and to the Arab political and cultural response to the colonial encounter, termed Nahḍah (Awakening) or Iḥyāʾ (Revival).

THREE

Aḥmad Shawqī and the Reweaving of the Mantle

Introduction

The third of our Mantle Odes is Nahj al-Burdah (The Way of the Mantle),[1] which, as its title indicates, is a contrafaction (*muʿāraḍah*), that is, a formal imitation in rhyme and meter, of al-Būṣīrī's Burdah composed by Aḥmad Shawqī (1868–1932), the most celebrated of the Egyptian Neo-Classical poets.[2] Termed in Arabic "Shuʿarāʾ al-Iḥyāʾ" (Poets of the Revival), the Neo-Classical poets formed an integral part of the mid-nineteenth–mid-twentieth-century renascence of Classical Arabic language, literature, and culture termed the Arab Awakening (al-Iḥyāʾ, literally "revival") or Renaissance (al-Nahḍah).

AḤMAD SHAWQĪ AND THE NAHḌAH

Aḥmad Shawqī was born in Cairo in 1868 to a family of mixed Arab, Turkish, Greek, and Circassian origins. His family had close ties to the court of the Khedives. Descendants of the great mid-nineteenth-century Albanian reformist ruler of Egypt, Muḥammad ʿAlī Pāshā (r. 1805–1845), the Khedives ruled Egypt under more or less nominal Ottoman suzerainty. In 1883 Shawqī completed his secondary studies at the Khedival School and enrolled at the Law School in 1885, where he studied for two years followed by two years in its Division of Translation, graduating in 1889. In 1890 he was appointed to the Khedival Secretariat of Khedive Tawfīq, who then sent him to study law and literature in France from 1891 to 1893, first in

Montpelier and then in Paris. Upon his return to Egypt, he was reappointed to the Khedival Secretariat. He remained there under Tawfīq's successor, ʿAbbās Ḥilmī II (r. 1892–1914), whom he served as court poet until the Khedive's dethronement and Shawqī's own exile to Spain, in 1914. Upon his return from exile in 1919, Shawqī was unable to gain a position at court but became an increasingly popular poet throughout the Arab world. Proclaimed by the Arab poetic establishment "Prince of Poets" (Amīr al-Shuʿarāʾ) in 1927, Shawqī died, after a long illness, in 1932.[3]

Shawqī's extraordinarily rich and varied poetic production ranges from imitations of French and European models in his early *Dīwān;* to the Neo-Classical court panegyric to the Khedive of Egypt and occasional poetry addressed to countless notables (including Lord Cromer) in his middle period; to the Neo-Classical masterpiece, his Sīniyyah in imitation of al-Buḥturī, on the monuments of Islamic Spain, the end product of his exile in Spain (1914–1919); to his experiments in verse drama, didactic poetry, etc.[4] His lifetime spans a dramatic transitional period in Egyptian and Arab culture: the emergence of Egyptian nationalism; the ʿUrābī Revolt of 1882, whose failure ushered in the British occupation of Egypt, 1882–1936; World War I, 1914–18; the Egyptian 1919 Revolution; and in the 1920s the Wafd party's establishment of a constitutional monarchy under diminished British authority—concomitant with the dissolution of the Ottoman Sultanate, and with it the Islamic Caliphate, in 1922, with the establishment of the Turkish Republic.

It has been widely recognized that the Nahḍah, or Arab Renaissance, arose largely as a response to Western imperialism and domination of the Arab world. In poetry, this led to the formation of the Neo-Classical school and took the form of attempting to recuperate a vision of Arab-Islamic hegemony through reprising the robust and majestic voices of the master poets of the High ʿAbbāsid era, often in the form of contrafactions (*muʿāraḍāt*) of established masterpieces.[5] A formative figure on the Egyptian scene was the Shaykh al-Ḥusayn al-Marṣafī (1815–90), who is regarded as the first to have formulated a renaissance (*nahḍah*) of Arabic literature, as seen in his influential study of Arabic language, grammar, and rhetoric, etc., *Al-Wasīlah al-Adabiyyah ilá al-ʿUlūm al-ʿArabiyyah* (vol. 1: 1289/1875; vol. 2: 1292/1879). There he espouses the revival of the art of writing or composition (*inshāʾ*), based largely on examples taken from the Umayyad and ʿAbbāsid prose masters, as essential for the rebirth and modernization of Egypt.[6] Worthy of mention here, too, is the poet and statesman Maḥmūd

Sāmī al-Bārūdī (1839–1904), one of the leaders of the failed nationalist ʿUrābī Revolt (1881–82). When British military intervention quashed the revolt and ushered in the British occupation of Egypt, Bārūdī was among the leaders exiled to Ceylon, where he spent the next seventeen years. It was there that he composed major parts of his *dīwān* and his voluminous and influential anthology of ʿAbbāsid poetry, *Al-Mukhtārāt,* both of which appeared posthumously and established him as major proponent of and formative influence on the Neo-Classical movement.[7]

Concomitant with this valorization of Classical, especially early ʿAbbāsid, poets was the Neo-Classical disparagement of the more immediate poetic precedents of what came to be termed ʿAṣr al-Inḥiṭāṭ (Age of Decline) or al-Jumūd (of Stagnation), that is, the Post-Classical period of Arab subjugation to "foreign," if Islamic, rule, such as the Ayyūbids, Mamlūks, and Ottomans. Charged with excessive artifice and artificiality, the late medieval tradition was taken to embody the degeneracy of Arab-Islamic culture that had, in turn, paved the way for non-Arab (Central Asian, Turkish, Kurdish, or Caucasian) Islamic and subsequently European Christian ascendancy and domination.

We must not forget that this literary movement was part and parcel of the broader cultural movement of the Nahḍah, the rebirth and reform of Arab and more generally Islamic culture under the influence of European liberal thought and scientific progress on the one hand and European imperialism and military domination on the other. In this respect, the work of intellectuals and reformers such as the Egyptian modernizer and educator Rifāʿah Rāfiʿ al-Ṭahṭāwī (d. 1873), the revolutionary pan-Islamist, Jamāl al-Dīn al-Afghānī (d. 1897), and, especially, the Egyptian Islamic modernizer Muḥammad ʿAbduh (d. 1905), must be kept in mind—particularly in light of Albert Hourani's point that the Islamic reformism of Muḥammad ʿAbduh, Rashīd Riḍá, and others "took place under the stimulus of European liberal thought, and led to the gradual reinterpretation of Islamic concepts so as to make them equivalent to the guiding principles of European thought."[8]

POETIC PRECEDENTS

What is curious about Shawqī's Nahj al-Burdah is that he has chosen not, as the usual Neo-Classical manner would suggest, a High ʿAbbāsid model for his contrafaction (*muʿāraḍah*), but rather the centerpiece of the poetry and piety of the Post-Classical era, al-Būṣīrī's Burdah, or Mantle Ode. Shawqī's Neo-Classical predecessor, al-Bārūdī, too, composed a *muʿāraḍah,* of sorts, of al-Būṣīrī's Burdah, namely his *madīḥ nabawī* of nearly 450 verses, Kashf al-Ghummah fī Madḥ Sayyid al-Ummah (The Banishment of Sorrow in Praise of the Master of the Ummah).[9] It opens with an unmistakable allusion to its poetic genealogy echoing the image and diction of al-Būṣīrī's base-text, the Mīmiyyah of Ibn al-Fāriḍ (see chapter 2 of this volume):

> O harbinger of lightning, make your way to Dārat al-ʿAlam
> And urge your flock of clouds to a tribe at Dhū Salam
>
> [59]

Although it begins with a lyrical *nasīb* or "*ghazal*" section, it is, as al-Bārūdī states in his prose introduction, basically a poetic rendition of Ibn Hishām's *Al-Sīrah al-Nabawiyyah.*[10] It thus represents a poetic undertaking altogether different from Shawqī's, one that has led to the debate over whether Kashf al-Ghummah is a *qaṣīdah* or an epic (*malḥamah*).[11] Further, we should note that Shawqī himself also composed a contrafaction of al-Būṣīrī's second most celebrated and imitated *madīḥ nabawī,* his Hamziyyah, known by its *incipit* Wulida al-Hudá (True Guidance Was Born).[12]

Yet another layer of literary influence must be taken into account. The intervening six centuries between al-Būṣīrī's Burdah as base-text and Shawqī's contrafaction of it in Nahj al-Burdah witnessed not merely the florescence of *madīḥ nabawī* as a major poetic genre, including myriad contrafactions and expansions of the Burdah, but also the peculiar genre of *badīʿiyyah,* that is, a contrafaction of al-Būṣīrī's Burdah that is composed in such a way that each verse exhibits a particular rhetorical device. Ṣafī al-Dīn al-Ḥillī (d. 749/1348 or 750/1349) is usually credited with creating the first such poem. Later practitioners, beginning with ʿIzz al-Dīn al-Mawṣilī (d. 789/1387), added the further proviso that each verse contain a *tawriyah* (pun) on the rhetorical term for the device exhibited therein. A number of these poems, especially those of Ṣafī al-Dīn al Ḥillī and Ibn Ḥijjah al-Ḥamawī (d. 837/1434), had a certain currency in the Neo-Classical period.[13] Inasmuch as their poems closely followed the thematic structure as well as rhyme and meter of al-Būṣīrī's Burdah, they, and the aesthetic rhetorical expectations they engendered, must have influenced both Shawqī's choice of base-text and his composition. Indeed, in his introduction to Nahj al-Burdah, Muḥammad al-Muwayliḥī states that Shawqī has taken the *badīʿiyyāt* type of *madīḥ nabawī* as his model.[14] Although Shawqī does not follow their programmatic practice, nevertheless his rhetorically ornate style creates a similar effect, and his poem shows the influence of this body of poetry. It should be noted, further, that especially since the technical term *badīʿiyyah* is sometimes used more loosely for rhetorically ornate *madīḥ nabawī*—usually contrafactions of, or strongly influenced by, al-Būṣīrī's Burdah—to Shawqī's contemporaries the *badīʿiyyah,* whether in the precise or looser sense, is the immediate genre-association for Nahj al-Burdah.

As we saw in chapter 2, al-Būṣīrī's Burdah is without question the preeminent example of *madīḥ nabawī,* one that, in addition to spawning the subgenre of the *badīʿiyyah,* was imitated, copied, commented upon, expanded upon, translated, etc., in an entirely unprecedented manner. Further, we must not forget the widespread popular belief in the Burdah's miraculous and talismanic powers, both spiritual and physical, that were both initiated and confirmed by the story associated with it, as follows. The poet, stricken with hemiplegia, composed this poem of *madīḥ nabawī.* He then saw the Prophet in a dream and recited the poem to him, whereupon the Prophet, in an expression of appreciation and delight, conferred his mantle upon the poet. The poet awoke the next morning cured of his ailment. The protection and blessings, in this world and the next, that the Burdah conferred resulted in its extensive incorporation into the everyday piety of the faithful—its recitation at *mawlid*s of the Prophet and various saints, at funerals, etc., and especially to its incorporation into Ṣūfī liturgies, where, as I understand it, its recitation is believed to evoke the presence of the Prophet even as it had for al-Būṣīrī (see chapter 2). Thus, in choosing to imitate al-Būṣīrī's Burdah, Shawqī was at once engaging a powerful and evocative model and creating for himself a formidable poetic challenge.

To understand Shawqī's purpose in following al-Būṣīrī's Burdah, then, we will once more invoke Connerton's concept of "mythic concordance," that is, the identification with an originary and authoritative model, whereby the imitator acquires, or coopts, for himself and his own work, the model's authenticity and authority. In the case of Shawqī's Nahj al-Burdah, we will refine the concept of mythic concordance to argue that Shawqī has chosen al-Būṣīrī's Burdah, and with it the centuries-old tradition of *madīḥ nabawī,* especially *badīʿiyyah,* associated with it, to appropriate for his "Iḥyāʾ Project" for the cultural and political revival of the Islamic Ummah the most compelling poetic and religious authority. As with any poetic contrafaction (*muʿāraḍah*), Shawqī's Nahj al-Burdah must be understood as a "performance" of the base-text, that is, a form of ritual reenactment that combines repetition and mimesis of the authority-conferring base-text on the one hand, but at the same time transforms and redirects it through the new text toward the poet's own contemporary goals and concerns (poetic, political, religious, etc., see below), on the other.

AUTHORIZING THE TEXT: THE KHEDIVE, THE SHAYKH, AND THE ADĪB

Shawqī's quest for authority—political and religious as well as poetic—comes to the fore extrapoetically in the prose dedication of Nahj al-Burdah to his patron, the Khedive ʿAbbās Ḥilmī II, to commemorate his Ḥajj of the year 1909/1327; this appears as the frontispiece, beneath the Khedival coat of arms, of the first edition (1910/1328).

> The Exalted King, My Lord the Ḥajjī ʿAbbās Ḥilmī II:
>
> God has thought it best for this humble servant, the poet of your noble house, to follow the light of the unrivaled luminary, the blessed al-Būṣīrī, the master of the celebrated qasida known as al-Burdah in praise of the best of all mankind, Muḥammad, pbuh. So I have composed this poem, which I ask Allāh and implore his Messenger to accept, and I have made it, my Lord, to commemorate your blessed Ḥajj of the year 1327, that people might spread the news of it each time it is read. Our lord the distinguished professor, the Shaykh of al-Azhar University, Shaykh Salīm al-Bishrī, has graciously undertaken to provide a commentary on it for the people. Thus, blessing has been added to its verses from every source and its favorable reception by the king <u>is the utmost goal of the originality and the beauty of [its composition]</u> [AND/OR] <u>would be the most marvelous and generous [reward]</u> [underlining mine].[15]

The prose dedication is composed in a rhetorically ornate stylized idiom that is designed with the utmost precision to enhance the prestige and authority of the royal gift that the poet proffers. While employing the conventional formulae of self-abasement, Shawqī first invokes the *madīḥ nabawī* tradition of divine or prophetic inspiration (as we saw in the case of al-Būṣīrī, chapter 2). Further, he specifies that this divine mandate is to compose a *madīḥ nabawī* following the model of the unrivalled master of that genre, al-Būṣīrī, which, in the Arabic poetic context of the time, means that the poem is technically a *muʿāraḍah,* a contrafaction that follows the same rhyme (*mīm*) and meter (*al-basīṭ*), and that its first religious and literary objective is therefore to be pleasing and acceptable to Allāh and the Prophet. In keeping with the Islamic hierarchical structure, it is only then that Shawqī introduces the statement that the poem has been composed in commemoration of his patron's Ḥajj of 1327/1909 and that it is intended to perpetuate among the people the memory of that blessed event. To further buttress the Islamic credentials of the poem, Shawqī adds that none other than the Shaykh al-Azhar of the period, the Mālikī *muftī* Salīm al-Bishrī (1832–1917) has deigned to compose the accompanying commentary, Waḍaḥ al-Nahj (Light of the Way), to explicate the poetic text to the reading public.[16]

This ranked hierarchy of religious figures—Allāh, the Prophet, al-Būṣīrī as the master of the greatest of all *madāʾiḥ nabawiyyah,* the Khedive-as-ḥajjī (i.e., the legitimate Islamic ruler in the performance of his religious duty), and the Shaykh al-Azhar—thus serves to authorize the poetic text in the religious, literary, and political spheres, an authorization or guarantee that Shawqī terms *barakah* (blessing). The rhetorically complex final sentence seems to me to be intentionally ambiguous. In a manner that charmingly encapsulates the panegyric pact (the ritual exchange of poem for prize) while at the same time exhibiting the convention of asking for no reward but the patron's satisfaction, Shawqī's closing statement reads both as: "the king's favorable reception of the poem is the utmost goal of the originality and beauty of its composition" and/or "the king's favorable reception of the poem should take the form of the most marvelous and generous [reward]."

We can contextualize the prose dedication more broadly. On the one hand, Shawqī's choice of al-Būṣīrī's Burdah as his model is natural, for in this period the visit to the Prophet's grave in Medina was still an integral part of the Ḥajj ritual and was traditionally an occasion for the composition of *madīḥ nabawī.* What seems strange, however, is that despite the prose dedication, in which the poet expresses his intention that the patron's

Ḥajj will be remembered as often as people recite the poem, there is no mention of the patron or his Ḥajj in the text of the poem itself. In fact, Shawqī had already performed his panegyric obligation of celebrating and commemorating his patron's Ḥajj in his *tāʾiyyah,* To [Mount] ʿArafāt, which takes as its themes the Khedive's Ḥajj to Mecca and subsequent visit to the tomb of the Prophet in Medina. Shawqī closes that poem, interestingly, by calling upon the Khedive to make a plea to the Prophet, bemoaning the backward and benighted state of the Islamic Ummah: "Your people . . . are in a deep slumber, like the Seven Sleepers snorting in their Den" (cf. QK 18:9 *Aṣḥāb al-Kahf*), and pleading for its awakening or revival.[17]

It is noteworthy that the prose dedication, which appears as the frontispiece of the original 1910 publication, is relegated in later editions of Nahj al-Burdah /Waḍaḥ al-Nahj to a footnote to al-Muwayliḥī's introduction, while in *Al-Shawqiyyāt* (as Shawqī's *dīwān* is conventionally titled), there is no mention at all of the occasion or patron.[18] That is, over time, the association of the Khedive with the poem has been obscured, omitted, and forgotten. Inasmuch as the normal celebratory or commemorative poem to one's patron is the *qaṣīdat al-madḥ*—the panegyric ode of praise to the patron—the fact is that in this case the earthly patron has been replaced as the *mamdūḥ* by the Prophet. What I would like to suggest is that there are political implications to not naming one's patron in a poem ostensibly dedicated to him: as we shall see from the poem itself, the poet does not place any political hopes in his patron nor, as is otherwise standard for a court poet, does he offer any praise of the patron or his rule. This is both very telling and very clever on the poet's part, for the Khedive could certainly not complain about the Prophet displacing him, and Shawqī's dedication declares that it was Allāh's bidding that he compose a *madīḥ nabawī* following al-Būṣīrī. As we noted, the Islamic credentials of the poem are further enhanced by the commentary by the Shaykh al-Azhar of the time, Salīm al-Bishrī. And yet in political terms, the Prophet as *mamdūḥ* and an idealized vision of past Islamic glory have completely displaced the court poet's contemporary patron and any expression of praise for or approval of his rule. In all, this suggests that Shawqī's dedication of Nahj al-Burdah to the Khedive in commemoration of his Ḥajj of 1909/1327 goes beyond performing the obligatory ceremony of allegiance incumbent upon a court poet; it further functions as an expedient to shield the poet from accusations of disloyalty or sedition that the poem's contents might invite.

In sum, in light of the 1,500-year court panegyric tradition of which Shawqī was the last great exemplar, his silence within the poetic text itself on the subject of the poem's proclaimed dedicatee and patron is telling. As I have demonstrated at length elsewhere, the principal role of the court panegyrist in the Arab-Islamic tradition is to substantiate and celebrate the legitimacy of his patron's rule.[19] Shawqī's silence on this subject in Nahj al-Burdah is therefore glaring. In fact, the poem as text does not do what the prose dedication says it is intended to do—i.e., immortalize the memory of the Khedive's Ḥajj. However prominent the placement of the dedication in the original 1328/1910 printing, by limiting mention of his patron to a prose dedication, Shawqī has made it not only distinct from, but also eminently detachable from, the poetic text—and this is precisely what happens in later editions and publications. In brief, over time any and all connection to the Khedive and his performance of the Ḥajj is lost.

The detachment of the compositional context from the poem in the case of Nahj al-Burdah is altogether in contrast to the inseparability of al-Būṣīrī's Burdah from the myth of the dream vision of the Prophet and the poet's cure, and from Kaᶜb ibn Zuhayr's Suᶜād Has Departed and the myth of the donation of the Prophet's mantle. In my reading, to the extent that the poem is at least for appearance's sake dedicated to ᶜAbbās Ḥilmī II, it functions as an unspoken but eloquent rebuke of the Khedive's rule—a virtual, or silent, *hijāʾ* (see below).

A final feature of the first printing of Nahj al-Burdah and its numerous reprintings is the introduction by the esteemed political journalist and litterateur (*adīb*) of the period, Muḥammad al-Muwayliḥī (1858?–1930). Most renowned for his *Ḥadīth ᶜĪsá ibn Hishām* (1907), the collection of his series of *maqāmāt*-inspired articles, originally published in his journal *Miṣbāḥ al-Sharq*, exposing the foibles of contemporary Egyptian society, al-Muwayliḥī himself was, as Roger Allen characterizes this work, for the most part Neo-Classical and conservative in his views. A staunch defender of Arab classicism in the face of the onslaught of Western—first French and then English Romantic—literature and literary theory on Arab letters, al-Muwayliḥī had ruthlessly attacked Shawqī in his reviews, also published in *Miṣbāḥ al-Sharq*. There he decried the young poet's first edition of *Al-Shawqiyyāt* (1898) for its espousal of Western (French) literary models such as Victor Hugo, Lamartine, and la Fontaine, whom he had read during his student years in France.[20] In this respect, Muwayliḥī's exuberant approbation in his Nahj al-Burdah introduction, with its defense of the timeless expressive capacities of the classical Arabic idiom in the face of Western-influenced modernists' claims that it is obsolete and inadequate, constitutes a Neo-Classical (or "Neo-Conservative") literary manifesto and, for Shawqī, imprimatur.[21]

THE COLONIAL DOUBLE BIND

A brief survey of the Egyptian political situation at the time of the composition of Nahj al-Burdah will, in my reading of the poem, shed light on Shawqī's silence on his patron's rule. Although under the British Agency Egypt experienced substantial material and economic improvements (regrettably at the expense of education, public health, etc.), particularly under the consulship of Lord Cromer (Sir Evelyn Baring, r. 1884–1907), it was otherwise in a state of political and cultural doldrums, as virtually all factions—the Ottomanists/pan-Islamists, the nationalists, the secularists—chafed under the British colonial yoke. The Khedive, although apparently nursing dreams of independently ruling Egypt, was in practical terms expecting to be deposed by the British Agency at any time (as in fact happened in 1914). Further, however trapped the Khedive was between the nominal suzerainty of the moribund Ottoman Sultan/Caliph (the notoriously despotic ʿAbd al-Ḥamīd II was deposed by the Young Turks in 1909 and replaced with Muḥammad V) and the actual control of the British Agency, nevertheless, the former guaranteed that Egypt could not be annexed, as India had been, into the British Empire. The French, to counter the influence of their British rivals, had supported the Khedive and the Nationalists, but the Anglo-French Entente of 1904 dashed any hopes of the French serving to end the British occupation. The Khedive, for his part, voiced support for Muṣṭafá Kāmil's Egyptian Nationalist Movement, inasmuch as it served as a threat to the Ottomans and British, but stopped short of espousing its idea of a constitutional monarchy, which did not accord with the Khedive's absolutist appetites.[22]

On the broader Egyptian scene, outside of the khedival court, the 1910 date of Nahj al-Burdah and its commentary Waḍaḥ al-Nahj by Shaykh Salīm al-Bishrī comes just four years after the crystallization of the Egyptian-British colonial experience in the notorious Dinshawāy Incident of May 1906 and its aftermath, and three years after Cromer's

1907 resignation, marked by his offensive and insulting Farewell Address.[23] Of the former, Hourani writes:

> the famous incident of Danishway (Dinshaway) brought to the surface the feeling of national humiliation. In 1906 a fight broke out between villagers of Dinshaway, near Tanta in the delta, and a group of British officers who were shooting pigeons in the neighborhood. Several officers were injured, and one died of shock and sunstroke; a peasant was beaten to death by the British soldiers who found the dead officer. Cromer was absent on leave, and those who were temporarily in charge lost their heads: a special court was set up, a number of peasants were condemned to be hanged, others to be flogged, and the sentences were carried out with barbarous publicity.[24]

The Egyptian reaction to the brutal and disproportionate British response (in a summary trial four villagers were condemned to be hanged, one to fifteen years in prison, others to shorter prison terms or flogging; the hangings and floggings were publicly carried out) is recorded in the oft-quoted remarks of Egyptian nationalist and reformer Qāsim Amīn:

> Every man I met had a broken heart and a lump in his throat. There was nervousness in every gesture—in their hands and their voices. Sadness was on every face, but it was a peculiar sort of sadness. It was confused, distracted and visibly subdued by superior force. . . . The spirits of the hanged men seemed to hover over every place in the city.[25]

Lord Cromer's Farewell Address was humiliating and patronizing: his statement that British control would need to continue indefinitely dashed hopes for Egyptian independence; his castigating the Egyptians for not showing gratitude to their British occupiers offended Egyptian sensibilities, as did his failure to mention the Khedive, the legitimate Islamic ruler of the land.[26]

If relations between the Khedive and Cromer (and later Kitchener, 1911–14) were unremittingly hostile, the rapprochement between him and the new consul general, Sir Eldon Gorst (r. 1907–11), who was under orders from the British Liberal government to give the Egyptian government more control over matters of policy and administration, did not entirely ease his situation. Rather, it opened the Khedive to more insistent attacks from the Nationalists for his conciliatory policy toward the British.

In the year 1910 itself, the political scene was dominated by the assassination on 10 February of Buṭrus Ghālī, the Coptic prime minister and a strong ally of the British, who had been the presiding judge in the Dinshawāy trial and who was now prepared to approve a British plan to extend the Suez Canal concession beyond 1968 for an additional forty years. The literary scene was dominated by the publication in July of the poetry collection, *Waṭaniyyatī* (My Patriotism), by the ardent nationalist and follower of Muṣṭafá Kāmil, ʿAlī al-Ghāyātī (d. 1956). The poems included vehement attacks on the British and Egyptian authorities, and the collection boasted three introductions: by Muḥammad Farīd, Muṣṭafá Kāmil's successor as leader of the National Party; ʿAbd al-ʿAzīz Shāwīsh, Kāmil's successor as editor of the party's paper, *Al-Liwāʾ*; and the poet himself. In August 1910 the three were brought to trial, convicted, and sentenced to imprisonment (for terms of six, three, and twelve months, respectively) for incitement against the government. Thus, al-Ghāyātī's *Waṭaniyyatī* provided Gorst with the occasion he had been looking for to crush the extreme wing of the Nationalist Party and its leaders.[27]

Beyond the political events and economic statistics, what is above all important is the moral condition of Egypt during the period of Shawqī's composition of Nahj al-Burdah. In this regard, I follow Husayn N. Kadhim in his astute choice of Albert Hourani's summation of the common characteristics of British and French control of Arab peoples in the nineteenth and twentieth centuries:

> First of all, it was imposed by acts of force, in opposition to such articulate political feeling as existed. In Egypt British control was imposed by the defeat of an inept but genuine national movement against older alien domination [the ʿUrābī Revolt, 1882]. . . . Secondly, this foreign control was not established primarily for the sake of the inhabitants of the Arab countries themselves. . . . What was important for them was the land and its resources. Those who happened to occupy the land were at best instruments for, at worst obstacles in the way of, purposes which were no concern of theirs. . . . Thirdly, foreign control was not only imposed by acts of force; it was always maintained by force. . . . It is this imposition of an alien rule upon an unwilling people which is called "imperialism." . . . The essence of imperialism is to be found in a moral relationship—that of power and powerlessness—and any material consequences which spring from it are not enough to change it.[28]

In light of this background, the categorization of Nahj al-Burdah under the rubric of Shawqī's *Islāmiyyāt,* as is sometimes done, must not blind us to its eminently political circumstances and polemical intent.

As we shall see, Shawqī's poem and the vitriolic political-polemical passages of al-Bishrī's commentary constitute an eloquent and cogent Arab-Islamic response to the moral and political double bind of a nation trapped between the moral and material decay of the Ottoman Muslim East on the one hand and the hypocrisy and oppression of the Christian West on the other. It is this situation of political and cultural paralysis, despondency, and humiliation that Shawqī's Nahj al-Burdah addresses and that his Iḥyāʾ Project of revival seeks to remedy.

We should also keep in mind that Arab literary modernism (*tajdīd*) of early twentieth-century Egypt, often termed Pre-Romantic, was espoused at this time by the Lebanese-born Khalīl Muṭrān (1872–1949). In his Neo-Classical poems Shawqī is moving against this growing trend, which would soon find more vocal support in the English and French Romantic-based movement composed of the triumvirate of Ibrāhīm al-Māzinī (1890–1949), ʿAbd al-Raḥmān Shukrī (1886–1958), and Maḥmūd ʿAbbās al-ʿAqqād (1889–1964), later named the Dīwān School after the 1921 publication of their literary manifesto of that title. Although in 1910 this movement was still in a formative stage, in the coming years the Dīwān School, especially al-ʿAqqād, would launch a sustained and virulent attack on Shawqī's Neo-Classicism as artificial, reactionary, and alienated from contemporary life and experience.[29] In this respect, Nahj al-Burdah, like Shawqī's other *muʿāraḍāt* of Classical Arabic masterpieces, should be understood as a challenge, not merely to the poet's Classical and Post-Classical forebears, but to his contemporary Modernist rivals as well.

Shawqī's Nahj al-Burdah: The Thematic Structure

The thematic structure of Shawqī's Nahj al-Burdah can best be understood through a comparison with that of the poem he has explicitly taken as his model or base-text, al-Būṣīrī's Burdah. As we saw in chapter 2, al-Būṣīrī's Burdah is traditionally, though not originally or always, divided into ten thematic sections, which for the purposes of a thematic and structural overview provide a useful starting point and frame of reference. Badr al-Dīn Muḥammad al-Ghazzī (d. 984/1577) in his commentary, *Al-Zubdah fī Sharḥ al-Burdah,* labels the sections as follows (emphasis mine):

Al-Būṣīrī's Burdah: Thematic Parts

1: Prophetic Nasīb (vv. 1–11) = lyric-elegiac prelude
2: Warning against the Desires of the Willful Self (vv. 11–28)
3: Praise of the Noble Messenger (vv. 29–58)
4: His Birth (vv. 59–71)
5: His Miracles (vv. 72–87)
6: The Noble Qurʾān (vv. 88–104)
7: The Night Journey and Ascension (vv. 105–117)
8: The Messenger's Jihād and Military Campaigns (vv. 118–139)
9: Supplication and Plea for Intercession (vv. 140–151)
10: Fervent Prayer and Petition (vv. 152–160)[30]

In chapter 2, on al-Būṣīrī's Burdah, I proposed that parts 1, 2, 3, 9 and 10 constitute that traditional structural framework of a courtly ode of supplication to which the Sīrah-related passages of parts 4–8 have been added as an extension of the *madīḥ* (praise) section. As Shawqī is avowedly following the example of the "Master of the Burdah," (in his prose dedication, above, and NB v. 101), we can assume that he is intimately aware of the structure of his model—even though he would not have expressed that awareness in the same terms as our contemporary studies—and undoubtedly he was familiar with the traditional division of the Burdah into ten thematic parts. With this in mind and, first, with the intention of revealing the structural and thematic relationship of Shawqī's poem to al-Būṣīrī's and, second, for the practical expedient of providing a structural and thematic overview of Shawqī's 190-line poem, I have divided Nahj al-Burdah into the following twelve parts and, as will be discussed below, two movements.

Shawqī's Nahj al-Burdah: Thematic Parts

Movement I: In the Path of al-Būṣīrī
1: Nasīb: Complaint of Unrequited Love (vv. 1–24)
2: Chiding the Unruly Soul—Warning against Worldly Temptations (vv. 25–38)
3: Repentance, Submission, and Supplication (vv. 39–46)
4: Prophetic Praise (vv. 46/7–74)
5: Sīrah Themes (vv. 75–99)
The Birth of the Prophet (vv. 75–82)
The Night Journey and Ascension (vv. 83–93)
The Miracle of the Cave (v. 94–99)
6: Metapoetic Recapitulation of Prophetic Praise (vv. 100–117)

Movement II: Deviation and Transformation
7: Polemic against Christians/Christianity (vv. 118–128)
8: Defense/Praise of Jihād and the Prophet's Military Campaigns (vv. 129–141)
9: The Sharīʿah (vv. 142–154)
10: The Glory of Baghdād (vv. 155–164)
11: The Orthodox Caliphs (vv. 165–176)
12: Benediction and Supplication (v. 177–190)

As the italics in the above list indicate, parts 1, 2, 3, 9, and 10 of al-Būṣīrī's Burdah, which constitute what I have termed the supplicatory framework of the poem, find their counterparts in parts 1, 2, 3, 4, 6, and 12 of Shawqī's Nahj al-Burdah. The sequence of supplicatory ode elements in Shawqī's poem is approximately: 1) Lyric-Elegiac Prelude (*nasīb*, consisting of the complaint of unrequited passion and resolving with chiding the self/soul and warning it against earthly temptations; 2–3) the poet's Self-Abasement and Supplication (repentance and submission) to the *mamdūḥ*/Prophet; 4) Praise of the *mamdūḥ*/Prophet; and, as we saw in al-Būṣīrī's Burdah, 5) Benediction with supplication, that is, asking for God's blessing upon the *mamdūḥ*/Prophet, etc. It should be noted here that, as we saw in chapter 2 for medieval *madīḥ nabawī* of the type of al-Būṣīrī's Burdah, the object of supplication is invariably (though not exclusively) the intercession (*shafāʿah*) of the Prophet on Judgment Day and, therefore, the gist of the supplicatory rite that the poem entails is the exchange of the poet's praise today for the Prophet's future intercession (see part 3, below).

As we shall see, Shawqī both complies with and transcends the dictates of the traditional form. Furthermore, Shawqī incorporates counterparts to what I have termed the Sīrah-related sections of al-Būṣīrī, i.e., Burdah parts 4–7, although in a truncated form, in what I have labeled as Nahj al-Burdah part 5. However, Būṣīrī's part 8, on the Prophet's jihād or military campaigns, takes on a new structural position in Shawqī's poem, where it forms part of the new extended political-polemical section that Shawqī has introduced into the traditional *madīḥ nabawī*—parts 7–11.

In sum, then, a comparison of the thematic structure of the two poems reveals that Shawqī has incorporated the main structural and thematic components of al-Būṣīrī's Burdah in parts 1–6 and 12 of his Nahj al-Burdah. He has then introduced a new extended section, parts 7–11, including a counterpart of al-Būṣīrī's part 8, in which he presents his own new political polemic against the Christian West and proposes, to counter Western military, political, cultural, and moral hegemony, a competing model for an Arab-Islamic hegemony grounded in a humanistic (re)vision of early Islam, the Sharīʿah, and the ʿAbbāsid Golden Age. Finally, in what is undoubtedly the most moving poetic and political achievement of Nahj al-Burdah, Shawqī closes his poem with a resounding plea, not for mercy on Judgment Day, but for the restoration of Islamic worldly dominion. This allows us to divide Shawqī's Nahj al-Burdah, for the sake of discussion and analysis, into two movements: movement I, in which the poet for the most part follows al-Būṣīrī's Burdah, and movement II, in which he departs from his model to redirect the poem toward his Iḥyāʾ Project of revival. A fuller comparison with specific points in al-Būṣīrī's Burdah follows in the discussion of the individual parts of Nahj al-Burdah.

Nahj al-Burdah Movement I: In the Path of al-Būṣīrī—Parts 1–6

The Way of the Mantle by Aḥmad Shawqī[31]

PART 1: *NASĪB:* COMPLAINT OF UNREQUITED LOVE (VV. 1–24)

1. On the plain between the ban-tree and the peak, a pale fawn
Has found it licit, in forbidden months, to shed my blood.

2. With the glance of fawn's eyes fate has shot a lion:
O gazelle of the plain, slay the lion of the thicket!

3. When the gazelle turned its gaze upon me, my soul said to me,
"Alas! Your heart has been struck by well-aimed arrow!"

4. I denied what my soul said and hid the arrow in my heart.* [*lit. "liver"]
For me, the wounds of lovers caused no pain.

5. You are endowed with the noblest of virtues
If you seek excuses for the sins of others.

6. O you who blame me for this love, though love is fate,
If passion so emaciated you, you would not be so quick to censure me.

7. I have lent you my ear, but it pays no heed;
For often, though the ear can hear, the heart is deaf.

8. O you with drowsy eye, may you never taste passion!
You've kept your lover awake, pining over passion, so sleep!

9. A thousand times would I be your ransom, and your
   night-phantom's, too,
Though the love that made you miserly to me has made it generous.

10. Your phantom came to me by night, found a bleeding wound,
   and healed it.
How many gifts do dreams to lovers bring!

11. Among the maidens that sway like ban-trees on a hill and, like
   spear-shafts, quiver,
Are those who make sport of my soul and spill my blood,

12. Those who, in the late morning, reveal faces like full moons,
Who, with their jewels and necklaces, stir to jealousy the
   forenoon sun,

13. Those who, with eyelids sick with languor, slay their lover—
For love-sickness is well-known to lead to death,

14. Those who trip over the hearts of men, and there is nothing
That can steady the coquettish tripping of their gait,

15. Those who inflame men's cheeks until they glow, revealing
The infatuation that inflames their hearts,* [*lit. "livers"][32]

16. Those who bear the banner of beauty, which,
However varied in its forms, is one and indivisible,

17. Every maiden, pale or dusky, adorned to the eye's delight,
For beauty is found in both the white gazelle and tawny
   mountain-goat,

18. How strange that they are frightened by a mere raised glance,
They who merely by pointing their ʿanam-twig fingers can capture
   the lion.

19. I abased my cheek to the gazelles and divided my heart among
   them in the hills;
In their coverts they grazed upon my heart, and on the rises.

20. O daughter of the full-maned lion of the well-guarded lair,
Shall I meet you in the forest or the palace?

21. I did not know, till I saw where he lived,
That death and desire pitch their tents in the same camp.

22. How did a swaying bough spring from a keen blade?
How did a white gazelle issue from a ravening lion?

23. Between you—my beloved—and me, brown spears block the way,
And likewise an ʿUdhrī veil of chastity.

24. I have never visited your abode, except in the folds of slumber;
Your abode, for him who desires you, is more distant than
many-columned Iram.

[60]

The challenge of the poet who chooses to imitate a great masterpiece is to evoke the power and majesty of the original while at the same time establishing his own distinct poetic identity. If we understand poetic imitation as a type of performance of the base-text, we must accept as well that every successful imitation, like every successful performance, transforms and transcends the base-text. The critical issue for discussing the opening section of Nahj al-Burdah is how Aḥmad Shawqī identifies Nahj al-Burdah with al-Būṣīrī's Burdah while establishing at the same time its, and his, own unique identity. We will take as our starting point Gian Biagio Conte's remarks on classical Greek and Latin poetry:

> [T]he "incipit" of poems . . . had all the importance of a title or heading; its function was that of the author's "signature." . . . [T]he opening of a work boasts a supreme position in composition because it is particularly memorable and *quotable* and is consequently an indispensable guide to interpretation for both reader and philologist. But for the author, poetic memory implicit in the opening verses is redeemed by the way it invests the very substance of the work with a literary identity. It is the quintessential literary act. The opening situates the poetic act and by situating it justifies it. The opening is, first and foremost, a bold signal asserting, "This is Poetry," because for our cultural tradition this is the way poetry begins. Once the word has issued from the living voice of the poet's personal invention and has entered the code of poetic tradition, it has the responsibility of imposing the emblematic *quality* of poetry upon its new host discourse. . . . The first line . . . acquires emblematic value and can stand for the work itself. . . . [I]t signals . . . the relation between a specific composition and its literary genre.[33]

The *incipit,* in the classical Arabic tradition the rhymed hemistichs of the opening verse, announces multiple aspects of the poem's identity. First, the rhymed hemistichs in the meter *basīṭ* identify the speech in terms of sonority as the opening line of a classical Arabic poem. The motif of a fawn shedding the poet-lover-speaker's blood identifies verse 1 as the opening of a *nasīb* dominated by the erotic or amatory (*tashbīb*) theme (as opposed to the elegiac icon of the abandoned campsite [*aṭlāl*] theme), modeled on an ʿAbbāsid conceit, and suggests that the poem is, potentially at least, a full-fledged *qaṣīdah* of traditional form. The antithesis (*ṭibāq*) between "licit" and "forbidden" further suggests the influence of the High ʿAbbāsid *badīʿ* style. As quickly becomes apparent, the heavily rhetoricized and conceptualized expression of the *nasīb* theme of the unattainability of the beloved throughout part 1 establishes Shawqī's Neo-Classical identification with the High ʿAbbāsid master poets. This broad sense of poetic ancestry and possibilities quickly yields, however, to a much more precise poetic genealogy: the combination of the meter *basīṭ* and the rhyme in the letter *mīm* already alludes to the most popular poem of the period, al-Būṣīrī's Burdah, but the phrase *al-bāni wa-al-ʿalami*, "the ban-tree and the mountain peak," explicitly identifies the new poem with its base-text, al-Būṣīrī's Burdah verse 5, and its base-text, Ibn al-Fāriḍ's Ṣūfī *ghazal,* Was That Laylá's Fire, verse 1 (see chapter 2). Ibn al-Fāriḍ's *ghazal* is further invoked by the second half of Shawqī's opening verse: "Has found it licit, in forbidden months, to shed my blood" *(ʾaḥalla safka damī fī al-ʾashhuri al-ḥurumi)*, which closely echoes that of the Ṣūfī poet's verse 17: "To shed my blood in both profane and sacred months" (*ʾaftá bi-safki damī fī al-ḥilli wa-al-ḥarami*). At the same time, of course, Shawqī is identifying his poem as one of the entire subgenre of *madīḥ nabawī* that takes the form of *muʿāraḍāt* of al-Būṣīrī's Burdah, whether explicitly *badīʿiyyāt* that programmatically exemplify a *badīʿ* device in each verse, or not.[34] Nevertheless, Shawqī's opening verse is strikingly different from al-Būṣīrī's, thereby staking out the new poet's original turf at the same time that he identifies his base-text.

In developing the ʿAbbāsid "hunt of love" conceit, in which the apparently weak and passive gazelle/beloved "slays" the mighty lion-poet, Shawqī stakes out his own individual poetic territory (vv. 1–5), distinct from both al-Būṣīrī's likewise ʿAbbāsid conceit of weeping tears of blood and Ibn al-Fāriḍ's Umayyad ʿUdhrī-derived "lightning-flash" that evokes the memory of the beloved. Nevertheless, at verse 6, with the poet's reproof of the blamer who censures him for his excessive passion, he forcefully reasserts his poetic lineage through this close variant of al-Būṣīrī's verse 9, itself a close variant of Ibn al-Fāriḍ's verse 10 (see chapter 2). Shawqī's verse 7, on lovers' deafness to sound advice, is likewise a close variant of al-Būṣīrī's verse 11. Shawqī then expands in verses 9–10 upon al-Būṣīrī's verse 8 one-line reference to the motif of the phantom of the beloved (*ṭayf al-khayāl*) before dilating further and with exquisite lyricism upon the lethal beauty of the gazelles/maidens (vv. 11–19). He then adds to this extended "hunt of love" another ʿAbbāsid conceit, that of the gazelle/maiden as the daughter of a fierce lion/father (vv. 20–22). Part 1 concludes on the theme of the dangers of love, and the how fulfillment of the lover's desires has been doubly blocked—by the beloved's kinsmen's spears and by her veil of chastity (v. 23). This leads to his sealing part 1 with the motif of the unattainable beloved (v. 24). Thus, in closing, Shawqī follows and develops al-Būṣīrī's verse 9 motif of chaste love, whereas al-Būṣīrī, for his part, concludes with reproach for both his censurer and himself (BB vv. 10–12).

The closure of Shawqī's *nasīb* exhibits a very curious transitional feature. Until verse 24, the *nasīb* has been purely lyric and erotic, with no religious—or Islamic—elements. It could just as well have served as the *nasīb* of a court panegyric. By closing it, however, with the Qurʾānic "the [many-]columned Iram" (*Irama dhati al-ʿimādi* [QK 89:7]), Shawqī creates a transition from the personal erotic loss and separation of lovers to the moral and mythic destruction of the pre-Islamic people of ʿĀd and their capital city of Iram, the object of divine retribution for their moral excesses. The Qurʾān warns: "Have you not seen how your Lord dealt with [the people of] ʿĀd of the many-columned Iram? . . . who committed transgressions in the lands and sowed much corruption in them, so that your Lord rained down on them the scourge of chastisement" (QK 89: 6–7, 11–13). This one word "Iram" thus serves as a pivot-point from the lyric-erotic *nasīb* to the moral admonitions of part 2.

In sum, Shawqī's part 1 is the more developed and the more lyrical of the two poems, and the emotional trajectory is somewhat different: al-Būṣīrī moves into the *ʿādhilah* (termagant, female reproacher) motif (vv. 9–12) to close his twelve-verse *nasīb,* whereas Shawqī develops the gazelle theme in delightful lyrical detail to end with an expression of the dangers and difficulties, both moral and practical, that make his desire/beloved unattainable. Although we may retroactively (after reading part 2) read this lyrical *nasīb* on the unattainability of the beloved and the poet's resultant suffering as an allegory of the vanity and unattainability of earthly desires, nothing forces us to do so at this point. To my mind, Shawqī's *nasīb* possesses an emotional immediacy and delicacy that mere allegory lacks. I prefer to look at it in a subtler light as the *introit* into the world of poetic emotions and sensibilities that, by evoking a deeply felt mood of loss and despair that begs for a remedy, sets the stage for the dramatic emotional and moral trajectory of the poem. Having clearly set his own poetic parameters and network of generic, historical, and stylistic identities, Shawqī has established his own authentic and authoritative poetic voice as well as the setting-off point for his poem's journey. Nahj al-Burdah "imitates" al-Būṣīrī's Burdah, but it does not reiterate it.

PART 2: CHIDING THE UNRULY SOUL—WARNING AGAINST WORLDLY TEMPTATIONS (VV. 25–38)

25. O my willful soul, your worldly abode conceals every tearful thing,
 However beautiful the smile that she reveals.

26. So break her teeth with your piety each time she laughs,
 As you would break the speckled viper's fangs to spill its venom.

27. She has been betrothed as long as mankind has existed, and betrothing;
 From time's beginning, she has never been widowed or unwed.

28. Time fades away, but her evil deeds remain
 A wound to Adam's flesh that forever makes him weep.

29. Don't be concerned with her fruits or with her crimes,
 For death with flowers is just like death with coals.

30. Many a man is asleep and does not see her, but she is ever wakeful.
 Were it not for hopes and dreams, he would not sleep.

31. At one time, she bestows on you prosperity and health;
 At another, she afflicts you with disease and misery.

32. How often has she led you astray! For, when she veils a man's sight,
 If he finds bitter colocynth, he drinks; if he finds acrid
 ʿalqam-plants, he grazes.

33. O woe is me for my soul! She is struck with fear and terror
 By the pages black with evil deeds on her white forelocks.

34. I raced her at a gallop to the lush pastures of disobedience and sin;
 I took no pious deeds to protect her from foundering.

35. She yearned after the traces of delight, seeking them;
 For the soul, when youthful passion calls, yearns after it.

36. For your own good, you must return to virtue;
 Straighten your soul with morals and it will follow the straight path.

37. It is best for the soul to graze on wholesome pasture-grounds;
The worst thing for the soul is to graze on noxious grass.

38. The soul, when emboldened by delight and passion,
Is as unruly as a fiery steed, champing at its bit.

[61]

With part 2 the tone of Nahj al-Burdah changes quite abruptly from the erotic lyrical-elegiac mood of the *nasīb* to that of a moral exhortation or admonition.[35] This may force us, retrospectively, to read part 1 allegorically, or at least to recognize that it has an allegorical level. Part 2 consists of a warning against worldly and fleshly temptations, much along the lines of al-Būṣīrī's part 2 but, again, longer. Al-Būṣīrī's sixteen-line part 2 contains the moral and emotional transition from admonition to repentance and submission. Shawqī, however, has expanded this process to what I have counted as two distinct passages: part 2 (vv. 25–38) and part 3 (vv. 39–45). These two Nahj al-Burdah passages differ strikingly in tone and style. Part 2 consists of traditional hortatory sermonizing (*waʿẓ*) couched in metaphors or allegories of physical appetites (e.g., vv. 37, 38) and the temptations they present to what I have translated as the "willful soul" (*nafs*), quite in keeping with al-Būṣīrī's model. In both poems, the reference is to the Qurʾānic Sūrat Yūsuf, *ʾinna al-nafsa la-ʾammāratun bi-al-sūʾi* (surely the willful soul commands one to do evil [QK 12:53]), although al-Būṣīrī keeps the willful self in the third person and addresses the reader, whereas Shawqī apostrophizes the soul/self. The result is that where al-Būṣīrī commands the reader, "Defy your wicked self and Satan, disobey them!" (al-Būṣīrī, v. 24), Shawqī, with, I believe, greater dramatic effect, urges the his self/soul against the world, "Break her teeth with your piety each time she laughs," (v. 26). This admonition continues until verse 33 with its plaintive "O woe is me for my soul! . . . ." Here Shawqī departs from al-Būṣīrī's metaphor of taming the soul in terms of weaning a child (BB v. 18) to develop as a metaphor for curbing the soul's appetites the breaking in of a horse, perhaps deriving from al-Būṣīrī's verse 20 with its image of grazing a steed. The effect of the depiction of youthful passion in terms of an unruly steed champing at the bit (NB vv. 35, 38), whatever its association with Platonic imagery, is, in the Arabic tradition, to evoke the oft-cited metaphor for the loss of youth and its impetuousness of the Jāhilī master Zuhayr ibn Abī Sulmá:

"And the steeds of youth and its camels have been stripped of their saddles" (*wa-ʿurriya ʾafrāsu al-ṣibā wa-rawāḥiluh*).[36] In both Shawqī and his predecessor al-Būṣīrī we thus find clearly articulated the classical *qaṣīdah* movement from the emotional and moral abandon of youthful passion to the realization of its futility and the concomitant shouldering of the responsibilities of maturity: self-control and the submission to a higher (moral) authority.

PART 3: REPENTANCE, SUBMISSION, AND SUPPLICATION (VV. 39–46)

39. If my sin is too grave to be forgiven,
    Yet I have hope that God will grant me the best of refuges.

40. When God the Savior appears in His terrible might, I will place my hope
    In Muḥammad, the dispeller of cares and sorrows in this world and the next.

41. When I lower the wing of submission before him, asking for the precious gift
    Of intercession, to him my request will be a paltry thing.

42. And if the pious man comes before him with good deeds,
    I will present before him tears of remorse.

43. I hereby cling to the door of Muḥammad, the Prince of Prophets,
    For he who holds tight to the key of God's door will prosper.

44. For every act of virtue, charity, or favor, whether performed freely
    Or compelled, comes through him.

45. I hereby grab tight to the rope of praise for him, which will avail me on a day
    When bonds of lineage and kinship are of no avail.

46. My poetry, when I praise the Prophet, disdains Zuhayr's,
    For the dew of Harim's gifts cannot compare with the bounty that will pour down on me.

[62]

At verse 39, part 3 is set off from part 2 by the change to the first person and by the abrupt transition from the hortatory tone of part 2 to a language that is highly emotively charged, simplified, transparent, and direct—stylistic qualities which, as I have demonstrated elsewhere, are characteristic of what we have termed the poem's "ritual core" (see chapters 1 and 2). Part 3 sets forth explicitly the ritual of supplication that constitutes the performative heart of the *madīḥ nabawī*, and in this respect part 3 of Shawqī's Nahj al-Burdah bears a close resemblance, poetically and ritually, to al-Būṣīrī's Burdah Part 9: Supplication and Plea for Intercession (BB vv. 140–151). It is essentially a ritual of exchange whereby a relationship of mutual obligation, the panegyric pact, is established: the poet offers submission to and praise of the Prophet in return for the Prophet's intercession on the Day of Judgment. With regard to the performative aspects of language, it is essential to realize that "repentance," "submission," and "supplication" are not the mere subjects or themes of part 3; they are, above all, speech acts whose (poetic) utterance changes the moral status of the poet (see chapters 1 and 2). The poet in uttering these lines is *ipso facto* performing those very acts of repentance, submission, and supplication that they entail. Furthermore we must keep in mind that this ritual is not unique to Shawqī, or even to *madīḥ nabawī* as a genre of devotional poetry, but is fully and extensively grounded in the structure of what we have termed the Supplicatory Ode, which was already fully developed in the Jāhiliyyah and, as early as Kaʿb ibn Zuhayr's Suʿād Has Departed, totally assimilated into the Islamic poetic tradition, for both courtly and religious purposes (see chapter 1).

It behooves us to examine these verses in detail. Verses 39–40 explicitly express the twinned emotions of hope and fear that are essential to the act of submission to the patron: through them the poet-supplicant throws himself on the patron's mercy. If there is no fear, there is no virtue in the poet's expression of hope. Self-abasement is also essential to the supplicatory ritual, and we find the poet performing his act of self-abasement most explicitly in verse 41, "When I lower the wing of submission . . ." where it is intimately tied to the object of supplication—"the most precious gift of intercession." The metaphoric expression "lower the wing of submission," or "humility" is of Qurʾānic provenance (QK 17:24), thus adding a spiritual dimension to the image of physical self-abasement. The shedding of "tears of remorse" of verse 42 is likewise a bodily enactment of remorse, not merely a verbal expression. But the "tears of remorse," like the "pious man's good deeds," are also the offering that the poet makes to the Prophet in a gift-exchange ritual to obtain his intercession. Al-Bishrī explains it thus:

"When the pious benefit from the good deeds that they have done beforehand and the virtuous acts that they have performed in advance, I will implore the Messenger of God (pbuh) with my weeping and remorse for my misdeeds, so that he will accept me and intercede for me" (WN v. 42). On a metapoetic level, of course, the "tears of remorse" that the poet presents to the Prophet are these very verses of poetry.

Graphic physical images and acts (i.e., bodily enactments or *performances*) of submission, self-abasement, and supplication continue in the following verses (vv. 43–45), which form an effective expansion and development of al-Būṣīrī's verse 37. Let us note first that the verbs *lazimtu* (43) and *ʿaliqtu* (45) are best understood in what Arab grammarians tell us is the performative use of the Perfect Tense, hence: "I hereby cling . . .," "I hereby grab tight . . ." graphically conveying in their physicality the strength of the moral and spiritual commitment that the poet is thereby establishing: the first, in the image of the supplicant clinging to the door of his patron; the second, a compelling encapsulation of the panegyric pact (cf. BB vv. 148–149). Paul Connerton's discussion of the performativity of physical postures will help us to grasp the rhetorical effectiveness of the "verbal acts" that the poet "performs." He says, taking kneeling as his example:

> To kneel in subordination is not to state subordination, nor is it just to communicate a message of submission. To kneel in subordination is to display it through the visible, present substance of one's body. Kneelers identify the disposition of their body with their disposition of subordination. Such performative doings are particularly effective, because unequivocal and substantial.[37]

The supplicatory intent of verse 43 is stated explicitly by al-Bishrī: "'Clinging to his door' is a metonymy (*kināyah*) for seeking refuge in his generosity and not ceasing to implore him to grant his requests" (WN v. 43). Verse 45 is striking for its performative immediacy as well as its metaphorical power: the praise of the Prophet, which the poet is at this instant uttering, is the figurative "rope" to which the poet clings. The verse, simple as it is in terms of diction, is rhetorically complex. The "rope" (*ḥabl*) to which the poet clings is first of all a metaphor for the "bond" of mutual obligation instituted by the praise-for-prize exchange of the panegyric pact (i.e., the poet's praise obligates the Prophet to grant intercession to him on Judgment Day, as discussed in chapter 2 in BB, part 9, vv. 140–151). This rope is also intended to contrast with the failed "bonds" of lineage and kinship, which, on Judgment Day, will be of no avail. At the same time, to hold tight to a rope (*ḥabl*) that guarantees salvation has the effect of identifying the act of *madīḥ nabawī* with the Qurʾānic "firm handle" (*al-ʿurwah al-wuthqá*), much as al-Būṣīrī has alluded to the use of this expression as an epithet for Muḥammad (see BB v. 37). Again, the performative aspects of these poetic utterances indicate that to compose *madīḥ nabawī* is not merely to compose a devotional poem; it is, moreover, in and of itself an "act of faith."

Finally, verse 46 follows the established convention of *madīḥ nabawī*, particularly that which imitates al-Būṣīrī in its rhyme and meter, of contrasting purely material and worldly panegyric pact, invariably exemplified by the pre-Islamic panegyrist Zuhayr ibn Abī Sulmá and his lavishly munificent patron Harim ibn Sinān (apparently aided by the suitability of "Harim" to the rhyme and meter), to the spiritual and otherworldly panegyric pact of *madīḥ nabawī* (see BB v. 151). In other words, the poet's praise poem to the Prophet is part of a ritual exchange for which the poet will receive as counter-gift a downpour of (spiritual) bounty (intercession on Judgment Day, salvation) that would put Harim ibn Sinān to shame.

Thus with great beauty, simplicity, and precision Shawqī has performed the supplicatory ritual and established the panegyric pact between poet and Prophet. In this respect verses 43–46 serve as the ritual and poetic preamble to the ensuing panegyric sections of Nahj al-Burdah, wherein the poet fulfills his end of the bargain by offering his gift of praise: parts 4, Prophetic Praise; 5, Sīrah Themes, which we can understand as an extension of the Prophetic Praise theme; and 6, Metapoetic Recapitulation of Prophetic Praise. These parts of Nahj al-Burdah constitute Shawqī's reprise of parts 3–7 of al-Būṣīrī's Burdah, namely: 3, Prophetic Praise; and the Sīrah-derived sections; 4, The Prophet's Birth; 5, His Miracles; 6, the Qurʾān; and 7, The Night Journey and Ascension—excluding Būṣīrī's Part 8, The Messenger's Jihād and Military Campaigns (see below, Nahj al-Burdah, part 8).

PART 4: PROPHETIC PRAISE (VV. 47–74)

47. Muḥammad, the chosen of the Creator, His mercy to mankind,
The goal of God's desire from among creation and mankind,

48. The Master of the Basin on the day when even God's Messengers are supplicants,
When the time has come for drink and even the trusty Jibrīl is thirsty.

49. The Prophet's majesty and glory are like the sun when it rises,
For the celestial orb runs high in its heavenly sphere, and yet its light illuminates the world below.

50. And even the stars in the heavens fall far short
Of his forefathers' lofty dominion and haughty mien.

51. When his forebears' lineage was traced to him, their nobility among men increased,
For sometimes the root is traced in glory to a branch!

52. Before their time he was preserved in two lights of "primordial adoration"[38]
The way a man is preserved in his ancestors' loins and wombs.

53. When the monk Baḥīrā beheld him, he said, "We recognize him
From the names and signs we have preserved."

54. Ask Mt. Ḥīrāʾ and [Jibrīl] the Holy Spirit, whether they knew
The guarded secret that was concealed from all but Muḥammad.

55. How often was Mecca's pebbled flood-plain honored
By his coming and going at morning and night!

56. How often did Muḥammad ibn ʿAbd Allāh desire seclusion with Mt. Ḥīrāʾ and Jibrīl
More than the company of friends and servants?

57. Waiting through the night for inspiration to descend,
For he who is given glad tidings is marked for great things.

58. When the Companions, out of thirst, called out for water,
A vessel-filling stream gushed forth from your two hands.

59. There shaded him, then came to seek the shade of his protection,
A cloud that was drawn along by the best of continuous rains.

60. A love for God's Messenger suffused the hearts of both
The monastery's cloistered monks and the hermit monks on mountain-tops.

61. For if one's character is gentle it can sway
Both obdurate rock and all creatures that have breath.

62. A voice called out to Muḥammad, "Recite!" Great is God the Speaker of these words,
Which, before they were revealed to him, had never crossed any man's lips.

63. Thereupon he called mankind to the Most Merciful
And filled the Meccans' ears with the pure tones of his voice.

64. Don't ask about Quraysh! How in their confusion
They fled to plain and mountain,

65. Asking each other, "What calamity has befallen us?!"
It left both young and old distraught.

66. O you impetuous fools [*jāhilīna*] who attack the Guide and his Call,
How can you ignore [*tajhalūna*] the rank of this great and truthful man?

67. In his youth you used to call him "Honest,"
And the word of an honest man is not to be doubted.

68. In beauty he exceeds the moon; in virtue, the prophets;
How great then are his form and character!

69. The other prophets brought miracles that are done and gone,
But you brought us a wisdom that is never ending—the Qurʾān.

70. Its miraculous verses, however much time passes, remain forever new,
Yet an ancient and primordial splendor adorns them still.

71. A single sublime utterance from it may suffice
To guide a man toward truth and piety and mercy.

72. O most eloquent of all who utter *ḍād*,* [* = the Arabs]
Your speech is honey to him who tastes and understands.

73. With its jewels you adorned the naked neck of eloquence
Until every phrase of prose bore poetic beauty.

74. With every noble word you utter, you revive men's hearts
And bring dead aspirations back to life.

[63]

As we have seen in the case of al-Būṣīrī's Burdah, the purpose of the praise section of *madīḥ nabawī* is not a random enumeration of laudable traits; rather, just as in Arab-Islamic court panegyric the poet's goal is to establish and confirm the unique authority and legitimacy of his patron as caliph or emir, etc., so in the case of *madīḥ nabawī*, the poet's aim in his praise is to establish the unique position of Muḥammad as the last and best of God's prophets. Further, as in caliphal panegyric the poet sought to prove his patron's supreme position as ruler of the Islamic Ummah vis-à-vis rival claimants, whether within or without Islamdom, so too in *madīḥ nabawī*, the poet's goal is to establish the prophethood of Muḥammad and the truth of Islam and its superiority over its main contenders for religious truth—that is, Judaism, or more explicitly in the case of Nahj al-Burdah, Christianity, as the religion of Western imperialism and colonialism. In reading this section, then, we will see that Shawqī is not merely establishing the authority and truth of Muḥammad's prophecy, but effecting a transition from prophetic praise to the Iḥyāʾ Project of Arab-Islamic cultural revival which lays the groundwork for the later more explicitly polemical and political parts of Nahj al-Burdah (parts 7–12).

Shawqī opens the praise section (v. 47) invoking Muḥammad's unique position as Allāh's Chosen One (as his epithet Muṣṭafá conveys, here alluded to in the noun of the same root, *ṣafwah*), that Allāh sent him as an act of mercy to mankind (*wa-mā ʾarsalnāka ʾillā raḥmatan lil-ʿālamīna* [QK 21:107]), and, in accord with the tenets surrounding the doctrines of al-Ḥaqīqah al-Muḥammadiyyah (the Muḥammadan Truth), the idea that Muḥammad is the ultimate goal or purpose of Allāh's creation (see below v. 52). He then turns in v. 48 to Muḥammad's position on Resurrection Day when, as his epithet Ṣāḥib al-Ḥawḍ al-Mawrūd (Master of the Watering-Basin) indicates, he will preside over a basin.[39] This doctrine is not based in the Qurʾānic text, except inasmuch as the Ḥawḍ comes to be identified with the paradisical spring of Kawthar, but rather in Ḥadīth. It is said that the Ummah will gather there on Resurrection Day. While the details are unclear, we can gather from the general symbolism of this figure that water represents life, that is, salvation, and that Muḥammad plays a crucial role in dispensing it, with even other Messengers or Prophets coming to him as supplicants (WN v. 48).[40] Again, Muḥammad's superiority over other Prophets and Messengers is the crucial point here.

The next two verses (49–50) shift from theological to ʿAbbāsid-style poetic-astrological images to describe Muḥammad with the paradox of the sun—that is at once the highest orb in the distant heavens, yet its light illumines the earth below; likewise, the stars fall short of his lofty ancestry.[41] With this, the poet shifts to the Prophet's noble ancestry (v. 51), which was, of course, further ennobled by its glorious descendent, to conclude (v. 52) with Muḥammad's supernatural antecedents—that is the (Post-Classical) doctrines of al-Nūr al-Muḥammadiyyah (the Muḥammadan Light) and the related al-Ḥaqīqah al-Muḥammadiyyah (the Muḥammadan Truth, the Archetypal, Pre-Existent Muḥammad; see chapter 2, BB v. 33). Al-Bishrī explains:

> It is related that God Almighty created the Muḥammadan Truth (*al-ḥaqīqah al-muḥammadiyyah*) from His light and that it revolved around the throne, and the lights of His epiphanies flooded over it; and those are the two lights which contained Muḥammad, pbuh, before he was contained in the loins and wombs of his ancestors. . . . ʿAbd al-Razzāq related that Jābir ibn ʿAbd Allāh al-Anṣārī said: I said, "Oh Messenger of God, by my father and mother, tell me about the first thing that God Almighty created before all other things!" He replied, "O Jābir, before all other things, God Almighty created the light of your Prophet from His light." (WN v. 52)

With verse 53 Shawqī returns to the Sīrah lore of the predictions of Muḥammad's coming, especially that of the Christian monk Baḥīrā. Al-Bishrī cites a tradition related by al-Bayhaqī and Abū Nuʿaym that the monk Baḥīrā was in his cell when he saw Muḥammad among a group of approaching riders, and a white cloud was shading him alone. They approached until they alighted in the shade of a tree near where Baḥīrā was, whereupon the branches of the tree bent to provide shade for Muḥammad. So Baḥīrā queried him about certain signs he had read about and found that Muḥammad agreed with the descriptions in the predictions, and he saw the seal of prophethood on his shoulder as had been predicted. Thereupon he embraced him and declared that this was the prophet whose coming the signs foretold (WN v. 53).

The theme of Muḥammad's coming being foretold in the Torah and the Gospels (*al-Tawrāh wa-al-Injīl*) had long been a potent element of Muslim polemic against the Christians and Jews. The prophet foretold by Moses in Deut. 18:5 ("The LORD thy God will raise up unto thee a Prophet from the midst of thee, of thy brethren, like unto me; unto him ye shall hearken"; King James Version) is identified by Muslims as Muḥammad. Under the name of Aḥmad, an etymological variant of Muḥammad, he is identified with the Biblical *paracletos* (counselor, helper), read by Muslims as *pericletos* (most praiseworthy = *aḥmad*), of John 14:16 ("And I will pray the Father, and he shall give you another Comforter, that he may abide with you for ever"; King James Version). Hence in the Qurʾān we read, "Those who follow the Messenger, the unlettered Prophet, whom they find written of among them in the Torah and the Gospel. . . ." (QK 7:157), and "When Jesus the son of Maryam said: O Children of Israel, I am the Messenger of God, confirming what came before me in the Torah and proclaiming the glad tidings of a Messenger who will come after me whose name is Aḥmad. . . ." (QK 61: 6; WN v. 60).[42] These predictions surrounding the name Aḥmad and physical signs such as the "seal of prophethood" mark on the shoulder, then, are what the poet succinctly conveys in verse 53 with the *jinās* between the phonetically and semiotically proximate *asmāʾ* (names; s. *ism,* root *s-m-y*) and its metathetic mate *siyam* (signs; s. *sīmah,* root *s-y-m*).

Verses 54–57 and 62–67 offer a summation of Muḥammad's divine revelation and mission to the doubting Meccans or Qurashīs. Shawqī begins by evoking Muḥammad's long period of waiting in the cave on Mount Ḥirāʾ for divine revelation to come to him through Jibrīl (the archangel Gabriel). As al-Bishrī notes, Muḥammad had to spend a doubt-filled and anxious thirty-six months of prayer from the initial revelation, "Recite in the name of your Lord. . . ." (QK 96:1), until Jibrīl appeared to him and cried, "You are truly the Messenger of God," and then a further period of waiting until he received the revelation "O you who are wrapped in your cloak, rise and warn [mankind]" (QK 74:1), whereupon he began his prophetic mission (WN v. 57).

This is followed by two verses of popular Sīrah-derived "standard miracles," of which al-Bishrī tells us there are many examples and/or variants, of water gushing from the Prophet's two hands (v. 58) and of a cloud following over the Prophet's head to shade him (WN v. 58). Within the poetic, as opposed to narrative prose, formulation of these events, however, a symbolic meaning emerges. The thirst of the Prophet's companions, especially in the context of verse 48, becomes a spiritual thirst, and his quenching their thirst thus becomes a spiritual life-giving, adumbrating the Prophet's powers of revival with which this section culminates (v. 73). Similarly, "the best of continuous rains" of verse 59 takes on the standard Arabic poetic connotation to refer to the Prophet's unequalled generosity and magnanimity.[43]

Verses 60–61 take up once more the persuasive effect of Muḥammad's mission on Christian monks—again a powerful polemical element in the colonial context. This continues with verses 62–67, which ostensibly relate to Muḥammad's efforts to convert the Meccans and his tribe Quraysh but would seem in the present colonial context to refer to all who would foolishly reject the Prophet's message. For example, verse 66 combines root-play on *jāhilīn* (ignorant) and *tajhalūn* (ignore) to imply the falsehood and error of the Jāhiliyyah (Age of Ignorance, i.e., the pre-Islamic period) with a double antithesis, first with *al-hādī* (the guide, also an epithet of the Prophet) and *al-ṣādiq* (truthful). The verse is addressed in its immediate context to the Meccan or Qurashī polytheists but, by extension, equally and allegorically to the poet's contemporaries who ignore or deny the true faith.

The remaining verses of this section, 68–74, focus in on the uniqueness of Muḥammad's message and miracle, which are one. That is, in keeping the Islamic doctrine of Iʿjāz al-Qurʾān (the unsurpassable rhetorical beauty of the Qurʾān), it is the divine origin of the Qurʾān revealed to Muḥammad that is the essential proof of his Prophethood, in addition to which he possesses among his *shamāʾil*, or virtues, extraordinary personal eloquence. In this respect, verse 69 echoes al-Buṣīrī's Burdah verses 91–93 in propounding a key element of Iʿjāz al-Qurʾān, namely that while other prophets' miracles—such as Moses' changing a staff into a serpent or Jesus' raising the dead—are one-time occurrences that are now over, the miraculous rhetorical power of the Qurʾān is eternal and permanently effective. That is, as Shawqī states in verse 69, the *āyāt* (s. *āyah*; the word means both "Qurʾānic verses" and "miracles"), are ancient, indeed pre-eternal, and at the same time forever new—that is, forever efficacious, so that even a single word or sentence may lead a man to "truth, piety, and mercy," that is, salvation. To exemplify this last proposition, al-Bishrī adduces the renowned episode of the conversion of the Meccan oligarch al-Walīd ibn al-Mughīrah (father of the illustrious general of the Islamic conquests, Khālid ibn al-Walīd). Upon hearing Muḥammad recite: "God commands justice, good deeds, and generosity to one's kin, and He forbids foul deeds, loathsome acts, and injustice, admonishing you so that perhaps you will take heed" (QK 16:90), he said, "By God, [these words] possess a sweetness and elegance, the least of which is a copious downpour, the best of which is abundant fruit. Surely these are not the words of a mere mortal," whereupon he converted to Islam (WN v. 71). The continued efficacy of Muḥammad's message is, of course, the crux of Shawqī's message in Nahj al-Burdah.

Shawqī closes part 4 with a poignant and powerful three-verse (72–74) apostrophe to the Prophet in which he brings the precept of the eternal veracity and efficacy of Muḥammad's miracle—the Qurʾān—and the Prophet's own personal eloquence to bear on the present condition of the Islamic Ummah. What is essential here is the identification of eloquence—and in these verses the poet has shifted from the Qurʾān itself to Muḥammad's own personal eloquence—with the power to revive. This curative, restorative power of the beauty/truth of Muḥammad's eloquence is first introduced in verse 72 in calling his speech "honey" or "honeycomb" (*shahd*). As al-Bishrī astutely points out, "honey" is intended here not merely to convey the sweetness and beauty of Muḥammad's speech, but also its properties as a spiritual restorative, that is, his words cure the soul just as honey is used medicinally to cure the body (WN v. 72). Shawqī adds rhetorical intensity to create a sense of momentum as he reaches the climax and closure of part 4. Employing a double *ṭibāq* (adorned/naked// prose/poetry), he praises the eloquence of Muḥammad as so powerful that his prose utterances have all the beauty of poetry (v. 73). Finally, the poet brings all his rhetorical might to bear in the closing verse of part 4 (v. 74), where, through the root-play on "word/utter" (*qawl/qāʾil*), intensifying repetition of *tuḥyī* (revive, bring back to life), and the antithesis between life and death (*tuḥyī/mayyit*), he drives home his message of the revival of the spiritually dead and politically moribund Islamic Ummah through the word of the Prophet (cf. BB v. 46; NB vv. 116 and 190).

Further, we should note that *himam* (aspirations, sing. *himmah*) of the phrase *tuḥyī mayyita al-himami* ("revive dead aspirations," lit.: "those whose aspirations are dead") is a literarily and culturally loaded term rooted as far back as Jāhilī poetry. It denotes determination, ambition, and resolution, with an energetic forward-looking zeal that distinguishes it diametrically from its root-mate *hamm*, pl. *humūm*, which denotes paralyzing cares and anxieties. The choice of *himam*, then, in this context points toward quite worldly political and military ambitions, as indeed al-Bishrī comments: that the words of the Prophet "made the ambitions (*himam*) of his Companions and Successors reach the Gemini, until kingdoms became subject to them and difficult obstacles were easily overcome" (WN v. 74). What is above all important in the context of the present argument is that Shawqī has mustered carefully chosen elements of traditional *madīḥ nabawī* to bring them at last to bear on his climactic conclusion: that the Prophet Muḥammad's words (that is, Qurʾān and Ḥadīth Nabawī) are a source for Islamic political and cultural revival.

A further level of discourse is at play here as well. Inasmuch as Shawqī is a, or the, leading proponent of the school of poetry termed Iḥyāʾ (Revival; conventionally translated as Neo-Classical), his reiterative insistence on its verbal form *tuḥyī* (revive) should alert us to the fact that this poem, indeed the entire project of the Shuʿārāʾ al-Iḥyāʾ (Poets of the Revival), is not the mere resuscitation of classical Arabic poetry and language, but above all, the revitalization of a moribund Arab-Islamic civilization through the recuperation of the cultural values of the classical (normally the High ʿAbbāsid Golden Age) period. Furthermore, then, Shawqī sees himself as the poetic counterpart of the Prophet in the Iḥyāʾ Project. In this respect, verse 74, as indeed its rhetorical highlighting indicates, is a key structural marker in the poem, pointing the way to the polemical-political sections of parts 7–12.

PART 5: SĪRAH THEMES (VV. 75–99)

[The Birth of the Prophet]

75. Glad tidings of the Guide and his birth spread east and west,
Like light that penetrates the dark of night,

76. It snatched the blood from Arab despots' hearts,
And put to flight the foreign tyrants' souls.

77. It so alarmed the battlements of Īwān Kisrá that they cracked,
From the shock of truth, not the shock of bold warriors' advance.

78. When you came you found mankind in chaos,
Like stone idols enthralled by stone idols,

79. And the earth was filled with injustice
And subjected to every despot who held sway over mankind.

80. The Persian overlord oppressed his subjects,
While pride left Rome's Caesar blind and deaf to his people's plight.

81. They tortured God's worshippers on false pretexts,
And slaughtered them like sacrificial sheep.[44]

82. Among mankind, the strong shed the blood of the weak,
Like lions killing sheep or whales killing minnows.

[The Night Journey and Ascension]

83. God conveyed you by night to the Farthest Mosque,
Where His angels and Messengers stood gathered to receive you.

84. When you strode in, they thronged around you, their master,
Like stars around the full moon, or troops around their flag.

85. Each one of noble station, they followed you in prayer,
For whoever follows God's beloved will triumph.

86. Passing close by them, you traversed the heavens—or what lies above them—
On a luminous mount with a bridle of pearl.

87. Yours was a mount that, due to your might and dignity, has no equal
Among swift steeds or hard-treading she-camels that leave traces on the ground.

88. Burāq is of the Maker's will and of His make,
And God's power is above all suspicion and doubt.

89. Until you reached a heaven to which
No wing can fly, no foot can walk.

90. As if a voice had said, "Let every prophet stand according to his rank,"
And, "O Muḥammad, this is God's throne, so touch it!"

91. You have written out the sciences for both religion and the world,
O reader of the Tablet! O holder of the Pen!

92. Your mind comprehends the secrets of both religion and the world;
The stores of science and knowledge were laid open before you.

93. Your closeness to God has multiplied beyond reckoning
The pendants of favor bestowed upon you, and the necklaces of grace.

[The Miracle of the Cave]

94. Then ask the band of polytheists who were pasturing their herds round the cave
(Who, except to pursue God's Chosen One, would not have pastured there):

95. Did they see the pure trace or hear the whisper
Of voices glorifying God or reciting the Qurʾān?

96. Did they think the spider's web was a forest
And the dappled doves that hovered there were vultures

97. So that they turned back, cursed by the very ground they traversed,
Like falsehood put to flight by the majesty of truth?

98. But for God's hand, the two companions would not have been safe;
But for His watchful eye, the pillar of religion would not still stand.

99. They were concealed and covered by the wing of God,
And whoever is enfolded in God's wing will not be harmed.

[64]

In the structural configuration of al-Būṣīrī's Burdah, as we saw in chapter 2, the Sīrah-derived passages (BB parts 4–9) function primarily as extensions of the Prophetic Praise (BB part 3) and lead into Supplication and Plea for Intercession (BB part 9). Shawqī configures his poem somewhat differently: his Sīrah themes (NB part 5) are also extensions of the Prophetic Praise (NB part 4), but they lead into a further Metapoetic Recapitulation of Prophet Praise (NB part 6). In part 5, which I have labeled Sīrah Themes, we find that in contrast to parts 1–3 of Nahj al-Burdah (vv. 1–45), where Shawqī has expanded upon al-Būṣīrī's parts 1–2, his treatment of Sīrah themes is more condensed than that of his predecessor, and, indeed, only three themes are developed in this part: The Birth of the Prophet (vv. 75–82); The Night Journey and Ascension (al-Isrāʾ wa-al-Miʿrāj, vv. 83–93); and The Miracle of Muḥammad and Abū Bakr in the Cave (vv. 94–99). Other Sīrah themes of al-Būṣīrī's Burdah have been given condensed treatment elsewhere in Nahj al-Burdah—such as the miraculous nature of the Qurʾān and other, lesser, miracles (NB part 5), and the Prophet's Jihād and Military Campaigns (BB part 8), which we find in Nahj al-Burdah thematically reconfigured in the polemic-political section, part 8. The effect of Shawqī's condensation is to bring each Sīrah theme to focus on a particular idea.

1) The Birth of the Prophet (vv. 75–82). Notice, that, especially compared with al-Būṣīrī (BB part 4, vv. 59–71), who presents a rhetorically dense passage designed to foreground the cosmic and miraculous effects of the Prophet's birth, Shawqī mentions only one of these—the cracking of the Sasanian Arch of Chosroes at Ctesiphon (v. 77). Shawqī opens his passage (v. 75) with the description of the birth of the Prophet as light penetrating darkness. This sets the stage for the thematic focus of the passage around the theme that Islam brought mankind "light," that is "enlightenment" of truth, justice, and civilization, to replace the "darkness" of falsehood, tyranny, and chaos that had up until then oppressed them.

In fact, however, this passage does not deal much with the birth of the Prophet, focusing instead on the chaos and tyranny that mankind suffered before his coming.[45] It is not rhetorically complex, but rather the poet drives home his message by densely lading it with what we might term the "diction of oppression": *ẓulam* (darknesses, s. *ẓulmah*—closely related to *ẓulm,* oppression) (v. 75); *al-ṭāghūn* (despots), *al-bāghūn* (tyrants) (v. 76); *fawḍá* (chaos) (v. 78); *jawr* (persecution, injustice, oppression), *ṭāghiyah* (despot) (v. 79); *yabghī* (oppress, tyrannize), *aṣamm* ([morally] deaf), *ʿamī* (for *ʿamin*; [morally] blind) (v. 80)—the last two inevitably evoke the Qurʾānic condemnation of those who refuse Muḥammad's message as "deaf, dumb, and blind" (*ṣummun bukmun ʿumyun* [QK 2:18, 2:171]); *yuʿadhdhibān* (torture)—; *yadhbaḥān* (slaughter) (v. 81); *yaftiku* (shed blood) (v. 82).

As contextualized in the poem, these catch-words of violence and tyranny are associated with Arab as well as foreign (or Persian, *ʿajam*) despots, but the overall emphasis is on the Persian (Sasanian) and especially Roman empires, the main contenders for power at the advent of Islam, but especially the Romans. On the one hand, the Caesars of Rome had become a byword for tyranny, and verse 81 in particular seems to refer to their persecution of the early Christians, especially in the gladiatorial arena. More important for Shawqī, however, in the context of the British occupation of Egypt, is that the British Empire and the Christian West generally are perceived as the heirs to the Roman Empire. Therefore Roman persecution, torture, and slaughter, of *ʿibād Allāh* (God's worshippers), that is, the early Christians (v. 81), reads allegorically as contemporary British persecution of Muslims. Certainly, in the aftermath of the Dinshawāy Incident (1906, 1907—see above) with its rigged courts, brutal sentences, and barbaric public floggings and executions, for the Egyptians of 1910 this reading is inescapable. This passage concludes its description of the reign of injustice by citing the "law of the jungle" whereby the strong shed the blood of the weak (v. 82).

Shawqī's redirection of al-Būṣīrī's model to focus on the reign of tyranny before the coming of Islam is clearly not arbitrary; rather, it is intended allegorically to identify Persian and especially Roman tyranny at the time of the advent of Islam with the current state of Egypt and the Islamic world generally under the yoke of Western domination. This allegory entails a crucial corollary: that just as the light of Islam came to dispel the darkness of pre-Islamic, Persian and Roman, oppression and tyranny, so too should the revival of Arab-Islamic civilization in the twentieth century put an end to Western oppression of the Islamic East.

In this respect, then, the theme of the Birth of the Prophet in Shawqī's Nahj al-Burdah is meticulously constructed to pave the way toward his political-polemical formulation of Iḥyāʾ (Revival) in the final sections of the poem.

2) The Night Journey and Ascension (al-Isrāʾ wa-al-Miʿrāj). We have already seen in al-Būṣīrī's Burdah, Part 7: The Night Journey and Ascension (vv. 105–117), how Shawqī's predecessor narrowed the rich body of material associated with the Prophet's Night Journey from Mecca to Jerusalem and back, and his Ascension from Jerusalem to the heavens, where he approached God's throne, to a precise poetic formulation of those elements that highlight the poet's central concern: the superiority of Muḥammad to all other prophets and the concomitant superiority of his Ummah to all other (religious) communities. Again, as we have noted before, this performs the contractual obligation of *madīḥ nabawī*, establishing and confirming through its "praise" the unique authority of the Prophet Muḥammad and the veracity of his message. Shawqī follows al-Būṣīrī's lead in likewise leaving aside much of the vast lore associated with the Prophet's initiatory journey (see BB part 7) to focus on those elements that establish Muḥammad's unrivalled and unique authority as the Seal of the Prophets, and then further directs the topic toward his own Iḥyāʾ-determined poetic-polemic purposes.

The Qurʾānic textual foundations for the Sīrah literature and popular lore of the Night Journey and Ascension are, for the former, "Glory to Him who took His servant by night from the Sacred Place of Prayer (*masjid al-ḥaram*) to the Furthest Place of Prayer (*al-masjid al-aqṣā*), whose precinct We blessed so that We might show him some of Our signs. . . ." (*āyātinā* = signs, also: miracles, Qurʾānic verses [QK 17:1]). Associated with the Ascension are the verses:

> By the star when it falls, your companion has not erred or gone astray, and he does not speak out of personal desire, but rather from inspiration that has come down to him. There instructed him one [Jibrīl or Allāh] of great power, imbued with strength, who stood on the highest horizon, then approached and drew near, until he was two bow-lengths away or closer. Then he revealed to his servant his revelation. The heart has not lied about what it saw. Will you then dispute with him over what he sees? And he saw him in another descent by the Lote-Tree of the Furthest Limit near which is the Garden of the Refuge. Then the Lote-Tree was shrouded,

> but his sight did not swerve or stray. He saw the greatest of the signs of his Lord. (QK 53:1–11)

This second Qurʾānic passage with its short rhymed verses (*sajʿ/fawāṣil*) has a lapidary, incantatory style that is extremely rhetorically effective in its evocation of the mystery and majesty of divine revelation. However, in strictly prosaic expository terms (which, of course, are not the purpose of the Qurʾān) it is somewhat obscure, especially as regards the antecedents of pronouns.

At this point, Qurʾānic commentary, Sīrah literature, and popular lore take over to generate cohesive prose narratives of these events.[46] From the Qurʾān itself, though, the essential message is clear and strikingly phrased. For the first passage, God has taken his servant Muḥammad on a nocturnal journey and showed him some of His signs. For the second, the antecedents of the pronouns are open to interpretation, but again, it strikingly conveys the message that Muḥammad's revelations are of divine inspiration. The prose narratives add the miraculous mount, Burāq, described as a white riding beast between the size of a donkey and a mule, whose hoof-steps carry it as far as its eye can see.[47] This beast carries the Prophet to Jerusalem, where he leads in prayer, that is, serves as leader or *imām* to, the other prophets, specified in some narratives as Ibrāhīm, Mūsá, ʿĪsá, Dāʾūd, and Sulaymān.[48] Muḥammad's superiority to the other Prophets is presented quite explicitly in the Ascension narratives where, leading a procession of angels, he systematically greets and then bypasses each of the seven heavens with its associated Prophet (1, Ādam; 2, ʿĪsá and Yaḥyá; 3, Yūsuf; 4, Idrīs; 5, Hārūn; 6, Mūsá; 7, Ibrāhīm), until he comes within two bow-lengths of Allāh and approaches His throne, where he receives knowledge that has been imparted to no human being but him (see chapter 2, BB part 7).

Like the Qurʾānic text, the poetic text eschews the narrative cohesion of the prose renditions in favor of a rhetorically focused insistence on the message. In the case of *madīḥ nabawī*, of course, both literary and popular versions of al-Isrāʾ wa-al-Miʿrāj are already well known to the poet's audience and require merely to be evoked, not reiterated. Against this background, then, as well as such well-known poetic antecedents as al-Būṣīrī's Burdah, Shawqī's verses 83–85 effectively encapsulate the Night Journey. He conveys the superior status of Muḥammad through his images of ritual or bodily practice. The communicative effect of such postures is termed by Connerton "the choreography of authority," as he explains:

> The importance of posture for communal memory is evident. Power and rank are commonly expressed through certain postures relative to others; from the way in which people group themselves and from the position of their bodies relative to the bodies of others, we can deduce the degree of authority which each is thought to enjoy or to which they lay claim. We know what it means when one person sits in an elevated position when everyone around them stands; when one person stands and everyone else sits. . . . There will of course be disparities between cultures in the meanings ascribed to some postures, but, in all cultures, much of the choreography of authority is expressed through the body.[49]

It is just such postures and positions that the poet exploits to convey the superior status of the Prophet Muḥammad: v. 83: the angels and prophets stand in attendance, waiting to receive Muḥammad; v. 84 Muḥammad strides before them, as we would imagine a general surveying his troops, and they throng around him as stars around a full moon, or troops around a flag. Finally, in v. 85, the angels and prophets, however exalted their own status, are ranked behind Muḥammad as they follow him in prayer, where he serves as leader, *imām*. The emphasis on bodily practice as an expression of rank and authority in the images and diction of these verses should remind us of Shawqī's similar methods in describing his own submission and clinging to the Prophet in verses 42–44, as discussed above. The final hemistich of v. 85, with its inverted expression (*qalb*), succinctly encapsulates in its antithesis of triumph (*yafuz*) and submission (*yaʾtamimi*) of the hierarchy of power: to triumph, even for prophets and angels, one must submit to the authority of Allāh's chosen Prophet.

Verses 86–90 constitute Shawqī's reprise of Muḥammad's Ascension. The first three verses, much to al-Bishrī's consternation, feature Muḥammad's magical mount, Burāq. Al-Bishrī is at pains to insist that Burāq served as the Prophet's mount for the Night Journey from Mecca to Jerusalem, but that the Ascension was accomplished by means of a ladder or stairway (*miʿrāj*) (WN vv. 86, 89). For poetry, however, popular imagination trumps theological learning. We can appreciate Shawqī's choice when we consider the iconographic primacy in manuscript illustrations of Muḥammad mounted on Burāq (often portrayed with a female human face) and surrounded by angels. Although technically this may be meant to illustrate the Night Journey (and other pictures show Muḥammad being carried on the back of Jibrīl ascending the heavens), it has become in popular Islam the emblematic referent to al-Isrāʾ wa-al-Miʿrāj and an iconic representation of Muḥammad's exalted status. We can understand, too, that the image of Muḥammad mounted on Burāq does not merely serve as a pictorial illustration of a narrative element, but comes to function iconographically as an Islamic religious equivalent of the equestrian statue: that is, the monumental representation of power and authority. Now translated from a horse to a divinely created mythical-magical mount and from the earth to the heavens with an entourage of angels, the image of Muḥammad mounted on Burāq adds to the political and military authority conveyed by the equestrian statue an apotheotic aura entirely consistent with the belief in Muḥammad's unrivalled status among God's creatures. The Ascension culminates in verses 89–90, in which Muḥammad's preeminent rank is conveyed through his reaching a heaven that no wing or foot has ever reached before (89), and he alone of all the prophets approaches and, it seems, touches God's throne. Again, al-Bishrī is concerned with the theological detail and insists that Muḥammad could not really touch God's throne (WN v. 90). Poetically, of course, what is intended is Muḥammad's unique proximity to and favor with Allāh (see v. 93).

The most interesting verses of this passage in terms of the Iḥyāʾ Project are verses 91–92. The culmination of the Ascension, as the original Qurʾānic passage states quite explicitly, is Allāh's revelation/inspiration to Muḥammad, that is, revealing some of His *āyāt*—"signs" in this context, but otherwise equally miracles or Qurʾānic verses. Shawqī, in accordance with the Iḥyāʾ imperative, eschews the common esoteric and/or mystical readings of such "signs" to interpret them rather in Enlightenment terms of both moral and practical science, knowledge, and wisdom. The discourse of the Western-influenced thinking of the nineteenth- and early twentieth-century Egyptian liberal intellectuals commonly associated traditional Islamic concepts of al-Lawḥ al-Maḥfūẓ (the Preserved Tablet) and al-Qalam (the Pen), whereby all God's decrees have been written,[50] with the poplular fatalism of the Islamic world which they saw as the main source of its backwardness (*jumūd*) and the major obstacle to modern enlightened development. Quite remarkably, Shawqī has reconceived the Preserved Table and the Pen in such as way as to identify them with precisely those terms that have in his day become associated with progressive and liberal modern thinking: *ʿulūm* (sciences) (v. 91), *ʿilm* (science), *ḥikam* (knowledge) (v. 92). By invoking the otherwise clichéd expression of Islam as *al-dīn wa al-dunyā* ("religion and world"—that is, as offering precepts both for religious and practical, political, life) in verse 91, Shawqī transforms or extends its sense to embrace the religious sciences and moral precepts on the one hand, and the modern sciences on the other. This continues in verse 92, where the secret (*sirr*) revealed to the Prophet now conjoins religious and scientific precepts, as does the store of knowledge that has been uncovered for him.

The importance of Shawqī's interpretation of Islam in these verses should not be underestimated. What he has done is to resolve the conflict between those Muslims who cling to traditional religion and reject modern secular liberalism as godless and those modern liberal secularists who condemn Islam as a stronghold of backwardness, fatalism, and superstition. Shawqī does this in the manner of the Iḥyāʾ/Nahḍah intellectuals and Islamic reformers, such as Jamāl al-Dīn al-Afghānī and Muḥammad ʿAbduh, by defining Islam as essentially enlightened, scientific, and just—and this, in turn, he accomplishes by a quite stunning conjoining (vv. 91–92) of the most traditional Islamic terms *al-dīn wa al-dunyā, al-Lawḥ, al-Qalam, al-sirr, inkashafat* (religion and world, the Tablet, the Pen, the secret, be revealed) with terms such as *ʿulūm, ʿilm, ḥikam* (sciences, science, knowledge), which, however rooted they are in the religious tradition, have become by the late nineteenth and early twentieth centuries bywords for Western science and learning. In brief, Shawqī has achieved in poetry the Islamic Reformist identification of Islamic tradition and Western Enlightenment humanism and science, which he will develop at length in the later sections of the poem (especially parts 9, 10, and 11).

Verse 93 seals this passage by invoking Muḥammad's closeness to Allāh as the source of the countless favors and graces bestowed upon him. Although this verse sounds altogether lyrical in its metaphors of "pendants of favor," "necklaces of grace," it is interesting to note that al-Bishrī takes these favors and graces to be *ʿulūm* (sciences or knowledge) (WN v. 93).

3) The Miracle of Muḥammad and Abū Bakr in the Cave. In the prose accounts of the Prophet's miracles, God's protection of the two

companions as they hid in the cave from the pursuing Meccan polytheists is quite simply presented. Al-Qāḍī ʿIyāḍ writes:

> It is related on the authority of Anas, Zayd ibn Arqam, and al-Mughīrah ibn Shuʿbah that the Prophet (pbuh) said: "On the night of the Cave, God commanded a tree to grow in front of the Prophet (pbuh) and conceal him; and he ordered two doves to stop at the mouth of the cave." And another *ḥadīth* says, "the spider wove its web at the cave's entrance, so that when his pursuers came and saw this they said, 'If there were anyone inside the cave the two doves would not be at its entrance,' and the Prophet (pbuh) heard what they said. Then they departed."[51]

Shawqī, in his poetic rendition, follows in part al-Būṣīrī's cognate passage (BB part 5, vv. 76–81), where this event serves to undergird the poet's oath that he has never come as a supplicant to the Prophet except that his request, for justice, protection, physical or spiritual bounty, has been granted. At the same time, however, Shawqī changes the rhetorical emphasis to begin by first foregrounding the Meccan polytheists who rejected and persecuted God's Chosen Prophet (vv. 94–97). To his rhetorical question, following al-Bishrī's interpretation, "Ask the polytheists what frightened them away—did the Prophet's footprints or the voices reciting the Qurʾān strike fear in their hearts?—In their terror, did they think the spider's web a forest? The doves vultures?" (WN vv. 94–97), he answers that it was God alone that protected them.

Much as al-Būṣīrī did, Shawqī extends this one-time miracle to an abiding religious principle. In each of verses 97–99, the first hemistich refers specifically to the Miracle of the Cave, while the second presents an abiding Islamic truth (*ḥikmah* or aphorism). Thus the fleeing Meccan polytheists (97a) are "like falsehood put to flight by the majesty of truth" (97b); God's hand protecting Muḥammad and Abū Bakr (98a) is followed by the aphoristic: "But for His watchful eye, the pillar of religion would not stand" (98b); finally, in a lovely lyrical verse in which the poet extends the doves' wings to a metaphor of divine protection: the "wing of God" conceals the Companions (99a), and moreover, the passage concludes, "Whoever is enfolded in God's wing will not be harmed" (99b). The careful rhetorical structure of verse 99 gracefully balances the repetition of "wing of God" (*jināḥ Allāh*) in the middle of each hemistich and brings the passage to a sonorous and semantically concise closure through the alliteration of liquids (*l, m, n*) and the combined *jinās* and *ṭibāq* of *yaḍummu* (protect, enfold) and *yuḍami* (be harmed).

The effect of the repeated movement from the particular to the general in verses 97–99 is to extract a permanent truth from even the passing miracle. Further, within the colonial context of Shawqī's day, the polytheists who persecute Muḥammad and Abū Bakr find an analog in the British occupation and its persecution of contemporary Muslims. The Miracle of the Cave thus is transformed from an episode in the Sīrah of the Prophet to an exemplar of Allāh's abiding protection of the Believers.

PART 6: METAPOETIC RECAPITULATION OF PROPHETIC PRAISE (VV. 100–117)

100. O Aḥmad of goodness, I have the dignity of being named for you,
And how can one named for the Messenger not reach exalted rank?

101. The panegyrists and the lords of passion* are all followers [* = Ṣūfīs]
Of the preeminent Master of the redolent Mantle.*
[* = al-Būṣīrī, al-Burdah]

102. His praise for you springs from sincere love and passion,
For true love dictates true words.

103. As God is my witness, I do not strive to surpass him,
For who could vie with the downpour of so widespread a cloud?

104. I am merely one of those who emulate him, and surely he who tries
To emulate your saint is not to be rebuked or blamed.

105. Praise of the Prophet is a station conferred by the Most Merciful;
Its awful dignity strikes dumb even the most silver-tongued Saḥbān,

106. For the full moon falls short of you in beauty and nobility;
The sea falls short of you in bounty and munificence.

107. The haughty mountains, if you challenged them in height, would sink;
If you vied in beauty with the gleaming stars, you would outshine them;

108. The lion when it pounces is not as bold as you
When you march against an iron-clad warrior bristling with weapons.

109. Though in war you make the hearts' black grains bleed,
Yet the hearts of the brave and valiant yearn for you.

110. Wherever armies clashed, God threw His love and dread
Behind Āminah's son, Muḥammad.

111. Your face amidst the battle-dust is like the full moon [*badr*] on a dark night:
Whether it is veiled by clouds or not, it shines.

112. Like a full moon [*badr*], Muḥammad rose at Badr and his radiant countenance
Was like the new moon of victory shining through the gloom of night.

113. In the Qurʾān you were called an orphan to honor you,
For the uniquely precious pearl is called an "orphan."

114. When God apportioned His blessings among mankind,
You were allowed to choose your blessings and your lot.

115. Whether you say "no" concerning an affair or "yes,"
God's choice is in that "no" and in that "yes."

116. Your brother Jesus called a dead man back to life and he arose,
But you revived whole generations of decaying bones.

117. Ignorance is death, so if another miracle is granted you,
Then raise mankind from ignorance or from the grave.

[65]

Part 6 forms not only both climax and metapoetic recapitulation of the theme of Prophetic praise, but also the completion of movement I of the poem. As such, it concludes the more traditional *madīḥ nabawī* themes and structure (with the partial exception of part 12) that follow the model of al-Būṣīrī's Burdah and sets the stage for Shawqī's new Iḥyāʾ-informed political-polemical passages (NB parts 7–11, and 12) that form the second movement of the poem. We are alerted to the heightened emotional urgency of this passage by the change from the third-person "he" that has dominated parts 4 and 5, to the second person "you" and the dramatic apostrophe, "O Aḥmad!" that opens part 6.

Shawqī's evocation in verse 100 of his base-text, al-Būṣīrī's verse 146, both establishes the cognation between the two texts and highlights the dramatic effect of Shawqī's rhetorical choices. The metapoetic substance of the opening passage (NB vv. 100–105) concerns the complex dynamic between the identities of Aḥmad Shawqī, Aḥmad/Muḥammad the Prophet, and Muḥammad al-Būṣīrī, the Master of the Burdah. The initial "O Aḥmad!" thus has three possible referents, until further defined. For just as we noted above (NB part 4) that Shawqī sees himself as the poetic counterpart to the Prophet in bringing a message of redemption/Iḥyāʾ

to the Islamic Ummah, a shared name suggests some measure of shared identity, as the blessing traditionally associated with being named after the Prophet, Muḥammad or Aḥmad, indicates.[52] This (con)fusion of identities on the principle that *nomen est omen* is rhetorically mimicked in the three-fold root-play of v. 100: *tasmiyah* and *samī* ("naming" and "namesake," from the root *s-m-y*) and *yatasāmā* ("reach exalted rank" from the root *s-m-w*). The other issue of identity is one of imitation, that Shawqī (NB v. 101), like all the other poets of *madīḥ nabawī* and the passionate devotees of the Prophet (Ṣūfīs), is following the model of the "preeminent Master of the Burdah," that is, al-Būṣīrī. The intensity of the praise passage and the intimate association of the Prophet with *madīḥ nabawī* and its practitioners is further suggested in the metathetic root-play (the roots *ḥ-m-d* and *m-d-ḥ* both denote "praise") of the opening words of vv. 100–102: *yā ʾAḥmadu, al-mādiḥūna, madīḥuhu* (Aḥmad "the most praiseworthy," "the praise-poets," "his praise"). Furthermore, in a manner that is, no doubt, intended to reflect Shawqī's own motivations and intentions, he states in v. 102 that al-Būṣīrī's praise for the Prophet is a pure, sincere expression of his love for him, unadulterated by any worldly or material motives or goals.

Inasmuch as the Arabic term *muʿāraḍah* (contrafaction) conveys opposition and challenge—to try to outdo a rival—Shawqī is careful to define his present poetic undertaking with regard to al-Būṣīrī. He insists, therefore, in vv. 103–104 that Nahj al-Burdah is an attempt not to surpass al-Būṣīrī's masterpiece, but merely to emulate Muḥammad's "saint" or "friend" (*walī*). Finally, in v. 105, Shawqī concludes this metapoetic passage on the nature of *madīḥ nabawī* by declaring that to praise one so great as the Prophet is beyond human capacity; it is, rather, an awful dignity conferred by God, or, as we might say, a humbling responsibility. As al-Bishrī explains, even the greatest of proverbial orators, Saḥbān, would be struck dumb by this task, which can only be accomplished with divine help (WN v. 105).

In metapoetic terms, Shawqī has defined the elements of the formidable double challenge that he faces in composing a *madīḥ nabawī* following the model of al-Būṣīrī's Burdah. The first is the undisputed preeminence of that work in the genre of *madīḥ nabawī*. Shawqī claims that he would not presume to try to surpass it, but what, we should ask, would be the point of composing a lesser poem? Clearly there is a poetic competition involved, for poetic contrafaction by its very nature calls for a comparison and evaluation of the base-text and the new text, and Shawqī has followed al-Būṣīrī's Burdah so closely that such a comparison is inevitable, as we will discuss in the conclusion. The second challenge has to do with the *mamdūḥ*—that is, that the subject and recipient of the praise is the Prophet Muḥammad, who surpasses all mankind in every praiseworthy quality and virtue, whose enumeration and description therefore exceed the poet's expressive capacities. Shawqī's response or resolution to this double challenge, that to compose *madīḥ nabawī* is a "station conferred by the All-Merciful" (*maqāmun min al-raḥmāni muqtabasun*), is then altogether stunning, For just as the synonymity of his name and the Prophet's of verse 100 has insinuated some level of identification or correspondence between the two, so too "a station conferred by the All-Merciful" is a phrase eminently applicable to prophethood as well as to the composition of prophetic praise poetry. Thus, Shawqī is at once establishing a bond of identification between himself and the Prophet and suggesting that his poem is the result of divine inspiration or aid. The latter proposition has the effect of undermining Shawqī's modest demurral of vv. 103–104. However much his personal modesty or sense of intimidation may make him refrain from challenging the Master of the Burdah, divine aid, needless to say, makes anything possible.

In light of this reading of vv. 100–105, then, the remaining verses of part 6 (106–117) in particular, and the entire Nahj al-Burdah in general, constitute Shawqī's response to this double challenge: one whose outstanding (even superior) poetic beauty he does not attribute to his own presumption of superior talent, but rather to divine aid—what we might otherwise understand as "(poetic) inspiration." It is as if, after v. 105, he says, "Here goes!" as he throws all his poetic and rhetorical skills, particularly the *badīʿ*-style rhetoric of High ʿAbbāsid court panegyric, into demonstrating the impossibility of describing that which is above and beyond all description. The rhetorical sleight of hand he engages in here, especially in vv. 106–108, is that in ostensibly demonstrating the impossibility of expressing the Prophet's virtues, he in fact expresses them. In other words, the poet achieves the impossible, a sort of poetic "*iʿjāz*." This he accomplishes through a negation of all the conventional similes of beauty, generosity, etc. The effect of the simplicity and beauty of verse 106 with its parallelism of the two hemistichs and its emphatic reiteration of *dūnaka* ("falls short of you," literally, beneath you, below you) is not merely to express the unrivalled beauty and generosity of the Prophet, but to declare the inadequacy of the Arabic poetic idiom to express it. The verse is a conundrum inasmuch as it beautifully expresses this idea and thereby contradicts it. Verses 107–108 follow a similar logic, declaring that the Prophet's (metaphorical) height makes lofty mountains sink; that he outshines the stars and is bolder than the lion. That is, all the conventional similes fall short.

Verses 109–112 describe the Prophet's valor on the battlefield, culminating in verses 111–112 with a dense word-play centering around the full moon (*badr*) as a symbol of the Prophet and the miraculous early Muslim victory over the Meccan polytheists at the Battle of Badr (2 AH), and related terms for luminosity and darkness. This picks up the light versus darkness imagery and diction of the Birth of the Prophet passage (NB part 5, vv. 75–82); thus, v. 111, *badru dujan* (full moon of a dark night); *yuḍīʾu* (shine), *multathim* (veiled [twice]); v. 112, with even more intensity: *badr* (full moon), *taṭallʿa* (rise [of a heavenly body]), Badr (proper name of the battle-place), *ghurrah* (bright face, luminosity [twice]), *tajlū* (appear, shine), *dājī* (dark), *al-ẓulami* (darknesses). The imagery of luminosity is joined to the concept of Muḥammad's unique status in verse 113 through a pun and root-play on *yatīm* ("orphan," but also "unique, peerless," here in the substantive form *yutm/yutum*). Invoking the Qurʾānic verse that refers to Muḥammad's orphanhood (his father, ʿAbd Allāh, died before Muḥammad was born), "Did He not find you an orphan (*yatīm*) and give you shelter?" (QK 93:6), the poet then proceeds to adduce another meaning for *yatīm,* that is "a matchless, precious pearl." In verse 115 Shawqī invokes al-Būṣīrī's v. 35 about the justice of the Prophet's judgments ("no" and "yes"), adding, through the near parallelism and repetition of "no" and "yes" in each hemistich, a divine choice that undergirds and confirms the Prophet's decisions.

Perhaps the most interesting verses of this passage are 116–117, in which Shawqī concludes part 6 with an Iḥyāʾ-inspired plea for the revival and recuperation of the Islamic Ummah, thereby forming a transition to movement II of Nahj al-Burdah, Shawqī's poetic rendition of the Iḥyāʾ Project. Verse 116 reiterates the standard Iʿjāz al-Qurʾān doctrine (above NB vv. 69–70 and BB v. 93) that the miracles of other prophets are one-time events, whereas Muḥammad's message and miracle (the Qurʾān) is forever and continuously in force to guide and save mankind. At the same time it invokes, through the key terms "revive" (*aḥyā, aḥyayta*) and "decaying bones" (*al-rimami*—the rhyme-word), verse 46 of al-Būṣīrī's Burdah and its Qurʾānic referent (see chapter 2). The "generations of decaying bones" refers to the generations of mankind who, through the salvific effect of Muḥammad's message, will be called back to life on Resurrection Day. However, in the present context, as al-Bishrī explains with great concision, Shawqī is using "revival" (*al-iḥyāʾ*) and "revive" (*aḥyayta*) metaphorically to mean "awaken men's hearts and lead them out from the darkness of ignorance to the path of following Islam" (WN v. 116). Shawqī's *iḥyāʾ* (revival) clearly refers to the Iḥyāʾ Project of the cultural revival of the Islamic Ummah, and forcefully echoes in both sense and diction the Iḥyāʾ proclamation of verse 74. Verse 117 then closes this passage with a rhetorically complex and powerfully condensed formulation of the Iḥyāʾ Project: it equates ignorance (*jahl*) with death and, therefore, political and cultural revival with resurrection. This is particularly effective because, as we saw with verse 66, *jahl*, with its etymological relation to Jāhiliyyah, the Age of Ignorance prior to the coming of Islam, bears a religious significance in this context—ignorance or denial of the true religion (Islam). But further, in the Iḥyāʾ/Nahḍah context, it conveys the idea that the contemporary fatalism and superstition of the Muslim masses and the backwardness of Islamic society constitute a falling away from true Islam, which in turn has now become identified with Western-derived concepts of science, progress, and civilization—as we will see in movement II.

This constitutes a dramatic change of direction and orientation for *madīḥ nabawī*. For whereas the sort of *madīḥ nabawī* that al-Būṣīrī's Burdah exemplifies and has spawned has an otherworldly goal, the plea for the Prophet's intercession on Judgment Day, Shawqī changes the focus from otherworldly concerns to worldly political, intellectual, and cultural "revival."[53] Opening the verse with the proclamation that "Ignorance is death," Shawqī employs a network of antithesis (*ṭibāq*) and repetition (*takrār*): *jahl* (ignorance) occurs twice, as does the imperative *fa-ibʿath* (resurrect, revive); death occurs as *mawt* (death) and *rimam* (decayed bones) to equate the (earthly) eradication of ignorance and backwardness with the (otherworldly) raising of dead bodies from the grave on Resurrection Day.[54] This then paves the way thematically for most of the remainder of the poem, our parts 7–12, in which Shawqī sets out his vision of an essentially Islamic humanism that serves as the foundation for his Iḥyāʾ Project.

In structural terms, we can observe that part 6, for all its metapoetic preoccupations, nevertheless performs a recapitulation of the supplicatory ritual, beginning with the direct address to the one supplicated, "O Aḥmad!" of v. 100, Shawqī's (poetic) Self-Abasement: "I do not strive to surpass. . . I am merely one of those who emulate. . ." (vv. 103–104), Praise of the *mamdūḥ* (vv. 105–116), and, finally, the Supplication: ". . . if [a] miracle is granted you, // Then raise mankind from ignorance. . ." (v. 117).

Nahj al-Burdah Movement II: The Iḥyāʾ Project—Parts 7–12

In a radical restructuring of his base-text, Shawqī subordinates the otherworldly concerns (the Prophet's intercession on Judgment Day) that dominate the supplicatory framework of al-Būṣīrī's Burdah to complete the Nahj al-Burdah supplicatory pattern with elements based on the Islamic Manifest Destiny themes of al-Būṣīrī's Sīrah-derived parts, especially Part 8: The Messenger's Jihād and Military Campaigns, to create what I have labeled movement II of Nahj al-Burdah. Shawqī begins with a poetic polemic against Western Christian imperialism as a preamble to his vision of an idealized and paradigmatic Islamic past; he then presents in his supplicatory closing a plea for the restitution in this world of the dignity and dominion of the Islamic Ummah. Hourani offers a concise formulation of the traditional Sunnī Muslim view of Islamic history and thereby provides a prose context for our reading of Shawqī's poetic work in movement II:[55]

> For an orthodox Muslim, history was the process by which the society of religious ignorance, directed to worldly ends, held together by natural solidarity and ruled by kings, was replaced by the ideal Muslim society. In a sense the struggle had been going on throughout history, wherever and whenever God had sent prophets to a specific *umma*. In a sense too it was still happening, wherever the *umma* faced the unconverted world. There had however been one period of particular importance, when the final revelation was fully embodied in the institutions of society. To devout Muslims, at the time and later, there lay a special significance in the early history of Islam, when the community was expanding and flourishing, the Quran and the Prophet's words were taken as principles of action, and the *umma* was one in outer manifestation as well as in spirit. For the

moral imagination of Sunnis, the early centuries of Islam have always been a compelling drama in three acts: the early days of the Prophet and his immediate successors, the golden age when the *umma* was as it should be; the Umayyad period when the principles of Islamic piety were overlaid by the natural human tendency towards secular kingship; and the early ʿAbbasid age when the principles of the *umma* were reasserted and embodied in institutions of a universal empire, regulated by law, based on the equality of all believers, and enjoying power, wealth, and culture which are the reward of obedience. In later ages this period of history served as a norm for rulers and ruled alike, a lesson of what God had done for His people, a lesson too of the evils of division and the rejection of God's will.[56]

PART 7: POLEMIC AGAINST CHRISTIANITY (VV. 118–128)

118. The Christians say that you conducted raids, but that God's Messengers
Were not sent to kill souls nor to shed blood.

119. This is ignorance, the delusion of dreams, and sophistry,
For you conquered by the sword only after you conquered by the pen.

120. Only after every man of high degree came to you of his own accord,
Was the sword charged with subduing the ignorant masses,

121. For if you meet evil with goodness, you will not withstand it;
But if you meet it with evil, it will be cut down.

122. So ask meek Christianity how often it has drunk
The bitter colocynth of wanton tyrants' lusts,

123. A prey to paganism that persecuted it
And at every turn attacked with fury.

124. Were it not for the protectors who took up the sword in its defense,
Its kindness and mercy would have been to no avail.

125. Were it not for Jesus' high rank with Him who sent him
And a sacred bond established to the Spirit from the beginning of time,

126. His noble and inviolate body would have been nailed to the cross's two boards
And his tormentor would have felt no dread or fright.

127. But the Messiah was too great for this! It was his enemy who suffered on the cross,
For punishment is in proportion to one's sins and crimes.

128. Jesus, the Prophet's brother and inspired by God, holds an honored rank
Above the heavens but below God's Throne.

[66]

Part 7: Polemic against Christianity serves largely as an introduction—or apologia—for Part 8: Defense/Praise of Jihād and the Prophet's Military Campaigns (*ghazawāt*). It is particularly interesting to compare Shawqī's part 8 with al-Būṣīrī's counterpart (BB part 8), which is pure and unabashed praise and celebration of the Prophet's military prowess and accomplishments without any need for apology or explanation, as indeed the traditional prophetic epithet "Prophet of Fierce Battle(s)" (*nabī al-malḥamah/al-malāḥim*) indicates.[57] It is indicative of the degree to which the colonial subject's identity is formed by the colonizer[58] and the defensive anticolonial posture of Neo-Classical poetry that Shawqī feels obliged to preface his praise of the Prophet's jihād with a refutation of Christian anti-Islamic polemic, namely their claim that God's messengers should promote peace (like Jesus), not war (like Muḥammad). Shawqī exposes the hypocrisy of their deluded claims in a largely self-explanatory argument (118–128). The poet's vindication of Islam is set out in two basic steps: Muḥammad conquered by the sword only after he conquered by the pen—that is, as a last resort—while men of rank converted to Islam of their own accord (119–120); and that meekness cannot prevail in the face of violence, but rather violence must be met with violence for the sake of righteousness—as, indeed, the persecution of the early Christians has shown (121–124). He concludes in verses 125–128 with a reiteration of the Islamic doctrines concerning Jesus: that he was a prophet, but was not crucified, and his rank, though exalted, is below that of Muḥammad, as verses 128 so succinctly states (see this in light of v. 90: Muḥammad, alone of God's prophets, approached the Throne).

PART 8: DEFENSE/PRAISE OF JIHĀD AND THE PROPHET'S MILITARY CAMPAIGNS (VV. 129–141)

129. You, Muḥammad, taught the Muslims everything of which they were ignorant,
Even how to do battle and honor the covenants of war.

130. You called them to a jihād by which they won dominion,
For war is the basis of the order of the world and of its nations.

131. But for jihād we never would have seen, through time's calamities,
Long-standing columns nor steadfast buttresses.

132. The evidence for this is clear in age after age,
Whether eras of enlightenment or benighted times.[59]

133. Of old, some thrones declined while others were erected;
Without bombs they would never have been breached or cracked.

134. The followers of Jesus have prepared every weapon of destruction,
While we have prepared for nothing but to be destroyed.

135. Muḥammad, whenever you were called to battle, you arose
Hurling warriors like lions, while God hurled demons like meteors from the sky.

136. Beneath your battle-standard there gathered every warrior
Avenging for God, advancing to meet Him, determined,

137. Glorifying God, his heart ablaze with passion to meet Him,
Mounted on a battle-steed like lightning's blaze,

138. Who, if he encountered time itself trying to get past him,
Then shot the arrow of his determination at its mount, time would not budge.

139. They are gleaming white swords, notched from combat;
They are the swords of God, not Indian blades.

140. How many a man, when you searched the battle-dust for dead,
Died true to his solemn promise and loyal to his oath!

141. Were it not that God bestowed His gifts on some more than on others,
Men would not differ in rank and worth.

[67]

It is only after the poet has refuted imperialist Christian claims, pointing out that the early Christianity's kindness and meekness led only to persecution until its protectors took up the sword in its defense (vv. 123–124), that Shawqī feels free to launch into his praise of Muḥammad's *ghazawāt* (raids, military campaigns) and the role of jihād in establishing and spreading Islam. Even here, however, verses 130–134 are essentially defensive and polemical. Declaring that war is the way of the world and the means by which dominions are won and civilizations developed, Shawqī clinches his argument in verse 134, exposing with bitter sarcasm the hypocrisy of "Christian meekness." The irony of Christian violence versus Islamic passivity is captured with biting rhetorical, in this case morphological, precision in the contrast of the active (Form I active participle: *fāʿil*) *qāṣimah* "crushing, destroying, shattering" [blow or weapon]) for the Christians, as opposed to the passive (Form VII—this form is passive in meaning—active participle: *munfaʿil*) *munqaṣim* "crushed, destroyed, shattered" for the Muslims: the Christians have all the weapons of destruction, while the Muslims wait passively to be destroyed. Shawqī's morphological contrast of active and passive forms provides a stunningly accurate formulation of the colonial experience, one that finds its prose counterpart in Albert Hourani's epitome (cited above), "The essence of imperialism is to be found in a moral relationship—that of power and powerlessness. . . ."

This passage, and verse 134 in particular, elicits from al-Bishrī a compelling and vehement prose diatribe against the hypocrisy of the Christian West (which, in light of the intervening century, seems almost prophetic):

> In this verse the poet intends to compare the people of the Christian religion with those of the Islamic religion. So he mentions that today the adherents of Christianity, "the religion of tranquility and peace," are the people of military power who devote themselves to preparing lightning-like weapons of destruction in wars, until it seems as if they have no occupation other than extracting gold from the bowels of the earth and spending it on iron and steel factories to produce the instruments of war throughout the length of the land and the breadth of the sea. They have mastered the manifold forms of destruction and demolition, and nothing—not the oaths they have sworn nor any virtues of their character—has prevented them from destroying the people and visiting scourges upon them, from behind their backs or under their feet, *until they have subjugated the very winds* (*taskhīr al-riyāḥ*) so they can rain down upon their heads every crushing disaster. While the people of the Islamic religion, whom their oppressors accuse of loving conquest and jihād, and whose reputation they besmirch by claiming they love nothing more than fighting and battle and the taste of human blood, today *they* are the people of tranquility and peace. Far be it from them to even come close to the people of the Christian religion in a contest for love of conquest and war, or even begin to match them in amassing weapons or in devising the instruments of war. (WN v. 134) [emphasis mine]

The passage is especially effective for the Muslim reader in its use of expressions associated with the unfettered might and dominion of

Sulaymān (King Solomon) as he is described in the Qurʾān, Qurʾānic commentary, and popular Islamic legends of the prophets (*qiṣaṣ al-anbiyāʾ*). In the Islamic tradition Sulaymān was endowed by Allāh with supernatural powers. He knew the language of birds and animals (QK 27:16, 19); unruly winds were subjected to his command ("Then We subjected the wind to him so that it would blow gently according to his command wherever he directed it" [*fa-sakhkharnā lahu al-rīḥa tajrī bi-ʾamrihi rukhāʾan ḥaythu ʾaṣāba*], QK:38:36); a fountain of molten brass was put at his service (QK 34:12); and he subdued the jinn to do his bidding, to work on his building projects (QK 34:12–13). His vast and irresistible army was composed of men, jinn, and birds (QK 27:17).[60] The awe and horror that the Muslims feel at the (almost) supernatural power of European economic, industrial, and military might are intensified by the evocation of the cosmic and God-given "superpower" of its Islamic analog and the realization that such might is not in the hands of a prophet of Islam and forerunner of Muḥammad, but rather in those of their arch-foe—the Christian West. In other words, the battle takes on cosmic proportions. There is also a subliminal logic evinced by al-Bishrī's shrewd phraseology. For inasmuch as Sulaymān is a mythic-symbolic prefiguration or analog of the Prophet Muḥammad, al-Bishrī's Qurʾānic phrase points to Muḥammad as the Islamic counterforce to the Christian West, which is precisely where the poem takes us.

The humiliation and passivity of the contemporary Muslim world provides the perfect foil for the Prophet's bold military action. Thus, with verse 135 there is a dramatic transition from the first person contemporary Muslim submissiveness of verse 134 to direct address of the Prophet responding to the call to war. The rhetorically effective contrast of active and passive voices ("whenever you were called by God to battle . . . you arose") stresses both the Prophet's divine mission and military action. The parallel structure of the Prophetic and divine "hurling" (*tarmī . . . yarmī Allāhu*) of weapons (v. 135) again reinforces the divine agency behind the Prophet's actions, in a manner that invokes both Qurʾānic and poetic antecedents: "It was not you who slew them, but God slew them, and you did not hurl when you hurled, but God hurled. . . ." (*fa-lam taqtulūhum wa-lākinna Allāha qatalahum wa-mā ramayta ʾidh ramayta wa-lakinna Allāha ramá* [QK 8:17]) and Abū Tammām's famous Amorium *qaṣīdah* (v. 41):

God hurled you against Amorium's two towers and destroyed them;
If anyone other than God had hurled you, he would have missed the mark.[61]

[68]

Verse 135 opens a passage (135–140) describing the Prophet and his Muslim warriors in battle that stands out for its explicit employ of the heightened rhetorical style of the High ʿAbbāsid panegyric. What is most interesting here is that we are dealing with a double-layered imitation. For Shawqī's model al-Būṣīrī, as we have seen in chapter 2, casts his Burdah Part 8: The Messenger's Jihād and Military Campaigns quite precisely in the style and motifs terms of a High ʿAbbāsid military panegyric. Thus Shawqī is imitating al-Būṣīrī, who is in turn imitating Abū Tammām and his ilk. What is curious about this is that the Neo-Classical poets most often preferred to emulate and write contrafactions of High ʿAbbāsid panegyrists in the first place. Therefore, although Shawqī has initially chosen a medieval Post-Classical model for his contrafaction, he shares with his model al-Būṣīrī the appropriation of High ʿAbbāsid "hegemonic discourse." This is true for even the lyrical sections of Nahj al-Burdah, as discussed above, but is particularly striking in this martial section, as is likewise true of the martial sections of al-Būṣīrī's Burdah and Ṣafī al-Dīn al-Ḥillī's Badīʿiyyah (chapter 2, BB part 8).

Achieving its consummate expression in his celebrated ode to the Caliph al-Muʿtaṣim on the conquest of the Byzantine city of Amorium (223/838), Abū Tammām's distinctive style of self-confident and robust rhetorical derring-do, termed *badīʿ*, and the Amorium Ode in particular, came to be synonymous with Islamic triumph and triumphalism.[62] Therefore, not only is the use of this distinctive style in itself rhetorically powerful, but it inevitably, and indeed essentially, evokes the Islamic triumphalism of the Amorium Ode, and in particular the spectacular and eternal victory of Islam over Christianity that that ode conveys. Verse 136 recalls Abū Tammām's oft-cited and oft-imitated "signature verse" describing the caliph al-Muʿtaṣīm (Amorium, v. 37):

Directed by one relying on God, avenging for God,
Striving and yearning toward God.[63]

[69]

Likewise, in verse 138, the convoluted playing with abstractions—personifying time, giving it a mount, then shooting "determination" at it—are typical of Abū Tammām's *al-madhhab al-kalāmī* ("dialectical mannerism"), what I have termed elsewhere "mental gymnastics." What is involved in such expressions, however, is not an empty rhetorical display. Rather, in Abū Tammām's and other ʿAbbāsid panegyrists' verses of caliphal panegyric, the ability of the patron (*mamdūḥ*) to defeat (the personifications of) time/fate (*dahr, zamān* [=death]) conveys a message of foreordained victory, cosmic power, and immortality (see chapter 2 and the introduction). It is not surprising that such rhetoric should make its way into *madīḥ nabawī.* Al-Bishrī cites as an antecedent of Shawqī's verse 138 another example from Abū Tammām:

> You rained down upon them such arrows of resolve
> That if you had shot them in battle at fate's foundation, it would have crumbled. (WN v. 138)[64]
>
> [70]

What needs to be noted here is that the tradition of transposition of the High ʿAbbāsid *badīʿ* style to the passages describing the military campaigns of the Prophet in *madīḥ nabawī* seems to have been initiated, or at least popularized, by al-Būṣīrī and to have become a standard stylistic practice of the genre, as we see, for example, in the Abū Tammāmian style of *badīʿ* that dominates the passages on the Prophet's battles in Ṣafī al-Dīn al-Ḥillī's Badīʿiyyah.[65]

Verse 139 employs the convention of terming the Muslim warriors who fight in the path of Allāh "God's swords" (*asyuf Allāh*), evoking verse 48 of Kaʿb's Suʿād Has Departed, which describes Muḥammad as "one of the swords of God, an Indian blade unsheathed" (*muhannadun min suyūfi Allāhi maslūlu*). But curiously, Shawqī denies them the equally conventional epithet *muhannad* (Indian, referring to the prized Indian tempered steel), declaring them emphatically "not Indian" (*lā al-hindiyyatu*). Yaseen Noorani has suggested in a similar Neo-Classical context that the conventional *muhannad* has now become associated with Britain's Indian subalterns who fight on her behalf.[66] Thus with his own *badīʿ*-twist, Shawqī adds a contemporary colonial political commentary: the Muslims fight out of commitment to their religion (as is indeed made emphatic in verse 140), whereas British Indian troops are—as the (subliminal) change of a dot in *khudhum* (cutting) to *khadam* (servants) suggests—mere servile subalterns. As we observed in our discussion of the cognate passage of al-Būṣīrī's Burdah (BB part 8) and as Shawqī's anticolonial stance requires, the Muslim warriors fighting at Muḥammad's side serve synecdochically for all Muslims fighting jihād in the service of Islam.

Verses 140 and 141 work in combination to convey the idea that the highest rank and glory are achieved by those who fall in jihād—who give their lives to honor their promise to fight unflinchingly *fī sabīl Allāh* (in the way of God). If we insist on our reading of verse 139, then this must be read in contrast to those subalterns, such as the Indians, who fight and die in abject service to their British overlords.

PART 9: THE SHARĪʿAH (VV. 142–154)

142. Muḥammad, with your Sharīʿah you made the minds of men
Burst forth with all kinds of knowledge, like a bounding sea.

143. Its gem-like essence sparkles round God's resplendent Unity
As jewels adorn a sword, or embroidery a banner.

144. It is a law of toleration, around which hover souls and minds;
He who thirsts for wisdom is drawn to its sweet water.

145. It is the light on the path, by which the worlds are guided;
It is men's surety in the youth of time and time's old age.

146. Fate and its decrees run according to the sentence it hands down,
Which is forever in force and inscribed upon creation.

147. When the dominion of Islam arose and spread
Its kingdoms walked in the Sharīʿah's perfect light.

148. It taught a nation of desert-dwellers,
After herding sheep and camels, to herd Caesars.

149. How many a domain, proud in its might, east and west,
Did the Reformers, enacting the Sharīʿah, build?

150. For the sake of knowledge, justice, and civilization,
They resolved upon their actions and girded their loins.

151. How quickly they conquered the world for their religion
And led mankind to drink of the Sharīʿah's cool sweet water.

152. As mankind's guides, they followed the Sharīʿah;
Through them it became man's clear path to prosperity.

153. Time cannot topple the column their justice erected,
But the wall of tyranny, if you touch it, will collapse.

154. They obtained felicity in both abodes,
And all partook of the general distribution of God's favor.

[71]

Shawqī pursues his polemic with a twelve-verse passage devoted to the Sharīʿah (Islamic law). This passage is the thematic counterpart to the first passage of Part 5: Sīrah Themes, on the Birth of the Prophet (vv. 75–82), where Shawqī dwelt on the tyranny, oppression, and ignorance that reigned before the coming of the Prophet. In part 9, by contrast, he demonstrates the justice, prosperity, and learning brought by Islamic rule under the Sharīʿah. The choice and meaning of the term in this context require some clarification—or at least exploration. In many ways, this passage seems to be Nahj al-Burdah's counterpart to al-Būṣīrī's Burdah Part 6: The Noble Qurʾān (BB vv. 88–104). For al-Būṣīrī, in keeping with classical and medieval Islamic theology, as well as rhetorical precepts, the Qurʾān is Muḥammad's evidentiary miracle, the proof of his Prophethood and of the Islamic faith. In my reading of al-Būṣīrī's Burdah, part 6 constitutes the culmination of the panegyric and the literary centerpiece of the poem. Although Shawqī duly recognizes the preeminence of the Qurʾān as Muḥammad's evidentiary miracle (NB part 4, vv. 69–71), nevertheless the Sharīʿah is given pride of place. Shawqī has essentially shifted the balance of his poetic intentions in Nahj al-Burdah to the politics of this world—the *dunyā* half of the *al-dīn wa-al-dunyā* formulation. Hence his emphasis on the Sharīʿah—that is, the institutional means for the establishment of Islamic dominion and the perpetuation of an Islamic polity. I argue, in other words, that Shawqī foregrounds the Sharīʿah rather than the Qurʾān because of his concern, in Nahj al-Burdah, with the Iḥyāʾ Project of the recuperation of the worldly dominion of Islam.

What does Shawqī mean by the Sharīʿah? When we examine the attributes promulgated in this passage, it becomes clear that Shawqī's vision, as we would expect from the Neo-Classical era, is deeply informed by the values of the Nahḍah, the Arab Awakening, what we could probably accurately term Enlightenment values, i.e., Western humanistic ideas. In Shawqī's intellectual formation these have been received as part of the Nahḍah and Islamic reformist discourse concerning contemporary Western enlightenment, humanism, social justice, science, and progress, as opposed to current Eastern superstition, despotism, ignorance, and backwardness. His achievement here is to create, as did the Islamic reformers, an Arab-Islamic vision or model of justice, knowledge, and prosperity—in a word, civilization—that conceives of these values as essentially Islamic and as recuperable from Arab-Islamic history, especially of the Golden Age of the ʿAbbāsid caliphate. What is perhaps most interesting here is that by his exposure of the hypocrisy and violence of the Christian West in parts 7 and 8, Shawqī has stripped them of their moral claim to these liberal values, which he now reassigns to, or projects back upon, the Islamic past. This he accomplishes in two steps. First, in Part 9: The Sharīʿah, he establishes the principle; and second, in Part 10: The Glory of Baghdād, he adduces the historical evidence and model.

In its general understanding, the term Sharīʿah, "Within Muslim discourse . . . designates the rules and regulations governing the lives of Muslims, derived in principal [sic] from the Ḳurʾān and *ḥadīth*."[67] Shawqī refines this general usage to create his own Iḥyāʾ Project vision of the Sharīʿah as embodying the highest ideals of justice, knowledge, and civilization as understood in Western-derived humanist terms. His formulation is more intellectual or ideological than historical, but his purpose is clear: to propose an Arab-Islamic model—one for which he claims or creates a historical precedent—of enlightenment, humanism, and progress to counter both the current climate of oppression and backwardness of the Islamic world and the Christian West's current domination and claim to a superior (vision of) civilization. Here we should cite once more Hourani's remark cited above that these Reformist ideas "took place under the stimulus of European liberal thought, and led to the gradual reinterpretation of Islamic concepts so as to make them equivalent to the guiding principles of European thought."

However much it is informed by contemporary Western expressions of enlightenment and humanistic values, Shawqī's formulation must be understood above all in the context of his twin experience of the brutality, injustice, and hypocrisy of Western colonial domination, which professed universally recognized values such as knowledge, justice, etc., on the one hand, and the appalling backwardness and ineptness of Ottoman rule, which claimed the Islamic caliphate, on the other.

It is worth noting, first of all, that Shawqī opens this section by binding the idea of the Sharīʿah to knowledge and learning. This is thematically consistent with his understanding of Muḥammad's message, as he has described it toward the end of the Night Journey and Ascension passage of Part 5: Sīrah Themes: "You have written out the sciences for both religion and the world," etc. (vv. 91–92). Here in part 9, Shawqī employs a subtle etymological manipulation to combine *sharīʿah* in the sense of "path to water" with the image of a (metaphorical) "sea of knowledge" (v. 142). His further images, too, are grounded in the classical lexical and etymological understanding of *sharīʿah:*

> *Sharīʿah* signifies a *place of descent to water* or *a way to water,* and signifies *al-Dīn* ([Islamic] religion), because it is a way to the means of eternal life. . . . *The religious law of God; consisting of such ordinances as those of fasting and prayer and pilgrimage and the giving the poor-rate and marriage and other acts of piety, or of obedience to God, or of duty to Him, and to men. . . .* [italics in original][68]

In terms of images, Shawqī's passage plays on this well-established etymological and semantic link: depictions of the Sharīʿah as "the way to water"—that is life, nourishment, eternal life, salvation, etc. Thus the Sharīʿah is depicted as "a bounding sea bursting with all kinds of knowledge" (*zājirin bi-ṣunūfi al-ʿilmi multaṭimi*) (v. 142); "sweet water of wisdom" (*salsalan min ḥikmatin*) (v. 144); "cool sweet water" (*salsālihā al-shabimi*) (v. 151); and further, as a "light on the path by which the worlds are guided" (*nūru al-sabīli yusāsu al-ʿālamūna bihā*) (v. 145), and again, the Islamic kingdoms walked "in its perfect light" (*fī nūrihā al-tamimi*) (v. 147). The most striking rhetorical achievement is Shawqī's use of the lexicon of humanistic values in his poetic formulation of the Sharīʿah to create a total fusion of the concepts of humanism and Sharīʿah: "minds bursting with all kinds of knowledge" (*fajjarta al-ʿuqūla . . . bi-ṣunūfi al-ʿilmi*) (v. 142) must perhaps first be read as a response to the poet's lament for the current state of ignorance of the Islamic world (v. 117); "wisdom" (*ḥikmah*) (v. 144); "knowledge, justice, civilization" (*lil-ʿilmi wa-al-ʿadli wa-al-tamdīni*) (150); and ultimately, in a term intimately associated with the Islamic call to prayer, but also in the Iḥyāʾ context of combating contemporary material as well as spiritual backwardness and poverty, "prosperity" (*al-falāḥ*) (v. 152).

Two particular elements can be highlighted as specific responses to the standard Christian and Western polemic against Islam: "tolerant" (*samḥāʾ*, the adjectival form of the more common Form VI verbal noun *tasāmuḥ*, "[religious] tolerance") (v. 144), in the first place evokes the traditional epithet of Islam as *al-ḥanīfah al-samḥāʾ* ("the true tolerant religion," i.e., Islam); but in the colonial context it takes on a further urgency in countering Christian claims to the contrary, and Christian cooption of the term. The second is the invocation of *zamān* (time or fate), which operates poetically as a synonym for *dahr,* thereby invoking the poetic convention of fate or time controlling all things (v. 146). Here, however, Shawqī follows the same *badīʿ*-inspired model on which he constructed verse 138, in which the convention is overturned. There Shawqī declares that Muḥammad can stop inexorable fate dead in its tracks—that is, the divinely appointed and inspired Prophet determines the course of events, not blind fate. Similarly in verse 146, in Shawqī's Iḥyāʾ formulation of the course of history, "time" or "fate" itself and its decrees (*aḥkām*) are subject to the decision or sentence (*ḥukm*) that the Sharīʿah hands down. That is to say, Islamic dominion and governance in accordance with the Sharīʿah (now understood to promote justice, prosperity, and the promotion of culture and science [below, part 10]), not inexorable fate, determines the course of events.

Conversely, we are to understand that the current state of decline of the Islamic world is not an act of fate, nor even something divinely preordained, but rather the result of failure to enact the Islamic principles of the Sharīʿah. Shawqī meticulously constructs his verse 146 not to contradict divine determination of events; the second hemistich refers to a divine sentence (law, decree) that does not take the form of predestination resulting in fatalism and passivity. As I understand Shawqī's formulation, in the Sharīʿah, Allāh has instituted or inscribed a law that is in force or effective (*nāfidh,* literally "piercing"—almost an antonym of "passive") among His creation. Therefore, like "natural law," divine law is inexorable ("What goes up must come down"; if a polity enacts and follows the Sharīʿah, it will prosper), but it is not predestined. Verse 146 must therefore be understood as Shawqī's Nahḍah/Iḥyāʾ response to Western Christian claims that Islam is responsible for the fatalism and passivity, the mentality of blind imitation (*taqlīd*), and the resultant stagnation (*jumūd*) that characterize the Islamic world of his day. For Shawqī,

Islam—particularly the Sharīʿah as the embodiment or enactment of Islam in the world—is not the problem, but the solution.

In keeping with Shawqī's political vision, the elements of dominion and conquest are included here (vv. 147, 149, and 151). What is of note, however, is that, in contrast to the brutality, materialism, and hypocrisy of Western imperialism, Islamic dominion is presented as the vehicle for the promotion of justice, prosperity, and civilization. (In fairness, I can think of no empire in history that claimed to be spreading oppression, poverty, and ignorance, though many did, and are.) In Shawqī's formulation, the Islamic worldly conquest was "for the sake of knowledge, justice, and civilization" (v. 149–150). Ironically, the concept of "civilization" (*al-tamdīn*) is itself a derivation from the West. Hourani writes, concerning the seminal Reformist thought of al-Afghānī:

> At this point we become aware of a novelty in al-Afghani's thought, or at least a new emphasis. The centre of attention is no longer Islam as a religion, it is rather Islam as a civilization. The aim of man's acts is not the service of God alone; it is the creation of human civilization flourishing in all its parts. The idea of civilization is indeed one of the seminal ideas of nineteenth-century Europe, and it is through al-Afghani above all that it reaches the Islamic world. It was given its classical expression by Guizot, in his lectures on the history of civilization in Europe, and al-Afghani had been impressed by him. The book was translated into Arabic in 1877, and al-Afghani inspired ʿAbduh to write an article welcoming the translation and expounding the doctrine of the book.[69]

It is of note, too, that the builders of the Islamic empire(s), what we would normally term "conquerors" or "rulers," are termed *muṣliḥūn* (v. 149), which conveys the meaning of "reformers," "restorers," "those who bring peace and prosperity." In Shawqī's vision of Islamic dominion, might and justice are inseparable. Here, too, we can see Shawqī's formulation as derivative of the ideas of al-Afghānī as they had penetrated Egyptian intellectual thought of his time. Hourani writes of al-Afghānī's formulation of Islamic civilization:

> In its great days, the *umma* had all the necessary attributes of a flourishing civilization: social development, individual development, belief in reason, unity and solidarity; later it lost them. Being of fiery and political temperament, he tended to see both the greatness and the decline in political and military terms, but in reality the military successes of early Islam

> were for him only a symbol of the flowering of Islamic civilization. What had once been achieved could be achieved again: on the one hand by accepting those fruits of reason, the sciences of modern Europe, but also, and more fundamentally, by restoring the unity of the *umma*.[70]

As I see it, in Shawqī's case at least, particularly within the context of the British military occupation of Egypt, the political and military successes of early Islam were not merely symbolic of the flowering of Islamic civilization, but part and parcel of it, just as any recuperation of Islamic civilization would require a political and/or military solution to the British occupation and Western domination in general.

In historical terms, then, Shawqī sees the Sharīᶜah, the earthly embodiment or enactment of Islam, as both the means and the ends for the rise of Arab-Islamic civilization, through which the sheep- and camel-herders of the desert learned how to "herd Caesars" and rule over a just and prosperous realm (v. 148). Al-Bishrī spells this out for us in his commentary on verse 148:

> This verse and the one before it serve as proof for the preceding verses about the universality of the Islamic Sharīᶜah and its revealing the means for success and prosperity [*al-fawz wa-al-falāḥ*] for all mankind in every age and in every circumstance. For the first of mankind to receive it were the Arabs, who were at that time a people of the barren desert,[71] mired in utter ignorance, and abased by grinding poverty. They had become so familiar with the means of death and destruction and committing outrages against one another that there was no one left among them who was not seeking vengeance or sought for it—so much so that if it were not for their paying the blood-wite, there would not have been a man left standing in the Arab Peninsula. Such was their state when Allāh the Most High sent them the Sharīᶜah of Islam: then the corrupt among them became virtuous, the poor became rich, the ignorant became learned, their few became many, their humbled became mighty. So, when Allāh granted them victory, subjected the nations of the earth to them, and put the reins of kingdoms in their hands, they administered their domains soundly on the basis of religion, treated their subjects well in accordance with the Sharīᶜah, and led them to the utmost felicity and prosperity.—Not to mention the brilliant civilization they achieved in their rule over al-Andalus, the flourishing of the sciences and arts in their age, and the industries they promoted for the people, etc., all of which the people of the West took from them and made the basis of their civilization with which they try to subdue and confound us [*yuᶜājizūnanā*] today. (WN v. 148)

Of note are al-Bishrī's subtle rhetorical employ of evocative Islamic diction in support of his Iḥyāʾ anticolonial manifesto. In Qurʾānic usage, the word *fawz* (success, triumph, victory) is invariably, in the formulae *al-fawz al-ʿaẓīm* (the great triumph; QK 4:13, etc.), *al-fawz al-mubīn* (the clear victory; QK 6:16, etc.), *al-fawz al-kabīr* (the big success, QK 85:11), an expression of salvation and felicity in the heavenly garden. The word *falāḥ* denotes simply prosperity or success, but through its use in the call to prayer (*hayyā ʿalá al-ṣalāh, hayyā ʿalá al-falāḥ* / Come to prayer, Come to salvation) has also come to connote salvation. In the Iḥyāʾ-determined context of al-Bishrī's commentary, these words are redirected (or directed back) to their ordinary denotations to express the worldly success and prosperity, i.e., dominion and civilization, that the application of the Sharīʿah has conferred upon the Arabs. Likewise he effectively employs the Form III verb *ʿājaza* (*to attempt* to confound or debilitate) for Western attempts to subdue the Muslim world, as opposed to the Form IV verb *ʾaʿjaza* (to confound, debilitate), which in Islamic parlance is used for the confounding or debilitating effect of the Qurʾān on those who would dare to imitate it (the doctrinal principle of the inimitability of the Qurʾān, Iʿjāz al-Qurʾān). Al-Bishrī is well aware of the irony of the West's borrowings, especially in science and technology, from Arab-Islamic civilization now being turned against their source, but his subtle juxtaposition of the attemptive Form III *ʿājaza* for the West as opposed to the causative/effective Form IV *iʿjāz* of the Qurʾān/Islam leaves no doubt in our minds that he has put his faith in the ultimate victory of Islam.

Needless to say, Shawqī is presenting an idealized vision of Islamic history, one that derives from the Islamic Reformist and Arab Nahḍah identification of Islamic civilization with Western humanistic ideals. Verse 153 states with compelling eloquence the permanence of justice as opposed to the fragility of tyranny—a hopeful message to an oppressed people. Finally, part 9 concludes by declaring that those who conquered in the name of Islam and ruled in accordance with the Sharīʿah "achieved felicity in both abodes" (*nālū al-saʿādata fī al-dārayni*, v. 154). Again, we can understand this as an expression of Iḥyāʾ or Nahḍah ideas that rejected the backwardness and fatalism that aimed at felicity solely in the next world while settling for political, moral, and physical degradation in this one. At the same time, this celebration of a past Islamic dominion characterized by "knowledge, justice, and civilization" serves as a "silent *hijā*ʾ" or implied invective against the failed Islamic polities of Shawqī's own day—his own Khedive and his despotic Ottoman sovereign.

In sum, we must understand Shawqī's attempt to identify Islam with justice and knowledge as his response to the colonial period's characterization of Islam, or Islamic societies, as despotic and backward. In this regard, it is of note that Shawqī makes no attempt to defend the Islam of his own day, and its rulers, from these charges, but feels compelled to return to an idealized image of a Golden Age. Above all, in Shawqī's formulation, justice, knowledge, and civilization are not presented as borrowings from Western humanist thought; rather he has construed them through a process of rhetorical fusion as essential, historically grounded, Islamic values. This he seeks to demonstrate in part 10.

PART 10: THE GLORY OF BAGHDĀD (VV. 155–164)

155. Forget the glories of Rome and Athens,
For all the sapphires are in Baghdād, and all the pearls.

156. Let Chosroes and the Arch in which he took such pride
Go up in smoke on the ashes of the Zoroastrian fires!

157. Don't speak of Ramses, for the true sign of dominion
Is instituting justice, not erecting pyramids.

158. Whenever Baghdād, the House of Peace, is mentioned,
Rome, the House of Laws, throws up her hands in surrender.

159. Rome could not equal Baghdād in eloquence at council,
Nor could she match her adjudication of disputes.

160. And the ranks of her Caesars never contained
A Rashīd, or a Maʾmūn, or a Muʿtaṣim,

161. Of those who, when their battalions went forth to conquer,
Imposed their will upon the borders and the boundaries of the earth.

162. They held councils devoted to science and knowledge;
Their intellect and understanding no man approached.

163. The scholars, when they addressed a session, bowed their heads
In awe of knowledge, not in awe of sovereign power.

164. They poured forth so profuse a rain of bounty
That the land knew no drought; its people knew no want.

[72]

In part 10, Shawqī takes the battle to the enemy to address the West and/or its supporters. He moves the celebration of justice and knowledge from the generalized depiction of Islamic civilization of Part 9: The Sharīʿah to a more explicit celebration of what he sees as the pinnacle of Islamic civilization (dominion, justice, learning) in the early ʿAbbāsid Caliphate at Baghdād. In this respect we should keep in mind that the Nahḍah and Iḥyāʾ movement for the recuperation of the Islamic Ummah did not take the period of the Prophet and his Companions as their model, but rather, in keeping with their need to respond to current Western humanistic ideas of civilization, they turned to the periods of greatest "worldly" achievement, in terms of dominion, learning, and scientific and literary production. For this they chose the ʿAbbāsid and Andalusian periods.[72] The poet perfunctorily dismisses the boasts of the West—Rome and Athens—and also the Persian Chosroes and his Arch at Ctesiphon, and even Ramses and the Pyramids of Ancient Egypt. Baghdād outshone them all in the two principles Shawqī most esteems: justice and the promotion of science and knowledge. Among the ʿAbbāsid caliphs he singles out three for special mention: Hārūn al-Rashīd (r. 170/786–193/809), whose name, perhaps more in the popular imagination of the *Thousand and One Nights* than in the historical record, is associated with the Golden Age of Islamic glory and justice;[73] al-Maʾmūn (r. 198/813–218/833), who is renowned for the scientific and cultural accomplishments of his rule, notably the establishment of the Bayt al-Ḥikmah (House of Wisdom) academy for science, especially the translation of Hellenistic philosophical and scientific works from Greek into Arabic, and the theological debates at his court;[74] and al-Muʿtaṣim (r. 218/833–227/842), whose name suits the rhyme, but also, through whose military conquests, such as that over the Byzantine Christian city of Amorium, or more precisely their poetic celebrations by panegyrists such as Abū Tammām, became proverbial of Arab-Islamic dominion (see above). In brief: Hārūn al-Rashīd, especially in his folkloric persona, exemplifies justice; al-Maʾmūn, the promotion of science; and al-Muʿtaṣim, military conquest, particularly against a Christian aggressor. The three together thus epitomize Shawqī's Iḥyāʾ-based conception of ideal Islamic rule.

The three-verse passage 161–163 encapsulates Shawqī's vision of the early ʿAbbāsid period as a model Islamic polity: it begins with military conquest and the expansion of Islamic dominion (v. 161), but joins this immediately to the holding of scientific councils and the expansion of knowledge (v. 162). Perhaps the most compelling expression of Shawqī's vision of an Islamic Enlightenment is verse 163, describing scholars bowing their heads as they addressed the caliphs' sessions: "In awe of knowledge, not in awe of sovereign power." The last two of these verses are striking for the sheer intensity of Iḥyāʾ-inspired diction of science and learning: science, knowledge, intellect, understanding, scholars, knowledge (*ʿilm, maʿrifah, ʿaql, fuhum, ʿulamāʾ, al-ʿilm*) (vv. 162–163).

The concluding verse (164) works at several levels to encapsulate the virtue of ʿAbbāsid rule: in the more immediate sense, the "pouring forth of profuse rain" means the lavish gifts and prizes that the ʿAbbāsid caliphs bestowed on the scholars and men of letters who adorned their courts and attended their sessions. The meaning quickly expands, however, to refer more broadly and archetypally to the fertility and prosperity, both literal and figurative, of their realms. At this point we should notice that Part 9: The Sharīʿah and Part 10: The Glory of Baghdād both follow the same three-step conceptual trajectory: the Islamic conquest of vast domains; the institution of an Islamic rule that promotes justice, science, and civilization; and, as a result, an Islamic polity that prospers both materially and spiritually.

We must keep in mind, however, that Shawqī's presentation of the early ʿAbbāsid caliphate is idealized, or at least extremely selective, and does not reflect the political, military, and religious turmoil of the period in question: Hārūn al-Rashīd's massacre of the Barmakid vizierial family and the roots of the disintegration of the empire under his rule; the civil war between his sons al-Amīn and al-Maʾmūn; the perennial Islamic controversy over the Muʿtazilite doctrines, with the accompanying Miḥnah (inquisition) introduced by al-Maʾmūn and pursued by al-Muʿtaṣim; as well as the many military uprisings of the period, to give but a few examples. That is, Part 10: The Glory of Baghdād falls under the rubric of panegyric, not history, and like all Arab-Islamic panegyric presents a "legitimizing vision" (Tarif Khalidi's term) of its subject. It is worth noting that the original vision of an ʿAbbāsid Golden Age is the creation of the great ʿAbbāsid court panegyrists.[75] What is striking in Nahj al-Burdah is that the subject of the panegyric of part 10 is not the dedicatee of the poem, Shawqī's patron the Khedive ʿAbbās Ḥilmī II, but a long-gone Golden Age.

Taken together, Part 9: The Sharīʿah and Part 10: The Glory of Baghdād, one more conceptual, the other more historically embodied, constitute Shawqī's vision of an alternative empire or imperialism, one that combines the enlightened humanist values professed but not enacted by the West with the Islamic legitimacy and divine sanction currently claimed by the backward, debilitated and debilitating, Ottomans. That is, within the contemporary political context, Shawqī on the one hand challenges the hypocrisy of the West/British by establishing a historical (Islamic) precedent for the political enactment and realization of the values to which they merely give lip service. With respect to the Ottomans, Shawqī's reaching to the distant Islamic past for a vision of legitimate and enlightened rule constitutes an unstated challenge to—or denial of—their legitimacy. Certainly as official panegyrist to the Khedival court, Shawqī would have been expected to portray the Islamic legitimacy and effectiveness of his patron's rule, *and his allegiance to it,* through an idealized, indeed adulatory, vision of his realm. His silence in this respect is an eloquent condemnation. We are reminded in this respect of al-Buḥtūrī's renowned *Sīniyyah* describing the Arch of Chosroes, a similar case in which, I argue, the poet's silence concerning his contemporary ʿAbbāsid masters and rhapsodic praise of the lost Persian past can only be read as a complaint against or condemnation of his erstwhile ʿAbbāsid patrons.[76]

PART 11: THE ORTHODOX CALIPHS (VV. 165–176)

165. God's Caliphs are too great to be measured against others,
So don't compare them with mere worldly kings.

166. For who among mankind resembles al-Fārūq* [*=ʿUmar ibn al-Khaṭṭāb]
In justice, or humble, modest Ibn ʿAbd al-ʿAzīz?* [*=ʿUmar II]

167. Or the Imām ʿAlī when he scattered a crowd
With tears that gathered in the corners of his men's eyes?

168. ʿAlī, abundant sweet water in science and letters,
Victorious and vigorous in war and peace.

169. Or ʿUthmān ibn ʿAffān, in his hand the Qurʾān
Over which he bends, yearning like a mother over her new-weaned babe,

170. Gathering its verses in order, and arranging them
In a string of pearls, never to be scattered, on the neck of the nights.

171. Two wounds in the heart* of Islam have never healed: [*lit. "liver"]
The wound of the martyred ʿUthmān and the wound that bloodied the Holy Book.

172. The valor of Abū Bakr can never be doubted
After his glorious achievements in deeds and services.

173. With resolve and determination he protected Religion
From trials that tested the patience of mature, forbearing men.

174. Trials that led astray even the right-guided ʿUmar al-Fārūq
Concerning death, which is certain and not subject to doubt.

175. ʿUmar contended with the people, drawing his Indian blade,
Concerning the greatest of prophets, how could he not live forever?

176. Don't blame him for being bewildered:
The beloved Prophet had died, and an ardent lover, despite himself, erred.

[73]

Verse 165, on the superiority of God's caliphs to ordinary rulers, serves as a transition from the ʿAbbāsid caliphs of Baghdād in the preceding part 10 to the Orthodox Caliphs (al-Khulafāʾ al-Rāshidūn), i.e., the first four caliphs to succeed the Prophet Muḥammad in leading the Islamic state, in part 11. These are, in chronological order: Abū Bakr (r. 11–13/632–634); ʿUmar ibn al-Khaṭṭāb (r. 13–23/634–644); ʿUthmān ibn ʿAffān (r. 23–35/644–656); and ʿAlī ibn Abī Ṭālib (r. 35–39 or 40/656–659 or 660). The invocation of the Orthodox Caliphs serves to complement the praise of the ʿAbbāsids of the preceding section. For although the ʿAbbāsid and also Andalusian periods are celebrated as the pinnacles of Islamic civilization and its attendant accomplishments in arts, sciences, and governance, etc., the Sunnī Islamic construction of history normally gives precedence to the Orthodox Caliphs in terms of closeness—physical, moral, and spiritual—to the Prophet and of establishing the foundations of the Islamic polity. Further, inasmuch as the recognition of all four Orthodox Caliphs is Sunnī as opposed to Shīʿī doctrine (the Shīʿah consider the Prophet's cousin and son-in-law ʿAlī ibn Abī Ṭālib the rightful successor to the Prophet and hence reject the first three Orthodox Caliphs), part 11 serves as the poet's Sunnī *credo* and pledge of allegiance, in keeping with the staunch Sunnism of the Ottoman Empire.

At this point we should note that the Ottoman sultans had long entertained claims to the title of caliph, which was explicitly proclaimed by Sultan ʿAbd al-Ḥamīd II. Although as suzerain of Shawqī's patron, Khedive ʿAbbās Ḥilmī II, Sultan ʿAbd al-Ḥamīd II had been the recipient of the poet's panegyric, by the time of the composition of Nahj al-Burdah he had just been deposed by the Young Turks (1909) and replaced with Sultan Muḥammad V. Shawqī, while praising the Arab Orthodox and ʿAbbāsid caliphs, is as remarkably mute on the subject of the contemporary Ottoman title-holders as he is on his patron the Khedive.

Shawqī does not present the Orthodox Caliphs in a historical, chronological, or narrative form. Rather he presents rhetorical epitomes of their significance to Islamic history that, in the end, move chronologically backward to conclude with their response to the death of the Prophet. In verse 166, employing a rhetorical form of riddle with the pun word omitted, he invokes the two celebrated caliphs named ʿUmar without mentioning their shared name: "al-Fārūq" (traditionally taken to mean "he who distinguishes between truth and falsehood") is the epithet of the second Orthodox Caliph, the stern and uncompromising ʿUmar [I] ibn al-Khaṭṭāb, "a driving force behind the early conquests and the creation of the early Islamic empire."[77] "Ibn ʿAbd al-ʿAzīz" is ʿUmar I's Umayyad namesake, the proverbially pious ʿUmar [II] ibn ʿAbd al-ʿAzīz (r. 99–101/717–720), traditionally considered the saving grace of the otherwise worldly and self-indulgent Umayyad "kings."[78] Verse 167 introduces the Prophet's cousin and son-in-law, the fourth caliph, ʿAlī ibn Abī Ṭālib, through a complex word-play involving a pun on *faḍḍa* (meaning both to shed tears and to disperse a crowd) and *jinās* (root-play) of *muzdaḥam* (crowded, gathered, crowded place) and *muzdaḥim* (crowding, gathering). Al-Bishrī's commentary is silent concerning the occasion to which this refers. It is related however, that when battles against "erring" Muslims ended, ʿAlī "showed his grief, wept for the dead, and even prayed over his enemies."[79] Further, as verse 168 relates, he was renowned for his eloquence, his learning, and his bravery in battle, the last evidenced by his epithet Ḥaydar, "lion."[80]

Verses 169–171 encapsulate the identity of the third Orthodox Caliph, ʿUthmān ibn ʿAffān (r. 23–35/644–656), who is credited with ordering the first recension of the Qurʾānic text. It is said that his murder, which set off Islam's First Civil War (al-Fitnah al-Ūlá), took place while he was reading the Qurʾān, so that his blood spilled on the Holy Book.[81] In Nahj al-Burdah, these events are not narrated, but rhetorically encapsulated. In verse 170, using diction and similes more often applied to poetry, Shawqī describes the now-ordered verses of the Qurʾān as forming a necklace on the neck of the nights (i.e., of time or fate), which is to say, an eternal order, never to be broken. Similarly, in a complex rhetorical interplay of figurative and literal wounds, Shawqī expresses not merely the "facts" of ʿUthmān's murder but also its profoundly disturbing effect on the Islamic community. The image of spilled blood defiling the Qurʾān, here grammatically inverted for rhetorical emphasis, as al-Bishrī notes (WN v. 171; literally, "a wound bloodied by the Book," *jurḥun bi-al-kitābi damī*), serves metonymically to express an outrage against Islam itself.

The closing verses (172–176) of part 11 open with the first caliph, who had also been during the Prophet's lifetime his closest friend and staunchest ally and defender, Abū Bakr (r. 11–13/632–634; cf. The Miracle of the Cave, NB Part 5: Sīrah Themes, vv. 94–99), before returning to the second caliph, ʿUmar ibn al-Khaṭṭāb. Verse 173 may refer primarily to the major accomplishment of Abū Bakr's caliphate, that is, his preserving the Islamic community through his dealing with the Ḥurūb al-Riddah (Wars of Apostasy) against tribes that withdrew their allegiance to the nascent Islamic state and religion when the Prophet died.[82] However, the following verse (174) connects these "trials" to the crucial moment of Islamic religion and history. The death of the Prophet in the year 11/632 triggered a profound spiritual and political crisis in his community. Al-Bishrī relates from the Sīrah of the Prophet that ʿUmar ibn al-Khaṭṭāb, when he heard people say that the Prophet had died, took up his sword and threatened to cut off their hands and feet. It was Abū Bakr who then arose and famously declared: "Let him who worships Muḥammad know that he is dead; let him who worships Allāh know that He lives forever." (WN v. 175).[83]

It is revealing to compare Ibn Hishām's *Al-Sīrah* narration with Shawqī's poetic presentation. In *Al-Sīrah*, ʿUmar's disbelief expresses the incredulity of a religious community that, up until that moment, was defined by its Prophet's guiding presence among them. The violence of

ʿUmar's response is an expression of his passion and devotion. However, in doctrinal, as well as narrative, terms it serves as a dramatic foil for Abū Bakr, the closest and most loyal of Muḥammad's followers, to make the pronouncement that defines the Islamic faith—and that ultimately distinguishes it from Christianity—that the Prophet Muḥammad is a mortal and that Allāh alone is immortal and divine. In Shawqī's passage the dramatic tension of the scene and the lapidary eloquence of Abū Bakr's formulation are replaced by a subdued and sympathetic explanation of, or excuse for, ʿUmar's error. The word-play in verse 174—concerning right guidance and error, certainty and ambiguity—sets the stage for the confusion and error of *al-rāshid al-Fārūq* (the rightly-guided one who distinguishes between truth and falsehood), and the closing verse, 176, then offers a plea for forgiveness for him, on the grounds that his fervent love for the Prophet was what led him to err.

Curiously, Part 11: The Orthodox Caliphs opens with the exaltation of the caliphs (v. 165) but, unlike Part 10: The Glory of Baghdād, does not present an idealized vision of the justice and prosperity of their age. Instead, the blasphemous murder of the third caliph, ʿUthmān, is mourned as a wound to Islam that will never heal (v. 171), and, moreover, the final lines about ʿUmar's response to the Prophet's death close the section on a melancholy note of ardent love, bewilderment, and error—and a plea for forgiveness, "Don't blame him" (vv. 174–176). We can now begin to understand the reason for this curious emotional trajectory. The poet asks forgiveness for ʿUmar for the greatest of all Islamic sins, *shirk* (polytheism, assigning partners to Allāh, which is how Muslims understand the Christian belief in the divinity of Jesus, and how they would understand a claim for the immortality of Muḥammad); he pleads for this forgiveness on the grounds that the source of this error was ardent love for the Prophet.

In the context of the Nahḍah and the Islamic Reformist ideology of his period, Shawqī's description of ʿUmar's mistake is identical to that of the devout Muslims of the Post-Classical "Age of Decline" (ʿAṣr al-Inḥṭāṭ) and of the popular Islam of his own day, who were excessive in their veneration of the Prophet: they are ardent lovers of the Prophet who have nevertheless, out of bewilderment, erred. As the poet pleads for forgiveness for ʿUmar, it is really the excesses of the Post-Classical veneration of the Prophet that he has in mind. For certainly if the pious and noble rightly guided (*al-rāshid*) al-Fārūq, "he who distinguishes between truth and falsehood,"

(v. 174) can fall into error, how much more can an ordinary believer? Shawqī is commenting on the Modernists' criticism of the medieval and popular tradition of *madīḥ nabawī*, of which al-Būṣīrī's Burdah is the preeminent example, as entailing an excessive veneration of the Prophet Muḥammad that is dangerously close to *shirk* and intimately bound up with the sort of *khurāfāt* (popular superstitions) evidenced in the *khaṣāʾiṣ* (Burdah-based philters and amulets) we saw in al-Bājūrī's *Ḥāshiyah* (chapter 2).[84] At this point we must reconsider Shawqī's claim (part 6, vv.103–104) that he is not competing with al-Būṣīrī's Burdah, but merely emulating it. Clearly Shawqī has coopted the Burdah, with its associations with what were in the Islamic Reformists' eyes the fatalism, superstition, and backwardness of popular piety, in an attempt to redirect it toward a Reformist formulation of Islamic humanism. In this light, we are prepared for the moving and eloquent plea for the recuperation of Islamic dignity and dominion that seals Nahj al-Burdah.

PART 12: BENEDICTION AND SUPPLICATION (VV. 177–190)

177. O Lord, Your blessing and peace for as long as You desire
Upon him who dwells at Your throne, the best of all Messengers.

178. Who kept prayer alive through the night,
Uninterrupted except by tears of apprehension flowing down,

179. Glorifying You beneath the wing of night,
Enduring sleeplessness and the pain of swollen feet.

180. His soul content, with no complaint of weariness,
For if your love is true, it never grows weary.

181. And bless, my Lord, his family, the elect, among whom
You set Muḥammad, the banner of the House of the Kaʿbah and of
Mecca's Sacred Precinct,

182. Their faces white when fate's face is pitch-black;
Their heads aloof from hot-headed fortune's blows.

183. Bestow your best blessing on those four of the Prophet's Companions
Whose friendship was a bond inviolate,

184. Who rode forth when the Prophet summoned them
To dreadful exploits and fearsome deeds,

185. Who stood fast when the very earth was shaking;
Who laughed as they plunged, reckless, into perils.

186. O Lord, peoples before have risen from death,
And nations have awakened from the slumber of privation.

187. Good- and ill-fortune and dominion, You are their master!
Your decree confers both blessings and chastisements.

188. In its wisdom Your divine decree has passed its judgment on us.
How noble is your countenance as judge and as avenger!

189. So, for the sake of the Messenger of the worlds, be gracious unto us;
Do not deepen the humiliation of his people and their disgrace.

190. O Lord, in him you gave the Muslims a good beginning,
Now complete your grace and grant them a good end.

[74]

In the final part of Nahj al-Burdah Shawqī returns to and completes the ritual and poetic requirements specific to *madīḥ nabawī,* especially as they have been established in the paradigm for the genre and the base-text for his poem, al-Būṣīrī's Burdah. At the same time, of course, he is fulfilling the broader generic dictates of the classical Arabic *qaṣīdat al-madḥ* (panegyric ode) of the supplicatory sort, that vast literary tradition to which he, the major proponent of Arabic Neo-Classical poetry (Shiʿr al-Iḥyāʾ), and his Nahj al-Burdah belong. The Benediction (*duʿāʾ*), whereby the poet calls on Allāh to bless the *mamdūh,* grant him long life and prosperity, etc., is a standard feature of Arab-Islamic court panegyric. It is worth noting that despite its explicitly religious formulation, the *duʿāʾ* functions, perhaps above all politically, as a sort of declaration or oath of allegiance. This is especially clear if we keep in mind the awful efficacy attributed to such speech acts as the blessing and curse in traditional societies.

It is crucial to remember that in Arabic panegyric the Benediction is a prayer to Allāh to bless, protect, and prolong the life of the patron to whom the praise poem is addressed—that is, the *mamdūḥ,* as well as his progeny, etc. In court panegyric, the Supplication (stated or otherwise) consists of the poet supplicating the patron. In *madīḥ nabawī,* then, the standard as set by and seen in al-Būṣīrī's Burdah is that the Supplication consists of the poet asking the Prophet for intercession (*shafāʿah*) on Judgment Day, and the Benediction is, in the first place, for Allāh to bless the Prophet Muḥammad and, further, his family. The benediction is then often extended to call down Allāh's blessing upon the Companions of the Prophet, upon the Orthodox Caliphs in Sunnī *madīḥ nabawī*, to the Muslims in general, and often to the poet himself and his family. Let us remember, too, that, as we have established in general (see chapters 1 and 2, and chapter 3, Part 3: Repentance, Submission, Supplication, vv. 39–46) the parts that I have termed the "ritual core" of the poem, which are performative in nature, are characterized by rhetoric that is simple, direct, transparent, and highly emotively charged.

In Part 12: Benediction and Supplication, then, Shawqī achieves a strikingly moving and effective ritual and emotional climax in what is perhaps both the most traditional and, at the same time, most original passage of Nahj al-Burdah. Part 12 is clearly set off from the preceding Part 11: The Orthodox Caliphs. Part 11 is constructed of third-person encapsulations of the Orthodox Caliphs and thus addressed to the reader. The change of tone and direction is signaled in the opening of part 12 by the emotive and dramatic second-person address to Allāh, "O Lord" (*yā Rabbi,* literally "O my Lord" [v. 177]), a phrase whose repetition in this part of the poem (vv. 186, 190) serves to build momentum toward the final climax. This use of apostrophe is comparable to Shawqī's "O Aḥmad" (v. 100) to create an effective and dramatic opening to Part 6: Metapoetic Recapitulation of Prophetic Praise.

The Benediction (*duʿāʾ*—the term denotes as well any personal prayer) begins with the *taṣliyah* (God bless him [the Prophet] and give him peace), the speech act that, as we discussed with regard to al-Būṣīrī's Burdah, is an essential ritual component in traditional Islam to guarantee the efficacy of a prayer (chapter 2, part 10). In verse 177, therefore, Shawqī is explicitly following obligatory religious as well as poetic (ritual) practice. At the same time, the Benediction (vv. 177 to 185), which like all benedictions and curses is a speech act, is a carefully formulated declaration of religious and political allegiances. Again, this is not description, but the performance of the speech act of declaring allegiance, that is, establishing a spiritual and political bond of mutual obligation between the poet and those upon whom he calls down Allāh's blessing. The poet's allegiances are hierarchically ranked and exclusive.

Allāh, as the source of all the blessings for which the poet pleads, is first. At the head of the list to be blessed comes, of course, the Prophet

Muḥammad, the prophet nearest to God's throne and the best of God's Messengers (v. 177). Muḥammad is invoked here, not for his miracles or message or military prowess, as in earlier parts of Nahj al-Burdah, but as the exemplar of pious devotion stemming from his sincere love for God. Al-Būṣīrī's image and diction of the Prophet's praying through the night until his feet became swollen (BB v. 29) is quite explicitly echoed in verses 178–179: *aḥyā/muḥyī* (revive, keep alive); *ḍurr* (harm, pain), *waram* (swelling). With verses 181–182 Shawqī adds the Prophet's family (Āl al-Bayt), conveying their nobility and superiority with precisely the diction and image we found in Kaᶜb ibn Zuhayr's (chapter 1) description of the Emigrants (Muhājirūn) toward the end of Suᶜād Has Departed (vv. 51–52): "haughty, high-nosed" (*shumm*) and "white" (*bīḍ*), that is, noble. The next three verses (183–185) confirm or establish Shawqī's Sunnī allegiance with the plea for God's blessing on the four Orthodox Caliphs. Here, too, verses 183–184 remind us of Kaᶜb's Suᶜād Has Departed verses 54–55 in their description of the reckless heroism of those fighting in the way of God. Once more, it is noteworthy in the context of Shawqī's prose dedication of Nahj al-Burdah to the Khedive ᶜAbbās Ḥilmī II that there is no mention in this "pledge of allegiance" section of the poet's worldly patron or his Ottoman overlords.

The ritual and poetic climax of the poem comes at the end, verses 186–190, which fall under the heading of Supplication. What is extraordinary in Nahj al-Burdah is that it does not end with the Benediction—neither for the Prophet, nor the Muslims altogether, nor the poet and his family. Nor is the Supplication what we have come to expect in *madīḥ nabawī*. In al-Būṣīrī's Part 10: Fervent Prayer and Petition (BB vv. 152–160) the first three verses are Supplication to the Prophet for intercession on Judgment Day (BB vv. 152–154), followed by a plea to God for forgiveness and mercy on Judgment Day, and His grace in both abodes (BB vv. 156–158). Al-Būṣīrī closes his Burdah with an exquisitely lyrical *nasīb*-derived Benediction (vv. 159–160), appealing for God's blessing upon the Prophet,

> For as long as the eastern breeze stirs the boughs of the ben-tree
> And the camel-driver stirs his light-hued beasts with song. (BB v. 160)

Shawqī, by contrast, does not provide a final lyrical resolution or emotional release; rather he maintains, indeed intensifies, the highly charged emotive urgency right through to the end. By reiterating in verse 186 and again in verse 190 the "O Lord" of verse 177, he builds his poem toward its conceptual and emotional climax. Here he gathers the Iḥyāʾ threads that run throughout Nahj al-Burdah to seal the poem with an eloquent and moving plea for the revival of the Islamic Ummah. The diction of this section achieves through its eloquence and transparency a direct and forceful expression of the Iḥyāʾ or Nahḍah call for cultural revival and awakening. Thus verse 186, with its "peoples before have risen from death" (*habbat shuʿūbun min maniyyatihā*) and "nations have awakened from the slumber of privation" or of "nonexistence." (*wa-istayqaẓat ʾumamun min raqdati al-ʿadami*), echoes the key formulations of part 4 verse 74 ("bring dead aspirations back to life") and part 6 verses 116–117 ("revive whole generations of decaying bones," "raise mankind from ignorance or from the grave") of the spiritual and cultural revival and renewal of the Islamic world. Whereas in parts 4 and 6 the plea for revival is addressed to the Prophet, in the closing passage the plea is addressed directly to Allāh (vv. 186–190). Verse 186 is a plea by indirection: other peoples have arisen from [cultural] death, so why not we?

There follows in verses 187–188 a careful formulation of divine power with respect to the rise and fall of nations. In terms of the panegyric component of the supplicatory ritual, these two verses recognize Allāh's power and authority and the concomitant submission of the Islamic Ummah, and the poet, to it. Verse 187 invokes Allāh's mastery of the fate of nations through distinctly Qurʾānic diction and locutions. Thus: "a dominion" of which "You are . . . master" (*mulkun ʾanta mālikuhu*) evokes the Qurʾānic verse: "Say: 'O God! Master of Dominion. You confer dominion on whomever You will and you strip dominion from whomever you will. . . .'" (*quli Allahumma mālika al-mulki tuʾtī al-mulka man tashāʾu wa-tanziʿu al-mulka mimman tashāʾu. . . .* [QK 3:26]). Likewise the verb *tudīlu* (Form IV = to confer [ascendency]) evokes the Form III verb of the same root, *dāwala* (to make alternate between) in the Qurʾānic: ". . . those days [of good- and ill-fortune] We give to men by turns. . . ." (*. . . wa tilka al-ʾayyāmu nudāwiluhā bayna al-nāsi. . . .* [QK 3:140]; see WN v. 187). Through what is essentially a double entendre on the loaded word *qaḍāʾ*, which can mean either "divine decree" or "fate," verse 188 performs an Iḥyāʾ-inspired verbal feat of establishing Allāh's *qaḍāʾ* not as predestined fate, but as an expression of His wisdom (*ḥikmah*) and judgment. In brief, Shawqī makes it clear that the so-called "vicissitudes of fate" are not the work of "blind fate" but of divine decree and judgment. Further, by invoking Allāh's might and justice, the poet implies that the current degraded state of the Islamic Ummah is a divine judgment for their having abandoned true Islam. Having established a divine judgment in this world, the poet then appropriates for *himself* the role of intercessor and pleads for mercy for his community.

Perhaps the most moving verse of Nahj al-Burdah is verse 189, the poet's Iḥyāʾ-inspired plea, not for mercy on Judgment Day, but for the Islamic Ummah's release in this world from its current state of "humiliation" and "disgrace" (*khasf*). In the context of Shawqī's Egypt, that disgrace is the combination of the failure of the Ottoman and Khedival states to create an advanced, prosperous, and powerful Islamic polity and the particular humiliation experienced by Egypt under British (Western, Christian) occupation. In terms of the panegyric pact of the ritual of supplication, we can perceive in these verses of praise to Allāh not only the elevation of the deity but also the self-abasement of the worshipper. In other words, a supplicatory ritual—now addressed to Allāh rather than to the Prophet—is being performed in this brief but extraordinarily powerful passage. Allāh's omnipotence (vv. 187–188) and His worshipper's humiliation (v. 189), define the two in their respective roles as supplicated and supplicant. The role of Muḥammad as Intercessor is presented in inverted form, as the poet, who appropriates the role of intercessor for the earthly judgment, beseeches Allāh for Muḥammad's sake to be gracious unto his, that is, Muḥammad's, people. The poet's employ of the first person plural adds poignancy and intimacy, but also a communal element, to this verse.

Shawqī's prayer for the restitution of Islamic dignity and dominion in this world reaches its climax in the closing verse. Verse 190 opens reiterating the "O Lord" of verses 177 and 186 to bring the poem to its emotive peak. The structure of this verse itself, however simple it appears, provides an encapsulated panegyric pact: the first hemistich is praise: "You gave the Muslims a good beginning"; the second is the petition, "now grant them a good end."

Perhaps the most striking element of the closure (vv. 186–190) is the manner in which Shawqī establishes a worldly judgment as the earthly counterpart to the Last Judgment and then appropriates for himself the role of intercessor that the Prophet will perform on Judgment Day, pleading for

God's mercy on the community of believers. This is the culmination of the identification or correspondence of poetic and prophetic roles that Shawqī introduced in Part 6: Metapoetic Recapitulation of Prophetic Praise.

The simple transparent diction of verse 190 combines with a rhetorically complex but eminently lucid verbal play—the antithesis between "beginning" and "end" (*badʾ/mukhtatam*), the root-play between "make good or beautiful" and "goodness or beauty" (*aḥsanta/ḥusn*)—that provides a striking example of the type of directness and transparency of expression that typifies the ritual core of supplicatory poetry. At the same time, however, Shawqī is invoking, however lightly and elegantly, the tradition of the *badīʿiyyah,* that distinctive subgenre of *madīḥ nabawī* which, like Shawqī's Nahj al-Burdah, consists of a *muʿāraḍah* imitation of al-Būṣīrī's Burdah, but with the added programmatic requirement that each verse must exemplify a particular rhetorical (*balāghah* or *badīʿ*) device. In fact, Shawqī here invokes the later development of this subgenre, first produced by ʿIzz al-Dīn al-Mawṣilī (d. 789/1387), in which each verse must, additionally, contain a pun (*tawriyah*) on the name of the device being demonstrated (chapter 3, introduction). In Shawqī's closing verse, then, he pays homage to this Post-Classical poetic tradition through his word-play on the rhetorical devices of *ḥusn al-ibtidāʾ* (beautiful opening) and *ḥusn al-khitām* (beautiful closure) are employed in the form of a pun (*tawriyah*)(*ʾaḥsanta al-badʾa, ḥusna mukhtatami*) to provide a "beautiful beginning" and "beautiful ending" not merely for the verse and the poem, but for the Islamic Ummah.

At first glance it seems ironic that Shawqī would seal his Iḥyāʾ Project with a rhetorical turn so distinctive of the poetics of what was termed ʿAṣr al-Inḥiṭāṭ (the Age of Decline). However, a comparison of his closure with that of Ibn Ḥijjah al-Ḥamawī's (d. 837/1434) closure of the *badīʿiyyah* around which he composed his celebrated *Khizānat al-Adab* (Storehouse of Literature) has the effect of highlighting the difference between the otherworldly concerns of the ʿAṣr al-Inḥiṭāṭ and the earthly political goals of the Iḥyāʾ Project of the Nahḍah. Ibn Ḥijjah closes his *badīʿiyyah:*

> By my beautiful beginning [*ḥusnu ibtidāya*] of this poem, I hope to escape [*al-takhalluṣ*]
> From Hellfire, and I hope for a beautiful end [*ḥusna mukhtatamī*].[85] [75]

In it, Ibn Ḥijjah, following his model al-Mawṣilī, first puns on the names of three rhetorical figures: beautiful beginning or opening (*ḥusn al-ibtidāʾ*), beautiful transition (*ḥusn al-takhalluṣ*), and beautiful closure (*ḥusn al-khitām*): thus, he at once sums up and seals the poem with an epitome of its poetic structure. At the same time, however, these terms refer to the final disposition of his immortal soul, for through this poem of *madīḥ nabawī* with its praise of the Prophet and petition for his Intercession on Judgment Day, the poet hopes to escape (*takhalluṣ*) Hellfire and perdition and to achieve salvation—a "beautiful end" in the heavenly Garden. In sum, Ibn Ḥijjah's closing verse encapsulates the entire *madīḥ nabawī* project of the Post-Classical Age.

Taken out of its Nahḍah-period poetic context, Shawqī's closure verse, with its puns on "beautiful beginning" and "beautiful end" reads much like Ibn Ḥijjah's:

> O Lord, in him you gave the Muslims a good beginning (*ʾaḥsanta badʾa*),
> Now complete your grace and grant them a good end (*ḥusna mukhtatami*).

Within the context of the Iḥyāʾ Project of Nahj al-Burdah, however, we understand that here the "good beginning" is the mission of the Prophet Muḥammad and the "good end" for which the poet pleads is not otherworldly salvation on Judgment Day, but the restoration of Islamic military, political, and cultural dominion in this world. This redirection of Burdah-derived *madīḥ nabawī* away from the Post-Classical concern with otherworldly intercession and salvation toward a Neo-Classical Nahḍah-inspired call for the restitution of an Islamic Golden Age is brilliantly and movingly achieved in Shawqī's closing verse.

Conclusion

UMM KULTHŪM, AL-QARAḌĀWĪ, AND NAHJ AL-BURDAH

The power of Shawqī's Nahj al-Burdah has not diminished with the passage of time, nor, conversely, have the political events of the past century made its message obsolete. In addition to its appearance in the several editions of *Al-Shawqiyyāt,* its separate publication with al-Muwayliḥī's introduction and al-Bishrī's commentary has never gone out of print. It has been adapted, too, to the arts and technologies of the century since its composition. Throughout the Arab-Islamic world, Shawqī's Nahj al-Burdah is best and most widely known through recordings of its rendition by the beloved and immensely popular Egyptian songstress, Umm Kulthūm (d. 1975).[86] Composed by Riyāḍ al-Sunbāṭī and first performed by Umm Kulthūm in 1946, its plea for the restoration of Arab-Islamic political power and dignity coincided with the aspirations of Arab and Egyptian nationalism, through the Nasserite era, and resonates all the more in the period of sustained demoralization the Arab world has suffered since the 1967 defeat. As Huda Fakhreddine has established in her analysis of Umm Kulthūm's performance of al-Sunbaṭī's musical composition, the thirty verses that al-Sunbāṭī has selected from Shawqī's 190-verse text belong to what I have termed the "ritual core" of the poem and are performed in such a way that "the anticolonial polemic is transformed into a profound spiritual performance through which the audience is guided."[87]

A search of the Internet reveals that Shawqī's Nahj al-Burdah continues to inform the contemporary understanding of the anticolonial situation of the Arab-Islamic world. The same self-defensive stance against Western Christian attacks that shaped both Shawqī's poem and al-Bishrī's commentary informs in the 2002 discussion of the Egyptian Islamic scholar Shaykh Yūsuf al-Qaraḍāwī on the Al Jazeera TV channel program, "Al-Sharīʿah wa-al-Ḥayāh" (The Sharia and Life), a transcript of which has been translated and posted on the website of "UK Charity Organisation, Jam'iat Ihyaa' Minhaaj al-Sunnah (JIMAS)," as the site says, "due to the continued and increasingly virulent attacks now being directed against the honour and sanctity of the final messenger of God to mankind, Muhammad (pbuh)."[88] Posted under the title: "Weapons Used by the Other Religions to Wage War on Islam," an excerpt reads:

> Some of them say that Islām was spread by the sword. Our Shaykh al-Ghazālī—may Allāh have mercy on him—used to say, "On the contrary, Islām was not victorious by the sword, it was victorious *over* the sword, because the sword was raised to it, and it countered the sword with the sword, for force can only be defeated with force." And Shawqī—may Allāh have mercy on him—has a few beautiful lines of poetry in *Nahj al-Burdah* in which he says,

They said the battles, and the Messengers of Allāh were not sent
To kill a person, nor did they come with bloodshed,
Lies and misguidance, dreams and sophistry,
Conquests with the sword came after conquests with the pen.
If you meet evil with good, it cannot bear it,
And if you meet it with evil, it will be erased. [Italics in original].[89]

APPENDIX OF ARABIC TEXTS

[1] **قال عَلْقَمَةُ الفَحْل**

١ طَحا بِكَ قَلْبٌ في الحِسانِ طَرُوبُ   بُعَيْدَ الشَّبابِ عَصْرَ حانَ مَشِيبُ
٢ يُكَلِّفُني لَيْلَى وَقَدْ شَطَّ وَلْيُها   وَعادَتْ عَوادٍ بَيْنَنا وَخُطُوبُ
٣ مُنَعَّمَةٌ ما يُسْتَطاعُ كِلامُها   عَلَى بابِها مِنْ أَنْ تُزارَ رَقِيبُ

[2] **قال عَلْقَمَةُ الفَحْل**

٨ فَإِنْ تَسْأَلوني بِالنِّساءِ فَإِنَّني   بَصيرٌ بِأَدْواءِ النِّساءِ طَبِيبُ
٩ إذا شابَ رَأْسُ المَرْءِ أَوْ قَلَّ مالُهُ   فَلَيْسَ لَهُ مِنْ وُدِّهِنَّ نَصِيبُ
١٠ يُرِدْنَ ثَراءَ المالِ حَيْثُ عَلِمْنَهُ   وَشَرْخُ الشَّبابِ عِنْدَهُنَّ عَجِيبُ

[3] **قال عَلْقَمَةُ الفَحْل**

١١ فَدَعْها وَسَلِّ الهَمَّ عَنْكَ بِجَسْرَةٍ   كَهَمِّكَ فيها بِالرِّدافِ خَبِيبُ
١٢ إلى الحارِثِ الوَهّابِ أَعْمَلْتُ ناقَتي   لِكَلْكَلِها وَالقُصْرَيَيْنِ وَجِيبُ

[4] **قال عَلْقَمَةُ الفَحْل**

١٧ إِلَيْكَ أَبَيْتَ اللَّعْنَ كانَ وَجِيفُها   بِمُشْتَبِهاتٍ هَوْلُهُنَّ مَهِيبُ
١٨ هَداني إِلَيكَ الفَرْقَدانِ وَلاحِبٌ   لَهُ فَوقَ أَصْواءِ المِتانِ عُلُوبُ
١٩ بِها جِيَفُ الحَسْرَى فَأَمّا عِظامُها   فَبِيضٌ وَأَمّا جِلْدُها فَصَلِيبُ

[5] **قال عَلْقَمَةُ الفَحْل**

٢١ فَـلا تَحْرِمَنِّي نـائِـلاً عَــنْ جَنابَةٍ　　فَـإِنِّي ٱمْـرُؤٌ وَسْـطَ القِبابِ غَرِيبُ

٢٢ وَأَنْـتَ ٱمْـرُؤٌ أَفْضَتْ إِلَيْكَ أَمانَتِي　　وَقَـبْـلَـكَ رَبَّتْنِي فَضِعْتُ رُبُوبُ

٢٣ فَـأَدَّتْ بَنُو كَعْبِ بْنِ عَـوْفٍ رَبِيبَها　　وَغُــودِرَ في بَعْضِ الجُنُودِ رَبِيبُ

[6] قال عَلْقَمَةُ الفَحْل

٢٥ تُـقَـدِّمُـهُ حَـتّـى تَـغـيـبَ حُجولُهُ　　وَأَنْــتَ لِبَيْضِ الـدّارِعِـينَ ضَرُوبُ

٢٦ مُظاهِرُ سِرْبَـالَيْ حَـديـدٍ عَلَيْهِما　　عَقِيلاً سُـيـوفٍ مِـخْـذَمٌ وَرُسُوبُ

[7] قال عَلْقَمَةُ الفَحْل

٣٥ وأَنْــتَ الَّــذي آثـارُهُ في عَدُوِّهِ　　مِنَ البُؤْسِ والنُّعْمَى لَهُنَّ نُدُوبُ

٣٦ وَفِي كُلِّ حَـيٍّ قَـدْ خَبَطْتَ بِنِعْمَةٍ　　فَـحُـقَّ لِـشَـأْسٍ مِـنْ نَـداكَ ذَنُوبُ

٣٧ وَمـا مِـثْـلُـهُ في الـنَّـاسِ إلاّ أَسِيرُهُ　　مُــدَانٍ وَلا دانٍ لِــذَاكَ قَرِيبُ

[8] قال النّابِغَةُ الذُّبْيانِيّ

١ يـا دارَ مَـيَّـةَ بالعَلْياءِ فالسَّنَدِ　　أَقْـوَتْ وطـالَ عَلَيْها سالِفُ الأَبَدِ

٢ وَقَـفْـتُ فِيها أُصَـيْـلانـاً أُسائِلُها　　عَيَّتْ جَواباً وما بالرَّبْعِ مِن أَحَدِ

. . . .

٦ أَمْسَتْ خَلاءً وأَمْسَى أهلُها احْتَمَلوا　　أَخْنَى عليها الذي أخْنَى على لُبَدِ

٧ فعَدِّ عـمّا تَـرَى إذْ لا ارْتِـجـاعَ له　　وَانْــمِ الـقُـتُـودَ عـلى عَـيْرانـةٍ أُجُدِ

[9] قال النّابِغَةُ الذُّبْيانِيّ

٣٧ فلا لَعَمْرُ الـذي مَسَّحْتُ كَعْبَتَهُ　　وما هُرِيقَ على الأَنْصابِ من جَسَدِ

٣٨ والمُؤْمِنِ العائذاتِ الطَّيْرَ يَمْسَحُها　　رُكْـبـانُ مَكَّةَ بين الغَيْلِ والسَّعَدِ

٣٩ ما قُلْتُ مِـن سَيِّءٍ مِـمّا أُتِـيْـتَ به　　إذاً فلا رَفَـعَـتْ سَـوْطِـي إِلَيَّ يَدِي

٤٠ إلاّ مَـقـالَـةَ أقْــوامٍ شَـقِـيـتُ بها　　كانتْ مَقالَتُهُمْ قَرْعاً على الكَبِدِ

[10] قال النّابِغَةُ الذُّبْيانِيّ

٤١ أُنْـبِـئْـتُ أَنَّ أبـا قـابُـوسَ أَوْعَدَنِي　　ولا قَــرارَ عــلى زَأْرٍ مِـنَ الأَسَدِ

٤٢ مَـهْـلاً فِــداءً لـكَ الأَقْــوَامُ كلُّهُمُ　　ومــا أُثَـمِّــرُ مِــن مـالٍ ومِــن وَلَدِ

٤٣ لا تَـقْـذِفَـنِّـي بـرُكْـنٍ لا كِـفـاءَ له　　وإنْ تَـأَثَّـفَـكَ الأَعْــداءُ بالرِّفَدِ

[11] قال النّابِغَةُ الذُّبْيَانِيّ

٢٠ فتلك تُبْلِغُنِي الـنُّـعْـمانَ إنّ له   فَضْلاً على النَّاسِ في الأَدْنَى وفي البَعَدِ

. . . .

٢٧ أَعْـطَـى لـفـارِهَـةٍ حُـلْـوٍ تَوابِعُها   مِن المـواهِـبِ لا تُعْطَى على نَكَدِ

٢٨ الـواهِـبُ المائـةَ المِـعْـكـاءَ زَيَّنَها   سَعْدانُ تُوضِحَ في أَوْبـارِهـا اللِّبَدِ

٢٩ والأُدْمَ قد خُيِّسَتْ فُتْلاً مَرافِقُها   مَـشْـدُودةً بـرِحـالِ الـحِـيرَةِ الجُدُدِ

٣٠ والرَّاكِضاتِ ذُيُـولَ الرَّيْطِ فانَقَها   بَـرْدُ الهَواجِرِ كالغِزْلانِ بالجَرَدِ

٣١ والـخَـيْـلَ تَمْـزَعُ غَـرْبـاً في أَعِنَّتِها   كالطَّيرِ تَنْجُو مِنَ الشُّؤْبوبِ ذي البَرَدِ

. . . .

٤٤ فما الـفُـراتُ إذا هَـبَّ الـرِّيـاحُ له   تَرْمي غَـوارِبُـهُ الـعِـبْرَيْـنِ بالزَّبَدِ

٤٥ يَمُـــدُّه كـلُّ وادٍ مُـــتْرَعٍ لَجِبٍ   فيه رُكـامٌ مِن اليَنْبُوتِ والخَضَدِ

. . . .

٤٧ يَـوْمـاً بـأَجْـوَدَ منه سَـيْـبَ نافِلَةٍ   ولا يَـحُـولُ عَطاءُ اليومِ دُونَ غَدِ

[12] قال النّابِغَةُ الذُّبْيَانِيّ

٢٤ فَمَن أَطـاعَـكَ فانْفَعْه بطاعتِهِ   كما أَطـاعَـكَ وَادْلُـلْـهُ على الرَّشَدِ

٢٥ وَمَـــنْ عَـصـاكَ فَعاقِبْهُ مُعاقَبَةً   تَنْهَى الظَّلُومَ ولا تَقْعُدْ على ضَمَدِ

[13] قال النّابِغَةُ الذُّبْيَانِيّ

٤٨ هذا الثَّناءُ فـإنْ تَسْمَعْ به حَسَناً   فلم أُعَـرِّضْ أَبَيْتَ اللَّعْنَ بالصَّفَدِ

٤٩ ها إنَّ ذِي عِـذْرَةٌ إلاّ تكنْ نَفَعَتْ   فَـإنَّ صاحِبَها مُـشـارِكُ النَّكَدِ

[14] قال زُهَيْرُ بْنُ أَبِي سُلْمَى

١ إنَّ الخَلِيطَ أَجَـدَّ الـبَـيْنَ فأنْفَرَقا   وعُلِّقَ القَلْبُ مِن أَسْماءَ ما عَلِقا

٢ وفـارَقَـتْـكَ بـرَهْـنٍ لا فِـكـاكَ لَهُ   يـومَ الـوَداعِ فأَمْسَى رَهْنُها غَلِقا

٣ وأَخْلَفَتْكَ ابنةُ البَكْرِيِّ ما وَعَدَتْ   فأَصْبَحَ الحَبْلُ منها واهِياً خَلَقا

[15] قال زُهَيْرُ بْنُ أَبِي سُلْمَى

٥ بِجِيدِ مُـغْـزِلَـةٍ أَدْمـــاءَ خاذِلَةٍ   مِـنَ الظِّباءِ تُـراعِـي شـادِنـاً خَرِقا

٦ كأَنَّ رِيقَتَها بعد الكَرَى ٱغْتَبَقَتْ   مِنْ طَيِّبِ الـرّاحِ لمّا يَعْدُ أَنْ عَتُقا

[16] **قال زُهَيْرُ بْنُ أَبِي سُلْمَى**

٨ ما زِلْتُ أَرْمُقُهُمْ حتّى إِذا هَبَطَتْ   أَيْدِي الرِّكابِ بهِمْ مِن راكِسٍ فَلَقا

. . . .

١٠ كـأَنَّ عَـيْـنَـيَّ في غَـرْبَيْ مُقَتَّلَةٍ   مِنَ النَّواضِحِ تَسْقِي جَنَّةً سُحُقا

[17] **قال زُهَيْرُ بْنُ أَبِي سُلْمَى**

١٧ فَعَـدِّ عـمّا تَـرَى إِذْ فـاتَ مَطْلَبُهُ   أَمْسَى بِـذاكَ غُـرابُ البَيْنِ قد نَعَقا

١٨ وَانْـمِ القُتُودَ على وَجْـنـاءَ دَوْسَرَةٍ   يَـشْرَى الجَدِيلُ إِذا ما دَأْيُها عَرِقا

١٩ كـأَنَّ كُـورِي وأَنْـسـاعـي ومِيثَرَتِي   كَـسَـوْتُـهُـنَّ مُشِبًّا ناشِطاً لَهَقا

. . . .

٢٤ فـأَدْرَكَـتْـه سَـمـاءٌ بينها خَلَلٌ   تُرْوِي الثَّرَى وتُسِيلُ الصَّفْصَفَ القَرِقا

٢٥ فبات مُعْتَصِمًا من قُـرِّهـا لَثِقًا   رَشَّ السَّحابُ عليه المـاءَ فاطَّرَقا

. . . .

٢٨ لَيلتَه كلَّها حـتّـى إذا حَسَرَتْ   عنْه النُّجومُ أَضاء الصُّبْحُ فانْطَلَقا

٢٩ فصبَّحتْه كِـلابٌ شَـدُّهـا خَطِفٌ   وقـانِـصٌ لا تَـرى في فِعْلِه خُرُقا

. . . .

٣١ حتّى إذا ظَنَّ قَـرْنَ الشَّمسِ غالبةً   وخاف من جانِبَيْه النَّهْزَ والرَّهَقا

٣٢ كَـرَّ فـفـرَّجَ أُولاهـا بنافذةٍ   نَـجْـلاءَ تُتْبِعُ رَوْقَـيْـه دَمـاً دَفَقا

[18] **قال زُهَيْرُ بْنُ أَبِي سُلْمَى**

٣٣ بل أَذْكُـرَنْ خَـيْرَ قَيْسٍ كلِّها حَسَباً   وخَـيْرَهـا نـائـلاً وخَـيْرَهـا خُلُقا

[19] **قال زُهَيْرُ بْنُ أَبِي سُلْمَى**

٣٥ فَضْلَ الجَوادِ على الخَيْلِ البِطاءِ فلا   يُعْطِي بذلك مَمْنوناً ولا نَزِقا

٣٦ قد جَعَلَ المُبْتَغُون الخَيْرَ في هَرِمٍ   والـسّـائـلـون إلى أبْـوابِـهِ طُرُقا

. . . .

٤٣ أَغَـرُّ أَبْـيَـضُ فَـيّـاضٌ يفكُّك عنْ   أَيْـدِي العُنَاةِ وعن أَعْناقِها الرِّبَقا

٤٤ مَـنْ يَلْقَ يوماً على عِـلاَّتِـهِ هَرِمًا   يَلْقَ السَّماحةَ منه والنَّدَى خُلُقا

٤٥ ولَيس مانِعَ ذي قُـرْبَى ولا نَسَبٍ   يومًا ولا مُعْدِمًا من خابِطٍ وَرَقا

[20] **قال زُهَيْرُ بْنُ أَبي سُلْمَى**

٣٧ القائدُ الخَيْلَ منْكوبًا دَوابِرُها   قد أُحْكِمتْ حَكَماتِ القِدِّ والأَبَقا

٣٨ غَـزَتْ سِمانًا فآبتْ ضُمَّرًا خُدُجًا   مِـنْ بَعْدِ ما جَنَبُوها بُدَّنًا عُقُقا

٣٩ حتَّى يَـؤوبَ بها شُعْثًا مُعَطَّلَةً   تَشْكو الدَّوَابِرَ والأَنْساءَ والصُّفُقا

. . . .

٤٦ لَـيْـثٌ بِـعَـثَّرَ يَصْطادُ الـرِّجـالَ إذا   ما اللَّيْثُ كَذَّبَ عن أَقْرانِه صَدَقا

٤٧ يَطْعَنُهُمْ ما ٱرْتَمَوا حتَّى إذا اطَّعَنُوا   ضـارَبَ حتّى إذا ما ضارَبُوا ٱعْتَنَقا

٤٨ هـذا ولَـيْـسَ كمَنْ يَعْيَا بخُطَّتِه   وَسْـطَ الرِّجالِ إذا ما ناطِقٌ نَطَقا

[21] **قال زُهَيْرُ بْنُ أَبي سُلْمَى**

٤٠ يطْلُبُ شَـأْوَ ٱمْـرَأَيْـنِ قَدَّمَا حَسَنًا   نـالا المـلـوكَ وبَـذَّا هـذه السُّوَقا

٤١ هو الـجَـوَادُ فـإنْ يَلْحَقْ بشَأْوِهِما   عـلى تَـكَـالـيـفِـهِ فـمِـثْـلُـه لَحِقا

٤٢ أو يَسْبِقاه على ما كان من مَهَلٍ   فمِثْلُ ما قَدَّما من صالِحٍ سَبَقا

[22] **قال زُهَيْرُ بْنُ أَبي سُلْمَى**

٤٩ لو نـال حَـيٌّ مِـن الدُّنيا بمَكْرُمةٍ   أُفْـقَ الـسَّـماءِ لنالت كَفُّه الأُفُقا

[23] **قال زُهَيْرُ بْنُ أَبي سُلْمَى**

٢٧ فلا تَكْتُمُنَّ اللهَ ما في صُدُورِكُمْ   لِيَخْفَى ومَهْما يُكْتَمِ اللهُ يَعْلَمِ

٢٨ يُـؤَخَّـرْ فيُوضَعْ في كِتابٍ فَيُدَّخَرْ   لِيَوْمِ الحِسابِ أوْ يُعَجَّلْ فيُنْقَمِ

[24] **قال زُهَيْرُ بْنُ أَبي سُلْمَى**

١ دَعْ ذا وعَـدِّ الـقَـوْلَ في هَرِمٍ   خَـيْرِ الـكُـهُـولِ وسَـيِّـدِ الحَضَرِ

٢ لـو كـنـتَ مـن شَيْءٍ سِـوى بَشَرٍ   كُـنْـتَ المُـنَـوِّرَ لـيـلـةَ البَدْرِ

٣ ولأنـت أَوْصَـلُ مَـنْ سَـمِـعْـتُ به   لـشَـوابِـكِ الأرْحــامِ والصِّهْرِ

٤ وَلَـنِـعْـمَ حَـشْـوُ الـدِّرْعِ أنـتَ إذا   دُعِـيَـتْ نَـزالِ ولُـجَّ في الذُّعْرِ

٥ وأراكَ تَفْرِي ما خَلَقْتَ وبَعـ   ضُ القَوْمِ يَخْلُقُ ثُمَّ لا يَفْرِي
٦ أُثْنِي عَلَيْكَ بما عَلِمْتُ وما   أَسْلَفْتَ في النَّجَداتِ من ذِكْرِ
٧ والسِّتْرُ دون الفاحِشاتِ ولا   يَلْقاكَ دون الخَيْرِ مِن سِتْرِ

[25] قال كَعْبُ بْنُ زُهَيْر

١ ألا أَبْلِغا عنِّي بُجَيْراً رِسالةً   فهَلْ لكَ فيما قلْتُ بالخَيْفِ هَلْ لَكَا
٢ شَرِبْتَ مع المأمونِ كأساً رَوِيَّةً   فأَنْهَلَكَ المأمونُ منها وعَلَّكا
٣ وخالَفْتَ أَسْبابَ الهُدَى وتَبِعْتَه   على أيِّ شيءٍ وَيْبَ غَيْرِكَ دَلَّكا
٤ على خُلُقٍ لم تُلْفِ أُمًّا ولا أبًا   عليه ولم تُدْرِكْ عليه أَخًا لَكَا

[26] قال بُجَيْرُ بْنُ زُهَيْر

١ مَنْ مُبْلِغٌ كَعْبًا فَهَلْ لَكَ في الّتي   تَلُومُ عليها باطلاً وَهْيَ أَحْزَمُ
٢ إلى اللهِ لا العُزَّى واللاّتِ وَحْدَهُ   فتَنْجُو إذا كان النَّجاءُ وتَسْلَمُ
٣ لَدَى يَوْمٍ لا يَنْجُو وليس بمُفْلِتٍ   من النَّارِ إلاّ طاهرُ القَلْبِ مُسْلِمُ
٤ فدِينُ زُهَيْرٍ وَهْوَ لا شيءَ دِينُه   ودِينُ أَبِي سُلْمَى علَيَّ مُحَرَّمُ

[27] قال دُرَيْدُ بْنُ الصِّمَّة

١ أَمَرْتُهُمُ أَمْري بمُنْعَرَجِ اللِّوَى   فلم يَسْتبِينوا الرُّشْدَ إلاَّ ضُحَى الغَدِ
٢ فلَمَّا عَصَوْني كنتُ منهم وقد أَرى   غَوايَتَهم وأَنَّني غيرُ مُهْتَدِ
٣ وهل أنا إلاَّ مِنْ غَزِيَّةَ إنْ غَوَتْ   غَوَيْتُ وإنْ تَرْشُدْ غَزِيَّةُ أَرْشُدِ

[28] بانَتْ سُعادُ لكَعْبِ بْنِ زُهَيْر

١ بانَتْ سُعادُ فَقَلْبِي اليومَ مَتْبولُ   مُتَيَّمٌ إثْرَها لم يُفْدَ مَكْبول
٢ وما سُعادُ غَداةَ البَيْنِ إذ رَحَلوا   إلاّ أَغَنُّ غَضيضُ الطَّرْفِ مَكْحولُ
٣ تَجْلُو عَوارِضَ ذي ظَلْمٍ إذا ابْتَسَمَتْ   كأنَّهُ مُنْهَلٌ بالرَّاحِ مَعْلُول
٤ شُجَّتْ بِذي شَبَمٍ مِنْ ماءِ مَحْنِيَةٍ   صافٍ بأَبْطَحَ أَضْحَى وَهْوَ مَشْمول
٥ تَجْلُو الرِّياحُ القَذَى عنهُ وأَفْرَطَه   مِن صَوْبِ سارِيَةٍ بِيضٌ يَعالِيل
٦ يا وَيْحَها خُلَّةً لو أنَّها صَدَقَتْ   ما وَعَدَتْ أوْ لَوَ انَّ النُّصْحَ مَقْبول
٧ لكِنَّها خُلَّةٌ قد سِيطَ مِن دَمِها   فَجْعٌ ووَلْعٌ وإخْلافٌ وتَبْديلُ

٨ فـما تَـدُومُ عـلى حـالٍ تـكـونُ بها   كـما تَـلَـوَّنُ في أَثْـوابِـهـا الغُولُ
٩ وما تَمَسَّكُ بالوَصْلِ الـذي زَعَمَتْ   إلاّ كـما تُمْـسِـكُ المـاءَ الغَرابِيلُ
١٠ كانت مَوَاعيدُ عُـرْقُـوبٍ لها مَثَلاً   ومـا مَـواعـيـدُهـا إلاّ الأَباطِيلُ
١١ أَرْجُـو وآمُـلُ أنْ يَعْجَلْنَ في أَبَدٍ   ومـا لَهُنَّ طَـوالَ الـدَّهْـرِ تَعْجيلُ
١٢ فلا يَغُرَّنْكَ ما مَنَّتْ وما وَعَدَتْ   إنَّ الأمــانِيَّ والأحْــلامَ تَضْليلُ

[29] **بانَتْ سُعادُ لِكَعْبِ بْنِ زُهَيْر**

١٣ أَمْـسَـتْ سُـعـادُ بـأَرْضٍ لا يُبَلِّغُها   إلاّ العِتاقُ النَّجيباتُ المَراسِيلُ
١٤ ولــن يُـبَـلِّـغَـهـا إلاّ عُذافِرَةٌ   فيها على الأَيْــنِ إرْقـالٌ وتَبْغيلُ
١٥ مِن كُلِّ نَضَّاخَةِ الذِّفْرَى إذا عَرِقَتْ   عُرْضَتُها طامِسُ الأعْـلامِ مَجْهولُ
١٦ تَرْمي الغُيُوبَ بِعَيْنَي مُفْرَدٍ لَهِقٍ   إذا تَـوَقَّـدَتِ الـحُـزَّانُ والمِيلُ
١٧ ضَـخْـمٌ مُقَلَّدُها فَـعْـمٌ مُقَيَّدُها   في خَلْقِها عن بَناتِ الفَحْلِ تَفْضيلُ
١٨ حَـرْفٌ أَخوها أبوها مِن مُهَجَّنَةٍ   وعَـمُّـهـا خالُها قَــوْداءُ شِمْليلُ
١٩ يَمْـشي الـقُـرادُ عليها ثـمَّ يُزْلِقُهُ   منها لَـبـانٌ وأقْــرابٌ زَهاليلُ
٢٠ عَيْرانَةٌ قُذِفَتْ في اللَّحْمِ عَنْ عُرُضٍ   مِرْفَقُها عن بَناتِ الـزَّوْرِ مَفْتولُ
٢١ كـأنَّ ما فـاتَ عَيْنَيْها ومَذْبَحَها   مِنْ خَطْمِها ومِن اللَّحْيَيْنِ بِرْطِيلُ
٢٢ تُمِرُّ مِثْلَ عَسيبِ النَّخْلِ ذا خُصَلٍ   في غـارِزٍ لم تَـخَـوَّنْـهُ الأَحَالِيلُ
٢٣ قَـنْـواءُ في حُـرَّتَـيْـهـا للبَصيرِ بها   عِتْقٌ مُبينٌ وفي الخَدَّيْنِ تَسْهيلُ
٢٤ تَخْدِي على يَـسَراتٍ وَهْـيَ لاحِقَةٌ   ذَوابِــلٌ وَقْـعُـهُـنَّ الأرْضَ تَحْليلُ
٢٥ سُمْرُ العُجاياتِ يَتْرُكْنَ الحَصَى زِيَماً   لم يَـقِـهِـنَّ رُءُوسَ الأُكْـمِ تَنْعيلُ
٢٦ يوماً يَظَلُّ بِهِ الحِرْباءُ مُصْطَخِماً   كـأنَّ ضـاحِـيَـهُ بـالـنّـارِ مَمْلولُ
٢٧ كـأنَّ أوْبَ ذِراعَـيْـهـا وقـد عَرِقَتْ   وقـد تَـلَـفَّـعَ بـالـقُـورِ العَساقِيلُ
٢٨ وقالَ للقَوْمِ حادِيهِمْ وقد جَعَلَتْ   وُرْقُ الجَنادِبِ يَرْكُضْنَ الحَصَى قِيلُوا
٢٩ شَـدَّ النَّهارِ ذِراعَـا عَيْطَلٍ نَصَفٍ   قـامَـتْ فَجاوَبَها نُـكْـدٌ مَثاكِيلُ
٣٠ نَـوَّاحَـةٌ رِخْـوَةُ الضَّبْعَيْنِ ليسَ لها   لمّا نَعَى بِكْرَها النَّاعونَ مَعْقولُ
٣١ تَـفْـرِي اللَّبانَ بِكَفَّيها ومِدْرَعُها   مُـشَـقَّـقٌ عَــنْ تَـراقِـيـهـا رَعابِيلُ

[30] **بانَتْ سُعادُ لكَعْبِ بْنِ زُهَيْر**

* ما زِلْـتُ أَقْتَطِعُ البَيْداءَ مُدَّرِعًا   جُنْحَ الظَّلامِ وثَـوْبُ اللَّيْلِ مَسْبولُ

[31] **بانَتْ سُعادُ لكَعْبِ بْنِ زُهَيْر**

٣٢ يَسْعَى الوُشاةُ بِجَنْبَيها وقَوْلُهُمُ   إنَّـكَ يـاْبْـنَ أبي سُلْمَى لَمَقْتولُ
٣٣ وقـالَ كُـلُّ خَـليـلٍ كُـنْـتُ آمُلُهُ   لا أُلْـفِـيَـنَّـكَ إنِّي عَـنْـكَ مَشْغولُ
٣٤ فَقُلْتُ خَلُّوا طَريقي لا أبا لَكُمُ   فكلُّ ما قَـدَّرَ الـرَّحْـمٰـنُ مَفْعولُ
٣٥ كلُّ ٱبْـنِ أُنْثَى وإنْ طالَتْ سَلامَتُهُ   يـوماً عـلى آلَـةٍ حَـدْبـاءَ مَحْمولُ
٣٦ أُنْـبِـئْـتُ أنَّ رسـولَ الـلـهِ أَوْعَدَني   والعَفْوُ عندَ رَسـولِ اللهِ مَأْمولُ
٣٧ مَهْلاً هَداكَ الذي أَعْطاكَ نافِلَةَ الـ   ـقُـرآنِ فيها مَواعيظٌ وتَفْصِيلُ
٣٨ لا تَـأْخُـذَنِّي بـأَقْـوالِ الـوُشـاةِ ولَمْ   أُذْنِـبْ ولـو كَـثُرَتْ عنِّي الأَقاويلُ
٣٩ لـقـدْ أَقـومُ مَـقـامـاً لـو يـقـومُ بهِ   أَرَى وأَسْـمَـعُ ما لو يَسْمَعُ الفِيلُ
٤٠ لَـظَـلَّ يُـرْعَـدُ إلاَّ أنْ يَـكـونَ لهُ   مِـنَ الـرَّسـولِ بـإِذْنِ اللهِ تَنْويلُ
٤١ حتّى وَضَـعْـتُ يَميني لا أُنازِعُهُ   في كَـفِّ ذي نَـقِـماتٍ قِيلُهُ القيلُ
٤٢ لَـذاكَ أَهْـيَـبُ عندي إذْ أُكَلِّمُهُ   وقِـيـلَ إنَّـكَ مَـسْـبـورٌ ومَسْؤولُ
٤٣ مِن ضَيْغَمٍ من ضِراءِ الأُسْدِ مُخْدَرُه   بِـبَـطْـنِ عَـثَّـرَ غِـيـلٌ دونَـهُ غِيلُ
٤٤ يَغْدو فَيَلْحَمُ ضِرْغامَيْنِ عَيْشُهُما   لَحْمٌ مِـنَ القَوْمِ مَعْفورٌ خَرَاذيلُ
٤٥ إذا يُـسـاوِرُ قِـرْنـاً لا يَـحِـلُّ لَهُ   أنْ يَـتْرُكَ الـقِـرْنَ إلاّ وهْـو مَفْلولُ
٤٦ مِنْهُ تَظَلُّ حَميرُ الوَحْشِ ضامِزَةً   ولا تُمَـشِّي بِـواديـهِ الأَراجيلُ
٤٧ ولا يَـزالُ بِـواديـهِ أخـو ثِقَةٍ   مُـطَـرَّحُ الـبَزِّ والـدِّرْسـانِ مَأْكولُ
٤٨ إنّ الـرَّسـولَ لَسَيفٌ يُسْتَضاءُ بهِ   مُهَنَّدٌ من سُـيُـوفِ اللهِ مَسْلولُ
٤٩ في عُصْبةٍ من قُرَيشٍ قال قائلُهُمْ   ببَطْنِ مَـكَّـةَ لمّـا أسْـلَـمـوا زُولُوا
٥٠ زالـوا فما زالَ أَنْـكـاسٌ ولا كُشُفٌ   عند الـلِّـقـاءِ ولا مِـيـلٌ مَعازيلُ
٥١ شُـمُّ الـعَـرانـيـنِ أبْـطـالٌ لَبوسُهُمُ   من نَسْجِ داودَ في الهَيْجا سَرابيلُ
٥٢ بِيضٌ سَوابغُ قد شُكَّتْ لها حَلَقٌ   كأنّها حَـلَـقُ القَفْعاءِ مَجْدولُ
٥٣ يَمْشُونَ مَشْيَ الجِمالِ الزُّهْرِ يَعْصِمُهُمْ   ضَرْبٌ إذا عَـرَّدَ الـسُّـودُ التَّنابيلُ

٥٤ لا يَـفْـرَحـونَ إذا نـالَـتْ رِماحُهُمُ   قوماً ولَيْسوا مَجازيعاً إذا نِيلُوا

٥٥ لا يَـقَـعُ الطَّعْنُ إلاّ في نُحورِهِمُ   ما إنْ لَهُم عن حِياضِ الموتِ تَهْليلُ

[32] **قال الفَرَزْدَق**

* وَالفَحْلُ عَلْقَمَةُ الَّـذِي كانَتْ لَهُ   حُـلَـلُ الْـمُـلُـوكِ كَـلامُـهُ يُتَمَثَّلُ

[33] **قال حَسَّانُ بْنُ ثابِت**

١ بِطَيْبَةَ رَسْـمٌ لِـلـرَّسُـولِ وَمَعْهَدُ   مُنِيرٌ وَقَـدْ تَعْفُو الـرُّسُـومُ وَتَهْمُدُ

٢ ولا تَمْتَحِي الآيـاتُ مَـنْ دارِ حُرْمَةٍ   بها مِنْبَرُ الهادِي الَّذي كانَ يَصْعَدُ

٣ وواضِـــحُ آثـــارٍ وَبـاقِـي مَعالِمٍ   وَرَبْـــعٌ لَـهُ فِيهِ مُـصَـلًّى ومَسْجِدُ

[34] **قال حَسَّانُ بْنُ ثابِت**

٤٥ ولَـيْـسَ هَـــوايَ نـازِعًـا عـن ثَنائِهِ   لَـعَـلِّي بِـهِ في جَـنَّـةِ الخُلْدِ أَخْلُدُ

٤٦ مع المُصْطَفَى أَرْجُـو بِـذاكَ جِوارَهُ   وفي نَيْلِ ذاكَ اليَوْمِ أَسْعَى وأَجْهَدُ

[35] **قال أبو ذُؤَيْبٍ الهُذَلِيّ**

* وإذا المَـنِـيَّـةُ أَنْـشَـبَـتْ أَظْفارَها   أَلْـفَـيْـتَ كـلَّ تَمِـيـمـةٍ لا تَنْفَعُ

[36] **قال أبو تَمَّام**

* متى يَـأْتِـكَ المِـقْـدارُ لا تَـكُ هالِكاً   ولـكـنْ زَمـانٌ غـالَ مِـثْـلَـكَ هالِكُ

[37] **قال أبو تَمَّام**

٣٧ تَـدْبِـيرُ مُعْتَصِمٍ بِاللهِ مُنْتَقِمٍ   للهِ مُـرْتَـقِـبٍ في الـلـهِ مُرْتَغِبِ

[38] **قال أبو تَمَّام**

٢٦ غادَرْتَ فيها بَهِيمَ اللَّيْلِ وَهْوَ ضُحًى   يَشُلُّه وَسْطَها صُبْحٌ مِـنَ اللَّهَبِ

. . . .

٢٨ ضَـوْءٌ مِـنَ النَّارِ والظَّلْماءُ عاكِفَةٌ   وظُلْمَةٌ مِنْ دُخانٍ في ضُحًى شَحِبِ

[39] **قال أبو تَمَّام**

٦٥ كَمْ أَحْـرَزَتْ قُضُبُ الهِنْدِيِّ مُصْلَتَةً   تَهْتَزُّ مِـنْ قُضُبٍ تَهْتَزُّ في كُثُبِ

[40] **قال عُمَرُ بْنُ الفارِض**

١ هَلْ نَارُ لَيْلَى بَـدَتْ لَيْلاً بِذي سَلَمِ   أَمْ بـارِقٌ لاحَ في الـــزَّوْراءِ فالعَلَمِ

٢ أَرْوَاحَ نَعْمانَ هَلاَّ نَسْمةٌ سَحَراً وماءَ   وماءَ وَجْرةَ هَلاَّ نَهْلةٌ بِفَمِ
٣ يا سائِقَ الظَّعْنِ يَطْوِي البِيدَ مُعْتَسِفاً   طَيَّ السِّجِلِّ بِذاتِ الشِّيحِ مِنْ إضَمِ
٤ عُجْ بالحِمَى يا رَعاكَ اللهُ مُعْتَمِداً   خَميلةَ الضَّالِ ذاتَ الرَّنْدِ والخُزُمِ
٥ وَقِفْ بِسَلْعٍ وَسَلْ بالجِزْعِ هل مُطِرَتْ   بالرَّقْمَتَيْنِ أُثَيْلاتٌ بِمُنْسَجِمِ
٦ نَشَدْتُكَ اللهَ إنْ جُزْتَ العَقِيقَ ضُحًى   فَاقْرَ السَّلاَمَ عليهِمْ غيرَ مُحْتَشِمِ
٧ وقُلْ تَرَكْتُ صَرِيعاً في دِيَارِكُمُ   حَيّاً كَمَيْتٍ يُعِيرُ السُّقْمَ للسَّقَمِ
٨ فَمِنْ فُؤادي لَهيبٌ نابَ عَنْ قَبَسٍ   ومِنْ جُفونِيَ دَمْعٌ فاضَ كالدِّيَمِ
٩ وهذه سُنَّةُ العُشّاقِ ما عَلِقُوا   بِشَادِنٍ فخَلاَ عُضْوٌ مِنَ الأَلَمِ
١٠ يا لائِماً لاَمَني في حُبِّهِمْ سَفَهاً   كُفِّ المَلامَ فلَوْ أحْبَبْتَ لم تَلُمِ
١١ وَحُرْمَةِ الوَصْلِ والوِدِّ العَتيقِ وبِالـ   ـعَهْدِ الوَثيقِ وما قد كان في القِدَمِ
١٢ ما حُلْتُ عنهمْ بسِلْوَانٍ ولا بَدَلٍ   ليسَ التبدُّلُ والسِّلوانُ من شِيَمي
١٣ رُدُّوا الُرّقادَ لِعَيْنِي علَّ طَيْفَكُمُ   بِمَضْجَعِي زائرٌ في غَفْلةِ الحُلُمِ
١٤ آهاً لِأَيّامِنا بالخَيْفِ لوْ بَقِيَتْ   عَشْراً ووَاهاً عليها كيف لمْ تَدُمِ
١٥ هَيْهاتَ وَاأَسَفِي لوْ كانَ يَنْفَعُنِي   أوْ كانَ يُجْدِي على ما فاتَ وَانَدَمِي
١٦ عَنِّي إلَيْكُمْ ظِباءَ المُنْحَنَى كَرَماً   عَهِدْتُ طَرْفِيَ لمْ يَنْظُرْ لِغَيْرِهِمِ
١٧ طَوْعاً لِقاضٍ أَتَى في حُكْمِهِ عَجَباً   أَفْتَى بِسَفْكِ دَمي في الحِلِّ والحَرَمِ
١٨ أَصَمُّ لم يَسْمَعِ الشَّكْوَى وأَبْكَمُ لمْ   يُحْرِ جَواباً وعن حالِ المَشُوقِ عَمِي

[41] **بُرْدةُ الْبُوصِيرِيّ: القسم الأوّل: النَّسِيبُ النَّبَويّ**

١ أَمِنْ تَذَكُّرِ جِيرانٍ بذي سَلَمِ   مَزَجْتَ دَمْعاً جَرَى مِن مُقْلةٍ بِدمِ
٢ أَمْ هَبَّتِ الرِّيحُ مِنْ تِلْقاءِ كاظِمَةٍ   وأَوْمَضَ البَرْقُ في الظَّلماءِ مِن إضَمِ
٣ فما لِعَيْنَيْكَ إنْ قُلْتَ ٱكْفُفا هَمَتا   وما لِقَلْبِكَ إنْ قُلْتَ ٱسْتَفِقْ يَهِمِ
٤ أَيَحْسَبُ الصَّبُّ أَنَّ الحُبَّ مُنْكَتِمٌ   ما بَيْنَ مُنْسَجِمٍ مِنْهُ ومُضْطَرِمِ
٥ لَوْلا الهَوَى لم تُرِقْ دَمْعاً على طَلَلٍ   ولا أَرِقْتَ لِذِكْرِ البانِ والْعَلَمِ
٦ فَكَيْفَ تُنْكِرُ حُبًّا بَعْدَما شَهِدَتْ   بِهِ عَلَيْكَ عُدُولُ الدَّمْعِ والسَّقَمِ
٧ وأَثْبَتَ الْوَجْدُ خَطَّيْ عَبْرَةٍ وضَنىً   مِثْلَ الْبَهارِ على خَدَّيْكَ والْعَنَمِ

٨ نَعَمْ سرى طَيْفُ مَنْ أَهْوَى فَأَرَّقَني   والْحُبُّ يَعْتَرِضُ اللَّذّاتِ بالأَلَمِ
٩ يا لائِمي في الْهَوَى الْعُذْرِيِّ مَعْذِرَةً   مِنّي إِلَيْكَ ولو أَنْصَفْتَ لَمْ تَلُمِ
١٠ عَدَتْكَ حالي لا سِرِّي بِمُسْتَتِرٍ   عَنِ الْوُشاةِ ولا دائي بِمُنْحَسِمِ
١١ مَحَضْتَني النُّصْحَ لكن لَسْتُ أَسْمَعُهُ   إنَّ المُحِبَّ عَنِ العُذّالِ في صَمَمِ
١٢ إنّي ٱتَّهَمْتُ نَصيحَ الشَّيْبِ في عَذَلي   والشَّيْبُ أبْعَدُ في نُصْحٍ عَنِ التُّهَمِ

[42] بُرْدةُ الْبُوصِيرِيّ: القسم الثاني: التَحْذِيرُ مِنْ هَوَى النَّفْس

١٣ فإنَّ أَمّارتي بالسُّوءِ ما ٱتَّعَظَتْ   مِنْ جَهْلِها بِنَذيرِ الشَّيْبِ والْهَرَمِ
١٤ ولا أَعَدَّتْ مِنَ الْفِعْلِ الْجَميلِ قِرَى   ضَيْفٍ أَلَمَّ بِرَأْسي غَيْرَ مُحْتَشِمِ
١٥ لَوْ كُنْتُ أَعْلَمُ أنّي ما أُوَقِّرُهُ   كَتَمْتُ سِرًّا بدا لي مِنْهُ بِالْكَتَمِ
١٦ مَن لي بِرَدِّ جِماحٍ مِنْ غَوايَتِها   كما يُرَدُّ جِماحُ الْخَيْلِ باللُّجُمِ
١٧ فلا تَرُمْ بالْمَعاصي كَسْرَ شَهْوَتِها   إنَّ الطَّعامَ يُقَوّي شَهْوَةَ النَّهِمِ
١٨ والنَّفْسُ كالطِّفْلِ إنْ تُهْمِلْهُ شَبَّ على   حُبِّ الرَّضاعِ وإنْ تَفْطُمْهُ يَنْفَطِمِ
١٩ فَٱصْرِفْ هَوَاها وحاذِرْ أنْ تُوَلِّيَهُ   إنَّ الْهَوَى ما تَوَلَّى يُصْمِ أَوْ يَصِمِ
٢٠ وَراعِها وَهْيَ في الأَعْمالِ سائِمَةٌ   وإنْ هِيَ ٱسْتَحْلَتِ المَرْعَى فلا تُسِمِ
٢١ كَمْ حَسَّنَتْ لَذَّةً لِلْمَرْءِ قاتِلَةً   مِنْ حَيْثُ لَمْ يَدْرِ أَنَّ السُّمَّ في الدَّسَمِ
٢٢ وٱخْشَ الدَّسائِسَ مِنْ جُوعٍ ومِنْ شَبَعٍ   فَرُبَّ مَخْمَصَةٍ شَرٌّ مِنَ التُّخَمِ
٢٣ وٱسْتَفْرِغِ الدَّمْعَ مِنْ عَيْنٍ قَدِ ٱمْتَلأَتْ   مِنَ المَحارِمِ وٱلْزَمْ حِمْيَةَ النَّدَمِ
٢٤ وخالِفِ النَّفْسَ والشَّيْطانَ وٱعْصِهِما   وإنْ هُما مَحَضاكَ النُّصْحَ فٱتَّهِمِ
٢٥ ولا تُطِعْ مِنْهُما خَصْماً ولا حَكَماً   فأَنْتَ تَعْرِفُ كَيْدَ الْخَصْمِ والحَكَمِ
٢٦ أَسْتَغْفِرُ اللهَ مِنْ قَوْلٍ بلا عَمَلٍ   لَقَدْ نَسَبْتُ بِهِ نَسْلاً لِذي عُقُمِ
٢٧ أَمَرْتُكَ الخَيْرَ لَكِنْ ما ٱئْتَمَرْتُ بِهِ   وما ٱسْتَقَمْتُ فما قَوْلي لَكَ ٱسْتَقِمِ
٢٨ ولا تَزَوَّدْتُ قَبْلَ المَوْتِ نافِلَةً   وَلَمْ أُصَلِّ سِوَى فَرْضٍ وَلَمْ أَصُمِ

[43] بُرْدةُ الْبُوصِيرِيّ: القسم الثالث: مَدْحُ الرَّسُولِ الكَرِيم

٢٩ ظَلَمْتُ سُنَّةَ مَنْ أحيا الظَّلامَ إلى   أنِ ٱشْتَكَتْ قَدَماهُ الضُّرَّ مِنْ وَرَمِ
٣٠ وشَدَّ مِنْ سَغَبٍ إحْشاءَهُ وطَوَى   تَحْتَ الحِجارَةِ كَشْحاً مُتْرَفَ الأَدَمِ

٣١ وَراوَدَتْـهُ الجِبالُ الشُّمُّ مِنْ ذَهَبٍ   عَـنْ نَـفْـسِـهِ فـأراهـا أَيَّمـا شَمَمِ

٣٢ وأَكَّـدَتْ زُهْـدَهُ فيها ضَرورتُهُ   إنَّ الـضَّرورةَ لا تَعْدو على الْعِصَمِ

٣٣ وكَيْفَ تَدْعو إلى الدُّنْيا ضَرورةُ مَنْ   لَـوْلاهُ لَمْ تَخْرُجِ الدُّنْيا مِنَ الْعَدَمِ

٣٤ مُحَمَّدٌ سَيِّدُ الْكَـوْنَـيْنِ والثَّقَلَيْـ   نِ والْفَريقَيْنِ مِنْ عُرْبٍ وَمِنْ عَجَمِ

٣٥ نَبِيُّنا الآمِـرُ الـنَّـاهـي فلا أَحَدٌ   أَبَــرَّ في قَــوْلِ لا مِـنْـهُ ولا نَعَمِ

٣٦ هُوَ الحَبيبُ الذي تُرْجَى شَفاعَتُهُ   لِكُلِّ هَـوْلٍ مِـنَ الأَهْـوَالِ مُقْتَحَمِ

٣٧ دَعَـا إلى اللهِ فالْمُسْتَمْسِكُونَ بِهِ   مُسْتَمْسِكُونَ بِحَبْلٍ غَيْرِ مُنْفَصِمِ

٣٨ فـاقَ النَّبيِّينَ في خَـلْـقٍ وفي خُلُقٍ   ولم يُـدانُــوهُ في عِـلْـمٍ ولا كَرَمِ

٣٩ وكُلُّهُمْ مِـنْ رَسـولِ اللهِ مُلْتَمِسٌ   غَرْفاً مِنَ البَحْرِ أَوْ رَشْفاً مِنَ الدِّيَمِ

٤٠ وَواقِــفُــونَ لَـدَيْـهِ عِـنْـدَ حَدِّهِمُ   مِنْ نُقْطَةِ العِلْمِ أَوْ مِنْ شَكْلَةِ الْحِكَمِ

٤١ فَـهُـوَ الـذي تَـمَّ مَعْناهُ وصُورَتُهُ   ثُـمَّ ٱصْطَفاهُ حَبيباً بـارِئُ النَّسَمِ

٤٢ مُـنَـزَّهٌ عَـن شَريـكٍ في مَحاسِنِهِ   فَجَوْهَرُ الحُسْنِ فيه غَيْرُ مُنْقَسِمِ

٤٣ دَعْ ما ٱدَّعَـتْـهُ النَّصارَى في نَبيِّهِمُ   وٱحْكُمْ بما شِئْتَ مَدْحاً فيه وٱحْتَكِمِ

٤٤ وٱنْسُبْ إلى ذاتِهِ ما شِئْتَ مِنْ شَرَفٍ   وٱنْسُبْ إلى قَدْرِهِ ما شِئْتَ مِنْ عِظَمِ

٤٥ فـإنَّ فَـضْـلَ رَسـولِ اللهِ لَـيْسَ لَهُ   حَـدٌّ فَـيُـعْـرِبَ عَـنْـهُ نـاطِـقٌ بِفَمِ

٤٦ لَـوْ نـاسَـبَـتْ قَـدْرَهُ آيـاتُـهُ عِظَماً   أَحْيا ٱسْمُهُ حينَ يُدْعَى دارِسَ الرِّمَمِ

٤٧ لَـمْ يَمْتَحِنَّا بما تَعْيا الْعُقولُ بِهِ   حِرْصاً عَلَيْنا فَلَمْ نَرْتَبْ ولَمْ نَهِمِ

٤٨ أَعْيا الوَرَى فَهْمُ مَعْناهُ فَلَيْسَ يُرَى   في القُرْبِ والبُعْدِ فيه غَيْرُ مُنْفَحِمِ

٤٩ كالشَّمْسِ تَظْهَرُ لِلْعَيْنَيْنِ مِنْ بُعُدٍ   صغيرةً وتُـكِـلُّ الـطَّـرْفَ مِـنْ أَمَمِ

٥٠ وكَيْفَ يُـدْرِكُ في الدُّنْيا حَقيقَتَهُ   قَـوْمٌ نِـيـامٌ تَسَلَّوا عَـنْـهُ بِالْحُلُمِ

٥١ فَـمَـبْـلَـغُ الـعِـلْـمِ فيه أنَّـه بَشَرٌ   وأنَّــه خَـيْـرُ خَـلْـقِ الـلـهِ كُلِّهِمِ

٥٢ وكُـلُّ آيٍ أَتى الـرُّسْـلُ الـكِـرامُ بها   فـإنَّمـا ٱتَّـصَـلَـتْ مِـنْ نُــورِهِ بِهِمِ

٥٣ فإنَّهُ شَمْسُ فَضْلٍ هُـمْ كَواكِبُها   يُظْهِرْنَ أَنْوارَها لِلنَّاسِ في الظُّلَمِ

٥٤ أَكْـرِمْ بِخَـلْـقِ نَـبـيٍّ زانَــهُ خُلُقٌ   بالْحُسْنِ مُشْتَمِلٍ بالْبِشْرِ مُتَّسِمِ

٥٥ كالزَّهْرِ في تَـرَفٍ والـبَـدْرِ في شَرَفٍ   والبَحْرِ في كَـرَمٍ والـدَّهْـرِ في هِمَمِ

٥٦ كَأَنَّه وَهْوَ فَرْدٌ مِنْ جَلالَتِهِ   في عَسْكَرٍ حينَ تَلْقاهُ وفي حَشَمِ
٥٧ كأَنَّما اللُّؤْلُؤُ المَكْنونُ في صَدَفٍ   مِنْ مَعْدِنَيْ مَنْطِقٍ مِنْهُ ومُبْتَسَمِ
٥٨ لا طِيبَ يَعْدِلُ تُرْباً ضَمَّ أَعْظُمَهُ   طُوبَى لِمُنْتَشِقٍ مِنْهُ ومُلْتَثِمِ

[44] قال أبو تَمّام

* تَدْبِيرُ مُعْتَصِمٍ بِاللهِ مُنْتَقِمٍ   للهِ مُرْتَقِبٍ في اللهِ مُرْتَغِبِ

[45] قال البُحْتُرِيّ

* فَمِنْ لُؤْلُؤٍ تَجْلُوهُ عِنْدَ ٱبْتِسَامِها   ومِنْ لُؤْلُؤٍ عِنْدَ الْحَدِيثِ تُسَاقِطُهْ

[46] بُرْدةُ الْبُوصِيرِيّ: القسم الرابع: التَّحَدُّثُ عَن مَوْلِدِه

٥٩ أَبانَ مَوْلِدُهُ عَنْ طِيبِ عُنْصُرِهِ   يا طِيبَ مُفْتَتَحٍ مِنْهُ ومُخْتَتَمِ
٦٠ يَوْمٌ تَفَرَّسَ فيه الفُرْسُ أَنَّهُمُ   قَدْ أُنْذِرُوا بِحُلولِ البُؤْسِ والنِّقَمِ
٦١ وباتَ إيوانُ كِسْرَى وَهْوَ مُنْصَدِعٌ   كَشَمْلِ أَصْحَابِ كِسْرَى غَيْرَ مُلْتَئِمِ
٦٢ والنَّارُ خامِدَةُ الأَنْفاسِ مِنْ أَسَفٍ   عليهِ والنَّهْرُ ساهي ٱلعَيْنِ مِنْ سَدَمِ
٦٣ وساءَ ساوَةَ أنْ غاضَتْ بُحَيْرَتُها   ورُدَّ وارِدُها بالغَيْظِ حينَ ظَمِي
٦٤ كأنَّ بالنارِ ما بالماءِ مِنْ بَلَلٍ   حُزْناً وَبالماءِ ما بالنَّارِ مِنْ ضَرَمِ
٦٥ والجِنُّ تَهْتِفُ وَالأَنْوارُ ساطِعَةٌ   وَالحَقُّ يَظْهَرُ مِنْ مَعْنىً ومِنْ كَلِمِ
٦٦ عَمُوا وَصَمُّوا فإعْلانُ البَشائِرِ لَمْ   يُسْمَعْ وَبارِقَةُ الإِنْذارِ لَمْ تُشَمِ
٦٧ مِنْ بَعْدِ ما أَخْبَرَ الأَقْوامَ كاهِنُهُمْ   بِأَنَّ دِينَهُمُ المُعْوَجَّ لَمْ يَقُمِ
٦٨ وبَعْدَ ما عايَنُوا في الأُفْقِ مِنْ شُهُبٍ   مُنْقَضَّةٍ وَفْقَ ما في الأرْضِ مِنْ صَنَمِ
٦٩ حَتَّى غدا عَنْ طَرِيقِ الوَحْيِ مُنْهَزِمٌ   مِنَ الشَّياطِينِ يَقْفُو إِثْرَ مُنْهَزِمِ
٧٠ كأَنَّهُمْ هَرَباً أَبْطالُ أَبْرَهةٍ   أَوْ عَسْكَرٌ بالحَصَى مِنْ رَاحَتَيْهِ رُمِي
٧١ نَبْذاً بِهِ بَعْدَ تَسْبيحٍ بِبَطْنِهِما   نَبْذَ المُسَبِّحِ مِنْ أحْشاءِ مُلْتَقِمِ

[47] بُرْدةُ الْبُوصِيرِيّ: القسم الخامس: التَّحَدُّثُ عَن مُعْجِزاتِه

٧٢ جاءَتْ لِدَعْوَتِهِ الأَشْجارُ ساجِدَةً   تَمْشِي إِلَيهِ عَلَى ساقٍ بِلا قَدَمِ
٧٣ كأَنَّما سَطَرَتْ سَطْراً لِمَا كَتَبَتْ   فُرُوعُها مِنْ بَدِيعِ الخَطِّ في اللَّقَمِ
٧٤ مِثْلَ الغَمامَةِ أَنَّى سَارَ سائِرَةً   تَقِيهِ حَرَّ وَطِيسٍ لِلْهَجِيرِ حَمِي

٧٥ أَقْسَمْتُ بالقَمَرِ المُنْشَقِّ أَنَّ لَهُ   مِنْ قَلْبِهِ نِسْبَةً مَبْرُورَةَ القَسَمِ
٧٦ وَمَا حَوَى الغارُ مِنْ خَيرٍ وَمِنْ كَرَمِ   وكلُّ طَرْفٍ مِنَ الكُفَّارِ عنه عَمِي
٧٧ فالصِّدْقُ فِي الغارِ والصِّدِّيقُ لَمْ يَرِما   وَهُمْ يقولونَ ما بالغارِ مِنْ أَرِمِ
٧٨ ظَنُّوا الحَمامَ وظَنُّوا العَنْكَبُوتَ على   خَيْرِ البَرِيَّةِ لَمْ تَنْسُجْ ولَمْ تَحُمِ
٧٩ وِقايةُ اللهِ أغنَتْ عَنْ مُضَاعَفَةٍ   مِنَ الدُّرُوعِ وَعَنْ عالٍ مِنَ الأُطُمِ
٨٠ ما ضامَنِي الدَّهْرُ ضَيْماً وٱسْتَجَرْتُ به   إلاَّ ونِلْتُ جِواراً مِنْه لَمْ يُضَمِ
٨١ ولا ٱلْتَمَسْتُ غِنَى الدَّارَيْنِ من يَدِهِ   إلاّ ٱسْتَلَمْتُ النَّدَى مِنْ خَيْرِ مُسْتَلَمِ
٨٢ لا تُنْكِرِ الوَحْيَ مِنْ رُؤْيَاهُ إِنَّ لهُ   قَلْباً إذا نامتِ العَيْنانِ لَمْ يَنَمِ
٨٣ وذاكَ حِينَ بُلُوغٍ مِنْ نُبُوَّتِهِ   فليسَ يُنْكَرُ فيهِ حالُ مُحْتَلِمِ
٨٤ تَبَارَكَ اللهُ ما وَحْيٌ بِمُكْتَسَبٍ   وَلا نَبِيٌّ عَلَى غَيْبٍ بِمُتَّهَمِ
٨٥ كَمْ أَبْرَأَتْ وَصِباً باللَّمْسِ راحَتُهُ   وأَطْلَقَتْ أَرِباً مِنْ رِبْقَةِ اللَّمَمِ
٨٦ وأَحْيَتِ السَّنةَ الشَّهْبَاءَ دَعْوَتُهُ   حتّى حَكَتْ غُرَّةً فِي الأَعْصُرِ الدُّهُمِ
٨٧ بعارِضٍ جادَ أَوْ خِلْتَ البِطاحَ بها   سَيْبٌ مِنَ اليَمِّ أَوْ سَيْلٌ مِنَ العَرِمِ

[48] بُرْدةُ الْبُوصِيرِيّ: القسم السادس: التَّحَدُّثُ عَن القُرْآن الكَرِيم

٨٨ دَعْنِي وَوَصْفِي آياتٍ لهُ ظَهَرَتْ   ظُهورَ نارِ القِرَى لَيْلاً عَلَى عَلَمِ
٨٩ فالدُّرُّ يَزْدادُ حُسْناً وَهْوَ مُنْتَظِمٌ   وَليسَ يَنْقُصُ قَدْراً غيرَ مُنْتَظِمِ
٩٠ فما تَطَاوُلُ آمالِي المَدِيحَ إلى   ما فيهِ مِنْ كَرَمِ الأَخْلاقِ والشِّيَمِ
٩١ آياتُ حَقٍّ مِنَ الرَّحْمٰنِ مُحْدَثَةٌ   قَدِيمَةٌ صِفَةُ المَوْصوفِ بالقِدَمِ
٩٢ لَمْ تَقْتَرِنْ بِزَمانٍ وَهْيَ تُخْبِرُنا   عَنِ المَعادِ وعَنْ عادٍ وعَنْ إِرَمِ
٩٣ دامَتْ لَدَيْنا فَفاقَتْ كُلَّ مُعْجِزَةٍ   مِنَ النَّبِيِّينَ إِذْ جاءَتْ ولَمْ تَدُمِ
٩٤ مُحَكَّماتٌ فما يُبْقِينَ مِنْ شُبَهٍ   لِذِي شِقاقٍ وما يَبْغِينَ مِنْ حَكَمِ
٩٥ ما حُورِبَتْ قَطُّ إلاَّ عادَ مِنْ حَرَبٍ   أَعْدَى الأَعادِي إليها مُلْقِيَ السَّلَمِ
٩٦ رَدَّتْ بَلاغَتُها دَعْوَى مُعارِضِها   رَدَّ الغَيُورِ يَدَ الجَانِي عَنِ الحُرَمِ
٩٧ لها مَعانٍ كَمَوْجِ البَحْرِ فِي مَدَدٍ   وفَوْقَ جَوْهَرِهِ فِي الحُسْنِ والقِيَمِ
٩٨ فَلا تُعَدُّ وَلا تُحْصَى عَجَائِبُها   ولا تُسامُ عَلَى الإِكْثارِ بالسَّأَمِ

٩٩ قَرَّتْ بها عَيْنُ قارِيها فَقُلْتُ لهُ   لقد ظَفِرْتَ بِحَبْلِ اللهِ فَٱعْتَصِمِ
١٠٠ إنْ تَتْلُها خِيفَةً مِنْ حَرِّ نارِ لَظىً   أَطْفَأْتَ نارَ لَظىً مِنْ وِرْدِها الشَّبِمِ
١٠١ كَأَنَّها الحَوْضُ تَبْيَضُّ الوجوهُ به   مِنَ العُصاةِ وقد جاؤُوهُ كَالحُمَمِ
١٠٢ وَكَالصِّرَاطِ وكالمِيزانِ مَعْدِلَةً   فالقِسْطُ مِنْ غَيرِها في النَّاسِ لَمْ يَقُمِ
١٠٣ لا تَعْجَبَنْ لِحَسُودٍ راحَ يُنْكِرُها   تَجاهُلاً وهْوَ عَيْنُ الحاذِقِ الفَهِمِ
١٠٤ قد تُنْكِرُ العينُ ضَوْءَ الشَّمْسِ من رَمَدٍ   ويُنْكِرُ الفَمُ طَعْمَ الماءِ مِنْ سَقَمِ

[49] **بُرْدةُ الْبُوصِيرِيّ: القسم السابع: التَّحَدُّثُ عَن الإسْراء والمِعْراج**

١٠٥ يا خيْرَ مَنْ يَمَّمَ العافُونَ ساحَتَهُ   سَعْياً وفَوْقَ مُتونِ الأَيْنُقِ الرُّسُمِ
١٠٦ وَمَنْ هُوَ الآيَةُ الكُبْرَى لِمُعْتَبِرٍ   وَمَنْ هُوَ النِّعْمَةُ العُظْمَى لِمُغْتَنِمِ
١٠٧ سَرَيْتَ مِنْ حَرَمٍ لَيْلاً إلَى حَرَمِ   كما سَرَى البَدْرُ في داجٍ مِنَ الظُّلَمِ
١٠٨ وَبِتَّ تَرْقَى إلَى أنْ نِلْتَ مَنْزِلَةً   مِنْ قَابِ قَوْسَيْنِ لَمْ تُدْرَكْ وَلَمْ تُرَمِ
١٠٩ وقَدَّمَتْكَ جَميعُ الأَنْبِياءِ بِها   والرُّسْلِ تَقْدِيمَ مَخْدُومٍ عَلَى خَدَمِ
١١٠ وأَنْتَ تَخْتَرِقُ السَّبْعَ الطِّباقَ بهِمْ   في مَوْكِبٍ كُنْتَ فيهِ صاحِبَ العَلَمِ
١١١ حتّى إذا لَمْ تَدَعْ شَأْواً لِمُسْتَبِقٍ   مِنَ الدُّنُوِّ وَلا مَرْقىً لِمُسْتَنِمِ
١١٢ خَفَضْتَ كلَّ مَقامٍ بالإضافَةِ إذْ   نُودِيتَ بالرَّفْعِ مِثْلَ المُفْرَدِ العَلَمِ
١١٣ كَيْمَا تَفُوزَ بِوَصْلٍ أَيِّ مُسْتَتِرٍ   عَنِ العُيُونِ وَسِرٍّ أَيِّ مُكْتَتَمِ
١١٤ فَحُزْتَ كلَّ فَخَارٍ غَيْرِ مُشْتَرَكٍ   وَجُزْتَ كلَّ مَقامٍ غيرِ مُزْدَحَمِ
١١٥ وَجَلَّ مِقْدارُ ما وُلِّيتَ مِنْ رُتَبٍ   وعَزَّ إدْرَاكُ ما أُولِيْتَ مِنْ نِعَمِ
١١٦ بُشْرَى لَنَا مَعْشَرَ الإسْلامِ إنَّ لنا   مِنَ العِنَايَةِ رُكْناً غيرَ مُنْهَدِمِ
١١٧ لَمَّا دَعا اللهُ داعِينا لَطَاعَتِهِ   بأَكْرَمِ الرُّسْلِ كُنَّا أَكْرَمَ الأُمَمِ

[50] **بُرْدةُ الْبُوصِيرِيّ: القسم الثامن: التَّحّدُّثُ عَن جِهاد الرَّسول وغَزَواتِه**

١١٨ راعَتْ قُلوبَ العِدا أَنْباءُ بَعْثَتِهِ   كَنَبْأَةٍ أَجْفَلَتْ غُفْلاً مِنَ الغَنَمِ
١١٩ ما زالَ يَلْقاهُمُ في كلِّ مُعْتَرَكٍ   حتَّى حَكَوْا بالقَنا لَحْماً على وَضَمِ
١٢٠ وَدُّوا الفِرارَ فكادُوا يَغْبَطُونَ بهِ   أَشْلاَءَ شالَتْ مَعَ العِقْبَانِ والرَّخَمِ
١٢١ تَمْضِي اللَّيالِي وَلا يَدْرُونَ عِدَّتَها   ما لَمْ تَكُنْ مِنْ لَيالِي الأَشْهُرِ الحُرُمِ

١٢٢ كأنَّما الدِّينُ ضَيْفٌ حَلَّ سَاحَتَهُمْ　　بِكُلِّ قَرْمٍ إلَى لَحْمِ العِدا قَرِمِ
١٢٣ يَجُرُّ بَحْرَ خَمِيسٍ فوقَ سابِحَةٍ　　يَرْمِي بِمَوْجٍ مِنَ الأبْطالِ مُلْتَطِمِ
١٢٤ مِنْ كلِّ مُنْتَدِبٍ للهِ مُحْتَسِبٍ　　يَسْطو بِمُسْتَأْصِلٍ لِلْكُفْرِ مُصْطَلِمِ
١٢٥ حتَّى غَدَتْ مِلَّةُ الإسلامِ وَهْيَ بِهِمْ　　مِنْ بَعْدِ غُرْبَتِها مَوْصُولَةَ الرَّحِمِ
١٢٦ مَكْفُولَةً أَبَداً مِنْهمْ بِخَيْرِ أَبٍ　　وخَيْرِ بَعْلٍ فَلَمْ تَيْتَمْ وَلَمْ تَئِمِ
١٢٧ هُمُ الجِبالُ فَسَلْ عنْهمْ مُصادِمَهُمْ　　ماذا رأى مِنْهُمُ في كُلِّ مُصطَدَمِ
١٢٨ وسَلْ حُنَيْناً وسَلْ بَدْراً وَسَلْ أُحُداً　　فُصُولُ حَتْفٍ لهُمْ أَدْهَى مِنَ الوَخَمِ
١٢٩ المُصْدِرِي البِيضَ حُمْراً بعدَ ما وَرَدَتْ　　مِنَ العِدا كُلَّ مُسْوَدٍّ مِنَ اللِّمَمِ
١٣٠ وَالكاتِبِينَ بِسُمْرِ الخَطِّ مَا تَرَكَتْ　　أقْلامُهُمْ حَرْفَ جِسْمٍ غَيْرَ مُنْعَجِمِ
١٣١ شاكِي السِّلاحَ لهمْ سِيمَا تُمَيِّزُهُمْ　　والوَرْدُ يَمْتازُ بالسِّيمَا عَنِ السَّلَمِ
١٣٢ تُهْدِي إليكَ رِياحُ النَّصْرِ نَشْرَهُمُ　　فَتَحْسَبُ الزَّهْرَ في الأكْمامِ كُلَّ كَمِي
١٣٣ كأنَّهُمْ في ظُهُورِ الخَيْلِ نَبْتُ رُباً　　مِنْ شِدَّةِ الحَزْمِ لاَ مِنْ شَدَّةِ الحُزُمِ
١٣٤ طارَتْ قلوبُ العِدا مِنْ بَأْسِهِمْ فَرَقاً　　فما تُفَرِّقُ بينَ البَهْمِ والبُهَمِ
١٣٥ ومَنْ تَكُنْ بِرَسُولِ اللهِ نُصْرَتُهُ　　إنْ تَلْقَهُ الأُسْدُ في آجامِها تَجِمِ
١٣٦ ولَنْ تَرَى مِنْ وَلِيٍّ غَيْرَ مُنْتَصِرٍ　　بهِ ولا مِنْ عَدُوٍّ غيْرَ مُنْقَصِمِ
١٣٧ أَحَلَّ أُمَّتَهُ في حِرْزِ مِلَّتِهِ　　كاللَّيْثِ حَلَّ مَعَ الأَشْبالِ في أَجَمِ
١٣٨ كَمْ جَدَّلَتْ كَلِماتُ اللهِ مِنْ جَدِلٍ　　فيهِ وكَمْ خَصَّمَ البُرْهانُ مِنْ خَصِمِ
١٣٩ كفاكَ بالعِلْمِ في الأُمِّيِّ مُعْجِزَةً　　في الجاهِلِيَّةِ وَالتَّأْدِيبِ في اليُتُمِ

[51] **قال عَمْرُو بْنُ كُلْثوم**

* نَزَلْتُمْ مَنْزِلَ الأَضْيافِ مِنَّا　　فَعَجَّلْنا القِرَى أَنْ تَشْتِمُونا

[52] **قال بِشْرُ بْنُ أَبِي خازِم**

* وَٱسْأَلْ تَميماً بنا يَوْمَ الجِفارِ وَسَلْ　　عَنّا بني لأمٍ ٱذْ وَلَّوا ولمْ يَقِفُوا

[53] **قال أبو تَمّام**

٦٠ يا رُبَّ حَوْباءَ لَمَّا ٱجْتُثَّ دابِرُهُمْ　　طابتْ ولوْ ضُمِّخَتْ بالمِسْكِ لمْ تَطِبِ

[54] **قال أَبو تَمّام**

٦٩ إنْ كان بَيْنَ صُروفِ الدَّهْرِ مِنْ رَحِمٍ   مَوْصولةٍ أَوْ ذِمـامٍ غَـيْرِ مُنْقَضِبِ

٧٠ فَـبَـيْنَ أَيّـامِـكَ الـلاَّتي نُـصِرْتَ بِها   وبَـيْنَ أَيّـامِ بَـدْرٍ أَقْـرَبُ النَّسَبِ

[55] **بُرْدةُ الْبُوصِيرِيّ: القسم التاسع: التَّوَسُّلُ والتَّشَفُّع**

١٤٠ خَـدَمْـتُـهُ بِمَـديـحٍ أَسْـتَـقـيـلُ بِهِ   ذُنوبَ عُمْرٍ مَضَى في الشِّعْرِ والْخِدَمِ

١٤١ إذْ قَـلَّـدانِيَ مـا تُـخْـشَى عَواقِبُهُ   كأَنَّني بِـهِـما هَـدْيٌ مِـنَ النَّعَمِ

١٤٢ أَطَعْتُ غَيَّ الصِّبا في الحالَتَيْنِ وما   حَـصَـلْـتُ إلاّ عـلى الآثـامِ والنَّدَمِ

١٤٣ فيا خَـسـارَةَ نَـفْـسٍ في تِجارَتِها   لم تَشْتَرِ الدِّينَ بالدُّنْيا ولمْ تَسُمِ

١٤٤ وَمَــنْ يَـبِـعْ آجِـلاً مِـنْـهُ بِعاجِلِهِ   يَـبِنْ لَـهُ الْـغُـبْنُ في بَـيْـعٍ وفي سَلَمِ

١٤٥ إنْ آتِ ذَنْباً فما عَهْدي بِمُنْتَقِضٍ   مِــنَ الـنَّـبـيِّ ولا حَـبْـلي بِمُنْصَرِمِ

١٤٦ فَــإنّ لي ذِمَّــةً مِـنْـهُ بِتَسْمِيَتي   مُحَمَّداً وَهْـوَ أَوْفى الْخَلْقِ بِالذِّمَمِ

١٤٧ إنْ لم يَكُنْ في مَعادي آخِـذاً بِيَدي   فَـضْـلاً وإلاّ فَـقُـلْ يا زَلَّـةَ الْقَدَمِ

١٤٨ حاشاهُ أَنْ يُحْرِمَ الرّاجي مَكارِمَهُ   أَوْ يَـرْجِـعَ الْجارُ فيه غَـيْرَ مُحْتَرَمِ

١٤٩ ومُـنْـذُ أَلْـزَمْـتُ أَفْـكـاري مَدائِحَهُ   وَجَـدْتُـهُ لِـخَـلاصي خَـيْرَ مُلْتَزِمِ

١٥٠ وَلَنْ يَفوتَ الْغِنى مِنْهُ يَداً تَرِبَتْ   إنَّ الْحَيَا يُنْبِتُ الأَزْهـارَ في الأَكَمِ

١٥١ ولم أُرِدْ زَهْرَةَ الدُّنْيا التي اْقْتَطَفَتْ   يَـدا زُهَــيْرٍ بِمـا أَثْـنَـى عـلى هَرِمِ

[56] **قال الْبُحْتُرِيّ**

* وٱشْـــتِرائِي الْـعِـراقَ خُـطَّـةُ غَبْنٍ   بَـعْـدَ بَيْعي الـشَّـآمَ بَيْعَةَ وَكْسِ

[57] **بُرْدةُ الْبُوصِيرِيّ: القسم العاشر: المُناجاةُ والتَّضَرُّع**

١٥٢ يا أَكْـرَمَ الرُّسْلِ ما لي مَنْ أَلـوذُ بِهِ   سِواكَ عِنْدَ حُلولِ الْحادِثِ الْعَمِمِ

١٥٣ وَلَـنْ يَضيقَ رَسـولَ اللهِ جاهُكَ بي   إذا الْكَريمُ تَحَلَّى بِٱسْمِ مُنْتَقِمِ

١٥٤ فـإنَّ مِـنْ جُـودِكَ الدُّنْيا وضَرَّتَها   ومِـنْ عُلومِكَ عِلْمَ اللَّوْحِ والْقَلَمِ

١٥٥ يا نَفْسُ لا تَقْنَطي مِنْ زَلَّةٍ عَظُمَتْ   إنَّ الْكَبائِرَ في الْغُـفْـرانِ كاللَّمَمِ

١٥٦ لَـعَـلَّ رَحْـمَـةَ رَبّي حِـينَ يَقْسِمُها   تَأْتي على حَسَبِ الْعِصْيانِ في الْقِسَمِ

١٥٧ يا رَبِّ وٱجْعَلْ رَجائي غَيْرَ مُنْعَكِسٍ   لَدَيْكَ وٱجْعَلْ حِسابي غَيْرَ مُنْخَرِمِ

١٥٨ والْطُفْ بِعَبْدِكَ في الدَّارَيْنِ إنَّ لَهُ   صَبْرًا متى تَدْعُهُ الأَهْوالُ يَنْهَزِمِ

١٥٩ وَائْذَنْ لِسُحْبِ صَلاةٍ مِنْكَ دائِمَةٍ   على النَّبيِّ بِمُنْهَلٍّ ومُنْسَجِمِ

١٦٠ ما رَنَّحَتْ عَذَباتِ الْبانِ ريحُ صَبًا   وأَطْرَبَ الْعِيسَ حادي الْعِيسِ بِالنَّغَمِ

[58] قال الأَخْطَلُ التَّغْلِبِيّ

٥٢ سَقَى اللهُ أرْضاً خالدٌ خَيْرُ أهْلِها   بِمُسْتَفْرِغٍ باتَتْ عَزالِيهِ تَسْحَلُ

٥٣ إذا طَعَنَتْ رِيحُ الصَّبا في فُرُوجِهِ   تَحَلَّبَ رَيّانُ الأَسافِلِ أَنْجَلُ

٥٤ إذا زَعْزَعَتْهُ الرِّيحُ جَرَّ ذُيُولَهُ   كما زَحَفَتْ عُوذٌ ثِقالٌ تُطَفِّلُ

٥٥ مُلِحٌّ كأنَّ البَرْقَ في حَجَراتِهِ   مَصابيحُ أو أَقْرابُ بُلْقٍ تَجَفَّلُ

[59] قال مَحْمود سامي الْبارودِيّ

* يا رائِدَ البَرْقِ يَمِّمْ دارَةَ العَلَمِ   وَاحْدُ الغَمامَ إلى حَيٍّ بِذِي سَلَمِ

[60] نَهْجُ الْبُرْدة لأَحْمَد شَوْقِيّ: القسم الأوّل

١ رِيمٌ على القاعِ بَيْنَ البانِ وَالعَلَمِ   أَحَلَّ سَفْكَ دَمِي في الأَشْهُرِ الحُرُمِ

٢ رَمَى القَضاءُ بِعَيْنَي جُؤْذَرٍ أَسَدًا   يا ساكِنَ القاعِ أَدْرِكْ ساكِنَ الأَجَمِ

٣ لَمّا رَنا حَدَّثَتْني النَّفْسُ قائِلَةً   يا وَيْحَ جَنْبِكَ بِالسَّهْمِ المُصيبِ رُمِي

٤ جَحَدْتُها وَكَتَمْتُ السَهْمَ في كَبِدي   جُرْحُ الأَحِبَّةِ عِندِي غَيْرُ ذِي أَلَمِ

٥ رُزِقْتَ أَسْمَحَ ما في النَّاسِ مِن خُلُقٍ   إذا رُزِقْتَ الْتِماسَ العُذْرِ في الشِّيَمِ

٦ يا لائِمي في هَواهُ وَالهَوَى قَدَرٌ   لَوْ شَفَّكَ الوَجْدُ لَمْ تَعْذِلْ وَلَمْ تَلُمِ

٧ لَقَدْ أَنَلْتُكَ أُذْنًا غَيرَ واعِيَةٍ   وَرُبَّ مُنْتَصِتٍ وَالقَلْبُ في صَمَمِ

٨ يا ناعِسَ الطَّرْفِ لا ذُقْتَ الهَوَى أَبَدًا   أَسْهَرْتَ مُضْناكَ في حِفْظِ الهَوَى فَنَمِ

٩ أَفْدِيكَ أَلْفًا وَلا آلو الخَيالَ فِدًى   أَغْراكَ بِالبُخْلِ مَن أَغْراهُ بِالكَرَمِ

١٠ سَرَى فَصادَفَ جُرْحًا دامِيًا فَأَسا   وَرُبَّ فَضْلٍ عَلَى العُشّاقِ لِلحُلُمِ

١١ مِنَ المَوائِسِ بانًا بِالرُّبَى وَقَنًا   اللاعِباتُ بِرُوحي السّافِحاتُ دَمي

١٢ السافِراتُ كَأَمْثالِ البُدورِ ضُحًى   يُغِرْنَ شَمْسَ الضُّحَى بِالحَلْيِ وَالعِصَمِ

١٣ القاتِلاتُ بِأَجْفانٍ بِها سَقَمٌ   وَلِلمَنِيَّةِ أَسْبابٌ مِنَ السَّقَمِ

١٤ العاثِراتُ بِأَلْبابِ الرِّجالِ وَما   أُقِلْنَ مِن عَثَراتِ الدَّلِّ في الرَّسَمِ

١٥ المُضْرِماتُ خُدودًا أَسْفَرَتْ وَجَلَتْ   عَن فِتْنَةٍ تُسْلِمُ الأَكْبادَ لِلضَّرَمِ
١٦ الحامِلاتُ لِواءَ الحُسْنِ مُختَلِفًا   أَشْكالُهُ وَهوَ فَرْدٌ غَيرُ مُنْقَسِمِ
١٧ مِن كُلِّ بَيْضاءَ أَو سَمْراءَ زُيِّنَتا   لِلعَيْنِ وَالحُسْنُ في الآرامِ كَالعُصُمِ
١٨ يُرَعْنَ لِلبَصَرِ السَّامِي وَمِن عَجَبٍ   إذا أَشَرْنَ أَسَرْنَ اللَيْثَ بِالعَنَمِ
١٩ وَضَعْتُ خَدّي وَقَسَّمْتُ الفُؤادَ رُبًى   يَرْتَعْنَ في كُنُسٍ مِنهُ وَفي أَكَمِ
٢٠ يا بِنْتَ ذي اللِّبَدِ المَحْميِّ جانِبُهُ   أَلْقاكِ في الغابِ أَمْ أَلْقاكِ في الأُطُمِ
٢١ ما كُنْتُ أَعْلَمُ حَتّى عَنَّ مَسْكَنُهُ   أَنَّ المُنَى وَالمَنايا مَضْرِبُ الخِيَمِ
٢٢ مَن أَنْبَتَ الغُصْنَ مِن صَمْصامَةٍ ذَكَرٍ   وَأَخْرَجَ الرِّيمَ مِن ضِرْغامَةٍ قَرِمِ
٢٣ بَيْني وَبَيْنَكِ مِن سُمْرِ القَنا حُجُبٌ   وَمِثْلُها عِفَّةٌ عُذرِيَّةُ العِصَمِ
٢٤ لَمْ أَغْشَ مَغْناكِ إلاَّ في غُضونِ كَرًى   مَغْناكِ أَبْعَدُ لِلمُشْتاقِ مِنْ إرَمِ

[61] نَهْجُ الْبُرْدَة لأَحْمَد شَوْقِيّ: القسم الثاني

٢٥ يا نَفْسُ دُنْياكِ تُخْفِي كُلَّ مُبْكِيَةٍ   وَإِنْ بَدا لَكِ مِنْها حُسْنُ مُبْتَسَمِ
٢٦ فُضِّي بِتَقْواكِ فاهًا كُلَّما ضَحِكَتْ   كَما يُفَضُّ أَذَى الرَّقْشاءِ بِالثَّرَمِ
٢٧ مَخْطوبَةٌ مُنْذُ كانَ النَّاسُ خاطِبَةٌ   مِن أَوَّلِ الدَّهرِ لَمْ تُرْمِلْ وَلَمْ تَئِمِ
٢٨ يَفْنَى الزَّمانُ وَيَبْقَى مِن إساءَتِها   جُرْحٌ بِآدَمَ يَبْكي مِنْهُ في الأَدَمِ
٢٩ لا تَحْفِلي بِجَناها أَوْ جِنايَتِها   المَوْتُ بِالزَّهْرِ مِثْلُ المَوْتِ بِالفَحَمِ
٣٠ كَمْ نائِمٍ لا يَراها وَهْيَ ساهِرَةٌ   لَوْلا الأَمانِيُّ وَالأَحْلامُ لَم يَنَمِ
٣١ طَوْرًا تَمُدُّكَ في نُعْمَى وَعافِيَةٍ   وَتارَةً في قَرارِ البُؤْسِ وَالوَصَمِ
٣٢ كَمْ ضَلَّلَتْكَ وَمَنْ تُحْجَبْ بَصيرَتُهُ   إنْ يَلْقَ صابًا يَرِدْ أَوْ عَلْقَمًا يَسُمِ
٣٣ يا وَيلَتاهُ لِنَفْسي راعَها وَدَها   مُسْوَدَّةُ الصُّحْفِ في مُبْيَضَّةِ اللِّمَمِ
٣٤ رَكَضْتُها في مَريعِ المَعْصِياتِ وَما   أَخَذْتُ مِن حِمْيَةِ الطّاعاتِ لِلتُّخَمِ
٣٥ هامَتْ عَلى أَثَرِ اللَّذّاتِ تَطْلُبُها   وَالنَّفْسُ إنْ يَدْعُها داعي الصِّبا تَهِمِ
٣٦ صَلاحُ أَمْرِكَ لِلأَخْلاقِ مَرْجِعُهُ   فَقَوِّمِ النَّفْسَ بِالأَخْلاقِ تَسْتَقِمِ
٣٧ وَالنَّفْسُ مِن خَيْرِها في خَيْرِ عافِيَةٍ   وَالنَّفْسُ مِن شَرِّها في مَرْتَعٍ وَخِمِ
٣٨ تَطْغَى إذا مُكِّنَتْ مِن لَذَّةٍ وَهَوًى   طَغْيَ الجِيادِ إذا عَضَّتْ عَلى الشُّكُمِ

[62] نَهْجُ الْبُرْدة لأَحْمَد شَوْقِيّ: القسم الثالث

٣٩	إنْ جَلَّ ذَنْبي عَنِ الغُفْرانِ لي أَمَلٌ	في اللهِ يَجْعَلُني في خَيْرِ مُعْتَصَمِ
٤٠	أُلْقِي رَجائي إذا عَزَّ المُجيرُ عَلى	مُفَرِّجِ الكَرْبِ في الدّارَيْنِ وَالغُمَمِ
٤١	إذا خَفَضْتُ جَناحَ الذُّلِّ أَسْأَلُهُ	عِزَّ الشَفاعَةِ لَمْ أَسْأَلْ سِوى أَمَمِ
٤٢	وَإنْ تَقَدَّمَ ذُو تَقْوَى بِصالِحَةٍ	قَدَّمْتُ بَيْنَ يَدَيْهِ عَبْرَةَ النَدَمِ
٤٣	لَزِمْتُ بابَ أَميرِ الأَنْبِياءِ وَمَن	يُمْسِكْ بِمِفْتاحِ بابِ اللهِ يَغْتَنِمِ
٤٤	فَكُلُّ فَضْلٍ وَإِحْسانٍ وَعارِفَةٍ	ما بَيْنَ مُسْتَلَمٍ مِنْهُ وَمُلْتَزَمِ
٤٥	عَلِقْتُ مِن مَدْحِهِ حَبْلاً أُعَزُّ بِهِ	في يَوْمِ لا عِزَّ بِالأَنْسابِ وَاللُّحَمِ
٤٦	يُزْري قَرِيضي زُهَيْرًا حِينَ أَمْدَحُهُ	وَلا يُقاسُ إلى جُودي نَدَى هَرِمِ

[63] نَهْجُ الْبُرْدة لأَحْمَد شَوْقِيّ: القسم الرابع

٤٧	مُحَمَّدٌ صَفْوَةُ الباري وَرَحْمَتُهُ	وَبُغْيَةُ اللهِ مِن خَلْقٍ وَمِن نَسَمِ
٤٨	وَصاحِبُ الحَوْضِ يَوْمَ الرُّسْلُ سائِلَةٌ	مَتَى الوُرودُ وَجِبْريلُ الأَمينُ ظَمِي
٤٩	سَناؤُهُ وَسَناهُ الشَّمسُ طالِعَةً	فَالجِرْمُ في فَلَكٍ وَالضَّوْءُ في عَلَمِ
٥٠	قَدْ أَخْطَأَ النَّجْمَ ما نالَتْ أُبُوَّتُهُ	مِن سُؤْدَدٍ باذِخٍ في مَظْهَرٍ سَنِمِ
٥١	نُمُوا إلَيهِ فَزادوا في الوَرَى شَرَفًا	وَرُبَّ أَصْلٍ لِفَرْعٍ في الفَخارِ نُمِي
٥٢	حَواهُ في سُبُحاتِ الطُّهرِ قَبْلَهُمُ	نُورانِ قاما مَقامَ الصُّلْبِ وَالرَّحِمِ
٥٣	لَمّا رَآهُ بَحِيرًا قالَ نَعْرِفُهُ	بِما حَفِظْنا مِنَ الأَسْماءِ وَالسِّيَمِ
٥٤	سائِلْ حِراءَ وَرُوحَ القُدْسِ هَل عَلِما	مَصُونَ سِرٍّ عَنِ الإِدْراكِ مُنكَتِمِ
٥٥	كَم جِيئَةٍ وَذَهابٍ شُرِّفَتْ بِهِما	بَطْحاءُ مَكَّةَ في الإِصْباحِ وَالغَسَمِ
٥٦	وَوَحْشَةٍ لِابْنِ عَبْدِ اللهِ بَيْنَهُما	أَشْهَى مِنَ الأُنْسِ بِالأَحْبابِ وَالحَشَمِ
٥٧	يُسامِرُ الوَحْيَ فيها قَبْلَ مَهْبِطِهِ	وَمَن يُبَشَّرْ بِسِيما الخَيْرِ يَتَّسِمِ
٥٨	لَمّا دَعا الصَّحْبُ يَسْتَسْقُونَ مِنْ ظَمَإٍ	فاضَتْ يَداكَ مِنَ التَّسْنيمِ بِالسَّنَمِ
٥٩	وَظَلَّلَتْهُ فَصارَتْ تَسْتَظِلُّ بِهِ	غَمامَةٌ جَذَبَتْها خِيرَةُ الدِّيَمِ
٦٠	مَحَبَّةٌ لِرَسولِ اللهِ أُشْرِبَها	قَعائِدُ الدَّيْرِ وَالرُّهْبانُ في القِمَمِ
٦١	إنَّ الشَّمائِلَ إنْ رَقَّتْ يَكادُ بِها	يُغْرَى الجَمادُ وَيُغْرَى كُلُّ ذِي نَسَمِ

٦٢ وَنودِيَ اقْرَأْ تَعالَى اللهُ قائِلُها … لَمْ تَتَّصِلْ قَبْلَ مَنْ قيلَتْ لَهُ بِفَمِ
٦٣ هُناكَ أَذَّنَ لِلرَّحْمٰنِ فَامْتَلأَتْ … أَسْماعُ مَكَّةَ مِن قُدْسِيَّةِ النَغَمِ
٦٤ فَلا تَسَلْ عَن قُرَيْشٍ كَيفَ حَيْرَتُها … وَكَيْفَ نُفْرَتُها في السَّهْلِ وَالعَلَمِ
٦٥ تَساءَلوا عَنْ عَظيمٍ قَد أَلَمَّ بِهِمْ … رَمَى المَشايِخَ وَالوِلْدانَ بِاللَّمَمِ
٦٦ يا جاهِلِينَ عَلَى الهادِي وَدَعْوَتِهِ … هَلْ تَجْهَلونَ مَكانَ الصَّادِقِ العَلَمِ
٦٧ لَقَّبْتُموهُ أَمينَ القَوْمِ في صِغَرٍ … وَما الأَمينُ عَلى قَوْلٍ بِمُتَّهَمِ
٦٨ فاقَ البُدورَ وَفاقَ الأَنْبِياءَ فَكَمْ … بِالخَلْقِ وَالخُلْقِ مِن حُسْنٍ وَمِن عِظَمِ
٦٩ جاءَ النَّبِيُّونَ بِالآياتِ فَانْصَرَمَتْ … وَجِئْتَنا بِحَكيمٍ غَيْرِ مُنْصَرِمِ
٧٠ آياتُهُ كُلَّما طالَ المَدَى جُدُدٌ … يَزينُهُنَّ جَلالُ العِتْقِ وَالقِدَمِ
٧١ يَكادُ في لَفْظَةٍ مِنْهُ مُشَرَّفَةٍ … يُوصِيكَ بِالحَقِّ وَالتَّقْوَى وَبِالرَّحِمِ
٧٢ يا أَفْصَحَ النَّاطِقِينَ الضّادَ قاطِبَةً … حَديثُكَ الشُّهْدُ عِندَ الذّائِقِ الفَهِمِ
٧٣ حَلَّيْتَ مِن عَطَلٍ جِيدَ البَيانِ بِهِ … في كُلِّ مُنْتَثِرٍ في حُسْنِ مُنْتَظِمِ
٧٤ بِكُلِّ قَوْلٍ كَريمٍ أَنْتَ قائِلُهُ … تُحْيِي القُلوبَ وَتُحْيِي مَيِّتَ الهِمَمِ

[64] نَهْجُ الْبُرْدَة لأَحْمَد شَوْقِيّ: القسم الخامس

٧٥ سَرَتْ بَشائِرُ بِالهادي وَمَوْلِدِهِ … في الشَّرْقِ وَالغَرْبِ مَسْرَى النُّورِ في الظُّلَمِ
٧٦ تَخَطَّفَتْ مُهَجَ الطَّاغِينَ مِن عَرَبٍ … وَطَيَّرَتْ أَنْفُسَ الباغِينَ مِن عَجَمِ
٧٧ رِيعَتْ لَها شُرَفُ الإيوانِ فَانْصَدَعَتْ … مِن صَدْمَةِ الحَقِّ لا مِن صَدْمَةِ القُدُمِ
٧٨ أَتَيْتَ وَالنَّاسُ فَوْضَى لا تَمُرُّ بِهِمْ … إِلاَّ عَلى صَنَمٍ قَدْ هامَ في صَنَمِ
٧٩ وَالأَرْضُ مَمْلوءَةٌ جَوْرًا مُسَخَّرَةٌ … لِكُلِّ طاغِيَةٍ في الخَلْقِ مُحتَكِمِ
٨٠ مُسَيْطِرُ الفُرْسِ يَبْغِي في رَعِيَّتِهِ … وَقَيْصَرُ الرُّومِ مِن كِبْرٍ أَصَمُّ عَمِي
٨١ يُعَذِّبانِ عِبادَ اللهِ في شُبَهٍ … وَيَذْبَحانِ كَما ضَحَّيْتَ بِالغَنَمِ
٨٢ وَالخَلْقُ يَفْتِكُ أَقْواهُمْ بِأَضْعَفِهِمْ … كَاللَّيْثِ بِالبُهْمِ أَو كَالحُوتِ بِالبَلَمِ
٨٣ أَسْرَى بِكَ اللهُ لَيْلاً إِذْ مَلائِكُهُ … وَالرُّسْلُ في المَسْجِدِ الأَقْصَى عَلى قَدَمِ
٨٤ لَمّا خَطَرْتَ بِهِ التَفُّوا بِسَيِّدِهِمْ … كَالشُّهْبِ بِالبَدْرِ أَو كَالجُنْدِ بِالعَلَمِ
٨٥ صَلَّى وَراءَكَ مِنْهُمْ كُلُّ ذي خَطَرٍ … وَمَنْ يَفُزْ بِحَبيبِ اللهِ يَأْتَمِمِ

٨٦ جُبْتَ السَّماواتِ أَوْ ما فَوْقَهُنَّ بِهِمْ عَلى مُنَوَّرَةٍ دُرِّيَّةِ اللُّجُمِ

٨٧ رَكوبَةٌ لَكَ مِن عِزٍّ وَمِن شَرَفٍ لا في الجِيادِ وَلا في الأَيْنُقِ الرُّسُمِ

٨٨ مَشِيئَةُ الخالِقِ الباري وَصَنْعَتُهُ وَقُدْرَةُ اللهِ فَوْقَ الشَّكِّ وَالتُّهَمِ

٨٩ حَتَّى بَلَغْتَ سَماءً لا يُطارُ لَها عَلى جَناحٍ وَلا يُسْعَى عَلى قَدَمِ

٩٠ وَقيلَ كُلُّ نَبِيٍّ عِنْدَ رُتْبَتِهِ وَيا مُحَمَّدُ هَذا العَرْشُ فَاسْتَلِمِ

٩١ خَطَطْتَ لِلدِّينِ وَالدُّنْيا عُلُومَهُما يا قارِئَ اللَّوْحِ بَلْ يا لامِسَ القَلَمِ

٩٢ أَحَطْتَ بَيْنَهُما بِالسِّرِّ وَانْكَشَفَتْ لَكَ الخَزائِنُ مِن عِلْمٍ وَمِن حِكَمِ

٩٣ وَضاعَفَ القُرْبُ ما قُلِّدْتَ مِن مِنَنٍ بِلا عِدادٍ وَما طُوِّقْتَ مِن نِعَمِ

٩٤ سَلْ عُصْبَةَ الشِّرْكِ حَوْلَ الغارِ سائِمَةً لَوْلا مُطارَدَةُ المُخْتارِ لَمْ تَسُمِ

٩٥ هَل أَبْصَروا الأَثَرَ الوَضّاءَ أَمْ سَمِعوا هَمْسَ التَّسابيحِ وَالقُرْآنَ مِن أَمَمِ

٩٦ وَهَل تَمَثَّلَ نَسْجُ العَنْكَبُوتِ لَهُمْ كَالغابِ وَالحائِماتُ الزُّغْبُ كَالرَّخَمِ

٩٧ فَأَدْبَروا وَوُجُوهُ الأَرْضِ تَلْعَنُهُمْ كَباطِلٍ مِن جَلالِ الحَقِّ مُنْهَزِمِ

٩٨ لَوْلا يَدُ اللهِ بِالجارَيْنِ ما سَلِما وَعَيْنُهُ حَوْلَ رُكْنِ الدِّينِ لَمْ يَقُمِ

٩٩ تَوارَيا بِجَناحِ اللهِ وَاسْتَتَرا وَمَنْ يَضُمَّ جَناحُ اللهِ لا يُضَمِ

[65] نَهْجُ الْبُرْدَة لِأَحْمَد شَوْقِيّ: القسم السادس

١٠٠ يا أَحْمَدَ الخَيْرِ لي جاهٌ بِتَسْمِيَتي وَكَيْفَ لا يَتَسامَى بِالرَّسولِ سَمِي

١٠١ المادِحونَ وَأَرْبابُ الهَوَى تَبَعٌ لِصاحِبِ البُرْدَةِ الفَيْحاءِ ذي القَدَمِ

١٠٢ مَديحُهُ فيكَ حُبٌّ خالِصٌ وَهَوًى وَصادِقُ الحُبِّ يُمْلي صادِقَ الكَلِمِ

١٠٣ اللهُ يَشْهَدُ أَنّي لا أُعارِضُهُ مَنْ ذا يُعارِضُ صَوْبَ العارِضِ العَرِمِ

١٠٤ وَإِنَّما أَنا بَعْضُ الغابِطينَ وَمَنْ يَغْبِطْ وَلِيَّكَ لا يُذْمَمْ وَلا يُلَمِ

١٠٥ هذا مَقامٌ مِنَ الرَحْمٰنِ مُقْتَبَسٌ تَرْمي مَهابَتُهُ سَحْبانَ بِالبَكَمِ

١٠٦ البَدْرُ دونَكَ في حُسْنٍ وَفي شَرَفٍ وَالبَحْرُ دونَكَ في خَيْرٍ وَفي كَرَمِ

١٠٧ شُمُّ الجِبالِ إِذا طاوَلْتَها انْخَفَضَتْ وَالأَنْجُمُ الزُّهْرُ ما واسَمْتَها تَسِمِ

١٠٨ وَاللَّيْثُ دُونَكَ بَأْسًا عِندَ وَثْبَتِهِ إِذا مَشَيْتَ إِلى شاكِي السِّلاحِ كَمي

١٠٩ تَهْفُو إِلَيكَ وَإِنْ أَدْمَيْتَ حَبَّتَها في الحَرْبِ أَفْئِدَةُ الأَبْطالِ وَالبُهَمِ

١١٠ مَـحَـبَّـةُ الـلـهِ أَلْـقـاهـا وَهَيْبَتُهُ عَـلَى ابْـنِ آمِـنَـةٍ في كُـلِّ مُصْطَدَمِ
١١١ كَأَنَّ وَجْهَكَ تَحْتَ النَّقْعِ بَدْرُ دُجًى يُـضِيءُ مُـلْـتَـثِـمًا أَو غَـيْرَ مُلْتَثِمِ
١١٢ بَـــدْرٌ تَـطَـلَّـعَ في بَـــدْرٍ فَغُرَّتُهُ كَغُرَّةِ النَّصْرِ تَجْلُو داجِـيَ الظُّلَمِ
١١٣ ذُكِـرْتَ بِاليُتْمِ في الـقُـرْآنِ تَكْرِمَةً وَقِيمَةُ اللُّؤْلُؤِ المَكْنونِ في اليُتُمِ
١١٤ الـلـهُ قَـسَّـمَ بَـيْنَ الـنَّـاسِ رِزْقَهُمُ وَأَنْـتَ خُـيِّرْتَ في الأَرْزاقِ وَالقِسَمِ
١١٥ إِنْ قُلْتَ في الأَمْرِ لا أَو قُلْتَ فيهِ نَعَمْ فَـخِـيرَةُ اللهِ في لا مِـنْـكَ أَو نَعَمِ
١١٦ أَخُـوكَ عِيسَى دَعـا مَيْتًا فَقامَ لَهُ وَأَنْـتَ أَحْيَيْتَ أَجْيالاً مِـنَ الرِّمَمِ
١١٧ وَالجَهْلُ مَوْتٌ فَإِنْ أُوتِيتَ مُعْجِزَةً فَابْعَثْ مِنَ الجَهْلِ أَوْ فَابْعَثْ مِنَ الرَّجَمِ

[66] **نَهْجُ الْبُرْدَة لأَحْمَد شَوْقِيّ: القسم السابع**

١١٨ قالوا غَـزَوْتَ وَرُسْـلُ اللهِ ما بُعِثُوا لِقَتْلِ نَفْسٍ وَلا جـاؤُوا لِسَفْكِ دَمِ
١١٩ جَهْلٌ وَتَضْليلُ أَحْـلامٍ وَسَفْسَطَةٌ فَتَحْتَ بِالسَّيْفِ بَعْدَ الفَتْحِ بِالقَلَمِ
١٢٠ لَـمَّا أَتى لَـكَ عَفْوًا كُـلُّ ذي حَسَبٍ تَكَفَّلَ السَّيْفُ بِالجُهَّالِ وَالعَمَمِ
١٢١ وَالـشَّرُّ إِنْ تَلْقَهُ بِالخَيْرِ ضِقْتَ بِهِ ذَرْعًـا وَإِنْ تَلْقَهُ بِالشَّرِّ يَنْحَسِمِ
١٢٢ سَلِ المَسيحِيَّةَ السَّمْحاءَ كَمْ شَرِبَتْ بِالصَّابِ مِن شَهَواتِ الظَّالِمِ الغَلِمِ
١٢٣ طَرِيدَةُ الـشِّرْكِ يُؤْذِيها وَيُوسِعُها في كُـلِّ حِـينٍ قِتالاً ساطِعَ الحَدَمِ
١٢٤ لَـوْلا حُـماةٌ لَها هَـبُّـوا لِنُصْرَتِها بِالسَّيْفِ ما انْتَفَعَتْ بِالرِّفْقِ وَالرُّحُمِ
١٢٥ لَـوْلا مَكانٌ لِعِيسَى عِندَ مُرْسِلِهِ وَحُـرْمَـةٌ وَجَبَت لِلرُّوحِ في القِدَمِ
١٢٦ لَسُمِّرَ البَدَنُ الطُّهْرُ الشَّرِيفُ عَلَى لَوْحَيْنِ لَمْ يَخْشَ مُؤْذِيهِ وَلَمْ يَجِمِ
١٢٧ جَلَّ المَسيحُ وَذاقَ الصَّلْبَ شانِئُهُ إِنَّ العِقابَ بِقَدْرِ الذَّنْبِ وَالجُرُمِ
١٢٨ أَخـو الـنَـبِـيِّ وَرُوحُ الـلـهِ في نُزُلٍ فَوْقَ السَّماءِ وَدونَ العَرْشِ مُحْتَرَمِ

[67] **نَهْجُ الْبُرْدَة لأَحْمَد شَوْقِيّ: القسم الثامن**

١٢٩ عَلَّمْتَهُمْ كُـلَّ شَيْءٍ يَجْهَلونَ بِهِ حَتَّى القِتالَ وَما فيهِ مِنَ الذِّمَمِ
١٣٠ دَعَـوْتَـهُـمْ لِجِهادٍ فيهِ سُؤْدَدُهُمْ وَالحَرْبُ أُسُّ نِظامِ الكَوْنِ وَالأُمَمِ
١٣١ لَـــوْلاهُ لَـمْ نَـرَ لِـلـدُّوَلاتِ في زَمَنٍ ما طالَ مِن عَمَدٍ أَو قَرَّ مِن دَعَمِ
١٣٢ تِـلْـكَ الـشَّـواهِـدُ تَـتْرَى كُـلَّ آوِنَةٍ في الأَعْصُرِ الغُرِّ لا في الأَعْصُرِ الدُّهُمِ

١٣٣ بِالأَمْسِ مالَتْ عُرُوشٌ وَاعْتَلَتْ سُرُرٌ لَـوْلا القَنابِلُ لَم تَثْلَمْ وَلَـم تُصَمِ

١٣٤ أَشْـياعُ عِيسَى أَعَـدُّوا كُـلَّ قاصِمَةٍ وَلَـم نُعِدَّ سِـوَى حـالاتِ مُنْقَصِمِ

١٣٥ مَهْما دُعِيْتَ إِلى الهَيْجاءِ قُمْتَ لَها تَرْمي بِأُسْدٍ وَيَرْمِي اللهُ بِالرُّجُمِ

١٣٦ عَـلى لِـوائِـكَ مِنْهُمْ كُـلُّ مُنْتَقِمٍ للهِ مُسْتَقتِلٍ في الـلـهِ مُعْتَزِمِ

١٣٧ مُـسَـبِّـحٍ لِـلِـقـاءِ الـلـهِ مُضْطَرِمٍ شَوْقًا عَلى سابِحٍ كَالبَرْقِ مُضْطَرِمِ

١٣٨ لَوْ صادَفَ الدَّهْرَ يَبْغِي نُقْلَةً فَرَمَى بِعَزْمِهِ في رِحـالِ الـدَّهْـرِ لَـم يَرِمِ

١٣٩ بِيضٌ مَفاليلُ مِنْ فِعْلِ الحُروبِ بِهِمْ مِنْ أَسْيُفِ اللهِ لا الهِندِيَّةِ الخُذُمِ

١٤٠ كَمْ في الـتُّرابِ إِذا فَتَّشْتَ عَن رَجُلٍ مَنْ ماتَ بِالعَهْدِ أَو مَنْ ماتَ بِالقَسَمِ

١٤١ لَـوْلا مَـواهِـبُ في بَعْضِ الأَنـامِ لَمَا تَفاوَتَ النَّاسُ في الأَقْـدارِ وَالقِيَمِ

[68] **قال أبو تمّام**

* رَمَـى بِـكَ اللهُ بُرْجَيْها فَهَدَّمَها وَلَـوْ رَمَـى بك غَـيْرُ اللهِ لَـمْ يُصِبِ

[69] **قال أبو تمّام**

* تَـدْبِـيرُ مُعْتَصِمٍ بِاللهِ مُنْتَقِمٍ للهِ مُـرْتَـقِـبٍ في الـلـهِ مُرْتَغِبِ

[70] **قال أبو تمّام**

* أَمْطَرْتَهُمْ عَزَماتٍ لَـوْ رَمَيْتَ بها يَوْمَ الكَرِيهةِ رُكْنَ الدَّهْرِ لَانْهَدَمَا

[71] **نَهْجُ الْبُرْدة لأَحْمَد شَوْقِيّ: القسم التاسع**

١٤٢ شَرِيـعَـةٌ لَـكَ فَـجَّـرْتَ العُقُولَ بِها عَن زاخِـرٍ بِصُنوفِ العِلْمِ مُلْتَطِمِ

١٤٣ يَلُوحُ حَوْلَ سَنَا التَّوْحِيدِ جَوْهَرُها كَالحَلْيِ لِلسَّيْفِ أَو كَالوَشْيِ لِلعَلَمِ

١٤٤ سَمْحاءُ حامَتْ عَلَيْها أَنْفُسٌ وَنُهًى وَمَنْ يَجِدْ سَلْسَلاً مِن حِكْمَةٍ يَحُمِ

١٤٥ نورُ السَّبيلِ يُساسُ العالَمُونَ بِها تَكَفَّلَتْ بِشَبابِ الـدَّهْـرِ وَالهَرَمِ

١٤٦ يَجْرِي الزَّمانُ وَأَحْكامُ الزَّمانِ عَلَى حُكْمٍ لَهَا نافِذٍ في الخَلْقِ مُرْتَسِمِ

١٤٧ لَمَّا اعْتَلَتْ دَوْلَةُ الإِسْلامِ وَاتَّسَعَتْ مَشَتْ مَمالِكُهُ في نُـورِهـا التَّمِمِ

١٤٨ وَعَـلَّـمَـتْ أُمَّـةً بِـالـقَـفْـرِ نازِلَةً رَعْـيَ القَياصِرِ بَعْدَ الشَّاءِ وَالنَّعَمِ

١٤٩ كَمْ شَيَّدَ المُصْلِحونَ العامِلونَ بِهَا في الشَّرْقِ وَالغَرْبِ مُلْكًا باذِخَ العِظَمِ

١٥٠ لِلعِلْمِ وَالعَدْلِ وَالتَّمْدينِ ما عَزَموا مِـنَ الأُمُـورِ وَمـا شَـدُّوا مِـنَ الحُزُمِ

١٥١ سَرْعـانَ ما فَتَحُوا الدُّنْيا لِمِلَّتِهِمْ   وَأَنْهَلوا النَّاسَ مِن سَلْسالِها الشَبِمِ

١٥٢ سارُوا عَلَيْها هُداةَ النَّاسِ فَهْيَ بِهِمْ   إلى الفَلاحِ طَرِيقٌ واضِـحُ العِظَمِ

١٥٣ لا يَهْدِمُ الدَّهْرُ رُكْنًا شادَ عَدْلُهُمُ   وَحائِطُ البَغْيِ إنْ تَلْمِسْهُ يَنْهَدِمِ

١٥٤ نالوا السَعادَةَ في الدَّارَيْنِ وَاجْتَمَعوا   عَلَى عَميمٍ مِنَ الرِضْوانِ مُقْتَسَمِ

[72] نَهْجُ الْبُرْدة لأَحْمَد شَوْقِيّ: القسم العاشر

١٥٥ دَعْ عَنْكَ رُومَـا وَآثِينا وَمـا حَوَتا   كُـلُّ اليَوَاقِيتِ في بَـغْـدادَ وَالتُّوَمِ

١٥٦ وَخَــلِّ كِــسْرَى وَإيــوانًـا يُـدِلُّ بِهِ   هَـوًى عـلى أَثَـرِ الـنِّـيرانِ وَالأُيُمِ

١٥٧ وَاتْـرُكْ رَعْمَسِيسَ إنَّ المُلْكَ مَظْهَرُهُ   في نَهْضَةِ العَدْلِ لا في نَهْضَةِ الهَرَمِ

١٥٨ دارُ الـشَّرائِـعِ رُومَــا كُلَّما ذُكِرَتْ   دارُ السَّلامِ لَهَا أَلْقَتْ يَـدَ السَّلَمِ

١٥٩ ما ضارَعَتْها بَيانًا عِنْدَ مُلْتَأَمٍ   وَلا حَكَتْها قَضاءً عِنْدَ مُخْتَصَمِ

١٦٠ وَلا احْتَوَتْ في طِرازٍ مِن قَياصِرِها   عَـلَى رَشـيـدٍ وَمَـأْمـونٍ وَمُعْتَصِمِ

١٦١ مِـنَ الَّذينَ إذا سـارَتْ كَتائِبُهُمْ   تَـصَرَّفُـوا بِـحُـدودِ الأَرْضِ وَالتُّخُمِ

١٦٢ وَيَجْلِسونَ إلى عِلْمٍ وَمَعْرِفَةٍ   فَـلا يُـدانَـوْنَ في عَـقْـلٍ وَلا فَهَمِ

١٦٣ يُطَأْطِئُ العُلَماءُ الهامَ إنْ نَبَسوا   مِنْ هَيْبَةِ العِلْمِ لا مِنْ هَيْبَةِ الحُكُمِ

١٦٤ وَيُمْطِرونَ فَما بِـالأَرْضِ مِنْ مَحَلٍ   وَلا بِمَـنْ باتَ فَـوْقَ الأَرْضِ مِن عُدُمِ

[73] نَهْجُ الْبُرْدة لأَحْمَد شَوْقِيّ: القسم الحادِيَ عشر

١٦٥ خَلائِفُ اللهِ جَلُّوا عَن مُوازَنَةٍ   فَـلا تَقِيسَنَّ أَمْـلاكَ الـوَرَى بِهِمِ

١٦٦ مَن في البَرِيَّةِ كَالفَارُوقِ مَعْدَلَةً   وَكَابْنِ عَبْدِ العَزيزِ الخاشِعِ الحَشِمِ

١٦٧ وَكَـالإمـامِ إذا ما فَـضَّ مُزْدَحَمًا   بِمَـدْمَـعٍ في مَـآقِـي الـقَـوْمِ مُزْدَحِمِ

١٦٨ الزَّاخِرُ العَذْبُ في عِلْمٍ وَفي أَدَبٍ   وَالنَّاصِرُ النَّدْبُ في حَـرْبٍ وَفي سَلَمِ

١٦٩ أَوْ كَابْنِ عَفَّانَ وَالـقُـرْآنُ في يَدِهِ   يَحْنُو عَلَيْهِ كَما تَحْنُو عَلى الفُطُمِ

١٧٠ وَيَجْمَعُ الآيَ تَرْتِيبًا وَيَنْظِمُها   عِقْدًا بِجِيدِ اللَّيَالِي غَـيْرَ مُنْفَصِمِ

١٧١ جُرْحانِ في كَبِدِ الإسْـلامِ ما الْتَأَمَا   جُرْحُ الشَّهيدِ وَجُـرْحٌ بِالكِتابِ دَمِي

١٧٢ وَمــا بَــلاءُ أَبي بَـكْـرٍ بِمُتَّهَمٍ   بَعْدَ الجَلائِلِ في الأَفْـعـالِ وَالخِدَمِ

١٧٣ بِالحَزْمِ وَالعَزْمِ حاطَ الدِّينَ في مِحَنٍ   أَضَلَّتِ الحِلْمَ مِن كَهْلٍ وَمُحْتَلِمِ

١٧٤ وَحُدْنَ بِالراشِدِ الفَارُوقِ عَن رَشَدٍ　　في المَــوْتِ وَهْــوَ يَقينٌ غَـيرُ مُنْبَهِمِ
١٧٥ يُـجـادِلُ الـقَـوْمَ مُسْتَلاً مُهَنَّدَهُ　　في أَعْظَمِ الرُّسْلِ قَدْرًا كَيفَ لَمْ يَدُمِ
١٧٦ لا تَعْذِلوهُ إذا طافَ الذُّهُولُ بِهِ　　ماتَ الحَبيبُ فَضَلَّ الصَّبُّ عَن رَغَمِ

[74] **نَهْجُ الْبُرْدة لأَحْمَد شَوْقِيّ: القسم الثانيَ عشر**

١٧٧ يا رَبِّ صَلِّ وَسَلِّمْ ما أَرَدْتَ عَلَى　　نَـزِيـلِ عَـرْشِـكَ خَـيْرِ الـرُّسْـلِ كُلِّهِمِ
١٧٨ مُحْيِي اللَّيَالِي صَلاةً لا يُقَطِّعُها　　إلاَّ بِـدَمْـعٍ مِـنَ الإشْـفـاقِ مُنْسَجِمِ
١٧٩ مُسَبِّحًا لَكَ جُنْحَ اللَّيْلِ مُحْتَمِلاً　　ضُرًّا مِـنَ السُّهْدِ أو ضُرًّا مِـنَ الوَرَمِ
١٨٠ رَضِـيَّـةً نَفْسُهُ لا تَشْتَكي سَأَمًا　　وَما مَعَ الحُبِّ إنْ أَخْلَصْتَ مِن سَأَمِ
١٨١ وَصَــلِّ رَبِّي عَــلَى آلٍ لَــهُ نُخَبٍ　　جَعَلْتَ فيهِمْ لِـواءَ البَيْتِ وَالحَرَمِ
١٨٢ بِيضُ الوُجُوهِ وَوَجْهُ الدَّهْرِ ذو حَلَكٍ　　شُمُّ الأُنُـوفِ وَأَنْـفُ الحادِثاتِ حَمِي
١٨٣ وَأَهْــدِ خَـيْرَ صَـلاةٍ مِنْكَ أَرْبَعَةً　　في الصَّحْبِ صُحْبَتُهُم مَرْعِيَّةُ الحُرَمِ
١٨٤ الرَّاكِبينَ إذا نـادَى النَّبِيُّ بِهِمْ　　ما هالَ مِن جَلَلٍ وَاشْتَدَّ مِن عَمَمِ
١٨٥ الصَّابِرينَ وَنَفْسُ الأَرْضِ واجِفَةٌ　　الضَّاحِكينَ إلى الأَخْـطـارِ وَالقُحَمِ
١٨٦ يا رَبِّ هَبَّتْ شُعُوبٌ مِن مَنِيَّتِها　　وَاسْتَيْقَظَتْ أُمَـمٌ مِن رَقْـدَةِ العَدَمِ
١٨٧ سَعْدٌ وَنَحْسٌ وَمُلْكٌ أَنْتَ مالِكُهُ　　تُـديـلُ مِـن نِـعَـمٍ فيهِ وَمِــنْ نِقَمِ
١٨٨ رَأَى قَضاؤُكَ فِينا رَأْيَ حِكمَتِهِ　　أَكْـرِمْ بِوَجْهِكَ مِن قـاضٍ وَمُنْتَقِمِ
١٨٩ فَالْطُفْ لأَجْلِ رَسولِ العالَمِينَ بِنا　　وَلا تَـزِدْ قَـوْمَـهُ خَسْفًا وَلا تَسُمِ
١٩٠ يا رَبِّ أَحْسَنْتَ بَدْءَ المُسْلِمينَ بِهِ　　فَتَمِّمِ الفَضْلَ وَامْنَحْ حُسْنَ مُخْتَتَمِ

[75] **قال ابْنُ حِجَّة الحَمَوِيّ**

* حُسْنُ ٱبْتِدايَ بِهِ أَرْجو التَّخَلُّصَ مِنْ　　نارِ الجَحيمِ وأَرْجو حُسْنَ مُخْتَتَمي

NOTES

Preface

1. See Ibn Khaldūn, *The Muqaddimah: An Introduction to History [Kitāb al-ʿIbar]*, trans. and intro. Franz Rosenthal (New York: Pantheon, 1958), xliv and 42.

2. "The Prophet's Mosque," ArchNet Digital Library http://www.archnet.org/library/sites/one-site.jsp?site_id=10061. Accessed 31 July 2009.

1. Kaʿb ibn Zuhayr and the Mantle of the Prophet

1. On the use of the panegyric ode as a vehicle for the expression and perpetuation of ideals of legitimate Arab-Islamic rule, see Suzanne Pinckney Stetkevych, *The Poetics of Islamic Legitimacy: Myth, Gender, and Ceremony in the Classical Arabic Ode* (Bloomington: Indiana University Press, 2002).

2. I have dealt with the issue of the literary interpretative use of early Arabic materials at length in Suzanne Pinckney Stetkevych, "Archetype and Attribution in Early Arabic Poetry: al-Shanfarā and the *Lāmiyyat al-ʿArab*," *International Journal of Middle Eastern Studies* 18 (1986): 361–90; a revised version appears as ch. 4 of Suzanne Pinckney Stetkevych, *The Mute Immortals Speak: Pre-Islamic Poetry and the Poetics of Ritual* (Ithaca, N.Y.: Cornell University Press, 1993), 119–57.

3. For fuller study of this *qaṣīdah,* including an English translation of the entire poem, see Suzanne Pinckney Stetkevych, "Pre-Islamic Poetry and the Poetics of Redemption: *Mufaḍḍalīyah 119* of ʿAlqamah and *Bānat Suʿād* of Kaʿb ibn Zuhayr," in *Reorientations: Arabic and Persian Poetry,* ed. Suzanne Pinckney Stetkevych (Bloomington: Indiana University Press, 1994), 21–57. Other versions of the compilation of *Al-Mufaḍḍaliyyāt* are found as well; see Fuat Sezgin, *Geschichte des Arabischen Schrifttums, Band II: Poesie bis ca. 430 H.* (Leiden: E. J. Brill, 1973), 53.

4. See Irfan Shahid, "Lakhmids" and "Ghassānids," in *Encyclopaedia of Islam,* New Edition (Leiden: E. J. Brill, 1954–2004) [hereafter *EI2*].

5. Charles James Lyall, ed. and trans., *The Mufaḍḍalīyāt: An Anthology of Ancient Arabian Odes Compiled by Al-Mufaḍḍal Son of Muḥammad, According to the Recension and with the Commentary of Abū Muḥammad al-Qāsim ibn Muḥammad*

al-Anbārī, Vol. 1, Arabic Text; Vol. 2, Translation and Notes (Oxford: Clarendon Press, 1918), 1:786 and 2:333.

6. Lyall, *Mufaḍḍalīyāt,* 1:786 and 2:333.

7. Marcel Mauss, *The Gift: Forms and Functions of Exchange in Archaic Societies,* trans. Ian Cunnison (New York: Norton, 1967) [*Essai sur le don, forme archaïque de l'échange,* 1925)], 1.

8. Ibid., 37.

9. Ibid., 40.

10. Ibid., 35.

11. Ibid., 70.

12. Ibid., vii.

13. Ibid., 1.

14. Victor Turner, *The Ritual Process: Structure and Anti-Structure* (Ithaca, N.Y.: Cornell University Press, 1977), 94–95. I first proposed the interpretation of the Arabic *qaṣīdah* of the tripartite type, as well as certain variant forms, in terms of the van Gennepian rite of passage in my article "Structuralist Analyses of Pre-Islamic Poetry: Critique and New Directions," *Journal of Near Eastern Studies* 42 no. 2 (1983): 85–107, and subsequently in a series of articles and, most extensively, in my book *The Mute Immortals Speak.* See Arnold van Gennep, *The Rites of Passage,* trans. Monika Vizedom and Gabrielle L. Caffee (Chicago: University of Chicago Press, 1960) [*Les rites de passage,* 1908].

15. I have followed the text and commentary of Lyall, *Mufaḍḍalīyāt,* 1:762–86; and consulted [ʿAlqamah ibn ʿAbadah], *Dīwān ʿAlqamah al-Faḥl bi-Sharḥ . . . al-Aʿlam al-Shantamarī,* ed. Luṭfī al-Ṣaqqāl and Durriyyah al-Khaṭīb (Aleppo: Dār al-Kitāb al-ʿArabī bi-Ḥalab, 1969), 32–39. Al-Shantamarī's recension has thirty-nine verses presented in a different order, to close with the poet's plea, verse 21 of our *Muf.* version. This in no way invalidates the present argument, as there is in any case, as we will see throughout this study, considerable variation of order and overlap of what we have termed the Supplicatory Elements, especially within the final *madīḥ* section of the poem. The variation in order also does not affect the rite of passage pattern exhibited in this poem. The effect in al-Shantamarī's recension is to shift part of the weight of the abasement and supplication from the transition at the beginning of the *madīḥ* to its reiteration at the closure. On these issues, see James E. Montgomery, *The Vagaries of the Qaṣīdah: The Tradition and Practice of Early Arabic Poetry* (Cambridge, UK: E.J.W. Gibb Memorial Trust, 1997), whose interpretations are often at odds with mine.

16. On the performative aspects of the *qaṣīdah,* see especially S. Stetkevych, "The Poetics of Political Allegiance: Praise and Blame in Three Odes by al-Mutanabbī," 180–240, in *The Poetics of Islamic Legitimacy.* Further on Speech Act Theory as it applies to the ritual exchange of *qaṣīdah* for prize and the establishment of a pact of mutual allegiance and obligation between poet and patron, see Majd Yassir Al-Mallah, "Doing Things with Odes: A Poet's Pledges of Allegiance: Ibn Darrāj al-Qasṭallī's *Hāʾiyyah* to al-Manṣūr and *Rāʾiyyah* to al-Mundhir," *Journal of Arabic Literature* 34 nos. 1–2 (2003): 45–81. See also, Beatrice Gruendler, *Medieval Arabic Praise Poetry: Ibn al-Rūmī and the Patron's Redemption* (London: RoutledgeCurzon, 2003). Standard sources include J. L. Austin, *How to Do Things with Words* (Cambridge, Mass.: Harvard University Press, 1975) and Sandy Petrey, *Speech Acts and Literary Theory* (London: Routledge, 1990).

17. Mauss, *The Gift*, 10.

18. On the Supplicatory Ode, see especially S. Stetkevych, *The Poetics of Islamic Legitimacy*, chs. 1, 2, 4, and index. I first introduced the idea of the Supplicatory Ode in "Umayyad Panegyric and the Poetics of Islamic Hegemony: Al-Akhṭal's *Khaffa al-Qaṭīnu* ('Those Who Dwelt with You Have Left in Haste')," *Journal of Arabic Literature*, 28 no. 2 (1997): 89–122; and "Qaṣīdat al-Madḥ wa-Marāsim al-Ibtihāl: Fāᶜiliyyāt al-Naṣṣ al-Adabī," in *Al-Naqd al-Adabī fī Munᶜaṭaf al-Qarn (Papers Presented at the First International Conference on Literary Criticism, Cairo, October, 1997)*, ed. ᶜIzz al-Dīn Ismāᶜīl (Cairo, 1999), 3:175–96.

19. See A. Arazi, "al-Nābigha al-Dhubyānī," *EI2*.

20. Abū al-Faraj al-Iṣbahānī, *Kitāb al-Aghānī*, ed. Ibrāhīm al-Abyārī (Cairo: Dār al-Shaᶜb, 1969–79), 11:3799–800.

21. The full texts of al-Nābighah's two poems, the *dāliyyah* in which he describes al-Mutajarridah and his *dāliyyah* of apology to King Nuᶜmān, and much of the lore associated with them, are translated and discussed in S. Stetkevych, "Transgression and Redemption: Cuckolding the King," *The Poetics of Islamic Legitimacy*, 1–47. For the Arabic text of the poems, see al-Nābighah al-Dhubyānī, *Dīwān*, 3rd ed., ed. Muḥammad Abū al-Faḍl Ibrāhīm (Cairo: Dār al-Maᶜārif, 1990), 89–97 (al-Mutajarridah); 14–28 (*iᶜtidhāriyyah*); for the anecdotal materials, see al-Iṣbahānī, *Al-Aghānī*, 11: 3794–801.

22. The most engaging studies of this theme are Jaroslav Stetkevych, *The Zephyrs of Najd: the Poetics of Nostalgia in the Classical Arabic* Nasīb (Chicago: University of Chicago Press, 1993), and Jaroslav Stetkevych, "Toward an Arabic Elegiac Lexicon: The Seven Words of the *Nasīb*" in S. Stetkevych, *Reorientations*, 58–129.

23. I have followed the text and commentary in al-Nābighah, *Dīwān*, 14–28.

24. Abū al-Faḍl Aḥmad ibn Muḥammad al-Maydānī, *Majmaᶜ al-Amthāl*, 2nd ed., ed. Muḥammad Muḥyī al-Dīn ᶜAbd al-Ḥamīd (Cairo: Al-Maktabah al-Tijāriyyah al-Kubrá, 1959), 1:429. No. 2265.

25. Maḥmūd Shukrī al-Ālūsī al-Baghdādī, *Bulūgh al-Arab fī Maᶜrifat Aḥwāl al-ᶜArab*, ed. Muḥammad Bahjat al-Atharī (Beirut: Dār al-Kutub al-ᶜIlmiyyah, n.d.), 2:341–42.

26. Al-Iṣbahānī, *Al-Aghānī*, 11:3813–14.

27. See references in note 21.

28. On how the poet's speech act (the poem) creates a pact with the patron, see S. Stetkevych, *The Poetics of Islamic Legitimacy*, esp. 181–82, 208–9; see Al-Mallah, "Doing Things with Odes," 58–59.

29. On Zuhayr see Lidia Bettini, "Zuhayr b. Abī Sulmā Rabīᶜah b. Riyāḥ al-Muzanī," *EI2*; A. J. Arberry, *The Seven Odes: The First Chapter in Arabic Literature* (London: George Allen and Unwin, 1957), 90–113, and an English translation of his Muᶜallaqah, 114–18.

30. Bettini, "Zuhayr b. Abī Sulmā," and al-Iṣbahānī, *Al-Aghānī*, 10:3755–57, 3773.

31. Al-Iṣbahānī, *Al-Aghānī*, 10:3776, 3778.10:3778; Arberry, *The Seven Odes*, 98.

32. Al-Iṣbahānī, *Al-Aghānī*, 10:3753.

33. Ibid., 10:3769.

34. See, for example, Abū Bakr Muḥammad ibn al-Qāsim al-Anbārī [= Ibn al-Anbārī], *Sharḥ al-Qaṣāʾid al-Sabᶜ al-Ṭiwāl al-Jāhiliyyāt*, ed. ᶜAbd al-Salām Muḥammad Hārūn (Cairo: Dār al-Maᶜārif, 1969), 234–90.

35. Abū ʿAbbās Aḥmad ibn Yaḥyá ibn Zayd al-Shaybānī Thaʿlab, *Sharḥ Dīwān Zuhayr ibn Abī Sulmá* (Cairo: Al-Dār al-Qawmiyyah lil-Ṭibāʿah wa-al-Nashr, 1964 [photo-offset of Cairo: Dār al-Kutub, 1944]), 1–32. Further on Zuhayr, see Bettini, "Zuhayr b. Abī Sulmā"; al-Iṣbahānī, *Al-Aghānī,* 10:3752–61.

36. Thaʿlab, *Sharḥ Dīwān Zuhayr,* 33–55; passages are cited in al-Iṣbahānī, *Al-Aghānī,* 10:3762–63; 3767.

37. Abū Muḥammad ʿAbd Allāh ibn Muslim Ibn Qutaybah, *Kitāb al-Shiʿr wa-al-Shuʿarāʾ wa-qīla Ṭabaqāt al-Shuʿarāʾ,* ed. M. J. de Goeje (Leiden: E. J. Brill, 1902), 61.

38. I have followed the text and commentary of Thaʿlab, *Sharḥ Dīwān Zuhayr,* 33–55. I have also consulted the recension and commentary of al-Shantamarī in al-Aʿlam al-Shantamarī, *Shiʿr Zuhayr ibn Abī Sulmá,* ed. Fakhr al-Dīn al-Qabāwah (Aleppo: Al-Maktabah al-ʿArabiyyah, 1970), 59–73, which contains thirty-three verses as opposed to Thaʿlab's forty-nine. I hope to turn to a separate study of the full *qaṣīdah* on another occasion.

39. The pronouns are a bit ambiguous in this verse.

40. Thaʿlab's commentary mentions that the Baṣran philologist al-Aṣmaʿī (d. 213/828) considered this verse the *bayt al-qaṣīdah,* i.e., the gist or crux of the entire poem. Thaʿlab, *Sharḥ Dīwān Zuhayr,* 49.

41. Al-Iṣbahānī, *Al-Aghānī,* 10:3768.

42. Ibid., 10:3769.

43. I discuss this issue in S. Stetkevych, *The Mute Immortals Speak,* 42–45, 284–85, and esp. 50–54 on Labīd, his brother Arbad, and the great Jāhilī warrior-poet, ʿĀmir ibn al-Ṭufayl. There I note (51) that "the Qurʾān played . . . the 'New Testament' to the pre-Islamic poetic 'Old Testament,' at once abrogating and fulfilling it."

44. Zuhayr's Muʿallaqah, in Thaʿlab, *Sharḥ Dīwān Zuhayr,* 18, vv. 27, 28; and al-Anbārī, *Sharḥ al-Qaṣāʾid al-Sabʿ,* 266, vv. 27, 28.

45. Al-Ālūsī, *Bulūgh al-Arab,* 3:101.

46. Al-Iṣbahānī, *Al-Aghānī,* 10:3768. These verses correspond (with minor variants) to the following verses in the Thaʿlab recension, respectively: 4, 24, ?, 8, 17, 22, 21. It is not surprising that, given the Islamic proscription of wine and the Caliph ʿUmar's reputation for stern piety, Zuhayr's verse 6, on wine, is not among the ones that appear in this anecdote. Thaʿlab, *Sharḥ Dīwān Zuhayr,* 86–95.

47. Sezgin, *Poesie,* 229–35.

48. On the dates, history, and nature of the literature on the biography of the Prophet (Sīrah) and an academic review and bibliography, see W. Raven, "Sīra," *Encyclopaedia of Islam, Second Edition* (Leiden: E. J. Brill, 2009) Brill Online, http://www.brillonline.nl/subscriber/entry?entry=islam_COM-1089 [hereafter *EI2online*] (accessed: Indiana University, by subscription, 15 April 2009).

49. Abū Muḥammad ʿAbd al-Malik ibn Hishām, *Al-Sīrah al-Nabawiyyah* (Cairo: Dār al-Fikr [1980]).

50. Muḥammad ibn Sallām al-Jumaḥī, *Ṭabaqāt Fuḥūl al-Shuʿarāʾ,* ed. Maḥmūd Muḥammad Shākir (Cairo: Maṭbaʿat al-Madanī, 1394/1974), 7–8, 11. This is regularly cited; see, for example, Raven, "Sīra," and Maḥmūd ʿAlī Makkī, *Al-Madāʾiḥ al-Nabawiyyah* (Cairo: Al-Sharikah al-Miṣriyyah al-ʿIlmiyyah lil-Nashr/Longman, 1991), 7.

51. I have developed this idea in earlier work as it applies to the ʿAbbāsid *qaṣīdah* in the hands of Abū Tammām. See Suzanne Pinckney Stetkevych, "The

ʿAbbāsid Poet Interprets History: Three Qaṣīdahs by Abū Tammām," *Journal of Arabic Literature* 10 (1979): 49–65; and Suzanne Pinckney Stetkevych, *Abū Tammām and the Poetics of the ʿAbbāsid Age* (Leiden: E. J. Brill, 1991), 106–236.

52. Eric A. Havelock, *The Literate Revolution in Greece and Its Cultural Consequences* (Princeton, N.J.: Princeton University Press, 1982), 116–17; and S. Stetkevych, *The Mute Immortals Speak,* chs. 5, 6.

53. See S. Stetkevych, *The Mute Immortals Speak,* 81.

54. Eric A. Havelock, *The Muse Learns to Write: Reflections on Orality and Literacy from Antiquity to the Present* (New Haven, Conn.: Yale University Press, 1986), 70.

55. Ibid., 71.

56. This is not, by any means, to say that Kaʿb was the first or only poet to serve the Prophet. Pride of place in that respect goes to the Prophet's main panegyrist, formerly an acclaimed pre-Islamic panegyrist, Ḥassān ibn Thābit. It is of note, however, that the classical Arabic critics concur that Ḥassān's pre-Islamic oeuvre was artistically superior to that written for the Prophet. There are, in addition, the minor poets of Ibn Hishām's *Al-Sīrah al-Nabawiyyah,* such as Kaʿb ibn Malik, who were always at hand to compose praise (*madīḥ*), incitement (*taḥrīḍ*) or invective (*hijāʾ*) as needed, but on the whole not of outstanding quality. Panegyric (*madḥ*) in this period tends to be short, extemporaneous, and spontaneous, rather direct in style, and often without a preceding elegiac prelude (*nasīb*) or journey section (*raḥīl*). A good overview is Makkī, *Al-Madāʾiḥ al-Nabawiyyah,* 7–58. See also Wahb Rūmiyyah, *Qaṣīdat al-Madḥ ḥattá Nihāyat al-ʿAṣr al-Umawī: Bayn al-Uṣūl wa-al-Iḥyāʾ wa-al-Tajdīd* (Damascus: Manshūrāt Wizārat al-Thaqāfah wa-al-Irshād al-Qawmī, 1981), 274–76; and James T. Monroe, "The Poetry of the *Sīrah* Literature," in *The Cambridge History of Arabic Literature: Vol. 1: Arabic Literature to the End of the Umayyad Period,* ed. A. F. L. Beeston, T. M. Johnstone, R. B. Serjeant, and G. R. Smith, (Cambridge: Cambridge University Press, 1983), 368–73. Kaʿb ibn Zuhayr, by contrast, was something of a latecomer to the Islamic fold (see below). His Suʿād Has Departed, which bears the sobriquet The Mantle Ode, is the most celebrated *qaṣīdah* of its period and, throughout the centuries, one of the most revered and influential poems of the Arabic and Islamic traditions.

57. To be supplanted or supplemented from the fourteenth century onward by the immensely popular Mantle Ode of al-Būṣīrī, the subject of chapter 2 of this study. To avoid confusion, I will refer to Kaʿb's ode as "Suʿād Has Departed" and his successor's as "Al-Būṣīrī's Burdah" or "Mantle Ode."

58. See Sezgin, *Poesie,* 229–35.

59. Of the many recensions of and commentaries on Suʿād Has Departed, I have relied primarily on Abū Saʿīd al-Ḥasan ibn al-Ḥusayn al-Sukkarī, *Sharḥ Dīwān Kaʿb ibn Zuhayr* (Cairo: Dār al-Qawmiyyah, 1965), 3–25, which is largely derived from Ibn Hishām; and Yaḥyā ibn ʿAlī al-Tibrīzī, in Fritz Krenkow, "Tabrīzīs Kommentar zur Burda des Kaʿb ibn Zuhair," *Zeitschrift der Deutschen Morganländischen Gesellschaft* 65 (1911): 241–79; and Ibn Hishām, *Al-Sīrah al-Nabawiyyah,* 3:1353–66 (Ibn Hishām's work is actually an edition of the older *Sīrah* of Ibn Isḥāq (d. 150/767), which has been reconstructed by Guillaume in his translation, below). Other English versions of the *qaṣīdah* and its *akhbār* are found in M. Hidayat Husain, "Bānat Suʿād of Kaʿb bin Zuhair," *Islamic Culture* 1 (1927): 67–84; and A. Guillaume, trans., *The Life of Muhammad: A Translation of Ibn Isḥāq's Sīrat Rasūl Allāh* (Lahore: Oxford University Press, 1974), 597–601 (which quotes Reynold Nichol-

son's translation). A translation by Michael A. Sells has appeared as "*Bānat Suᶜād:* Translation and Interpretative Introduction," *Journal of Arabic Literature* 21, no. 2 (1990): 140–54. For further sources, see Sezgin, *Poesie,* 230–35.

60. Gregory Nagy, *Pindar's Homer: The Lyric Possession of an Epic Past* (Baltimore: Johns Hopkins University Press, 1991), 433.

61. Reading *qulta* for *qultu.*

62. Al-Sukkarī, *Sharḥ Dīwān Kaᶜb ibn Zuhayr,* 3–5. This story occurs with a number of minor variations. See the sources cited above, note 50. The *Sīrah* version dates these events quite explicitly as occurring after the capture of al-Ṭāʾif (8 H.), with Kaᶜb's conversion thus taking place in the year 9/630. See Ibn Hishām, *Al-Sīrah al-Nabawiyyah,* 3:1353; Guillaume, *The Life of the Prophet,* 597; Sezgin, *Poesie,* 229.

63. Al-Iṣbahānī, *Al-Aghānī,* 10:3472.

64. See, for example, Zakī Mubārak, *Al-Madāʾiḥ al-Nabawiyyah fī al-Adab al-ᶜArabī* (Cairo: Muṣṭafá al-Bābī al-Ḥalabī, 1354/1935), 22–24.

65. I have followed al-Sukkarī's recension, except where otherwise noted: al-Sukkarī, *Sharḥ Dīwān Kaᶜb ibn Zuhayr,* 3–25.

66. Reading *lam yufda.* See al-Sukkarī, *Sharḥ Dīwān Kaᶜb ibn Zuhayr,* 6.

67. For *s-ᶜ-d,* see Edward William Lane, *Arabic-English Lexicon,* 8 vols. (New York: Frederick Ungar, 1958) [London, 1863] [hereafter Lane].

68. Al-Sukkarī, *Sharḥ Dīwān Kaᶜb ibn Zuhayr,* 6.

69. For an engaging interpretation of the imagery and rhetorical techniques of the *nasīb* imagery of purity and limpidity, as well as perfidy, in Kaᶜb's Suᶜād Has Departed and several other early Arabic *qaṣīdahs*, see Michael A. Sells, "Guises of the *Ghūl:* Dissembling Simile and Semantic Overflow in the Classical Arabic *Nasīb,*" in S. Stetkevych, *Reorientations,*130–64.

70. See *gh-w-l,* in Muḥammad ibn Mukarram ibn Manẓūr, *Lisān al-ᶜArab,* 15 vols. (Beirut: Dār Ṣādir, 1955–56) [hereafter *Lisān*].

71. On the *ghūl* as a simile for fickleness and mutability in this poem, see the discussion of the *nasīb* in Sells, "Guises of the *Ghūl,*" 137–41. For a comparative study of Taʾabbaṭa Sharran and the *ghūl* with Oedipus and the Sphinx, see "Taʾabbaṭa Sharran and Oedipus: A Paradigm of Passage Manqué," in S. Stetkevych, *The Mute Immortals Speak,* 87–118.

72. Al-Maydānī, *Majmaᶜ al-Amthāl,* 2:311, no. 4071.

73. Al-Sukkarī, *Sharḥ Dīwān Kaᶜb ibn Zuhayr,* 10; Ibn Hishām, *Al-Sīrah al-Nabawiyyah,* 3:1358.

74. Verses 36–46; see al-Anbārī, *Sharḥ al-Qaṣāʾid al-Sabᶜ,* 553–65. See the translation and discussion in S. Stetkevych, *The Mute Immortals Speak,* 13–14, 31–32.

75. On this reading of the image, see Annemarie Schimmel, *And Muhammad Is His Messenger: The Veneration of the Prophet in Islamic Piety* (Chapel Hill: University of North Carolina Press, 1985), 179–80.

76. Ibn Hishām's recension adds another verse here:

I kept on across the wasteland,
  my only coat of mail
The wing of darkness, beneath
  the lowered veil of night,
[30]

Ibn Hishām, *Al-Sīrah al-Nabawiyyah,* 3:1363.

77. As the commentarists read it, this verse would translate:

They walk as the white camels walk,
  and their sword's blow
Protects them when
  the black runts flee the field.

See al-Sukkarī, *Sharḥ Dīwān Kaᶜb ibn Zuhayr,* 24–25; Krenkow, "Tabrīzīs Kommentar," 278. See the discussion of this verse below.

78. Makkī, *Madāʾiḥ Nabawiyyah,* 51.

79. Al-Sukkarī, *Sharḥ Dīwān Kaᶜb ibn Zuhayr,* 21, n. 2.

80. Paul Connerton, *How Societies Remember* (Cambridge: Cambridge University Press, 1989), 73–74; (see chapters 2 and 3 of this volume). See my discussion in *The Poetics of Islamic Legitimacy,* 247; and chapter 2, part 5, v. 40, and chapter 3, part 3, vv. 148–49 of this volume.

81. Krenkow, "Tabrīzīs Kommentar," 273.

82. See S. Stetkevych, "Pre-Islamic Poetry and the Poetics of Redemption," 13–15.

83. See al-Sukkarī, *Sharḥ Dīwān Kaᶜb ibn Zuhayr,* 24–25.

84. In reading the manuscript of this book Michael Sells has quite judiciously queried, "Does 'the Islamic context' refer to the time of the original performance of the poem or to later uses and canonization of it? Did Kaᶜb's reference to the Muhājirūn . . . also entail an understanding of and acceptance of the qurʾānic doctrines of physical resurrection and eternal afterlife at the time he recited the poem? If that is the case, why is there no trace of such doctrines in the poem itself—no reference to terms like *al-jannah, al-ākhirah, al-baᶜth, al-qiyāmah, al-ḥashr, yawm al-dīn* (the [heavenly] garden, the other world, the resurrection, etc.), or the other terms in the Qurʾān, any one of which would be enough to evoke the entire 'life everlasting' field." The answer is that we have no direct access to any original "text," its performance, or the events surrounding it, we have only literary compilations, dating to a century and a half or so after the events they record, of historically unverifiable orally transmitted materials, and those are what we are interpreting in this work. In my interpretation, and in what I take to be the understanding of the poem in the Islamic devotional tradition, both the prose narrative (which may well be a prosification of the poem) of the physical danger and saving of the poet's life and the poem itself are allegories or metaphors for spiritual transformation and salvation. As I have now pointed out in the text, in response to Sells's remarks, the Bujayr poem of the conversion narrative speaks explicitly about salvation on Judgment Day, thus contextualizing the poem in light of this belief. We cannot, of course, count on the narrative or its parts actually going back to the time of the Prophet.

85. Walter Burkert, *Homo Necans: The Anthropology of Ancient Greek Ritual and Myth,* trans. Peter Bing (Berkeley: University of California Press, 1983), 23. See also S. Stetkevych, *The Mute Immortals Speak,* 82–83.

86. Versions of this anecdote are found in Ibn Qutaybah, *Al-Shiᶜr wa-al-Shuᶜarāʾ,* 60; and Muḥammad ibn Sallām al-Jumaḥī, *Ṭabaqāt Fuḥūl al-Shuᶜarāʾ,* 2 vols., ed., Maḥmūd Muḥammad Shākir (Cairo: Maṭbaᶜat al-Madanī, 1974), 1:103. See Rudi Paret, "Die Legende der Verleihung des Prophetmantels (*burda*) an Kaᶜb ibn Zuhair," *Der Islam* 17 (1928): 9–14; and Sezgin, *Poesie,* 229–30. The most extensive study of the sources, variants, and politico-historical significance of the *burdah* anecdote is that of Zwettler, which serves as an update and corrective of Paret. Mi-

chael Zwettler, "The Poet and the Prophet: Towards an Understanding of the Evolution of a Narrative," *Jerusalem Studies in Arabic and Islam* 5 (1984): 313–87. Of particular interest is his tracing its development into a "Prophetic *ḥadīth*" in the early third century H., 334–72.

87. Cited in Paret, "Die Legende," 13.

88. Cited by al-Anbārī in Lyall, *Mufaḍḍalīyāt,* 1:764.

89. On the "witness value of symbolic objects," see Walter J. Ong, *Orality and Literacy: The Technologizing of the Word* (London: Methuen, 1982), 97.

90. Paret, "Die Legende," 12–13. Moreover, by expanding Paret's citation back to II Kings 2:8, it is clear that the mantle of Elijah that Elisha takes up is identified with the spirit of Elijah.

91. Ibn Qutaybah, *Al-Shiʿr wa-al-Shuʿarāʾ,* 51.

92. Al-Iṣbahānī, *Al-Aghānī,* 9:3219–21.

93. See my interpretation of the *akhbār* of Imruʾ Qays in S. Stetkevych, *The Mute Immortals Speak,* 241–49; 283–85. On the "proto-Islamic" reading of the pre-Islamic, see my discussion of Labīd and his brother Arbad, ibid., 42–54.

94. See the discussion of *ḍ-l-l* above.

95. Mauss, *The Gift,* 10.

96. Ibid., 43.

97. [Al-Walīd ibn ʿUbayd Allāh al-Buḥturī], *Dīwān al-Buḥturī,* 5 vols., ed. Ḥasan al-Ṣayrafī (Cairo: Dār al-Maʿārif, n.d.), 2:1070–73. No. 241 (rhyme *uʿdharu*).

98. The power of both Kaʿb's Suʿād Has Departed and al-Būṣīrī's Burdah to generate myths, relics, and miracles, is treated in my unpublished paper "From Text to Talisman: Myth, Relic, and Miracle in the Two Mantle Odes," presented at the annual meeting of the Middle East Studies Association, Washington, D.C., November 2005.

99. Ḥassān ibn Thābit, *Dīwān,* 2 vols., ed. Walīd ʿArafāt (Beirut: Dār Ṣādir, 1974), 1:455–58. See also Ibn Hishām, *Al-Sīrah al-Nabawiyyah,* 4:1525–1527. Needless to say, I (and I imagine most others) disagree with Zakī Mubārak's assessment that Ḥassān ibn Thābit's elegies for the Prophet are poetically weak. See Mubārak, *Al-Madāʾiḥ al-Nabawiyyah,* 29; by contrast, see Makki, *Al-Madāʾiḥ al-Nabawiyyah,* 22–26. On Ḥassān's Islamization of the Bedouin *nasīb* and the elegiac passages of this poem, see J. Stetkevych, *Zephyrs of Najd,* 59–64. I hope to turn to a fuller study of this elegy on another occasion.

100. Makkī, *Al-Madāʾiḥ al-Nabawiyyah,* 22; and W. ʿArafat, "Ḥassān ibn Thābit," *EI2online;* and his intro. to Ḥassān ibn Thābit, *Dīwān,* ed. ʿArafāt, 1:16–25.

101. Ḥassān ibn Thābit, *Dīwān,* ed. ʿArafāt, 1:455–58. See also Ibn Hishām, *Al-Sīrah al-Nabawiyyah,* 4:1525–27.

102. This is a major theme of my book *The Poetics of Islamic Legitimacy,* see esp. 180–240.

2. Al-Būṣīrī and the Dream of the Mantle

1. An earlier version of chapter 2 appeared in a two-part study published in the *Journal of Arabic Literature:* Suzanne Pinckney Stetkevych, "From Text to Talisman: Al-Būṣīrī's Qaṣīdat al-Burdah (Mantle Ode) and the Poetics of Supplication," *Journal of Arabic Literature* 37 no. 2 (2006): 145–89; and Suzanne Pinckney Stetke-

vych, "From Sīrah to Qaṣīdah: Poetics and Polemics in al-Buṣīrī's Qaṣīdat al-Burdah (Mantle Ode), *Journal of Arabic Literature* 38 no. 1 (2007): 1–52.

2. What I term "expansions" are derivative poems in which a second poet takes the base text—in this case al-Būṣīrī's Burdah—and adds a line or lines of his own to each line or hemistich of the base text. In *tashṭīr* the second poet adds one hemistich (*shaṭr*) for each of the original ones, in the order base + new = first line; new + base = second line; etc., with the new poet's second hemistichs maintaining the original rhyme. *Takhmīs* ("fiver") is by far the most common form of expansion of the Burdah and, vice-versa— the overwhelming majority of *takhmīsāt* have the Burdah as their base-text, to the extent that *takhmīsāt* of the Burdah are virtually a genre unto themselves. In *takhmīs* the new poet adds three hemistichs of his own, usually before each base line (though the other way is possible) in the rhyme of the first hemistich of each base line, for a total of five hemistichs per verse. The *tasbīᶜ* ("sevener") does the same thing, only adding five hemistichs to the base line's two. See Mubārak, *Al-Madāʾiḥ al-Nabawiyyah,* 161–70; and my unpublished study "Poetic Expansion as Verbal Reliquary: Shams al-Dīn al-Fayyūmī's *Takhmīs al-Burdah,*" presented at the annual meeting of the Middle East Studies Association, Cambridge, Mass., November 2006. For a curious case of a *madīḥ nabawī* that is an expansion, not of an Islamic *qaṣīdah,* but by the greatest and most scandalous examplar and poet of the Jāhiliyyah, see Schimmel, *And Muhammad is His Messenger,* 188 and n. 44., and the full study, Julie Scott Meisami, "Imruʾ al-Qays Praises the Prophet," in *Tradition and Modernity in Arabic Literature,* ed. Issa J. Boullata and Terri DeYoung (Fayetteville: Arkansas University Press, 1997), 223–45.

3. The *badīᶜiyyah* is a curious subgenre of *madīḥ nabawī.* Though commonly defined merely as a praise poem to the Prophet in which each verse exemplifies a particular rhetorical device (*fann min funūn al-badīᶜ*), in practical fact (a few early and anomalous examples notwithstanding), it is precisely a *muᶜāraḍah* (a contrafaction, or counter-poem, that follows the rhyme and meter of the base poem) of al-Būṣīrī's Burdah that exhibits a rhetorical device in each line. On this subject see Rajāʾ al-Sayyid al-Jawharī's introduction to her edition of Abū Jaᶜfar al-Andalusī's commentary on the *badīᶜiyyah* of Shams al-Dīn ibn Jābir al-Andalusī: Rajāʾ al-Sayyid al-Jawharī, ed., *Kitāb Ṭirāz al-Ḥullah wa-Shifāʾ al-Ghullah lil-Imām Abī Jaᶜfar Shihāb al-Dīn [. . .] al-Andalusī, Sharḥ al-Ḥullah al-Siyarā [. . .] Badīᶜiyyah naẓamahā Shams al-Dīn Abū ᶜAbd Allāh al-Andalusī* (Alexandria: Muʾassasat al-Thaqāfah al-Jāmiᶜiyyah, 1410/1990), 11–66. Usually considered prior to Ibn Jābir al-Andalusī's (d. 780/1378) *badīᶜiyyah,* the first full-fledged *badīᶜiyyah* is that of Ṣafī al-Dīn al-Ḥillī (d. 752(?)/1339): Ṣafī al-Dīn al-Ḥillī, *Dīwān* (Beirut: Dār Ṣādir/Dār Bayrūt, 1962), 685–702. I have dealt with the *badīᶜiyyah* in Suzanne Pinckney Stetkevych, "From Jāhiliyyah to *Badīᶜiyyah:* Orality, Literacy, and the Transformations of Rhetoric in Arabic Poetry," Papers of the Orality and Literacy VII Conference, Rice University, 12–14 April 2008, in a special issue of *Oral Tradition,* ed. Werner Kelber and Paula Sanders, 2010; and Suzanne Pinckney Stetkevych, "Al-Badīᶜiyyah bayn Fann al-Qaṣīdah wa-ᶜIlm al-Balāghah: Dirāsah fī Tadākhul al-Anwāᶜ al-Adabiyyah," 12th Literary Criticism Conference, Yarmouk University, Irbid, Jordan, 22–24 July 2008, unpublished conference paper.

4. The range may be suggested by two quite disparate examples: first, the courtly fifteenth-century CE Khwarizmian Turkic translation *Kashf al-Hudá* by

Kamāl al-Dīn Ḥusayn Khorezmī presented to Abū al-Khayr Khān in honor of his conquest of Khorezm; see Devin A. DeWeese, "The *Kashf al-Hudā* of Kamāl al-Dīn Ḥusayn al-Khorezmī: A Fifteenth-Century Sufi Commentary on the *Qaṣīdat al-Burdah* in Khorezmian Turkic (Text Edition, Translation, and Historical Introduction)," (Ph.D. diss., Indiana University, 1985). A second, contrasting example is the simple pietistic anonymous late nineteenth-century CE Swahili translation; see Jan Knappert, ed. and trans., *Swahili Islamic Poetry,* Vol. 2: *The Two Burdas* (Leiden: E. J. Brill, 1971), 165–225. See further the references in Stefan Sperl, translation, introduction, and notes, "Al-Būṣīrī's Burdah," poem no. 50, in Stefan Sperl and Christopher Shackle, eds., *Qasida Poetry in Islamic Asia and Africa: Vol. I: Classical Traditions and Modern Meanings; Vol. II: Eulogy's Bounty, Meaning's Abundance: An Anthology* (Leiden: E. J. Brill, 1996); 2: 388–411 (trans.); 2:470–76 (intro. and notes) at 2:471, and Vol. I: index, al-Būṣīrī.

5. See, for example, Carl Brockelmann, *Geschichte der Arabischen Litteratur* Vols. 1 and 2, 2nd ed. (Leiden: E. J. Brill, 1943) Suppl. 1 (Leiden: E. J. Brill, 1937), 1:308–13; Suppl. 1: 467–72 (hereafter *GAL*); Kātib Chalabī [= Kâtip Çelebi, known as Ḥājjī Khalīfah], *Kashf al-Ẓunūn ʿan Asāmī al-Kutub wa-al-Funūn,* 2 vols., ed. Muḥammad Sharaf al-Dīn Yāltaqyā and Riʿat Balīgah al-Kalīsa (Istanbul: Wikālat al-Maʿārif al-Jalīlah, 1360–63/1941–43), 2: 1331–36; W. Ahlwardt, *Verzeichniss der Arabischen Handschriften der Königlichen Bibliothek zu Berlin,* vol. 7 (Berlin: A. Asher, 1895), 43–59; Dār al-Kutub al-Miṣriyyah, *Fihris al-Kutub al-ʿArabiyyah,* (Cairo: Maṭbaʿat Dār al-Kutub al-Miṣriyyah, 1345/1927), part 3, 309–12.

6. See, for example, Mubārak, *Al-Madāʾiḥ al-Nabawiyyah,* 148–50; Ḥājjī Khalīfah, *Kashf al-Ẓunūn,* 2: 1331–36, and n. 1, 1331; Knappert, *Swahili Islamic Poetry,* 168; Sharaf al-Dīn Abū ʿAbd Allāh Muhḥammad ibn Saʿīd al-Būṣīrī, *Dīwān al-Būṣīrī,* 2nd ed., ed. Muḥammad Sayyid Kīlānī (Cairo: Muṣṭafá al-Bābī al-Ḥalabī, 1972), 29–30; ʿAbd al-ʿAlīm al-Qabbānī, *Al-Būṣīrī: Ḥayātuh wa-Shiʿruh* (Cairo: Dār al-Maʿārif, 1968), 3–5, 131–32. For a broad overview in English, see Annemarie Schimmel, "Poetry in Honor of the Prophet," in *And Muhammad Is His Messenger,* 176–215; esp. 178–87. See also, Sperl, "Al-Būṣīrī's Burdah," 2:271; and Sperl and Shackle, *Qasida Poetry,* Vol. I: index, al-Būṣīrī. The performance traditions of the Burdah in popular Islam and especially in Ṣūfī practice are an important topic, but beyond the purview of the present study.

7. On the theme of praise of the Prophet Muḥammad in Shīʿite poetry to Āl al-Bayt, see Mubārak, *Al-Madāʾiḥ al-Nabawiyyah,* 53–140, and Makkī, *Al-Madāʾiḥ al-Nabawiyyah,* 57–95. On the Shīʿite use of the *qaṣīdah* for both devotional/liturgical and political aims, see Suzanne Pinckney Stetkevych, "Al-Sharīf al-Raḍī and the Poetics of ʿAlid Legitimacy: Elegy for al-Ḥusayn ibn ʿAlī on ʿĀshūrāʾ, 391 AH" in Festschrift for Jaroslav Stetkevych, *Journal of Arabic Literature* 38 (2007): 293–323.

8. The foregoing paragraph is quite speculative, as concerns the historical and literary relationships between these several genres of devotional poetry, but attempts to give at least an overview. It is noteworthy that Mubārak's *Al-Madāʾiḥ al-Nabawiyyah* does not treat extensively the rich body of medieval devotional *madāʾiḥ nabawiyyah,* for an anthology of which see especially Yūsuf ibn Ismāʿīl al-Nabhānī (d. 1350/1932), *Al-Majmūʿah al-Nabhāniyyah fī al-Madāʾiḥ al-Nabawiyyah,* 4 vols. (Beirut: Dār al-Kutub al-ʿIlmiyyah, n.d.) [Repr. of Beirut: Al-Maṭbaʿah al-Adabiyyah, 1903]. Particularly appealing examples of the lyrical-devotional

madāʾiḥ nabawiyyah are Muḥammad ibn Abī al-ʿAbbās al-Abīwardī's (d. 507 AH) *lāmiyyah*, a *muʿāraḍah* of Kaʿb ibn Zuhayr's Bānat Suʿād (al-Nabhānī, *Al-Majmūʿah*, 3:26–28) and ʿAfīf al-Dīn al-Tilimsānī's *bāʾiyyah* composed in 696 AH. (al-Nabhānī, *Al-Majmūʿah*, 1:357–58). Makkī presents medieval *madīḥ nabawī* in both the Mashriq and Maghrib/al-Andalus in the context of *mawlidiyyāt* (poems of the birth of the Prophet) and the growing popularity of the celebration of the Prophet's birth in this period (Makkī, *Al-Madāʾiḥ al-Nabawiyyah*, 96–106,125–140. The starting point for the exploration of Andalusian devotional poetry to the Prophet is Aḥmad ibn Muḥammad al-Maqqarī, *Nafḥ al-Ṭīb min Ghuṣn al-Andalus al-Raṭīb*, 8 vols., ed. Iḥsān ʿAbbās (Beirut: Dār Ṣādir, 1968); for *madīḥ nabawī*, see 7:432–516. I wish to thank Prof. Sulaymān al-ʿAṭṭār of Cairo University and Hassan Lachheb of Indiana University for their help and advice as concerns *madīḥ nabawī* in al-Andalus and the Maghrib. For further materials, see Makkī, *Madāʾiḥ Nabawiyyah*, bibliography. In English, Meisami's translation and analysis of Ḥāzim al-Qarṭājannī's (d. 684/1284) *madīḥ nabawī* in the form of a *tashṭīr* of Imruʾ al-Qays's Muʿallaqah provides an interesting basis for comparison in terms of themes and structure with al-Būṣīrī's Burdah, especially as concerns the military aspects. See Meisami, "Imruʾ al-Qays Praises the Prophet," passim.

9. Mubārak, *Al-Madāʾiḥ al-Nabawiyyah*, 20–24.

10. This is not to say that there are not other forms, particularly of the more purely lyrical-devotional type. Nevertheless a clear formulation of the genre characteristics of al-Būṣīrī's Burdah and its vast poetic progeny should be a necessary first step toward sorting out the poetic forms that have been gathered under the rubric of *madīḥ nabawī*.

11. ʿUmar Mūsá Bāshā, intro. to Badr al-Dīn Muḥammad al-Ghazzī, *Al-Zubdah fī Sharḥ al-Burdah*, ed. and intro. ʿUmar Mūsá Bāshā (Algiers: Al-Sharikah al-Waṭaniyyah lil-Nashr wa-al-Tawzīʿ, 1972), 36.

12. Bāshā, intro. to al-Ghazzī, *Al-Zubdah fī Sharḥ al-Burdah*, 34.

13. The *locus classicus* for the definition of *ʿamūd al-shiʿr* is that of al-Marzūqī (d. 421/1030) in his introduction to *Al-Ḥamāsah* of Abū Tammām. See Aḥmad ibn Muḥammad al-Marzūqī, *Sharḥ Dīwān al-Ḥamāsah*, 2nd ed., 4 vols., eds. Aḥmad Amīn and ʿAbd al-Salām Hārūn (Cairo: Maṭbaʿat Lajnat al-Taʾlīf wa-al-Tarjamah wa-al-Nashr, 1967), 8–9. For further references, see S. Stetkevych, *Abū Tammām*, 257–64; al-Marzūqī's passage is translated on p. 260.

14. The poets and scholars of rhetoric of the period did not see it this way. On this subject, see S. Stetkevych, "From Jāhiliyyah to *Badīʿiyyah*."

15. ʿAbd Allāh Ibn al-Muʿtazz, *Kitāb al-Badīʿ*, ed. Ignatius Kratchkovsky, E.J.W. Gibb Memorial Series No. X (London: Messrs. Luzac, 1935), 1 and passim. For discussion and further references, see S. Stetkevych, *Abū Tammām*, 19–37.

16. On Johnsonian "wit" and Metaphysical poetry, see Mustafa Badawi, "From Primary to Secondary *qaṣīdahs*," *Journal of Arabic Literature* 11 (1980), 23–24. The concept of "mannerism" as it might be applied to Arabic poetry, introduced by J. C. Bürgel and then Wolfhart Heinrichs, has been explored further by Sperl (although the issues of "classicism" versus "mannerism" as well as various concepts of "mimesis" as they apply in various periods of Arabic poetry remain problematic, Sperl's application, following Bürgel and Heinrichs, of H. Friedrich's observations concerning the Italian baroque lyric is a fruitful approach). See Stefan Sperl, *Manner-*

ism in Arabic Poetry: A Structuralist Analysis of Selected Texts (3rd Century AH/9th Century AD–5th Century AH/11th Century AD) (Cambridge: Cambridge University Press, 1989), esp. 155–80, references 155.

17. See S. Stetkevych, *Abū Tammām,* ch. 1, 5–37; based on my earlier study "Toward a Redefinition of *Badīʿ* Poetry," *Journal of Arabic Literature* 12 (1981): 1–29. Badawi's remarks on *al-madhhab al-kalāmī* appear to be influenced by my 1981 article (although he provides no reference), which, as editor of *JAL* at the time, he read prior to the publication of his 1980 article. See Badawi, "From Primary to Secondary *qaṣīdahs,*" 24.

18. My argument here generally follows that of earlier work in S. Stetkevych, *Abū Tammām,* 5–37.

19. See S. Stetkevych, *Abū Tammām,* ch. 3, passim, esp. 66, 81, 36; Abū al-Qāsim al-Ḥasan ibn Bishr al-Āmidī, *Al-Muwāzanah bayn Shiʿr Abī Tammām wa-al-Buḥturī,* 2 vols., ed. Aḥmad Ṣaqr (Cairo: Dār al-Maʿārif, 1972), 1:238–39; 1:511–12.

20. Abū Tammām [Ḥabīb ibn Aws al-Ṭāʾī], *Dīwān Abī Tammām bi-Sharḥ al-Khaṭīb al-Tibrīzī,* 4 vols., ed. Muḥammad ʿAbduh ʿAzzām (Cairo: Dār al-Maʿārif, 1951), 1:40–74; poem no. 3. For a translation and discussion of the full poem, see S. Stetkevych, *Abū Tammām,* 187–211; S. Stetkevych, *The Poetics of Islamic Legitimacy,* 152–79. This structural "defamiliarization" does not seem to bother al-Āmidī who, it is worth noting, considered the first verse of Abū Tammām's Amorium *qaṣīdah* his best opening line. See S. Stetkevych, *Abū Tammām,* 54; al-Āmidī, *Al-Muwāzanah,* 1:59–60.

21. Ibn al-Muʿtazz, *Kitāb al-Badīʿ,* 11; S. Stetkevych, *Abū Tammām,* 24.

22. Ibn al-Muʿtazz, *Kitāb al-Badīʿ,* 23; S. Stetkevych, *Abū Tammām,* 24. Abū Tammām, *Dīwān,* 3:167, gives *lā tudʿa hālikan* = "they will not say you have perished."

23. *Apud* Badawi, "From Primary to Secondary *qaṣīdahs,*" 23.

24. See S. Stetkevych, "Toward a Redefinition of *Badīʿ Poetry,*" and S. Stetkevych, *Abū Tammām,* 5–32.

25. See, for example, the passage on coining new terms, especially technical terms, that al-Jāḥiẓ cites, in ʿAmr ibn Baḥr al-Jāḥiẓ, *Al-Bayān wa-al-Tabyīn,* 4 vols., ed. ʿAbd al-Salām Hārūn (Cairo: Maktabat al-Khānjī, 1968), 1:138–141; see the translation in S. Stetkevych, *Abū Tammām,* 16–17.

26. See S. Stetkevych, "Toward a Redefinition *of Badīʿ Poetry,*" and S. Stetkevych, *Abū Tammām,* 3–49.

27. See S. Stetkevych, *The Poetics of Islamic Legitimacy,* 152–79 passim.

28. See S. Stetkevych, *The Poetics of Islamic Legitimacy,* 180–240 passim on al-Mutanabbī and, on the imitation of High ʿAbbasid *badīʿ* panegyrics as emblems of political legitimacy in the Umayyad court in Cordoba, 241–82. Also of note in this regard is the conscious employ of High ʿAbbāsid poetics and the many *muʿāraḍāt* of the ʿAbbāsid master panegyrists in Arabic Neo-Classical poetry.

29. See S. Stetkevych, "From Jāhiliyyah to *Badīʿiyyah,*" and S. Stetkevych, "Al-Badīʿiyyah bayn Fann al-Qaṣīdah wa-ʿIlm al-Balāghah."

30. See Cl. Cahen, "Ayyūbids," and P. M. Holt, "Mamlūks," *EI2.*

31. Modern biographies include Mubārak, *Al-Madāʾiḥ al-Nabawiyyah,* 140–49 (the most lively); Kīlānī's introduction, in Kīlānī, *Dīwān al-Būṣīrī,* 5–47 and his excerpts from al-Kutubī's *Fawāt al-Wafayāt*: al-Qazwīnī's *Al-Muqaffá;* and Ibn Taghrī

Birdī's *Al-Manhal al-Ṣāfī,* 282–92; al-Qabbānī, *Al-Būṣīrī.* For the primary sources for al-Būṣīrī's biography, see the notes in Kīlānī, *Dīwān al-Būṣīrī,* passim; the bibliography in al-Qabbānī, *Al-Būṣīrī,* 141–42; ʿUmar Riḍá al-Kaḥḥālah, *Muʿjam al-Muʾallifīn: Tarājim Muṣannifī al-Kutub al-ʿArabiyyah,* 15 vols. (Damascus: Maṭbaʿat al-Taraqqī, 1380/1960), 10:28–29; Khayr al-Dīn al-Ziriklī, *Al-Aʿlām: Qāmūs Tarājim li-Ashhar al-Rijāl wa-al-Nisāʾ . . .*, 2nd ed., 11 vols. (N.p.:n.d.), 7:11. Also see, "Al-Būṣīrī," *EI2* Suppl.

32. See Kīlānī, *Dīwān al-Būṣīrī,* 49–77 (*Umm al-Qurá*); 220–33 (*Dhukhr al-Maʿād*); al-Nabhānī, *Al-Majmūʿah,* 1:77–105 (*Umm al-Qurá*); 3:9–20 (*Dhukhr al-Maʿād*).

33. See references in note 31 above.

34. A more extensive exploration of the Burdah myth, its variants, and its relation to the Burdah myth associated with Kaʿb ibn Zuhayr's Burdah, is the subject of my unpublished paper "From Text to Talisman: Myth, Relic, and Miracle in the Two Mantle Odes."

35. Ibrāhīm ibn Muḥammad al-Bājūrī al-Kharpūtī, *Hādhā Kitāb Ḥāshiyat Ibrāhīm al-Bājūrī al-Kharpūtī . . . ʿalá matn al-Burdah li . . . al-Būṣīrī* ([Istanbul], 1290 [1872]), 2–3. According to Juynboll, it is a gloss (*ḥāshiyah*) on al-Muṣannifak's (d. 875/1470) commentary on the Burdah. See Th. W. Juynboll, "Bādjūrī, Muḥammad Ibrāhīm," *EI2*. The wide influence and popularity of al-Bājūrī's *Ḥāshiyah* is attested not only by the many printings (see, for example, Dār al-Kutub al-Miṣriyyah, *Fihris,* part 3, 80–81), but also Zakī Mubārak's remarks in his formative 1935 study of *madīḥ nabawī,* that the *ʿulamāʾ* of al-Azhar used to hold classes on al-Bājūrī's *Ḥāshiyat al-Burdah* every Thursday and Friday that were very popular with the students, although they were not required. See Mubārak, *Al-Madāʾiḥ al-Nabawiyyah,* 164.

36. Muḥammad ibn Shākir al-Kutubī, *Fawāt al-Wafayāt wa-al-Dhayl ʿAlayhā,* 4 vols., ed. Iḥsān ʿAbbās (Beirut: Dār Ṣādir, 1973–74), 3:368–69. See, e.g., Kīlānī, *Dīwān al-Būṣīrī,* 27, 284–85; Mubārak, *Al-Madāʾiḥ al-Nabawiyyah,* 147–48.

37. Kīlānī, *Dīwān al-Būṣīrī,* 27–28.

38. Sperl, "Al-Būṣīrī's Burdah," 2:470–71.

39. Ibn ʿAbd al-Salām, *Qāla al-Shaykh Ibn ʿAbd al-Salām fī Khawāṣṣ al-Kawākib al-Durriyyah fī Madḥ Khayr al-Bariyyah lil-Shaykh al-Būṣīrī.* Staatsbibliothek zu Berlin. Petermann II 105 folios 243–254a. Ahlwardt identifies the author as ʿAbd al-ʿAzīz ibn ʿAbd al-Salām d. 660/1262 and dates the ms. to ca. 1150/1737 (Ahlwardt, *Arabische Handschriften,* 60). Brockelmann cites the ms. as *Ḫawāṣṣ al-burda fī burʾ ad-dāʾ*, by ʿAbdassalām b. Idrīs al-Marrākošī, d. 660/1262 (Brockelmann, *GAL,* 1: 311, no. 71 Berlin 7823). This identification seems highly improbable to me, as the date seems rather too early. Further research is needed on the development of the *khaṣāʾiṣ al-Burdah* traditions.

40. See, for example, Mubārak, *Al-Madāʾiḥ al-Nabawiyyah,* 151. Sperl seems unaware of this, mentioning instead its common rhyme and meter with al-Mutanabbī's *mīmiyyah* "*wā ḥarra qalbāhu mimman qalbuhū shibamu*" ([Abū al-Ṭayyib al-Mutanabbī,] *Dīwān Abī al-Ṭayyib al-Mutanabbī bi-Sharḥ Abī al-Baqāʾ al-ʿUkbarī,* 4 vols., ed. Muṣṭafá al-Saqqā *et al.* [Cairo: Muṣṭafá al-Bābī al-Ḥalabī, 1971], 3:362–74, poem no. 222). Sperl, "Al-Būṣīrī's Burdah," 2:274.

41. ʿUmar ibn al-Fāriḍ, *Sharḥ Dīwān Ibn al-Fāriḍ li-Jāmiʿih Rashīd ibn Ghālib; min Sharḥay Ḥasan al-Būrīnī wa-ʿAbd al-Ghānī al-Nābulusī.* 2 vols. in 1, ([Cairo,]

Egypt: Al-Maṭbaʿah al-ʿĀmirah al-Sharīfah, 1306 [1888]), 1:39–47. See also the translation and notes, esp. on place-names, in A. J. Arberry, trans. and ann., *The Mystical Poems of Ibn al-Fāriḍ* (Dublin: Emery Walker, 1956), 96–97. I have followed the al-Būrīnī/al-Nābulusī *sharḥ* (p. 41) in taking *muʿtasifan* of v. 3 to be a *ḥāl* describing the desert ("random" = "wayless")—rather than describing the "rolling up" or "traveling" of the camel-driver, as Arberry (p. 95) has done—and reading the rhyme-word of v. 7 as *lil-saqami* (p. 43).

42. J. Stetkevych, *The Zephyrs of Najd*, 79–102.

43. Al-Ghazzī, *Al-Zubdah fī Sharḥ al-Burdah*, 6 and passim. I have corrected the editor's misnumbering of the lines.

44. On the Supplicatory Ode, i.e., the *qaṣīdah* as a supplicatory ritual, see chapter 1 of this book, and S. Stetkevych, *The Poetics of Islamic Legitimacy*, esp. "Supplication and Negotiation," 110–43; also 32–47, 75.

45. On the supplicatory panegyric *qaṣīdah* as a ritual exchange along the lines formulated by Mauss, see chapter 1 of this book; S. Stetkevych, *The Poetics of Islamic Legitimacy*, 18, 77–78, 120, 182–83; and S. Stetkevych, "Umayyad Panegyric and the Poetics of Islamic Hegemony." On his formulation, see Mauss, *The Gift*. See also S. Stetkevych, "Pre-Islamic Panegyric and the Poetics of Redemption," passim.

46. For the text, I have followed al-Ghazzī, *Al-Zubdah fī Sharḥ al-Burdah*, correcting the mistakes in numbering the verses. For vocalization and translation, I have relied on al-Ghazzī's text and commentary and also on al-Bājūrī, *Ḥāshiyah . . . ʿalá Matn al-Burdah*, and the Egyptian grammarian Khālid [ibn ʿAbd Allāh] al-Azharī [d. 905/1499], *Sharḥ Qaṣīdat al-Burdah lil-Shaykh Khālid al-Azharī* ([Istanbul]: Der Saadet/Sharikat Ṣaḥāfiyyah ʿUthmāniyyah, 1318 [1900]). As these exist in numerous other manuscripts and print editions, I have referred to verse numbers rather than page numbers. Of the several English translations available, the most accurate is probably that of R. A. Nicholson. I have consulted it as it appears in Arthur Jeffery, ed., *A Reader on Islam: Passages from Standard Arabic Writings Illustrative of the Beliefs and Practices of Muslims* ('S-Gravenhage: Mouton, 1962), 605–20. I have also referred to Stefan Sperl's translation and notes: Sperl, "Al-Būṣīrī's Burdah," 2: 388–411 (trans.); 2:470–76 (intro. and notes). Please note that some differences in translation are due to the variety of interpretations offered by various commentators, and some minor differences reflect minor textual variants.

47. More precisely, according to Yāqūt, Dhū Salam is a wadi on the way from Basra to Mecca (3:240); Kāẓimah is on the Bahrayni seashore on the way from Basra (4:431); and Iḍam is a wadi in the mountains of Tihāmah in which Medina lies (1:214–15). See Yāqūt al-Ḥamawī, *Muʿjam al-Buldān*, 5 vols. (Beirut: Dār Ṣādir, 1955–57). As others have noted, these places do not correspond to a pilgrimage route that al-Būṣīrī (or anyone) would have taken from Egypt. Hence my point that they form a poetic and spiritual genealogy rather than a geographical itinerary.

48. See al-Ghazzī, *Al-Zubdah fī Sharḥ al-Burdah*, v. 2. According to Maḥmūd ʿAlī Makkī, it was Mihyār al-Daylamī who introduced the Ḥijāzī place-names associated with the Islamic pilgrimage routes and rites (*manāzil al-ḥajj*) into the *nasīb*, which otherwise had been characterized by the evocative place-names associated with the poet's beloved or his tribal homeland, e.g., of Najd (verbal communication, Cairo, May 2001). It seems it may actually go back to Mihyār's teacher, al-Sharīf al-Raḍī (Arberry, *The Mystical Poems of Ibn al-Fāriḍ*, 96, n. 1). Although she does not mention

these earlier precedents, Schimmel provides a brief overview of the theme of the poet's longing for Medina in Arabic and other Islamic poetries (Schimmel, *And Muhammad Is His Messenger,* 189–94). See J. Stetkevych, *Zephyrs of Najd,* 80–89.

49. See Nicholson, "The Burdah of Al-Būṣīrī," 606, v. 5.

50. I have followed Sperl in translating *khaṣm* (enemy, opponent) as "litigant" to capture the play on *ḥakam* (arbiter, judge) and *khaṣm.* As Sperl notes, al-Būṣīrī derives this word-play from v. 12 of al-Mutanabbī's *mīmiyyah,* although he uses it quite differently. See al-Mutanabbī, *Dīwān,* 3:366; Sperl, "Al-Būṣīrī's Burdah," 2:474, n. 10.

51. Al-Ghazzī, *Al-Zubdah fī Sharḥ al-Burdah,* 52, n. 2; Sperl, "Al-Būṣīrī's Burdah," 2:474, n. 7. Sperl has a bit of a mix-up: the *second* hemistich of al-Būṣīrī's v. 14, not the first, is the quotation from al-Mutanabbī's opening hemistich of the poem. My interpretation of v. 14 of the Burdah differs somewhat from his. The quote (*taḍmīn*) is from al-Mutanabbī, *Dīwān,* 4:34, poem no. 233, v. 1.

52. M. Talbi, "ʿIyāḍ ibn Mūsā," *EI2.*

53. Al-Qāḍī ʿIyāḍ ibn Mūsá al-Yaḥṣubī al-Andalusī, *Al-Shifāʾ bi-Taʿrīf Ḥuqūq al-Muṣṭafá,* 2 vols., ed. Muḥammad Amīn Qurrah ʿAlī et al. (Damascus: Dār al-Wafāʾ lil-Ṭibāʿah wa-al-Nashr, 1392/1972), 1:280 (part 1, ch.2, sect. 22).

54. Schimmel succinctly explains this concept:

> In Sufism, after Ibn ʿArabi the preexistent essence of the Prophet, called *al-ḥaqīqa al-muḥammadiyya,* is considered to be the fountainhead of all prophetic activity. For this *ḥaqīqa muḥammadiyya*—a term often translated as "archetypal Muhammad"—manifests itself first in Adam, then in all the other prophets until it finds its full expression once more in the historical Muhammad, who thus becomes, as it were, the Alpha and Omega of creation. Muhammad the Prophet is the all-comprehensive and perfect manifestation of the primordial light, and with him the cycle of manifestations is completed, for he is the Seal of the Prophets.

Schimmel, *And Muhammad Is His Messenger,* 132; and see further, ch. 7 of the same book, "The Light of Muhammad and the Mystical Tradition," 123–43.

55. In Gerhard Böwering's words, "The origin of the *nūr Muḥammad* in pre-eternity is depicted as a luminous mass of primordial adoration in the presence of God which takes the shape of a transparent column, *ʿamūd,* of divine light and constitutes Muḥammad as the primal creation of God." Gerhard Böwering, "The Prophet of Islam," 49–50, as cited in Schimmel, *And Muhammad Is His Messenger,* 125.

56. Kīlānī, *Dīwān al-Būṣīrī,* 30–31; see also al-Qabbānī, *Al-Būṣīrī,* 121–23.

57. See al-Qāḍī ʿIyāḍ, *Al-Shifāʾ,* 1:454 (part 1, ch. 3, sect. 12).

58. Ibid., 1:424–27 (part 1, ch. 3, sect. 10).

59. On intercommunal polemic in al-Būṣīrī, see part 7 of the Burdah: The Night Journey and the Ascension, vv. 88–104; and his long polemical poem against the Christians and Jews, Al-Makhraj wa-al-Mardūd fī al-Radd ʿalá al-Naṣārá wa-al-Yahūd (Kīlānī, *Dīwān al-Būṣīrī,* 175–219; and al-Nabhānī, *Al-Majmūʿah al-Nabhāniyyah,* 3: 134–50; rhyme: *-lā*), and sections of his celebrated long *madīḥ nabawī,* Umm al-Qurá fī Madḥ Khayr al-Wará, commonly known by its rhyme as al-Hamziyyah (Kīlānī, *Dīwān al-Būṣīrī,* 49–77; al-Nabhānī, *Al-Majmūʿah al-Nabhāniyyah,* 1:77–105). See the discussion in al-Qabbānī, *Al-Būṣīrī,* 91–96.

60. Connerton, *How Societies Remember*, 73–74; S. Stetkevych, *The Poetics of Islamic Legitimacy*, 247; and see above, chapter 1, Kaʿb's vv. 39–41; and below, chapter 3, part 5, vv. 83–93.

61. Al-Ghazzī, *Al-Zubdah fī Sharḥ al-Burdah*, 75, n.1. The line is from Abū Tammām's celebrated *qaṣīdah* on al-Muʿtaṣim's conquest of the Byzantine city of Amorium (Ammūriyah). See Abū Tammām, *Dīwān*, 1:40–74; poem no. 3, v. 37 (see intro. to chapter 2).

62. I have given the line as it appears in al-Buḥturī, *Dīwān*, 2:1230; poem no. 486, v. 6.

63. See al-Qāḍī ʿIyāḍ, *Al-Shifāʾ*, 2:194–207 (part 2, ch. 4, sect. 9); Schimmel, *And Muhammad Is His Messenger*, 190–91.

64. Al-Qāḍī ʿIyāḍ, *Al-Shifāʾ*, 2:132 (part 2, ch. 3, sect. 9).

65. As noted above, parts 4–8 of the Burdah are, in terms of the *qaṣīdah* form of the poem, structurally appended to the *madīḥ* section proper (part 3).

66. See S. Stetkevych, *The Poetics of Islamic Legitimacy*, 145, 152, 169–70.

67. Schimmel, *And Muhammad Is His Messenger*, 33. Schimmel's book remains the best English-language resource as both a survey and bibliographic reference on this subject.

68. As mentioned above, the modern editions of al-Qāḍī ʿIyāḍ's *Al-Shifāʾ* provide detailed references to authoritative sources. The commentaries on al-Būṣīrī's Burdah likewise provide references, although not very systematically, for Sīrah-related events that appear in the poem. This does not, of course, prove that these are precisely the sources that the judge or the poet relied upon, but rather that their writings are in keeping with materials recognized and accepted as authoritative. It is interesting that al-Bājūrī also wrote a commentary on *Al-Shifāʾ*. See Juynboll, "Bādjūrī."

69. On the historical development of Islamic narratives concerning the birth of the Prophet, see Marion Holmes Katz, *The Birth of the Prophet Muḥammad* (London: Routledge, 2007), 6–62.

70. See S. Stetkevych, *Abū Tammām*, 154–55; indeed ʿAbd al-Qāhir al-Jurjānī takes Abū Tammām to task for what he considers his excessive affectation: that he could not pass by a place-name without producing *jinās* or other *badīʿ*-figure involving it. See ibid., 27; ʿAbd al-Qāhir al-Jurjānī, *Asrār al-Balāghah*, ed., Hellmut Ritter (Istanbul: Government Press, 1954), 15.

71. See al-Qāḍī ʿIyāḍ, *Al-Shifāʾ*, 1:715–733 (part 1, ch. 4, sects. 28–29); al-Ghazzī; al-Bājūrī.

72. See al-Qāḍī ʿIyāḍ, *Al-Shifāʾ*, 1:730 (part 1, ch. 4, sect. 29); al-Ghazzī; al-Bājūrī.

73. As far as I know, the crashing down of idols at the Kaʿbah is most commonly said to have occurred when Muḥammad entered the mosque of Mecca in the year of the conquest, when he pointed a staff at the sixty idols surrounding the Kaʿbah and declared, "The truth has come and falsehood has perished" (*jāʾa al-ḥaqqu wa-zahaqa al-bāṭilu*; QK 17:81), whereupon the idols fell over on their faces. See al-Qāḍī ʿIyāḍ, *Al-Shifāʾ*, 1:592 (part 1, ch. 3, sect.18).

74. See al-Qāḍī ʿIyāḍ, *Al-Shifāʾ*, 1:588 (part 1, ch. 4, sect. 16). It seems to me that there may be a conflation of the story of pebbles singing praises as in *Al-Shifāʾ*, where no mention is made of battle (and the notes give reference to Ibn ʿAsākir), with the accounts of Muḥammad's miraculously routing the enemy with a handful

of pebbles, which, as al-Ghazzī and al-Bājūrī tell us, occurred at the battle of Badr (according to al-Būkhārī) or Ḥunayn (according to Muslim).

75. The term "mythic concordance" I adopt from Connerton, *How Societies Remember,* 43 and passim. I have used this concept in an extended way in S. Stetkevych, *The Poetics of Islamic Legitimacy,* passim and index, with regard to the cognation established between different poets and also between their patrons through the employ of the ritual structure of the panegyric ode.

76. The second hemistich is a paraphrase of a *ḥadīth* that al-Ghazzī (v. 82) cites from *Al-Ṣaḥīḥān* (i.e., the *Ṣaḥīḥ*s of al-Bukhārī and Muslim), that the Prophet said, "My two eyes sleep but my heart sleeps not" (*ʾinna ʿaynayya tanāmāni wa-lā yanāmu qalbī*).

77. In the Arabic I have followed the variant *al-yamm* for sea or ocean, rather than al-Ghazzī's *al-baḥr.*

78. For an overview of traditional Islamic beliefs concerning the Prophet Muḥammad's miracles, special attributes, and signs of divine favor (*muʿjizāt, khaṣāʾiṣ, karāmāt*), see al-Qāḍī ʿIyāḍ, *Al-Shifāʾ,* 1:479–743 (part 1, ch. 4); Schimmel, *And Muhammad Is His Messenger,* 67–80 and references.

79. See al-Qāḍī ʿIyāḍ, *Al-Shifāʾ,* 1:573–80 (part 1, ch. 4, sect. 16) = trees; 1:593 (part 1, ch. 3, sect. 18) = cloud; 1: 543–50 (part 1, ch. 3, sect. 12), also 1:495–97 (part 1, ch. 4, sect. 3) = splitting the moon. See Schimmel, *And Muhammad Is His Messenger,* 69–70 and references on the splitting of the moon. See al-Ghazzī and al-Bājūrī, vv. 72–75.

80. See al-Qāḍī ʿIyāḍ, *Al-Shifāʾ,* 1:573–80 (part 1, ch. 4, sect. 16); al-Ghazzī and al-Bājūrī, vv. 72–73.

81. See Ibn Hishām, *Al-Sīrah al-Nabawiyyah,* 1:179–80, where the event takes place in Muḥammad's childhood; al-Qāḍī ʿIyāḍ, *Al-Shifāʾ,* 1:336–38 (part 1, ch. 3, sect. 1), where it is placed in the section on Muḥammad's place or status (*makānah*), which directly precedes the section on the Night Journey and Ascension but is related by the Prophet as part of his childhood; and 1:347 (part 1, ch. 3, sect. 2) where the author states that it did not occur at the time of the Night Journey, but in Muḥammad's childhood. See further, Schimmel, who notes that the splitting and cleansing of Muḥammad's breast "serves clearly as an initiatory preparation for his prophetic calling and mission" (69); see Schimmel, *And Muhammad Is His Messenger,* 67–69 and especially her references.

82. Al-Bājūrī objects that the verse should be understood to mean "I swear by [the Lord of] the moon," because legists forbid swearing by other than God. Obviously my reading differs from this.

83. See Ibn Hishām, *Al-Sīrah al-Nabawiyyah,* 2:423–24, part of al-Isrāʾ wa-al-Miʿrāj, the etiological anecdote of the Prophet giving Abū Bakr the sobriquet "al-Ṣiddīq" most explicitly because he *believed in* Muḥammad's description of Jerusalem in his Night Journey when others did not. The entire anecdote is an extended wordplay on *ṣadaqa* (to tell the truth); *ṣaddaqa* (to believe, give credence), and *ṣiddīq,* demonstrating both Abū Bakr's loyalty and his giving credence to Muḥammad.

84. See al-Qāḍī ʿIyāḍ, *Al-Shifāʾ,* 1:602 (part 1, ch. 4, sect. 19); al-Ghazzī and al-Bājūrī, vv. 76–77. The Miracle of the Cave is said to have as its Qurʾānic text-source QK 8:30: "[Remember how] the Unbelievers plotted against you, to keep you in bonds, or kill you, or expel you. They plot, but Allāh plots too, and Allāh is the best of all plotters."

85. Ibid., 1:617–24 (part 1, ch. 4, sect. 21).

86. See al-Qāḍī ʿIyāḍ, *Al-Shifāʾ*, 1:628 (part 1, ch. 4, sect. 22).

87. Ibid.

88. The basic tenets of Iʿjāz al-Qurʾān are summarized in al-Qāḍī ʿIyāḍ, *Al-Shifāʾ*, 1:500–52 (part 1, ch. 4, sects. 4–11), that is the first major block of materials concerning Muḥammad's miracles. See G. E. von Grunebaum, "Iʿdjāz," *EI2*.

89. I follow al-Azharī and al-Bājūrī in my reading of this line—i.e., that Muḥammad *passed by* the other prophets, which is more in keeping with the Ascension narratives (and my discussion of the Ascension as an initiatory contest, below), rather than Nicholson's more literal reading "With them [the other prophets] thou didst pierce through the seven heavenly spheres."

90. It seems to have inspired the academic imagination as well. For an extensive diachronic study of the development of the Ibn ʿAbbās version of the Night Journey and Ascension, plus translations and bibliography, see Frederick S. Colby, *Narrating Muḥammad's Night Journey: Tracing the Development of the Ibn ʿAbbās Ascension Discourse* (Albany: State University of New York Press, 2008). On pictorial expressions, see Christiane J. Gruber, *The Timurid Book of Ascension: A Study of Text and Image in a Pan-Asian Context* (Valencia, Spain: Patrimonio Ediciones, 2008). Further, see Brooke Olson Vuckovic, *Heavenly Journeys, Earthly Concerns: The Legacy of the Miʿrāj in the Formation of Islam* (New York: Routledge: 2005); and Christiane Gruber and Frederick Colby, eds., *The Prophet's Ascension: Cross-Cultural Encounters with the Islamic Miʿrāj Tales* (Bloomington: Indiana University Press, 2010). For a composite narrative of the Night Journey and Ascension, chronology, illustrations, basic bibliography, and interpretative essay, see Jamel Eddine Bencheikh, *Le Voyage Nocturne de Mahomet* followed by *L'Aventure de la Parole* (Paris: Imprimerie Nationale, 1988).

91. See B. Schrieke—[J. Horovitz] "Miʿrādj," part 1, and J. E. Bencheikh "Miʿrādj," part 2, and references *EI2;* Schimmel, *And Muhammad Is His Messenger,* 159–75. See further the discussion of the Night Journey and Ascension in Aḥmad Shawqī's Nahj al-Burdah, chapter 3 of this volume, part 5.

92. See Ibn Hishām, *Al-Sīrah al-Nabawiyyah,* 2:421–33; al-Qāḍī ʿIyāḍ, *Al-Shifāʾ*, 1:343–97 (part 1, ch. 3, sects. 2–7), and above, note 43.

93. See al-Qāḍī ʿIyāḍ, *Al-Shifāʾ*, 1:363 (part 1, ch. 3, sect. 3).

94. I have followed al-Bājūrī in identifying the third person masc. pl. pronoun as the enemy. There is some confusion in the commentaries (see al-Ghazzī and al-Bājūrī, v. 122) in identifying the antecedents of the pronouns in this passage: however, with careful attention to the context, I have taken the 3m pl. of verses 118–122 to refer to the enemies/Infidel; 123–133 to refer to the Muslim warriors/Companions.

95. Unlike al-Ghazzī and al-Bājūrī, I take *minhum* to be a case of *min al-bayān* and to refer to the warriors/Companions. This is consistent in terms of grammar and sense with the preceding and following verses (125 and 127).

96. As Nicholson points out (v. 138), "proof" (*burhān*) may be an allusion to QK 4:174, which also seems to refer to the Qurʾān itself. I take it to mean the Qurʾān.

97. Although he does not discuss the literary genesis of passages such as al-Būṣīrī's, Fawzī Amīn makes a similar point in his explanation of the appearance of the Prophet's battles and raids in *madīḥ nabawī* of the Mamlūk period: that they present an idealized picture of warriors of the faith that is equally applicable for all

periods. On this and on the contemporary polemic and political aspect of elements such as the Prophet's battles in *madīḥ nabawī* of the Mamlūk period, see Fawzī Muḥammad Amīn, *Adab al-ʿAṣr al-Mamlūkī al-Awwal: Malāmiḥ al-Mujtamaʿ al-Miṣrī* (Alexandria, Egypt: Dār al-Maʿrifah al-Jāmiʿiyyah, 2003), 93–98.

98. In chronological order: Badr, 2 AH, QK 3:123, Ibn Hishām, *Al-Sīrah al-Nabawiyyah*, 2:643–802; Uḥud, 3 AH, QK 3:121 (taken to refer to it, not named); Ibn Hishām, 3:837–967; Ḥunayn, 8 AH, QK 9:25, Ibn Hishām, 4:1283–1329.

99. See Abū Tammām, *Dīwān*, 1:40–74; poem no. 3, vv. 50–58; S. Stetkevych, *The Poetics of Islamic Legitimacy*, 172–73.

100. The Muʿallaqah of ʿAmr ibn Kulthūm, v. 79, in al-Anbārī, *Sharḥ al-Qaṣāʾid al-Sabʿ*, 367–427. I have taken *manzil* to be a *maṣdar mīmī* used as *mafʿūl muṭlaq lil-tashbīh*.

101. See Bishr ibn Abī Khāzim al-Asadī, *Dīwān*, 2nd ed., ed. ʿIzzat Ḥasan (Damascus: Manshūrāt Wizārat al-Thaqāfah, 1972), 137–41; poem no. 28, v.13. The rhetorical *sal* (or *isʾal*, ask) is commonly found in other poetic contexts (*hijāʾ*, *madīḥ*, etc.) as well, but its use in *fakhr* is nevertheless pronounced. Al-Ghazzī cites a Qurʾānic referent, *wa-isʾal al-qaryata* (QK 12:82), but the poetic *fakhr* convention seems much closer in this case.

102. See for example, the Muʿallaqah of ʿAmr ibn Kulthūm, vv. 58–61 and again vv. 74–77, in al-Anbārī, *Sharḥ al-Qaṣāʾid al-Sabʿ*, 367–427. On the poetics of these strings of active participial epithets, with particular references to elegy, see S. Stetkevych, *The Mute Immortals Speak*, 168–88.

103. Abū Tammām, *Dīwān*, 1:40–74; poem no. 3, v. 60.

104. Ibid., vv. 69–70.

105. See S. Stetkevych, *The Poetics of Islamic Legitimacy*, 73, 105–9.

106. On the general Muslim tenet that the Prophet was *ummī*, in the sense of unlettered, illiterate, and that this constitutes proof of his divine inspiration, plus references to scholarship that explores other interpretations, see Schimmel, *And Muhammad Is His Messenger*, 71–74 and references.

107. See chapter 1 of this volume; S. Stetkevych, "Pre-Islamic Panegyric and the Poetics of Redemption," 33–37; and S. Stetkevych, *The Poetics of Islamic Legitimacy*, 65–70.

108. *Dīwān al-Buḥturī*, 2:1153 (poem no. 470, v. 6).

109. See Al-Qāḍī ʿIyāḍ, *Al-Shifāʾ*, 1:398–407 (part 1, ch. 3, sect. 8).

110. Schimmel, *And Muhammad Is His Messenger*, 92; see also al-Qāḍī ʿIyāḍ, *Al-Shifāʾ*, 2:137–76 (part 2, ch. 4, sect. 1–5).

111. From al-Akhṭal's *lāmiyyah*,ʿAfā Wāsiṭun (Wāsiṭ Lies Deserted), in Fakhr al-Dīn Qabāwah, ed. *Shiʿr al-Akhṭal, Abī Mālik Ghiyāth ibn Ghawth al-Taghlibī*, in the recension of al-Sukkarī, 2nd ed., 2 vols. (Beirut: Dār al-Āfāq al-Jadīdah, 1979), 1:1–34. For a translation and analysis of the full poem, see S. Stetkevych, "Supplication and Negotiation: The Client Outraged," in *The Poetics of Islamic Legitimacy*, 110–43; or S. Stetkevych, "Umayyad Panegyric and the Poetics of Islamic Hegemony."

112. On *ṣabá* and Najd, see J. Stetkevych, *Zephyrs of Najd*, ch. 3, esp. 116–20, 128–32; see also, S. Stetkevych, *Abū Tammām*, 326–27.

113. See S. Stetkevych, "Poetic Expansion as Verbal Reliquary," S. Stetkevych, "From Jāhiliyyah to *Badīʿiyyah*," and S. Stetkevych, "Al-Badīʿiyyah bayn Fann al-Qaṣīdah wa-ʿIlm al-Balāghah."

3. Aḥmad Shawqī and the Reweaving of the Mantle

1. Under the title "Imperialisms and Identities: Aḥmad Shawqī's *Nahj al-Burdah*," parts of this study, in earlier versions, were presented at the annual meetings of the American Comparative Literature Association, Ann Arbor, Michigan, 17 April, 2004, and the Middle East Studies Association, Montreal, Canada, 17 November 2007.

2. In the present study I have relied primarily on the first printing of Nahj al-Burdah, with Muḥammad al-Muwayliḥī's introduction and Shaykh Salīm al-Bishrī's commentary: Aḥmad Shawqī, *Nahj al-Burdah wa-ʿalayh Waḍaḥ al-Nahj lil-Shaykh Salīm al-Bishrī* (Cairo: Maṭbaʿat al-Iṣlāḥ, 1328/1910). There are numerous later editions and reprints. It appears in the editions of Shawqī's *dīwān* with standard philological and explanatory commentaries, but with no reference to the occasion or circumstances of its composition. See, e.g., Aḥmad Shawqī, *Al-Shawqiyyāt,* intro. Muḥammad Ḥusayn Haykal, 4 vols. in 2 (Cairo: Al-Maktabah al-Tijāriyyah al-Kubrá, 1970), 1:190–208; Aḥmad Shawqī, *Al-Shawqiyyāt,* ed. and comment. ʿAlī ʿAbd al-Munʿim ʿAbd al-Ḥamīd (Cairo: Al-Sharikah al-Miṣriyyah al-ʿĀlamiyyah lil-Nashr/Longman: 2000), 212–28, where it falls under the rubric of "Islāmiyyāt."

3. Mounah A. Khouri, *Poetry and the Making of Modern Egypt,* 55–57; and, further, 54–102. For an extensive bibliography, see Arthur Goldschmidt, Jr., *Biographical Dictionary of Modern Egypt* (London and Boulder, Colo.: Lynne Rienner Publishers, 2000), 193–94.

4. For a literary and historical overview of Shawqī's life and work, see Shawqī Ḍayf, *Shawqī: Shāʿir al-ʿAṣr al-Ḥadīth,* 11th ed. (Cairo: Dār al-Maʿārif, 1986).

5. For an overview of the major characteristics and modernist literary disputes concerning Arabic Neo-Classical poetry, see S. Moreh, "The Neoclassical Qaṣīda: Modern Poets and Critics," in G. E. von Grunebaum, ed., *Arabic Poetry: Theory and Development,* Third Giorgio Levi Della Vida Biennial Conference, University of California, Los Angeles, 1971 (Wiesbaden: Otto Harrassowitz, 1973), 155–79; likewise, see S. Somekh, "The Neo-Classical Poets," in M. M. Badawī, ed., *The Cambridge History of Modern Arabic Literature* (Cambridge: Cambridge University Press, 1992), 36–81. Recently several important studies have brought Arabic Neo-Classical poetry fully into the purview of contemporary literary theory and interpretation. Most important in the present context are: Hussein N. Kadhim, *The Poetics of Anti-Colonialism in the Arabic Qaṣīdah* (Leiden: E. J. Brill, 2004), which deals with Arabic Neo-Classical and Modern poetry as a response to Western imperialism; Yaseen Noorani, "A Nation Born in Mourning: The Neoclassical Funeral Elegy in Egypt," *Journal of Arabic Literature* 28 no. 1 (March, 1997): 38–67; Yaseen Noorani, "The Rebellious Subject: Political Self-Fashioning in Arabic and Persian Poetry of the Colonial Period," *Journal of Arabic Literature* 29 no. 2 (July 1998): 1–30; Yaseen Noorani, "The Lost Garden of al-Andalus: Islamic Spain and the Poetic Inversion of Colonialism," *International Journal of Middle East Studies* 31 no. 2 (May 1999): 237–54. These three articles treat Arabic Neo-Classical poetry in terms of the formation of nationalism in the colonial context; the last especially is pertinent to the present study. See also Akiko Motoyoshi Sumi, "Poetry and Architecture: A Double Imitation in the Sīniyyah of Aḥmad Shawqī," *Journal of Arabic Literature* 39 no. 1 (2008): 72–122, which offers a reading of Shawqī's Neo-Classical

masterpiece in terms of Interarts Theory as an imitation of al-Buḥtūrī's Sīniyyah, on the one hand, and an ekphrastic portrayal of the Islamic monuments of al-Andalus, on the other.

6. G. Delanoue, "al-Marṣafī, al-Ḥusayn," *EI2*.

7. Khouri, *Poetry and the Making of Modern Egypt*, 9, 13–14.

8. Albert Hourani, *Arabic Thought in the Liberal Age 1798–1939* (Cambridge: Cambridge University Press, 1998 [Oxford, 1962]), 344; and passim for a general intellectual background for the period under discussion, especially on al-Ṭahṭāwī (ch. 4), al-Afghānī (ch. 5), ʿAbduh and his disciples (chs. 6 and 7), Egyptian nationalism (ch. 8).

9. Maḥmūd Sāmī al-Bārūdī, *Kashf al-Ghummah fī Madḥ Sayyid al-Ummah*, ed. and intro., Saʿd al-Ẓalām ([Cairo]: Maṭbūʿāt al-Shaʿb, 1978).

10. Al-Bārūdī, *Kashf al-Ghummah*, 43.

11. See Saʿd al-Ẓalām, introduction to al-Bārūdī, *Kashf al-Ghummah*, 32. An extended discussion of al-Bārūdī's Kashf al-Ghummah and its relationship to Shawqī's Nahj al-Burdah is beyond the purview of the present study. Zakī Mubārak has undertaken the comparison and evaluation of the three *madāʾiḥ nabawiyyah*, al-Būṣīrī's Burdah, al-Bārūdī's Kashf al-Ghummah, and Shawqī's Nahj al-Burdah; see Zakī Mubārak, *Al-Muwāzanah bayn al-Shuʿarāʾ* (Cairo: Dār al-ʿArabī lil-Ṭibāʿah wa-al-Nashr, n.d.), ch. 19 (al-Būṣīrī wa-Shawqī), 171–80; and esp. ch. 20 (Bayn al-Būṣīrī wa-Shawqī wa-al-Bārūdī), 181–95. His discussion does not go much beyond comparing individual lines or passages of the *nasīb*, especially for the first two; but he does have some interesting comparative examples from other poets.

12. *Al-Shawqiyyāt*, ed. Haykal, 1:34–41; and see chapter 2.

13. For example, the collection of five *badīʿiyyāt*, of Ibn Ḥijjah al-Ḥamawī, ʿImād al-Dīn Abū al-Fidā, ʿIzz al-Dīn al-Mawṣilī, ʿĀʾishah al-Bāʿūniyyah and Ṣafī al-Dīn al-Ḥillī, respectively; in *Al-Badīʿiyyāt al-Khams fī Madḥ al-Nabī al-Mukhtār wa-al-Ṣaḥābah al-Kirām* (Cairo: 1897). Likewise, Ibn Ḥijjah's literary and rhetorical compendium organized as a commentary to his *badīʿiyyah* was published in Egypt in this period: Taqī al-Dīn Abū Bakr ibn ʿAlī Ibn Ḥijjah al-Ḥamawī, *Khizānat al-Adab wa-Ghāyat al-Arab* (Cairo: Al-Maṭbaʿah al-Khayriyyah, 1304/1887).

14. Al-Muwayliḥī, introduction to Shawqī, *Nahj al-Burdah*, p. *ʿayn* (= iii).

15. Shawqī, *Nahj al-Burdah*, frontispiece. In later editions, such as the Cairo 1994, the frontispiece with the Khedival seal is gone, and the dedication is relegated to a footnote to al-Muwayliḥī's introduction. Shawqī, *Nahj al-Burdah* (Cairo: Maktabat al-Ādāb, 1994), 9.

16. For a brief biography of Salīm al-Bishrī and references, see Goldschmidt, *Biographical Dictionary of Modern Egypt*, 37–38. It is of note that as a student at al-Azhar al-Bishrī studied with al-Bājūrī, whose commentary on al-Būṣīrī's Burdah I discussed in chapter 2. What is most curious is that Mubārak notes a literary controversy over whether it was actually Salīm al-Bishrī who composed the Waḍaḥ al-Najh commentary or his son, Shaykh ʿAbd al-ʿAzīz al-Bishrī. The latter vehemently denies this (this is from after Salīm al-Bishrī's death). See Mubārak, *Al-Muwāzanah bayn al-Shuʿarāʾ*, 180. My point here is that Salīm al-Bishrī undoubtedly put his name to the Waḍaḥ al-Nahj and it is therefore his authority that the Waḍaḥ al-Nahj invokes.

17. *Al-Shawqiyyāt*, ed. Haykal, 1:98–102. Ḍayf, *Shawqī*, 132.

18. See notes 15 above and 31 below.

19. This is a major theme of S. Stetkevych, *The Poetics of Islamic Legitimacy.*

20. R. M. A. Allen, "al-Muwayliḥī, Muḥammad," *EI2*; Ḍayf, *Shawqī,* 95–96.

21. Muḥammad al-Muwayliḥī, introduction to Shawqī, *Nahj al-Burdah,* pp. *alif-zāʾ*.

22. For in-depth coverage of these circumstances, see Afaf Lutfi Al-Sayyid, *Egypt and Cromer: A Study in Anglo-Egyptian Relations* (New York: Praeger, 1969), passim, and Peter Mansfield, *The British in Egypt* (New York: Holt, Rinehart and Winston, 1972), chs. 14–17.

23. Hussein N. Kadhim, in his discussion and analysis of Shawqī's poetic responses to these two incidents, offers an eloquent and compelling formulation of the colonial experience in Egypt and the Arab world in light of post-colonial theory and provides an excellent backdrop and references. See Kadhim, *The Poetics of Anti-Colonialism,* preface and ch. 1.

24. Hourani, *Arabic Thought in the Liberal Age,* 201. See also Khouri, *Poetry and the Making of Modern Egypt,* 65.

25. As cited in Khouri, *Poetry and the Making of Modern Egypt,* 83.

26. Ibid., 65–75.

27. Ibid., 88–98. Oddly, Khouri, in tracing the political poetry of precisely this period—indeed, the very year 1910—makes no mention of Shawqī's Nahj al-Burdah. He writes, summarizing Shawqī's poetic production of the period from 1907–14:

> The reversal of Cromer's policies after his retirement and the conciliatory attitude adopted by Gorst toward the Khedive, who was able to reassert his authority, left their mark on Shawqī's poetry. From the violent attacks on Cromer in the early poems, the poet shifted gradually to the less bitter criticism reflected in the Dinshawāy poems. *These were followed by a long overwhelming silence* interrupted shortly after the dethronement of ʿAbbās by an ambiguous poem, which, as will be shown later, actually precipitated Shawqī's exile to Spain in December, 1914. [p. 88; emphasis mine]

28. Albert Hourani, "The Decline of the West in the Middle East—I," *International Affairs* 29 (1953): 22–44, at 29–31. See Kadhim, *The Poetics of Anti-Colonialism,* vii.

29. Moreh, "The Neoclassical Qaṣīda"; Khouri, *Poetry and the Making of Modern Egypt,* 135–95 passim; M. M. Badawi, *A Critical Introduction to Modern Arabic Poetry* (Cambridge: Cambridge University Press, 1975), 68–114 passim.

30. Al-Ghazzī, *Al-Zubdah fī Sharḥ al-Burdah,* 6 and passim.

31. I have relied on the text of the first printing (1910) of Nahj al-Burdah with Muḥammad al-Muwayliḥī's introduction and Shaykh Salīm al-Bishrī's commentary: Shawqī, *Nahj al-Burdah,* and have consulted Haykal, *Al-Shawqiyyāt,* 1:190–208; ʿAbd al-Ḥamīd, *Al-Shawqiyyāt,* 212–28.

32. Al-Bishrī takes this verse to mean that the girls have red cheeks that inflame men's hearts. I take it to mean rather that the sight of the beautiful maiden's make the men's cheeks blush, revealing the passion in their hearts. Al-Bishrī, *Waḍaḥ al-Nahj,* v. 15.

33. Gian Biagio Conte, *The Rhetoric of Imitation: Genre and Poetic Memory in Virgil and Other Latin Poets,* trans. Charles Segal (Ithaca, N.Y.: Cornell University

Press, 1986), 35 n. 5, 70, 76–77. See my discussion of Conte's ideas as they apply to the pre-Islamic *qaṣīdah* of al-Nābighah al-Dhubyānī in S. Stetkevych, *The Poetics of Islamic Legitimacy,* 25–26.

34. See above, note 13.

35. Although he does not explicitly divide Nahj al-Burdah into sections, al-Bishrī notes in his commentary to verse 25 that there is a transition (*takhalluṣ*) here as the poet makes an abrupt cut-off from *ghazal* and *tashbīb* (lyrical and amatory verse) to censuring worldly pleasures and warning against their temptations (*dhamm al-dunyā wa-al-taḥdhīr min kaydihā . . .*). Al-Bishrī, *Waḍaḥ al-Nahj,* v. 25.

36. As cited in Āmidī, *Al-Muwāzanah,* 1:269.

37. Connerton, *How Societies Remember,* 59. See, further, my discussion of Connerton's ideas with regards to al-Mutanabbī and the Arabic tradition, S. Stetkevych, *The Poetics of Islamic Legitimacy,* 185–86.

38. Gerhard Böwering's phrase, see chapter 2, part 3, vv. 52–53, and n. 55.

39. Al-Qāḍī ʿIyāḍ, *Al-Shifāʾ,* 1:455 (part 1, ch. 3, sect. 13).

40. Al-Bishrī, *Waḍaḥ al-Nahj,* v. 48. Al-Bishrī, typical of his theological nitpicking, notes that, technically speaking, angels do not thirst.

41. For a summary of the literature/lore concerning Muḥammad's ancestors, see al-Bishrī, *Waḍaḥ al-Nahj,* v. 51.

42. See also Schimmel, *And Muhammad Is His Messenger,* 109; Abdullah Yusuf Ali,. *The Holy Qurʾan: Text, Translation, Commentary,* (Elmhurst, N.Y.: Tahrike Tarsile Qurʾan, 1987), 385 n. 1127; al-Qāḍī ʿIyāḍ, *Al-Shifāʾ,* 1:445–46 (part 1, ch. 3, sect. 13).

43. On the miracles of Muḥammad of this sort, see al-Qāḍī ʿIyāḍ, *Al-Shifāʾ,* 1: 550–80 (part 1, ch. 5, sects. 15–17), and Schimmel, "Legends and Miracles," in *And Muhammad Is His Messenger,* 67–80.

44. V. 81 is in the dual, referring, apparently, to both the Romans and the Persians of v. 80.

45. This correlates quite precisely to Hourani's formulation of the Sunnī conception of Islamic history. See Hourani, *Arabic Thought in the Liberal Age,* 7.

46. See the discussion of and references for the Night Journey and Ascension, chapter 2, part 7, and notes.

47. See R. Paret, "al-Burāḳ," *EI2*.

48. Al-Qāḍī ʿIyāḍ, *Al-Shifāʾ,* 1:351 (part 1, ch. 3 sect. 2).

49. Connerton, *How Societies Remember,* 73–74. See my discussion of Connerton in the context of Arabic and Andalusian court ceremony and poetry, S. Stetkevych, *The Poetics of Islamic Legitimacy,* 247.

50. As it occurs in the Qurʾān, *lawḥ maḥfūẓ* (preserved tablet) appears to refer to the original heavenly Qurʾān (QK 85:22), but further, it was believed to be the tablet upon which were written all the decisions of the divine will, past, present, and future. Likewise *al-qalam* (the pen; QK 68:1; 96:4) is said in *ḥadīth*s cited by al-Ṭabarī to be the first thing that God created, so He could write down events to come. See A. J. Wensinck and C. E. Bosworth, "Lawḥ" and Cl. Huart and A. Grohmann, "Ḳalam," *EI2*.

51. Al-Qāḍī ʿIyāḍ, *Al-Shifāʾ,* 1:602 (part 1, ch. 4, sect. 19).

52. Schimmel, *And Muhammad Is His Messenger,* p. 109; al-Qāḍī ʿIyāḍ, *Al-Shifāʾ,* 1:445–46 (part 1, ch. 3 sect.13).

53. It is also quite distinct from the sort of Andalusian *madīḥ nabawī* that pleads for military intecession, whether divine or Mashriqī, against the military advances of the Reconquista.

54. In his commentary al-Bishrī takes *jahl* to be *shirk*, as though the verse is referring to Muḥammad's era; I take the verse to be referring primarily to the ignorance and backwardness of the Islamic East in Shawqī's own time. See al-Bishrī, *Waḍaḥ al-Nahj*, v. 117.

55. This is not to say that I have interpreted Shawqī's Nahj al-Burdah in light of Hourani's formulation, but rather that, after reading Shawqī's poem, it seemed to me to embody—perhaps more precisely to shape and/or enact—the Sunnī conception of Islamic history that Hourani has so concisely expressed. I by no means intend to suggest that Nahj al-Burdah is merely a poetic rendition of these ideas.

56. Hourani, *Arabic Thought in the Liberal Age*, 7. This passage also applies quite particularly to Shawqī's passage on the Birth of the Prophet, NB part 5, vv. 75–82.

57. Al-Qāḍī ʿIyāḍ, *Al-Shifāʾ*, 1:452–53 (part 1, ch. 3 sect. 13).

58. This issue as it applies to Shawqī is discussed by Noorani, "The Lost Garden of al-Andalus," esp. 239 and references.

59. In the second hemistich I have followed al-Bishrī's commentary, WN v. 132.

60. See J. Walker—[P. Fenton], "Sulaymān b. Dāwūd," *EI2;* Suzanne Pinckney Stetkevych, "Solomon and Mythic Kingship in the Arabo-Islamic Tradition," Solomon Katz Distinguished Lecture in the Humanities, University of Washington, Seattle, 13 May 1999 (in preparation for publication).

61. Abū Tammām, *Dīwān*, 1:40–74; v. 41.

62. For a translation of the full poem and a discussion of Abū Tammām's poetical transformation of a historical event, the conquest of Amorium, into a legitimizing myth of the ʿAbbāsid caliphate and a vehicle for the promulgation of an ideology of Arab-Islamic "manifest destiny," see. S. Stetkevych, *The Poetics of Islamic Legitimacy*, ch. 5 "Political Dominion as Sexual Domination," esp. 152–79.

63. Abū Tammām, *Dīwān*, 1:40–74; v. 37.

64. Ibid., 3:120; v. 21.

65. Al-Ḥillī, *Dīwān*, 693–97 (approx. vv. 65–99).

66. Noorani, "A Nation Born in Mourning," 49.

67. N. Calder, "Sharīʿa," *EI2*.

68. Lane, *sh-r-ʿ*; see also, *Lisān, sh-r-ʿ*; Calder, "Sharīʿa."

69. Hourani, *Arabic Thought in the Liberal Age*, 114–15. The work to which he refers is F. Guizot, *Histoire de la civilisation en Europe* (Paris, 1938).

70. Hourani, *Arabic Thought in the Liberal Age*, 115.

71. Reading *jardāʾ* (1994 ed.) for *ḥardāʾ* (1910 ed.), al-Bishrī, *Waḍaḥ al-Nahj*, v. 148.

72. On the Neo-Classical and Nahḍah vision, and appropriation, of al-Andalus, see Noorani, "The Lost Garden of al-Andalus," and Sumi, "Poetry and Architecture."

73. F. Omar, "Hārūn al-Rashīd," *EI2*.

74. M. Rekaya, "al-Maʾmūn b. Hārūn al-Rashīd," *EI2*.

75. See Stefan Sperl, "Islamic Kingship and Arabic Panegyric Poetry in the Early Ninth Century," *Journal of Arabic Literature* 8 (1977): 20–35; and S. Stetkevych, *Abū Tammām*, part II, 109–235, passim.

76. Al-Buḥturī, *Dīwān,* 2:1152–62 (poem no. 470).
77. G. Levi della Vida–[M. Bonner], "ʿUmar b. al-Khaṭṭāb," *EI2.*
78. P. B. Cobb, "ʿUmar b. ʿAbd al-ʿAzīz," *EI2.*
79. L. Veccia Vaglieri, "ʿAlī b. Abī Ṭālib," *EI2.*
80. Ibid.
81. G. Levi della Vida, "ʿUthmān b. ʿAffān," EI2.
82. W. Montgomery Watt, "Abū Bakr," *EI2.*
83. Al-Bishrī's version is a variant of that found in Ibn Hishām, *Al-Sīrah al-Nabawiyyah,* 4:1513–14.
84. This complaint about al-Būṣīrī's Burdah is made quite precisely and concisely by Mubārak. See Mubārak, *Al-Muwāzanah bayn al-Shuʿarāʾ,* 178.
85. Abū Bakr Muḥammad ibn ʿAlī ibn Ḥijjah al-Ḥamawī, *Khizānat al-Adab wa-Ghāyat al-Arab,* 2 vols., intro., ed., ann., Ṣalāḥ al-Dīn al-Hawwārī (Beirut: Al-Maktabah al-ʿAṣriyyah, 2006) 2:477; for al-Mawṣilī's closure, 2:486. See also, *Al-Badīʿiyyāt al-Khams,* 8 (Ibn Ḥijjah) and 22 (al-Mawṣilī). I have followed the latter version of Ibn Ḥijjah's second hemistich.
86. Umm Kulthūm, *Nahj al-Burdah,* Sono Cairo/Ṣawt al-Qāhirah no. 144, 1946. On Umm Kulthūm's performances of *qaṣīdah*s by Aḥmad Shawqī, including Wulida al-Hudá, see Virginia Danielson, *The Voice of Egypt: Umm Kulthūm, Arabic Song, and Egyptian Society in the Twentieth Century* (Chicago: University of Chicago Press, 1997), 110–21 passim; on Nahj al-Burdah, 112–14; 148–49.
87. Huda Fakhreddine, "Umm Kulthūm Sings Shawqī's Nahj al-Burdah: The Spiritualization of Polemics" (unpublished seminar paper, Indiana University, fall 2007), 9 and passim.
88. The site attributes the translated transcript, titled, "Weapons Used by the Other Religions to Wage War on Islam," as follows: posted on 18 October 2002 from an Al Jazeera interview of Dr. Yūsuf al-Qaraḍāwī, "Daʿi and Islamic Thinker" aired on 13 October 2002 by Mahir ʿAbdullah on the program, "Shariʿah and Life." Available at www.jimas.org/defence.htm (accessed 26 August 2009).
89. Al-Qaradāwī, "Weapons Used by the Other Religions," 17. The verses quoted are NB 118, 199, 121.

WORKS CITED

Abū Tammām [Ḥabīb ibn Aws al-Ṭāʾī]. *Dīwān Abī Tammām bi-Sharḥ al-Khaṭīb al-Tibrīzī*. 4 vols. Ed. Muḥammad ʿAbduh ʿAzzām. Cairo: Dār al-Maʿārif, 1951.

Ahlwardt, W. *Verzeichniss der Arabischen Handschriften der Königlichen Bibliothek zu Berlin*. Vol. 7. Berlin: A. Asher, 1895.

Ali, Abdullah Yusuf. *The Holy Qurʾan: Text, Translation, Commentary*. Elmhurst, N.Y.: Tahrike Tarsile Qurʾan, 1987.

Allen, R. M. A. "al-Muwayliḥī, Muḥammad." *EI2*.

Al-Mallah, Majd Yassir. "Doing Things with Odes: A Poet's Pledges of Allegiance: Ibn Darrāj al-Qasṭallī's *Hāʾiyyah* to al-Manṣūr and *Rāʾiyyah* to al-Mundhir." *Journal of Arabic Literature* 34 nos. 1–2 (2003): 45–81.

[ʿAlqamah ibn ʿAbadah]. *Dīwān ʿAlqamah al-Faḥl bi-Sharḥ . . . al-Aʿlam al-Shantamarī*. Ed. Luṭfī al-Ṣaqqāl and Durriyyah al-Khaṭīb. Aleppo: Dār al-Kitāb al-ʿArabī bi-Ḥalab, 1969.

Al-Sayyid, Afaf Lutfi. *Egypt and Cromer: A Study in Anglo-Egyptian Relations*. New York: Praeger, 1969.

al-Ālūsī al-Baghdādī, Maḥmūd Shukrī. *Bulūgh al-Arab fī Maʿrifat Aḥwāl al-ʿArab*. 3 vols. Ed. Muḥammad Bahjat al-Atharī. Beirut: Dār al-Kutub al-ʿIlmiyyah, n.d.

al-Āmidī, Abū al-Qāsim al-Ḥasan ibn Bishr. *Al-Muwāzanah bayn Shiʿr Abī Tammām wa-al-Buḥturī*. 2 vols. Ed. Aḥmad Ṣaqr. Cairo: Dār al-Maʿārif, 1972.

Amīn, Fawzī Muḥammad. *Adab al-ʿAṣr al-Mamlūkī al-Awwal: Malāmiḥ al-Mujtamaʿ al-Miṣrī*. Alexandria, Egypt: Dār al-Maʿrifah al-Jāmiʿiyyah, 2003.

al-Anbārī, Abū Bakr Muḥammad ibn al-Qāsim [= Ibn al-Anbārī]. *Sharḥ al-Qaṣāʾid al-Sabʿ al-Ṭiwāl al-Jāhiliyyāt*. Ed. ʿAbd al-Salām Muḥammad Hārūn. Cairo: Dār al-Maʿārif, 1969.

Arafat, W. "Ḥassān b. Th̲ābit." *EI2*online.

Arazi, A. "al-Nābigha al-Dhubyānī." *EI2*.

Arberry, A. J., trans. and ann. *The Mystical Poems of Ibn al-Fāriḍ*. Dublin: Emery Walker, 1956.
———. *The Seven Odes: The First Chapter in Arabic Literature*. London: George Allen and Unwin, 1957.
Austin, J. L. *How to Do Things with Words*. Cambridge, Mass.: Harvard University Press, 1975.
al-Azharī, Khālid [ibn ʿAbd Allāh]. *Sharḥ Qaṣīdat al-Burdah lil-Shaykh Khālid al-Azharī*. [Istanbul]: Der Saadet/Sharikat Ṣaḥāfiyyah ʿUthmāniyyah, 1318 [1900].
Badawi, M. M. *A Critical Introduction to Modern Arabic Poetry*. Cambridge: Cambridge University Press, 1975.
Badawi, Mustafa. "From Primary to Secondary *qaṣīdahs*." *Journal of Arabic Literature* 11 (1980): 1–31.
al-Bājūrī al-Kharpūtī, Ibrāhīm ibn Muḥammad. *Hādhā Kitāb Ḥāshiyat Ibrāhīm al-Bājūrī al-Kharpūtī . . . ʿalá matn al-Burdah li . . . al-Būṣīrī*. [Istanbul]: n.p., 1290/1872.
al-Bārūdī, Maḥmūd Sāmī. *Kashf al-Ghummah fī Madḥ Sayyid al-Ummah*. Ed. and intro., Saʿd al-Ẓalām. [Cairo]: Maṭbūʿāt al-Shaʿb, 1978.
Bencheikh, J. E. "Miʿrādj," part 2. *EI2*.
Bencheikh, Jamel Eddine. *Le Voyage Nocturne de Mahomet* followed by *L'Aventure de la Parole*. Paris: Imprimerie Nationale, 1988.
Bettini, Lidia. "Zuhayr b. Abī Sulmā Rabīʿah b. Riyāḥ al-Muzanī." *EI2*.
Bishr ibn Abī Khāzim al-Asadī. *Dīwān*, 2nd ed. Ed. ʿIzzat Ḥasan. Damascus: Manshūrāt Wizārat al-Thaqāfah, 1972.
Brockelmann, Carl. *Geschichte der Arabischen Litteratur*. Vols. 1 and 2. 2nd ed. Leiden: E. J. Brill, 1943; and Suppl. 1. Leiden: E. J. Brill, 1937. [= *GAL*]
[al-Buḥturī, al-Walīd ibn ʿUbayd Allāh]. *Dīwān al-Buḥturī*. 5 vols. Ed. Ḥasan al-Ṣayrafī. Cairo: Dār al-Maʿārif, n.d.
Burkert, Walter. *Homo Necans: The Anthropology of Ancient Greek Ritual and Myth*. Trans. Peter Bing. Berkeley: University of California Press, 1983.
"Al-Būṣīrī." *EI2* Suppl.
al-Būṣīrī, Sharaf al-Dīn Abū ʿAbd Allāh Muḥammad ibn Saʿīd. *Dīwān al-Būṣīrī*. 2nd ed. Ed. Muḥammad Sayyid Kīlānī. Cairo: Muṣṭafá al-Bābī al-Ḥalabī, 1972.
Cahen, Cl. "Ayyūbids." *EI2*.
Calder, N. "Sharīʿa." *EI2*.
Cobb, P. B. "ʿUmar b. ʿAbd al-ʿAzīz." *EI2*.
Colby, Frederick S. *Narrating Muḥammad's Night Journey: Tracing the Development of the Ibn ʿAbbās Ascension Discourse*. Albany: State University of New York Press, 2008.
Connerton, Paul. *How Societies Remember*. Cambridge: Cambridge University Press, 1989.
Conte, Gian Biagio. *The Rhetoric of Imitation: Genre and Poetic Memory in Virgil and Other Latin Poets*. Trans. Charles Segal. Ithaca, N.Y.: Cornell University Press, 1986.
Danielson, Virginia. *The Voice of Egypt: Umm Kulthūm, Arabic Song, and Egyptian Society in the Twentieth Century*. Chicago: University of Chicago Press, 1997.

Dār al-Kutub al-Miṣriyyah. *Fihris al-Kutub al-ʿArabiyyah.* Part 3. Cairo: Maṭbaʿat Dār al-Kutub al-Miṣriyyah, 1345/1927.
Ḍayf, Shawqī. *Shawqī: Shāʿir al-ʿAṣr al-Ḥadīth.* 11th ed. Cairo: Dār al-Maʿārif, 1986.
Delanoue, G. "al-Marṣafī, al-Ḥusayn." *EI2.*
DeWeese, Devin A. The *Kashf al-Hudā* of Kamāl al-Dīn Ḥusayn al-Khorezmī: A Fifteenth-Century Sufi Commentary on the *Qaṣīdat al-Burdah* in Khorezmian Turkic (Text Edition, Translation, and Historical Introduction). Ph.D. diss., Indiana University, 1985.
Encyclopaedia of Islam. New edition. Leiden: E. J. Brill, 1954–2004. [= *EI2*]
Encyclopaedia of Islam. 2nd edition. Brill, 2009. Brill Online. Indiana University Bloomington. 15 April 2009 http://www.brillonline.nl/subscriber/entry?entry=islam_COM-1089. [= *EI2*online]
Fakhreddine, Huda. "Umm Kulthūm Sings Shawqī's Nahj al-Burdah: The Spiritualization of Polemics." Unpublished seminar paper, Indiana University, Fall 2007.
al-Ghazzī, Badr al-Dīn Muḥammad. *Al-Zubdah fī Sharḥ al-Burdah.* Ed. and intro., ʿUmar Mūsá Bāshā. Algiers: Al-Sharikah al-Waṭaniyyah lil-Nashr wa-al-Tawzīʿ, 1972.
Goldschmidt, Arthur, Jr. *Biographical Dictionary of Modern Egypt.* Boulder, Colo.: Lynne Rienner, 2000.
Gruber, Christiane J. *The Timurid Book of Ascension: A Study of Text and Image in a Pan-Asian Context.* Valencia, Spain: Patrimonio Ediciones, 2008.
Gruber, Christiane, and Frederick Colby, eds. *The Prophet's Ascension: Cross-Cultural Encounters with the Islamic Miʿrāj Tales.* Bloomington: Indiana University Press, 2010.
Gruendler, Beatrice. *Medieval Arabic Praise Poetry: Ibn al-Rūmī and the Patron's Redemption.* London: RoutledgeCurzon, 2003.
Guillaume, A. trans. *The Life of Muhammad: A Translation of Ibn Isḥāq's Sīrat Rasūl Allāh.* Lahore: Oxford University Press, 1974.
Guizot, F. *Histoire de la civilisation en Europe.* Paris, 1938.
Ḥassān ibn Thābit. *Dīwān.* 2 vols. Ed. Walīd ʿArafāt. Beirut: Dār Ṣādir, 1974.
Havelock, Eric A. *The Literate Revolution in Greece and Its Cultural Consequences.* Princeton, N.J.: Princeton University Press, 1982.
———. *The Muse Learns to Write: Reflections on Orality and Literacy from Antiquity to the Present.* New Haven, Conn.: Yale University Press, 1986.
al-Ḥillī, Ṣafī al-Dīn. *Dīwān.* Beirut: Dār Ṣādir/Dār Bayrūt, 1962.
Holt, P. M. "Mamlūks." *EI2.*
Hourani, Albert. *Arabic Thought in the Liberal Age 1798–1939.* Cambridge: Cambridge University Press, 1998 [Oxford, 1962].
———. "The Decline of the West in the Middle East--I." *International Affairs* 29 (1953): 22–44.
Huart, Cl., and A. Grohmann. "Ḳalam." *EI2.*
Husain, M. Hidayat. "Bānat Suʿād of Kaʿb bin Zuhair." *Islamic Culture* 1 (1927): 67–84.
Ibn ʿAbd al-Salām. *Qāla al-Shaykh Ibn ʿAbd al-Salām fī Khawāṣṣ al-Kawākib al-Durriyyah fī Madḥ Khayr al-Bariyyah lil-Shaykh al-Būṣīrī.* Staatsbibliothek zu Berlin. Petermann II 105. folios 243–254a.

Ibn al-Fāriḍ, ʿUmar. *Sharḥ Dīwān Ibn al-Fāriḍ li-Jāmiʿih Rashīd ibn Ghālib; min Sharḥay Ḥasan al-Būrīnī wa-ʿAbd al-Ghānī al-Nābulusī.* 2 vols. in 1. [Cairo], Egypt: Al-Maṭbaʿah al-ʿĀmirah al-Sharīfah, 1306/1888.

Ibn Ḥijjah al-Ḥamawī, Abū Bakr Muḥammad ibn ʿAlī. *Khizānat al-Adab wa-Ghāyat al-Arab.* 2 vols. Intro., ed., ann. Ṣalāḥ al-Dīn al-Hawwārī. Beirut: Al-Maktabah al-ʿAṣriyyah, 2006.

Ibn Ḥijjah al-Ḥamawī, Taqī al-Dīn Abū Bakr ibn ʿAlī. *Khizānat al-Adab wa-Ghāyat al-Arab.* Cairo: Al-Maṭbaʿah al-Khayriyyah, 1304/1887.

Ibn Ḥijjah al-Ḥamawī, ʿImād al-Dīn Abū al-Fidā, ʿIzz al-Dīn al-Mawṣilī, ʿĀʾishah al-Bāʿūniyyah, and Ṣafī al-Dīn al-Ḥillī. *Al-Badīʿiyyāt al-Khams fī Madḥ al-Nabī al-Mukhtār wa-al-Ṣaḥābah al-Kirām.* Cairo, 1897.

Ibn Hishām, Abū Muḥammad ʿAbd al-Malik. *Al-Sīrah al-Nabawiyyah.* 4 vols. Cairo: Dār al-Fikr, [1980].

Ibn Khaldūn. *The Muqaddimah: An Introduction to History [Kitāb al-ʿIbar].* Trans. and intro. Franz Rosenthal. New York: Pantheon Books, 1958.

Ibn Manẓūr Muḥammad ibn Mukarram. *Lisān al-ʿArab.* 15 vols. Beirut: Dār Ṣādir, 1955–56. [= *Lisān*].

Ibn al-Muʿtazz, ʿAbd Allāh. *Kitāb al-Badīʿ.* Ed. Ignatius Kratchkovsky. E.J.W. Gibb Memorial Series No. X. London: Messrs. Luzac., 1935.

Ibn Qutaybah, Abū Muḥammad ʿAbd Allāh ibn Muslim. *Kitāb al-Shiʿr wa-al-Shuʿarāʾ wa-qīla Ṭabaqāt al-Shuʿarāʾ.* Ed. M. J. de Goeje. Leiden: E. J. Brill, 1902.

al-Iṣbahānī, Abū al-Faraj. *Kitāb al-Aghānī.* 32 vols. Ed. Ibrāhīm al-Abyārī. Cairo: Dār al-Shaʿb, 1969–79.

ʿIyāḍ ibn Mūsá al-Yaḥṣubī al-Andalusī, al-Qāḍī. *Al-Shifāʾ bi-Taʿrīf Ḥuqūq al-Muṣṭafá.* 2 vols. Ed. Muḥammad Amīn Qurrah ʿAlī et al. Damascus: Dār al-Wafāʾ lil-Ṭibāʿah wa-al-Nashr, 1392/1972.

al-Jāḥiẓ, ʿAmr ibn Baḥr. *Al-Bayān wa-al-Tabyīn.* 4 vols. Ed. ʿAbd al-Salām Hārūn. Cairo: Maktabat al-Khānjī, 1968.

al-Jawharī, Rajāʾ al-Sayyid, ed. *Kitāb Ṭirāz al-Ḥullah wa-Shifāʾ al-Ghullah lil-Imām Abī Jaʿfar Shihāb al-Dīn [. . .] al-Andalusī, Sharḥ al-Ḥullah al-Siyarā [. . .] Badīʿiyyah naẓamahā Shams al-Dīn Abū ʿAbd Allāh al-Andalusī.* Alexandria: Muʾassasat al-Thaqāfah al-Jāmiʿiyyah, 1410/1990.

al-Jumaḥī, Muḥammad ibn Sallām. *Ṭabaqāt Fuḥūl al-Shuʿarāʾ.* 2 vols. Ed. Maḥmūd Muḥammad Shākir. Cairo: Maṭbaʿat al-Madanī, 1974.

al-Jurjānī, ʿAbd al-Qāhir. *Asrār al-Balāghah.* Ed. Hellmut Ritter. Istanbul: Government Press, 1954.

Juynboll, Th. W. "Bādjūrī, Muḥammad Ibrāhīm." *EI2.*

al-Kaḥḥālah, ʿUmar Riḍá. *Muʿjam al-Muʾallifīn: Tarājim Muṣannifī al-Kutub al-ʿArabiyyah.* 15 vols. Damascus: Maṭbaʿat al-Taraqqī, 1957–61.

Kadhim, Hussein N. *The Poetics of Anti-Colonialism in the Arabic Qaṣīdah.* Leiden: E. J. Brill, 2004.

Kātib Chalabī [= Kâtip Çelebi, known as Ḥājjī Khalīfah]. *Kashf al-Ẓ unūn ʿan Asāmī al-Kutub wa-al-Funūn.* 2 vols. Ed. Muḥammad Sharaf al-Dīn Yāltaqyā and Riʿat Balīgah al-Kalīsa. Istanbul: Wikālat al-Maʿārif al-Jalīlah, 1360–63/1941–43.

Katz, Marion Holmes. *The Birth of the Prophet Muḥammad.* London: Routledge, 2007.

Khouri, Mounah A. *Poetry and the Making of Modern Egypt (1882–1922).* Leiden: E. J. Brill, 1971.

Knappert, Jan, ed. and trans. *Swahili Islamic Poetry.* Vol. 2, *The Two Burdas.* Leiden: E. J. Brill, 1971.

Krenkow, Fritz. "Tabrīzīs Kommentar zur Burda des Kaᶜb ibn Zuhair." *Zeitschrift der Deutschen Morganländischen Gesellschaft* 65 (1911): 241–79.

al-Kutubī, Muḥammad ibn Shākir. *Fawāt al-Wafayāt wa-al-Dhayl ᶜAlayhā.* 4 vols. Ed. Iḥsān ᶜAbbās. Beirut: Dār Ṣādir, 1973–74.

Lane, Edward William. *Arabic-English Lexicon.* 8 vols. New York: Frederick Ungar, 1958 [London, 1863] [= Lane].

Levi della Vida, G. "ᶜUthmān b. ᶜAffān." *EI2.*

Levi della Vida, G.–[M. Bonner]. "ᶜUmar b. al-Khaṭṭāb." *EI2.*

Lyall, Charles James, ed. and trans. *The Mufaḍḍalīyāt: An Anthology of Ancient Arabian Odes Compiled by Al-Mufaḍḍal Son of Muḥammad, According to the Recension and with the Commentary of Abū Muḥammad al-Qāsim ibn Muḥammad al-Anbārī.* Vol. 1, Arabic Text; Vol. 2, Translation and Notes. Oxford: Clarendon Press, 1918.

Makkī, Maḥmūd ᶜAlī. *Al-Madāʾiḥ al-Nabawiyyah.* Cairo: Al-Sharikah al-Miṣriyyah al-ᶜIlmiyyah lil-Nashr/Longman, 1991.

Mansfield, Peter. *The British in Egypt.* New York: Holt, Rinehart and Winston, 1972.

al-Maqqarī, Aḥmad ibn Muḥammad. *Nafḥ al-Ṭīb min Ghuṣn al-Andalus al-Raṭīb.* 8 vols. Ed. Iḥsān ᶜAbbās. Beirut: Dār Ṣādir, 1968.

al-Marzūqī, Aḥmad ibn Muḥammad. *Sharḥ Dīwān al-Ḥamāsah.* 4 vols. 2nd ed. Ed. Aḥmad Amīn and ᶜAbd al-Salām Hārūn. Cairo: Maṭbaᶜat Lajnat al-Taʾlīf wa-al-Tarjamah wa-al-Nashr, 1967.

Mauss, Marcel. *The Gift: Forms and Functions of Exchange in Archaic Societies.* Trans. Ian Cunnison. New York: Norton, 1967 [*Essai sur le don, forme archaïque de l'échange,* 1925)].

al-Maydānī, Abū al-Faḍl Aḥmad ibn Muḥammad. *Majmaᶜ al-Amthāl.* Ed. Muḥammad Muḥyī al-Dīn ᶜAbd al-Ḥamīd. 2nd ed. 2 vols. Cairo: Al-Maktabah al-Tijāriyyah al-Kubrá, 1959.

Meisami, Julie Scott. "Imruʾ al-Qays Praises the Prophet." In *Tradition and Modernity in Arabic Literature,* ed. Issa J. Boullata and Terri DeYoung. Fayetteville: University of Arkansas Press, 1997, 223–45.

Monroe, James T. "The Poetry of the *Sīrah* Literature." In *The Cambridge History of Arabic Literature: Vol. 1, Arabic Literature to the End of the Umayyad Period,* ed. A. F. L. Beeston, T. M. Johnstone, R. B. Serjeant, and G. R. Smith, Cambridge: Cambridge University Press, 1983, 368–73.

Montgomery, James E. *The Vagaries of the Qaṣīdah: The Tradition and Practice of Early Arabic Poetry.* Cambridge: E.J.W. Gibb Memorial Trust, 1997.

Moreh, Shmuel. "The Neoclassical Qaṣīda: Modern Poets and Critics." In *Arabic Poetry: Theory and Development,* ed. G. E. von Grunebaum. Third Giorgio Levi Della Vida Biennial Conference, University of California, Los Angeles, 1971. Wiesbaden: Otto Harrassowitz, 1973, 155–79.

Mubārak, Zakī. *Al-Madāʾiḥ al-Nabawiyyah fī al-Adab al-ᶜArabī.* Cairo: Muṣṭafá al-Bābī al-Ḥalabī, 1354/1935.

———. *Al-Muwāzanah bayn al-Shuʿarāʾ*. Cairo: Dār al-ʿArabī lil-Ṭibāʿah wa-al-Nashr, n.d.

[al-Mutanabbī, Abū al-Ṭayyib]. *Dīwān Abī al-Ṭayyib al-Mutanabbī bi-Sharḥ Abī al-Baqāʾ al-ʿUkbarī.* 4 vols. Ed. Muṣṭafá al-Saqqā et al. Cairo: Muṣṭafá al-Bābī al-Ḥalabī, 1971.

al-Nabhānī, Yūsuf ibn Ismāʿīl. *Al-Majmūʿah al-Nabhāniyyah fī al-Madāʾiḥ al-Nabawiyyah.* 4 vols. Beirut: Dār al-Kutub al-ʿIlmiyyah, n.d. [Repr. of Beirut: Al-Maṭbaʿah al-Adabiyyah, 1903].

al-Nābighah al-Dhubyānī, *Dīwān.* 3rd ed. Ed. Muḥammad Abū al-Faḍl Ibrāhīm. Cairo: Dār al-Maʿārif, 1990.

Nagy, Gregory. *Pindar's Homer: The Lyric Possession of an Epic Past.* Baltimore, Md.: Johns Hopkins University Press, 1991.

Nicholson, R. A., trans. "The Burdah of al-Būṣīrī." In *A Reader on Islam: Passages from Standard Arabic Writings Illustrative of the Beliefs and Practices of Muslims,* ed. Arthur Jeffery. 'S-Gravenhage: Mouton, 1962, 605–20.

Noorani, Yaseen. "The Lost Garden of al-Andalus: Islamic Spain and the Poetic Inversion of Colonialism." *International Journal of Middle East Studies* 31 no. 2 (May 1999): 237–54.

———. "A Nation Born in Mourning: The Neoclassical Funeral Elegy in Egypt." *Journal of Arabic Literature* 28 no. 1 (March 1997): 38–67.

———. "The Rebellious Subject: Political Self-Fashioning in Arabic and Persian Poetry of the Colonial Period." *Journal of Arabic Literature* 29 no. 2 (July 1998): 1–30.

Omar, F. "Hārūn al-Rashīd." *EI2.*

Ong, Walter J. *Orality and Literacy: The Technologizing of the Word.* London: Methuen, 1982.

Paret, R. "al-Burāḳ." *EI2.*

Paret, Rudi. "Die Legende der Verleihung des Prophetmantels (*burda*) an Kaʿb ibn Zuhair." *Der Islam* 17 (1928): 9–14.

Petrey, Sandy. *Speech Acts and Literary Theory.* London: Routledge, 1990.

"The Prophet's Mosque." ArchNet Digital Library http://www.archnet.org/library/sites/one-site.jsp?site_id=10061 (accessed 23 April 2009).

Qabāwah, Fakhr al-Dīn., ed. *Shiʿr al-Akhṭal, Abī Mālik Ghiyāth ibn Ghawth al-Taghlibī.* Recension of al-Sukkarī, 2nd ed. 2 vols. Beirut: Dār al-Āfāq al-Jadīdah, 1979.

al-Qabbānī, ʿAbd al-ʿAlīm. *Al-Būṣīrī: Ḥayātuh wa-Shiʿruh.* Cairo: Dār al-Maʿārif, 1968.

al-Qaraḍāwī, Yūsuf. "Weapons Used by the Other Religions to Wage War on Islam." Translation of discussion aired on "*Al-Sharīʿah wa-al-Ḥayāh,*" with Māhir ʿAbd Allāh, Al Jazeera 13/10/2002. www.jimas.org/defence.htm (accessed 26 August 2009).

Raven, W. "Sīra." *EI2online.*

Rekaya, M. "al-Maʾmūn b. Hārūn al-Rashīd." *EI2.*

Rūmiyyah, Wahb. *Qaṣīdat al-Madḥ ḥattá Nihāyat al-ʿAṣr al-Umawī: Bayn al-Uṣūl wa-al-Iḥyāʾ wa-al-Tajdīd.* Damascus: Manshūrāt Wizārat al-Thaqāfah wa-al-Irshād al-Qawmī, 1981.

Schimmel, Annemarie. *And Muhammad Is His Messenger: The Veneration of the Prophet in Islamic Piety.* Chapel Hill: University of North Carolina Press, 1985.

Schrieke, B.–[J. Horovitz] "Miʿrādj," part 1. *EI2.*

Sells, Michael A. "*Bānat Suʿād:* Translation and Interpretative Introduction." *Journal of Arabic Literature* 21 no. 2 (1990): 140–54.

———. "Guises of the *Ghūl:* Dissembling Simile and Semantic Overflow in the Classical Arabic *Nasīb.*" In *Reorientations: Arabic and Persian Poetry,* ed. S. Stetkevych. Bloomington: Indiana University Press, 1994, 130–64.

Sezgin, Fuat. *Geschichte des Arabischen Schrifttums, Band II: Poesie bis ca. 430 H.* Leiden: E. J. Brill, 1973.

Shahid, Irfan. "Lakhmids" and "Ghassānids." *EI2.*

al-Shantamarī, al-Aʿlam. *Shiʿr Zuhayr ibn Abī Sulmá.* Ed. Fakhr al-Dīn al-Qabāwah. Aleppo: Al-Maktabah al-ʿArabiyyah, 1970.

Shawqī, Aḥmad. *Nahj al-Burdah wa-ʿalayh Waḍaḥ al-Nahj lil-Shaykh Salīm al-Bishrī.* Cairo: Maṭbaʿat al-Iṣlāḥ, 1328/1910; and Cairo: Maktabat al-Ādāb, 1994.

———. *Al-Shawqiyyāt.* Ed. and comment. ʿAlī ʿAbd al-Munʿim ʿAbd al-Ḥamīd. Cairo: Al-Sharikah al-Miṣriyyah al-ʿĀlamiyyah lil-Nashr/Longman, 2000.

———. *Al-Shawqiyyāt.* Intro. Muḥammad Ḥusayn Haykal, 4 vols. in 2. Cairo: Al-Maktabah al-Tijāriyyah al-Kubrá, 1970.

Somekh, S. "The Neo-Classical Poets." In *The Cambridge History of Modern Arabic Literature,* ed. M. M. Badawī, Cambridge: Cambridge University Press, 1992, 36–81.

Sperl, Stefan. "Al-Būṣīrī's Burdah." In Sperl and Shackle, *Qasida Poetry,* 2:388–411 and 2:470–76.

———. "Islamic Kingship and Arabic Panegyric Poetry in the Early Ninth Century." *Journal of Arabic Literature* 8 (1977): 20–35.

———. *Mannerism in Arabic Poetry: A Structuralist Analysis of Selected Texts (3rd Century AH/9th Century AD–5th Century AH/11th Century AD).* Cambridge: Cambridge University Press, 1989.

Sperl, Stefan, and Christopher Shackle, eds. *Qasida Poetry in Islamic Asia and Africa: Vol. I, Classical Traditions and Modern Meanings; Vol. II, Eulogy's Bounty, Meaning's Abundance: An Anthology.* Leiden: E. J. Brill, 1996.

Stetkevych, Jaroslav. "Toward an Arabic Elegiac Lexicon: The Seven Words of the *Nasīb.*" In *Reorientations: Arabic and Persian Poetry,* ed. S. Stetkevych. Bloomington: Indiana University Press, 1994, 58–129.

———. *The Zephyrs of Najd: The Poetics of Nostalgia in the Classical Arabic* Nasīb. Chicago: University of Chicago Press, 1993.

Stetkevych, Suzanne Pinckney. "The ʿAbbāsid Poet Interprets History: Three Qaṣīdahs by Abū Tammām." *Journal of Arabic Literature* 10 (1979): 49–65.

———. *Abū Tammām and the Poetics of the ʿAbbāsid Age.* Leiden: E. J. Brill, 1991.

———. "Archetype and Attribution in Early Arabic Poetry: al-Shanfarā and the *Lāmiyyat al-ʿArab.*" *International Journal of Middle Eastern Studies* 18 (1986): 361–90.

———. "Al-Badīʿiyyah bayn Fann al-Qaṣīdah wa-ʿIlm al-Balāghah: Dirāsah fī Tadākhul al-Anwāʿ al-Adabiyyah." Unpublished paper presented at the

Twelfth Literary Criticism Conference, Yarmouk University, Irbid, Jordan, 22–24 July 2008.

———. "From Jāhiliyyah to *Badīʿiyyah:* Orality, Literacy, and the Transformations of Rhetoric in Arabic Poetry." Papers of the Orality and Literacy VII Conference, Rice University, 12–14 April 2008, in a special issue of *Oral Tradition.* Ed. Werner Kelber and Paula Sanders. 2010.

———. "From Sīrah to Qaṣīdah: Poetics and Polemics in al-Buṣīrī's Qaṣīdat al-Burdah (Mantle Ode)." *Journal of Arabic Literature* 38 no. 1 (2007): 1–52.

———. "From Text to Talisman: Al-Būṣīrī's Qaṣīdat al-Burdah (Mantle Ode) and the Poetics of Supplication." *Journal of Arabic Literature* 37 no. 2 (2006): 145–89.

———. "From Text to Talisman: Myth, Relic, and Miracle in the Two Mantle Odes." Unpublished paper presented at the annual meeting of the Middle East Studies Association, Washington, D.C., November 2005.

———. "Min al-Badīʿ ilá al-Badīʿiyyah: Dirāsah fī Dalālat al-Uslūb al-Balāghī." Presented at the Fourth International Conference on Literary Criticism, Cairo, November 2006.

———. *The Mute Immortals Speak: Pre-Islamic Poetry and the Poetics of Ritual.* Ithaca, N.Y.: Cornell University Press, 1993.

———. "Poetic Expansion as Verbal Reliquary: Shams al-Dīn al-Fayyūmī's *Takhmīs al-Burdah.*" Unpublished paper presented at the annual meeting of the Middle East Studies Association, Cambridge, Mass., November 2006.

———. *The Poetics of Islamic Legitimacy: Myth, Gender, and Ceremony in the Classical Arabic Ode.* Bloomington: Indiana University Press, 2002.

———. "Pre-Islamic Panegyric and the Poetics of Redemption: *Mufaḍḍalīyah 119* of ʿAlqamah and *Bānat Suʿād* of Kaʿb ibn Zuhayr." In *Reorientations: Arabic and Persian Poetry,* ed. S. Stetkevych. Bloomington: Indiana University Press, 1994, 1–57.

———. "Qaṣīdat al-Madḥ wa-Marāsim al-Ibtihāl: Fāʿiliyyāt al-Naṣṣ al-Adabī." In *Al-Naqd al-Adabī fī Munʿaṭaf al-Qarn (Papers Presented at the First International Conference on Literary Criticism, Cairo, October, 1997).* Ed. ʿIzz al-Dīn Ismāʿīl. 3 vols. Cairo, 1999, 3:175–96.

———, ed. *Reorientations: Arabic and Persian Poetry.* Bloomington: Indiana University Press, 1994.

———. "Al-Sharīf al-Raḍī and the Poetics of ʿAlid Legitimacy: Elegy for al-Ḥusayn ibn ʿAlī on ʿĀshūrāʾ, 391 AH." Festschrift for Jaroslav Stetkevych. *Journal of Arabic Literature* 38 (2007): 293–323.

———. "Solomon and Mythic Kingship in the Arabo-Islamic Tradition." Unpublished paper: Solomon Katz Distinguished Lecture in the Humanities, University of Washington, Seattle, 13 May 1999.

———. "Structuralist Analyses of Pre-Islamic Poetry: Critique and New Directions." *Journal of Near Eastern Studies* 42 no. 2 (1983): 85–107.

———. "Toward a Redefinition of *badīʿ* Poetry." *Journal of Arabic Literature* 12 (1981): 1–29.

———. "Umayyad Panegyric and the Poetics of Islamic Hegemony: Al-Akhṭal's *Khaffa al-Qaṭīnu* ('Those That Dwelt with You Have Left in Haste')." *Journal of Arabic Literature* 28 no. 2 (1997): 89–122.

al-Sukkarī, Abū Saʿīd al-Ḥasan ibn al-Ḥusayn. *Sharḥ Dīwān Kaʿb ibn Zuhayr.* Cairo: Dār al-Qawmiyyah, 1965.

Sumi, Akiko Motoyoshi. "Poetry and Architecture: A Double Imitation in the Sīniyyah of Aḥmad Shawqī." *Journal of Arabic Literature* 39 no. 1 (2008): 72–122.

al-Tabrīzī, Yaḥyā ibn ʿAlī. See: Krenkow, Fritz.

Talbi, M. "ʿIyāḍ ibn Mūsā." *EI2.*

Thaʿlab, Abū ʿAbbās Aḥmad ibn Yaḥyá ibn Zayd al-Shaybānī. *Sharḥ Dīwān Zuhayr ibn Abī Sulmá.* Cairo: Al-Dār al-Qawmiyyah lil-Ṭibāʿah wa-al-Nashr, 1964 [photo-offset of Cairo: Dār al-Kutub, 1944].

Turner, Victor. *The Ritual Process: Structure and Anti-Structure.* Ithaca, N.Y.: Cornell University Press, 1977.

Umm Kulthūm. *Nahj al-Burdah.* Sono Cairo/Ṣawt al-Qāhirah no. 144, 1946.

van Gennep, Arnold. *The Rites of Passage.* Trans. Monika Vizedom and Gabrielle L. Caffee. Chicago: University of Chicago Press, 1960 [*Les rites de passage,* 1908].

Veccia Vaglieri, L. "ʿAlī b. Abī Ṭālib." *EI2.*

Vuckovic, Brooke Olson. *Heavenly Journeys, Earthly Concerns: The Legacy of the Miʿrāj in the Formation of Islam.* New York: Routledge: 2005.

von Grunebaum, G. E. "Iʿdjāz." *EI2.*

Walker, J.–[P. Fenton]. "Sulaymān b. Dāwūd." *EI2.*

Watt, W. Montgomery. "Abū Bakr." *EI2.*

Wensinck, A. J., and C. E. Bosworth. "Lawḥ" *EI2.*

Yāqūt al-Ḥamawī. *Muʿjam al-Buldān.* 5 vols. Beirut: Dār Ṣādir, 1955–57.

al-Ziriklī, Khayr al-Dīn. *Al-Aʿlām: Qāmūs Tarājim li-Ashhar al-Rijāl wa-al-Nisāʾ . . . ,* 2nd ed. 11 vols. [Cairo], n.d.

Zwettler, Michael. "The Poet and the Prophet: Towards an Understanding of the Evolution of a Narrative." *Jerusalem Studies in Arabic and Islam* 5 (1984): 313–87.

INDEX

Aaron (*Hārūn*), 130
ʿAbbās Ḥilmī II, xiii, 152, 156, 159, 218, 221, 227
ʿAbbāsid, 75, 78, 80; ʿAbbāsid period, 91, 104, 106, 201, 217, 220; High ʿAbbāsid period, 75, 78, 80, 104, 109, 111, 134, 135, 137, 139, 141, 152, 166, 184, 218. *See also* caliphs, ʿAbbāsid
ʿAbd al-Ḥamīd II, 160, 221
ʿAbd Allāh (father of the Prophet Muḥammad), 113, 140, 198
ʿAbduh, Muḥammad, 153, 192
al-Abīwardī, Muḥammad ibn Abī al-ʿAbbās, 270n8
Abrahah, 54, 112, 115, 116
Abraham (*Ibrāhīm*), 101–102, 130, 189
Abū al-Khayr Khān, 269n4
Abū Bakr, 117, 119–20, 129, 186, 192–94, 220, 222–23, 277n83
Abū Dhuʾayb al-Hudhalī, 77
Abū Hurayrah, 101
Abū Nuwās, 74, 80
Abū Saʿīd Muḥammad ibn Yūsuf al-Thaghrī, 77
Abū Sulmá, 20, 34, 35, 36, 46
Abū Tammām, 74, 76–80, 104, 113–14, 135–40, 205–207, 217, 272n20, 276nn61,70
ʿĀd, 31, 121, 124, 170
al-Afghānī, Jamāl al-Dīn, 153, 192, 213
Age of Decline (*ʿAṣr al-Inḥiṭāṭ*), 66, 74, 153, 223, 230
Age of Ignorance (*Jāhiliyyah*), 1, 134, 140, 182, 199
Ahlwardt, W., 273n39
al-Akhṭal, 104, 146
ʿAlī ibn Abī Ṭālib, 72, 220, 221
Allāh, 17, 28, 29, 34, 35, 44, 47–48, 52–53, 79, 83, 86–88, 94–95, 97–98, 100–104, 112, 115–17, 119–22, 124–29, 130–35, 143–45, 147, 156–57, 165, 173, 176–80, 182, 184–86, 188, 189, 191–96, 200–203, 205–209, 211–14, 223, 225–30, 232, 275n55, 277nn50,84; caliphs of, 219–20; immortality of, 222–23; rope of, 122, 126; swords of, 48, 57, 139, 203, 207; throne of, 100, 185, 188, 191, 202, 227
allegiance, 9–10, 28, 32–33, 36, 38, 49, 51, 61, 62–63, 68–69, 84, 139, 222, 225, 227; between poet and patron, xii, 10, 16–17, 19, 91–92, 158, 219, 221, 226, 262n16; transfer of, 3, 9–10, 12, 22, 36, 60
Allen, Roger, 159
allusion, 53, 58, 80, 114, 121, 125, 126, 154, 278n96
ʿAlqamah ibn ʿAbadah, xii, 3–8, 10–15, 18–23, 25, 27, 44, 49, 51, 59–61, 63, 66, 91, 145

Suzanne Pinckney Stetkevych is Professor of Near Eastern Languages and Cultures and Adjunct Professor of Comparative Literature at Indiana University, Bloomington. She is author of *Abū Tammām and the Poetics of the ʿAbbāsid Age; The Mute Immortals Speak: Pre-Islamic Poetry and the Poetics of Ritual;* and *The Poetics of Islamic Legitimacy: Myth, Gender, and Ceremony in the Classical Arabic Ode* (Indiana University Press, 2002) and editor of *Reorientations: Arabic and Persian Poetry* (Indiana University Press, 1994) and *Early Islamic Poetry and Poetics.*

Printed and bound by CPI Group (UK) Ltd, Croydon, CR0 4YY

09/06/2025

14685939-0001